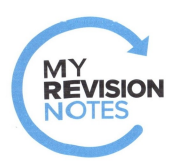

MY
REVISION
NOTES

AQA

A-level

PE
SECOND EDITION

Sue Young
Symond Burrows
Michaela Byrne

Boost

HODDER
EDUCATION
AN HACHETTE UK COMPANY

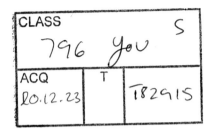
The Publishers would like to thank the following for permission to reproduce copyright material.

Photo credits

p.33 © Shutterstock/Maxisport; **p.34** © Shutterstock/Pal2iyawit; **p.43** © ALLSTAR PICTURE LIBRARY/Alamy Stock Photo; **p.123** © Andres Rodriguez – Fotolia; **p.130** © Undrey/Shutterstock; **p.141** Casey B. Gibson/Alamy Stock Photo; **p.149** l © Steve Russell/Toronto Star via Getty Images, r © Adam Pretty/Getty Images; **p.153** © Popperfoto/Getty Images; **p.156** © Jaroslav Uher/Fotolia.

Every effort has been made to trace all copyright holders, but if any have been inadvertently overlooked, the Publishers will be pleased to make the necessary arrangements at the first opportunity.

Although every effort has been made to ensure that website addresses are correct at time of going to press, Hodder Education cannot be held responsible for the content of any website mentioned in this book. It is sometimes possible to find a relocated web page by typing in the address of the home page for a website in the URL window of your browser.

Hachette UK's policy is to use papers that are natural, renewable and recyclable products and made from wood grown in well-managed forests and other controlled sources. The logging and manufacturing processes are expected to conform to the environmental regulations of the country of origin.

Orders: please contact Hachette UK Distribution, Hely Hutchinson Centre, Milton Road, Didcot, Oxfordshire, OX11 7HH. Telephone: +44 (0)1235 827827. Email: education@hachette.co.uk. Lines are open from 9 a.m. to 5 p.m., Monday to Friday. You can also order through our website: www.hoddereducation.co.uk.

ISBN: 978 1 3983 6059 4

© Sue Young, Symond Burrows, Michaela Byrne 2022

First published in 2017

This edition published in 2022 by
Hodder Education,
An Hachette UK Company
Carmelite House
50 Victoria Embankment
London EC4Y 0DZ

www.hoddereducation.co.uk

Impression number   10 9 8 7 6 5 4 3 2 1

Year   2026 2025 2024 2023 2022

Cover photo © Aida Servi - stock.adobe.com

Typeset by Integra Software Services Ltd, Pondicherry, India

Printed in Spain

A catalogue record for this title is available from the British Library.

Get the most from this book

Everyone has to decide their own revision strategy, but it is essential to review your work, learn it and test your understanding. These Revision Notes will help you to do that in a planned way, topic by topic. Use this book as the cornerstone of your revision and don't hesitate to write in it — personalise your notes and check your progress by ticking off each section as you revise.

Tick to track your progress

Use the revision planner on pages 4 and 5 to plan your revision, topic by topic. Tick each box when you have:

✚ revised and understood a topic
✚ tested yourself
✚ practised the exam questions and gone online to check your answers and complete the quick quizzes

You can also keep track of your revision by ticking off each topic heading in the book. You may find it helpful to add your own notes as you work through each topic.

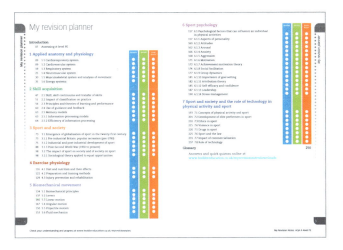

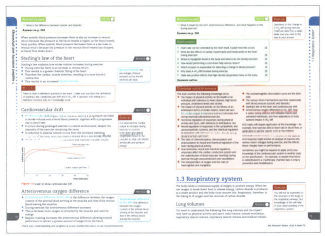

Features to help you succeed

Exam tips

Expert tips are given throughout the book to help you polish your exam technique in order to maximise your chances in the exam.

Now test yourself

These short, knowledge-based questions provide the first step in testing your learning. Answers are at the back of the book.

Definitions and key words

Clear, concise definitions of essential key terms are provided.

Key words from the specification are highlighted in bold throughout the book.

Making links

This feature identifies specific connections between topics and tells you how revising these will aid your exam answers.

Revision activities

These activities will help you to understand each topic in an interactive way.

Exam practice

Practice exam questions are provided for each topic. Use them to consolidate your revision and practise your exam skills.

Knowledge and skills summary

These summaries provide a quick-check bullet list for each topic.

Online

Go online to check your answers to the exam questions and try out the extra quick quizzes at **www.hoddereducation.co.uk/ myrevisionnotesdownloads**

My revision planner

Check your understanding and progress at **www.hoddereducation.co.uk/myrevisionnotes**

6 Sport psychology

7 Sport and society and the role of technology in physical activity and sport

Exam practice answers and quick quizzes online at
www.hoddereducation.co.uk/myrevisionnotesdownloads

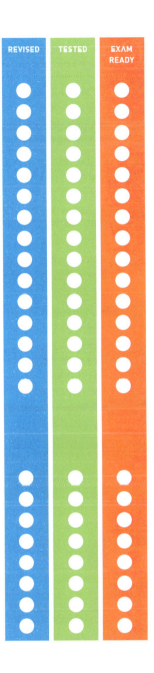

My revision planner

Countdown to my exams

6–8 weeks to go

+ Start by looking at the specification — make sure you know exactly what material you need to revise and the style of the examination. Use the revision planner on pages 4 and 5 to familiarise yourself with the topics.
+ Organise your notes, making sure you have covered everything on the specification. The revision planner will help you to group your notes into topics.
+ Work out a realistic revision plan that will allow you time for relaxation. Set aside days and times for all the subjects that you need to study, and stick to your timetable.
+ Set yourself sensible targets. Break your revision down into focused sessions of around 40 minutes, divided by breaks. These Revision Notes organise the basic facts into short, memorable sections to make revising easier.

REVISED ⬤

2–6 weeks to go

+ Read through the relevant sections of this book and refer to the exam tips, summaries and key terms. Tick off the topics as you feel confident about them. Highlight those topics you find difficult and look at them again in detail.
+ Test your understanding of each topic by working through the 'Now test yourself' questions in the book. Look up the answers at the back of the book.
+ Make a note of any problem areas as you revise, and ask your teacher to go over these in class.
+ Look at past papers. They are one of the best ways to revise and practise your exam skills. Write or prepare planned answers to the exam practice questions provided in this book. Check your answers online and try out the extra quick quizzes at **www.hoddereducation.co.uk/ myrevisionnotesdownloads**
+ Use the revision activities to try out different revision methods. For example, you can make notes using mind maps, spider diagrams or flash cards.
+ Track your progress using the revision planner and give yourself a reward when you have achieved your target.

REVISED ⬤

One week to go

+ Try to fit in at least one more timed practice of an entire past paper and seek feedback from your teacher, comparing your work closely with the mark scheme.
+ Check the revision planner to make sure you haven't missed out any topics. Brush up on any areas of difficulty by talking them over with a friend or getting help from your teacher.
+ Attend any revision classes put on by your teacher. Remember, they are experts at preparing people for examinations.

REVISED

The day before the examination

+ Flick through these Revision Notes for useful reminders, for example the exam tips, knowledge and skills summaries and key terms.
+ Check the time and place of your examination.
+ Make sure you have everything you need — extra pens and pencils, tissues, a watch, bottled water, sweets.
+ Allow some time to relax and have an early night to ensure you are fresh and alert for the examinations.

REVISED

My exams

A-level PE Paper 1

Date:...

Time: ....

Location: ....

A-level PE Paper 2

Date:...

Time: ....

Location: ....

Check your understanding and progress at **www.hoddereducation.co.uk/myrevisionnotes**

Exam breakdown

This book covers all the content for Papers 1 and 2 of the AQA A-level PE exam.

Paper 1: Factors affecting participation in physical activity and sport

+ Section A: Applied anatomy and physiology
+ Section B: Skill acquisition
+ Section C: Sport and society

Paper 2: Factors affecting optimal performance in physical activity and sport

+ Section A: Exercise physiology and biomechanics
+ Section B: Sport psychology
+ Section C: Sport and society and technology in sport

Assessment

+ Paper 1 and Paper 2 are both 2 hours long.
+ Each exam has a total of 105 marks available and they are both worth 35% of your A-level (i.e. 70% in total).
+ Each section (i.e. see Sections A–C above) on both papers has questions that total 35 marks.
+ The question format is also the same, with each section having two multiple-choice questions (2 marks), a number of short-answer questions (to a total of 10 marks) and two questions requiring extended writing in continuous prose (one worth 8 marks, the other worth 15 marks) – 35 marks in total per section of the exam paper.

The assessment objectives

Your answers will be marked by examiners who will look to see how well you have met the three assessment objectives set in your papers. These are explained below:

Assessment objective	Requirements
AO1: Knowledge and understanding	Identify/state/provide knowledge of the key term(s) mentioned in the question
AO2: Apply knowledge and understanding	Apply your knowledge and understanding to the example in the question (e.g. a particular sport or a sports performer)
AO3: Analyse and evaluate this knowledge	Analyse and evaluate your knowledge by: + giving advantages and disadvantages + stating the impact on the practical example in the question + providing reasons for the judgements made + offering alternative viewpoints

Specific question advice

Synoptic assessment will be assessed in each paper and will draw on content from any topic, regardless of which component that topic is predominantly assessed in (e.g. Paper 2 topics such as sports supplements, goal setting or theories of aggression could appear in Paper 1). These questions will always be extended-answer questions worth 8 marks or 15 marks. There is one 8-mark and one 15-mark question in each section so that is three 8-mark and three 15-mark questions in Paper 1 and the same for Paper 2.

'Synoptic' means that the question could ask for:
+ Knowledge, application and analysis/evaluation of two topics from the same section, for example:
    + Anatomy – muscles and movement and fibre type
    + Skill – types of practice and operant conditioning
    + Sport and society – sports legislation and strategies to control crowd violence
+ Knowledge, application and analysis/evaluation of two topics from different sections, for example:
    + Psychology/Exercise physiology
    + Exercise physiology/Sport and society and the role of technology
    + Sport and society and the role of technology/Psychology
+ Knowledge, application and analysis/evaluation of one topic from any section in Paper 1 with another topic from any section in Paper 2.

Specific exam skills including synoptic skills

+ Always look at the command word in the question and make sure you understand what the command word wants you to do. For example, if the command word is 'discuss' make sure you give both strengths and weaknesses or offer alternative views of a debate.
+ Synoptic questions are marked using level of response grids, so you are not awarded 1 mark for each correct answer. For example, there are 2 knowledge marks, 3 application marks and 3 analysis or evaluation marks for 8-mark questions and 4 knowledge marks, 5 application marks and 6 analysis/evaluation marks for 15-mark questions. The examiner will look at the depth and quality of your knowledge from the responses given and place you in one of the levels linked to your knowledge, application and analysis/evaluation.

1 Applied anatomy and physiology

1.1 Cardiorespiratory system

This topic explains the relationship between the cardiovascular system (below) and the respiratory system (pp. 19–25), and describes how these systems change prior to exercise, during exercise of differing intensities and during recovery. Taking part in physical activity can have a positive effect on both these systems. This relationship is therefore covered in the next two sections.

1.2 Cardiovascular system

The cardiovascular system is the body's transport system. It includes the heart and the blood vessels. During exercise, an efficient cardiovascular system is extremely important, as the heart works to pump blood through the various blood vessels to deliver oxygen and nutrients to the working muscles and gather waste products such as carbon dioxide.

Impact of physical activity and sport on health

REVISED

Heart disease

+ Exercise helps prevent coronary heart disease (CHD), which occurs when your coronary arteries, which supply the heart muscle with oxygenated blood, become hardened, blocked or start to narrow through a gradual build-up of fatty deposits. This process is called atherosclerosis and the fatty deposits are called atheroma.
+ High blood pressure, high levels of cholesterol, lack of exercise and smoking can all cause atherosclerosis, which limits the supply of oxygen to the heart, resulting in a heart attack.

High blood pressure

+ Blood pressure is the force exerted by the blood against the blood vessel wall. This pressure comes from the heart as it pumps the blood around the body.
+ High blood pressure puts extra strain on the arteries and heart, and if left untreated increases the risk of heart attack, heart failure, kidney disease, stroke or dementia.
+ Regular aerobic exercise can reduce blood pressure. It lowers both systolic and diastolic pressure by up to 5–10 mmHg, which reduces the risk of a heart attack by up to 20 per cent.

Effects of cholesterol

There are two types of cholesterol:

+ LDLs (low-density lipoproteins) transport cholesterol in the blood to the tissues, and are classed as 'bad' cholesterol since they are linked to an increased risk of heart disease.
+ HDLs (high-density lipoproteins) transport excess cholesterol in the blood back to the liver, where it is broken down. They protect the artery walls against LDL cholesterol and have a positive antioxidant effect. HDLs are classed as 'good' cholesterol since they lower the risk of developing heart disease.

> **Exam tip**
>
> While structure is not tested in the exam, a good grasp of how the components of the cardiovascular system are arranged and organised will enable you to better understand how the system functions.

> **Atherosclerosis** When arteries harden and narrow, and become blocked with fatty deposits.
>
> **Aerobic** A reaction that occurs in the presence of oxygen.

> **Exam tip**
>
> Be aware that heart disease can lead to a heart attack. Past questions have asked you to make this link.

9

Regular physical activity lowers bad LDL cholesterol levels, while significantly increasing good HDL cholesterol levels.

Stroke

The brain needs a constant supply of oxygenated blood and nutrients to maintain its function. The energy to work all the time is provided by oxygen delivered to the brain in the blood. A **stroke** occurs when the blood supply to part of the brain is cut off, causing damage to brain cells, which then start to die. This can lead to brain injury, disability and sometimes death.

There are two main types of stroke:
+ Ischaemic strokes are the most common form and occur when a blood clot stops the blood supply.
+ Haemorrhagic strokes occur when a weakened blood vessel supplying the brain bursts.

Research has shown that regular exercise can help to lower your blood pressure and help you maintain a healthy weight, which can reduce your risk of stroke by 27 per cent.

Now test yourself   TESTED ◯

1   What effect does regular physical activity have on blood pressure and cholesterol?

Answer on p. 260

> **Revision activity**
>
> Create a table to summarise how physical activity can have an effect on heart disease, high blood pressure, cholesterol levels and strokes.

Impact of physical activity and sport on fitness

REVISED ◯

Stroke volume

Stroke volume is the volume of blood pumped out by the heart ventricles in each contraction. On average, the resting stroke volume is approximately 70 ml.

Stroke volume will increase due to the following:
+ Venous return – when this increases then stroke volume will also increase.
+ The elasticity of cardiac fibres – this is concerned with the degree of stretch of cardiac tissue during the diastole phase (when the heart is relaxed) of the cardiac cycle. The more the cardiac fibres can stretch the greater the force of contraction will be.
+ The contractility of cardiac tissue (myocardium) – the greater the contractility of cardiac tissue, the greater the force of contraction.

Stroke volume in response to exercise

Stroke volume increases as exercise intensity increases. However, this is only the case up to 40–60 per cent of maximum effort. Once a performer reaches this point then stroke volume plateaus (evens out) because the ventricles simply do not have as much time to fill up with blood, and so cannot pump as much out.

Heart rate

Heart rate refers to the number of times the heart beats per minute. On average, the resting heart rate is approximately 72 beats per minute.

Heart rate range in response to exercise

Heart rate increases with exercise, but how much it increases depends on the intensity of the exercise. Heart rate will increase in direct proportion to exercise intensity. The higher the intensity, the higher the heart rate. Heart rate does eventually reach a maximum. Maximum heart rate can be

Check your understanding and progress at **www.hoddereducation.co.uk/myrevisionnotes**

calculated by subtracting your age from 220. An 18-year-old will therefore have a maximum heart rate of 202 beats per minute:

220 − 18 = 202

A trained performer has a greater heart rate range because their resting heart rate is lower than average, and their maximum heart rate is higher.

The graphs in Figure 1.1 illustrate what happens to heart rate during maximal exercise, such as sprinting, and submaximal exercise, such as jogging.

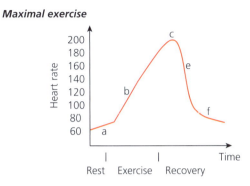

a = *Anticipatory rise* due to hormonal action of adrenaline which causes the SAN to increase heart rate

b = *Sharp rise* in heart rate due mainly to **anaerobic** work

c = Heart rate continues to rise due to maximal workloads stressing the anaerobic systems

d = *Steady state* as the athlete is able to meet the oxygen demand with the oxygen supply

e = *Rapid decline* in heart rate as soon as the exercise stops

f = *Slower recovery* as body systems return to resting levels; heart rate needs to remain elevated to rid the body of waste products, for example **lactic acid**

Figure 1.1 Heart rate responses to maximal and submaximal exercise

✦ Regular aerobic training will result in more cardiac muscle. When the cardiac muscle becomes bigger and stronger this is known as cardiac hypertrophy.
✦ Consequently, a bigger, stronger heart will enable more blood to be pumped out per beat (i.e. stroke volume). This is known as bradycardia, which means there is a decrease in resting heart rate to below 60 beats per minute. When this occurs oxygen delivery to the muscles improves because there is less oxygen needed for each contraction of the heart, as it beats less frequently.

Cardiac output

Cardiac output is the volume of blood pumped out by the heart ventricles per minute. It can be calculated using the following equation:

cardiac output (Q) = stroke volume (SV) × heart rate (HR)

$Q = 70\,\text{ml} \times 72$ beats per minute

$Q = 5040\,\text{ml}$ (5.04 litres)

It can be seen from this calculation that if heart rate or stroke volume increases, then cardiac output will also increase.

Cardiac output in response to exercise

During exercise there is a large increase in cardiac output due to an increase in heart rate and an increase in stroke volume. Cardiac output will increase as the intensity of exercise increases until maximum intensity is reached. Then it plateaus.

Exam tip

Maximum heart rate is calculated as 220 minus age.

Anaerobic A reaction that occurs without the presence of oxygen.

Lactic acid A by-product of anaerobic respiration. As it accumulates, it causes fatigue.

Cardiac hypertrophy When the heart becomes bigger and stronger due to a thickening of the muscular wall.

Bradycardia When there is a decrease in resting heart rate to below 60 beats per minute.

Table 1.1 shows the differences in cardiac output between a trained and untrained individual, both at rest and during exercise. The individual in this example is aged 18, so their maximum heart rate will be 202 beats per minute.

Table 1.1 Cardiac output during exercise and at rest

	stroke volume × heart rate = cardiac output (SV × HR = Q)	
	Exercise	**At rest**
Untrained	120 ml × 202 = 24.24 litres	70 ml × 72 = 5.04 litres
Trained	170 ml × 202 = 34.34 litres	84 ml × 60 = 5.04 litres

Impact of an increase in cardiac output on performance:
✚ Able to transport more blood to the working muscles and therefore more oxygen.
✚ Easier to continue working at a higher intensity for longer.

Exam tip

Do not be caught out by an exam question asking for the effects of a period of training on resting cardiac output. Resting cardiac output remains unchanged – it is *maximum* cardiac output that changes.

It is important to understand the impact of a bigger cardiac output on a performer for AO2.

> **Now test yourself** TESTED ◯
>
> 2 Define cardiac output and stroke volume, and explain the relationship between them.
>
> 3 Explain how and why the components of cardiac output would differ for an elite football player at rest.
>
> 4 How would maximal cardiac output differ between a trained performer and an untrained performer?
>
> **Answers on p. 260**

Regulation of responses during physical activity and sport

REVISED ◯

Heart rate increases with exercise, but how much it increases depends on the intensity of the exercise. The higher the intensity, the higher the heart rate.

Cardiac conduction system

When the heart beats, the blood needs to flow through it in a controlled manner – in through the atria and out through the ventricles. Heart muscle is described as being **myogenic** because the beat is generated in the heart muscle itself with an electrical signal in the SAN (Figure 1.2). This electrical signal then spreads through the heart in what is often described as a wave of excitation (similar to a Mexican wave), in the following order:
✚ The sinoatrial node (SAN) sends an impulse through the walls of the atria.
✚ This spreads as a wave of excitation.
✚ This causes atrial systole/the atria to contract.
✚ The impulse then passes to the atrioventricular node (AVN), which delays the impulse for around 0.1 seconds, enabling the atria to empty fully.
✚ The impulse passes down the bundle of His (in the septum of the heart) to the Purkinje fibres in the (walls of) the ventricles.
✚ Ventricular systole then occurs/the ventricles contract.

SAN A small mass of cardiac muscle (sinoatrial node or SAN) found in the wall of the right atrium that generates the heartbeat. It is more commonly called the pacemaker.

> **Now test yourself** TESTED ◯
>
> 5 Identify the correct order of events in a cardiac impulse.
>
> **Answer on p. 260**

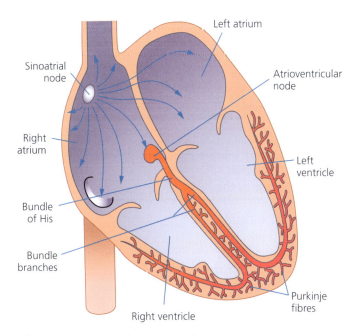

Left atrium

Sinoatrial
node

Atrioventricular
node

Right
atrium

Left
ventricle

Bundle
of His

Bundle
branches

Purkinje
fibres

Right ventricle

Figure 1.2 The cardiac conduction system

The conduction system ensures that heart rate increases during exercise to allow the working muscles to receive more oxygen. The rate at which the heart generates its own impulses from the SAN involves hormonal, neural and chemical regulation.

Sympathetic and parasympathetic control

The sympathetic and parasympathetic systems are part of the peripheral nervous system. Their role is to transmit information from the brain to the parts of the body that need to adjust what they are doing to prepare for exercise:

✚ The sympathetic nervous system prepares the body for exercise, and is often referred to as the 'fight or flight response'.

✚ The parasympathetic nervous system has the opposite effect and relaxes the body and slows down many high-energy functions. It is often described by the phrase 'rest and relax'.

> **Making links**
>
> Knowledge of the sympathetic and parasympathetic systems is needed in several topics: heart, blood flow, respiratory system and neuromuscular system.

Hormonal regulation

The hormone adrenaline is secreted by the adrenal gland and makes the heart beat faster and stronger.

Anticipatory rise

An anticipatory rise is when heart rate increases prior to exercise. It occurs when the hormonal adrenaline is released by the nervous system in anticipation of exercise. This stimulates the heart to increase both the speed and force of contraction, therefore increasing cardiac output. This results in more blood being pumped to the working muscles so they can receive more oxygen for the energy they need.

Neural and chemical regulation

Neural regulation involves the sympathetic and parasympathetic nervous systems. Chemical regulation involves the levels of oxygen and carbon dioxide in the blood and the pH of the blood. The sympathetic and parasympathetic systems are coordinated by the cardiac control centre located in the medulla oblongata of the brain.

> **Exam tip**
>
> When explaining the cardiac conduction system, make sure you can give the correct order of events involved in a cardiac impulse.

> **Exam tip**
>
> Make sure you do not confuse the sympathetic and parasympathetic systems. The sympathetic system is fight or flight – it fires up the body for exercise. The parasympathetic system is 'rest and relax' – it slows everything down.

> **Adrenaline** A stress hormone released by the nervous system to increase heart rate.

> **Medulla oblongata** The most important part of the brain, because it regulates the processes that keep us alive.

13

The cardiac control centre is stimulated by chemoreceptors, baroreceptors and proprioceptors. It will then send an impulse through either the sympathetic system to the SAN to increase heart rate or the parasympathetic system to the SAN to decrease heart rate.

Receptors involved in regulation of responses during physical activity

REVISED

+ Chemoreceptors are tiny structures in the carotid and aortic arch that detect changes in blood acidity caused by an increase or decrease in the concentration of carbon dioxide.
+ Proprioceptors are sensory nerve endings in the muscles, tendons and joints that detect changes in muscle movement.
+ Baroreceptors are special sensors in the aortic arch, carotid sinus, heart and pulmonary vessels that respond to changes in blood pressure to either increase or decrease heart rate.

How neural and chemical regulation works

+ chemoreceptors → increase in blood carbon dioxide → cardiac control centre → sympathetic system → SAN increases heart rate
+ baroreceptors → increase in blood pressure → cardiac control centre → parasympathetic system → SAN decreases heart rate
+ proprioceptors → increase in muscle movement → cardiac control centre → sympathetic system → SAN increases heart rate

Making links

Knowledge of the receptors is the same for the control of heart rate, blood flow and breathing.

Now test yourself

TESTED

6 Identify and explain the roles of chemoreceptors and proprioceptors in increasing heart rate.

Answer on p. 260

Exam tip

Do not be vague – tell the examiner what the receptors detect. For example, chemoreceptors detect an increase in carbon dioxide during exercise – do not just say chemical changes.

Redistribution of blood during exercise (vascular shunting)

The distribution of blood flow is different at rest compared with during exercise. During exercise the skeletal muscles require more oxygen, so more blood needs to be redirected to them to meet this increase in oxygen demand. The redirecting of blood flow to the areas where it is most needed is known as vascular shunting.

+ More blood goes to the heart because the heart muscle needs more oxygen to beat faster and with more force.
+ More blood goes to the muscles because they need more oxygen for energy.
+ More blood goes to the skin because more energy is needed to cool the body down.
+ Blood flow to the brain remains constant because it needs oxygen for energy to maintain function.
+ A full stomach would result in more blood being directed to the gut instead of the working muscles, and this would have a detrimental effect on performance because less oxygen is being made available.

Vascular shunting The redistribution of cardiac output to where oxygen is needed most.

Vasodilation and vasoconstriction

+ During exercise chemoreceptors detect an increase in carbon dioxide. Baroreceptors detect an increase in blood pressure. Proprioceptors detect an increase in muscle movement.

Check your understanding and progress at **www.hoddereducation.co.uk/myrevisionnotes**

+ These receptors send impulses to the vasomotor centre located in the medulla oblongata.
+ The medulla oblongata controls blood flow by sending out increased sympathetic nervous impulses to cause both vasoconstriction to the blood vessels and the closing of the pre-capillary sphincters surrounding the non-essential organs.
+ The medulla oblongata decreases sympathetic nervous impulses to cause both vasodilation to the blood vessels and the opening of the pre-capillary sphincters surrounding the working muscles.

Vasoconstriction The narrowing of the blood vessels to reduce blood flow into the capillaries.

Vasodilation The widening of the blood vessels to increase the flow of blood into the capillaries.

Now test yourself

TESTED

7 Why does blood flow to the skin and heart increase during exercise?

8 Explain why there is a need for an increase in blood flow to the skeletal muscles during exercise and how this is achieved.

Answers on p. 260

Transportation of oxygen

REVISED

Arteries, arterioles, veins, venules and capillaries transport blood from the heart, distribute it around the body and then return it back to the heart (systemic circulation). They also transport deoxygenated blood from the heart to the lungs and oxygenated blood back to the heart (pulmonary circulation).
+ Veins transport deoxygenated blood back to the heart (with the exception of the pulmonary vein), have thinner muscle/elastic tissue layers, contain blood at low pressure, and have valves and a wider lumen.
+ Arteries transport oxygenated blood around the body (with the exception of the pulmonary artery), have the highest pressure, thick and elastic outer walls, and have thick layers of muscle, a smaller lumen and a smooth inner layer.
+ Capillaries have a tiny lumen and are only wide enough to allow one red blood cell to pass through at a given time. This slows down blood flow and allows the exchange of nutrients with the tissues to take place by diffusion. They are also one cell thick, which allows for a short diffusion pathway.

Now test yourself

TESTED

9 Explain why arteries have the highest pressure.

10 How does the structure of capillaries help diffusion?

Answers on p. 260

Revision activity

Create a spider diagram to highlight the key structures of arteries, veins and capillaries.

Haemoglobin

Oxygen can be transported as follows:
+ 3 per cent dissolves into plasma.
+ 97 per cent combines with haemoglobin to form oxyhaemoglobin.

At the tissues oxygen is released from oxyhaemoglobin due to the lower pressure of oxygen that exists there. The release of oxygen from oxyhaemoglobin to the tissues is referred to as oxyhaemoglobin dissociation.

Myoglobin

In the muscles, oxygen is stored by myoglobin, which is often called 'muscle haemoglobin'. It is an iron-containing muscle pigment in slow-twitch muscle fibres that has a higher affinity for oxygen than haemoglobin. It stores the oxygen until it is used by the mitochondria in muscle cells.

Myoglobin A protein found in muscle cells which stores and provides oxygen.

Mitochondria Components of cells that are often referred to as the 'powerhouses' of the cells because respiration and energy production occur there.

15

Now test yourself   TESTED ◯

11 What is the difference between haemoglobin and myoglobin?

Answer on p. 260

Oxyhaemoglobin dissociation curve

The oxyhaemoglobin dissociation curve (Figure 1.3) helps us to understand how haemoglobin in our blood carries and releases oxygen. The curve represents the relationship between oxygen and haemoglobin.

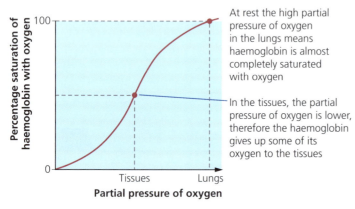

At rest the high partial pressure of oxygen in the lungs means haemoglobin is almost completely saturated with oxygen

In the tissues, the partial pressure of oxygen is lower, therefore the haemoglobin gives up some of its oxygen to the tissues

Figure 1.3 The oxyhaemoglobin dissociation curve

From this curve you can see that in the lungs there is almost full saturation (concentration) of haemoglobin but at the tissues the partial pressure of oxygen is lower.

The Bohr shift

During exercise this S-shaped curve shifts to the right. This is because when muscles require more oxygen the dissociation of oxygen from haemoglobin in the blood capillaries to the muscle tissue occurs more readily. This shift to the right is known as the Bohr shift (Figure 1.4).

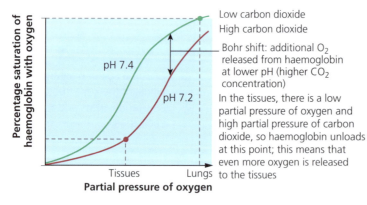

Low carbon dioxide
High carbon dioxide

Bohr shift: additional O_2 released from haemoglobin at lower pH (higher CO_2 concentration)

In the tissues, there is a low partial pressure of oxygen and high partial pressure of carbon dioxide, so haemoglobin unloads at this point; this means that even more oxygen is released to the tissues

Figure 1.4 The effect of changing acidity on the oxyhaemoglobin dissociation curve

Three factors are responsible for this increase in the dissociation of oxygen from haemoglobin, which results in more oxygen being available for use by the working muscles:

+ Increase in blood temperature – when the blood and muscle temperature increases during exercise oxygen will dissociate from haemoglobin more readily.
+ Increases in partial pressure of carbon dioxide – as the level of blood carbon dioxide rises during exercise oxygen will dissociate more quickly from haemoglobin.
+ A drop in pH – more carbon dioxide will lower the pH in the body; this causes oxygen to dissociate from haemoglobin more quickly (the Bohr shift — Figure 1.4).

> **Bohr shift** When an increase in blood carbon dioxide and a decrease in pH results in a reduction of the affinity of haemoglobin for oxygen.

> **Exam tip**
>
> When giving the causes of the Bohr shift, do not forget the word 'blood' – *blood* pH, *blood* carbon dioxide levels, *blood* temperature.

Check your understanding and progress at **www.hoddereducation.co.uk/myrevisionnotes**

Now test yourself

TESTED ◯

12 Describe the Bohr shift.

13 What causes the Bohr shift?

Answers on p. 260

Venous return

REVISED ◯

Venous return is the return of blood to the right side of the heart via the vena cava. Up to 70 per cent of the total volume of blood is contained in the veins at rest. This means that a large amount of blood can be returned to the heart when needed. During exercise the amount of blood returning to the heart (venous return) increases.

> **Venous return** The return of blood to the right side of the heart via the vena cava.

Venous return mechanisms

✚ The skeletal muscle pump (Figure 1.5) – when muscles contract and relax they change shape. This change in shape means that the muscles press on the nearby veins and cause a pumping effect that pushes the blood towards the heart.

✚ The respiratory pump – when muscles contract and relax during respiration pressure changes occur in the thorax (chest). These pressure changes compress the nearby veins and push blood back to the heart.

✚ Pocket valves prevent the back-flow of blood.

✚ Smooth muscle found in the walls of the veins contracts to push blood back towards the heart.

✚ The pumping of the heart results in suction, which pulls blood back towards the heart.

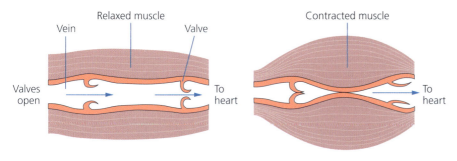

Figure 1.5 The skeletal muscle pump

> **Exam tip**
>
> Do not just identify a mechanism – explain what it does.

Relationship with blood pressure

Blood pressure is the force exerted by the blood against the blood vessel wall and is often referred to as:

blood flow × resistance

During exercise the heart contracts with more force, so that blood leaves the heart under high pressure in order for the muscles to receive the extra oxygen they require. This is the systolic pressure or pressure of contraction. The lower pressure as the ventricles relax is the diastolic pressure.

> **Systolic** The ventricles are contracting.
>
> **Diastolic** The ventricles are relaxing.

Blood pressure is measured at the brachial artery in the upper arm. A typical reading at rest is:

$\frac{120}{80}$ mmHg (millimetres of mercury)

Blood pressure is different in the various blood vessels, and is largely dependent on the distance of the blood vessel from the pumping action of the heart.

> **Exam tip**
>
> It is easy to remember that blood pressure increases during exercise, but make sure you can explain why.

17

Now test yourself   TESTED

14 What is the difference between systolic and diastolic?

Answer on p. 260

When systolic blood pressure increases there is also an increase in venous return because the pressure in the blood vessels is higher, so the blood travels more quickly. When systolic blood pressure decreases there is a decrease in venous return because the pressure in the various blood vessels has dropped, so blood flow slows down.

Starling's law of the heart   REVISED

Starling's law explains how stroke volume increases during exercise:
+ During exercise there is an increase in venous return.
+ This results in a greater diastolic filling of the heart.
+ Therefore the cardiac muscle stretches, resulting in a more forceful contraction.
+ This results in an increased ejection fraction.

Ejection fraction The percentage of blood pumped out by the left ventricle per beat.

Exam tip

There is often a definition question in the exam – make sure you learn the definitions of Starling's law, cardiovascular drift and A-VO$_2$ diff. A question only asking for a definition involves only AO1 knowledge recall.

Cardiovascular drift   REVISED

+ Cardiovascular drift (Figure 1.6) is characterised by a progressive decrease in stroke volume and arterial blood pressure, together with a progressive rise in heart rate.
+ It occurs during prolonged exercise in a warm environment, despite the intensity of the exercise remaining the same.
+ A reduction in plasma volume occurs from the increased sweating response of the body and this reduces venous return and stroke volume.
+ Heart rate then increases to compensate and maintain cardiac output.

Exam tip

It is important for cardiac output to increase during exercise to cool the body down and deliver oxygenated blood to the muscles so they can respire aerobically and produce energy.

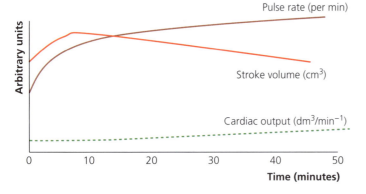

Figure 1.6 Graph to show cardiovascular drift

Arteriovenous oxygen difference   REVISED

+ Arteriovenous difference (A-VO$_2$ diff) is the difference between the oxygen content of the arterial blood arriving at the muscles and that of the venous blood leaving the muscles.
+ During exercise the arteriovenous difference increases.
+ This is because more oxygen is extracted by the muscles and used for energy.
+ Regular training increases the arteriovenous difference allowing trained performers to extract a greater amount of oxygen from the blood.

Arteriovenous difference (A-VO$_2$ diff) The difference between the oxygen content of the arterial blood arriving at the muscles and that of the venous blood leaving the muscles.

Check your understanding and progress at **www.hoddereducation.co.uk/myrevisionnotes**

15 What is meant by the term 'arteriovenous difference', and what happens to this during exercise?

Answer on p. 260

Questions on the change in A-VO$_2$ diff during exercise could use data from a table. Make sure you refer to the data in your answer.

Exam practice

1 Heart rate can be controlled by the heart itself. Explain how this occurs. [3]
2 What are the effects of cardiac hypertrophy and bradycardia on the heart during exercise? [3]
3 Where is myoglobin found in the body and what is its role during exercise? [2]
4 How would performing a cool-down help venous return? [2]
5 Which receptor is responsible for detecting a change in blood pressure? [1]
6 Why does A-VO$_2$ diff increase during exercise. [2]
7 State two positive effects that high-density lipoproteins have on the body. [2]

Answers online

Knowledge and skills summary

This topic involves the following knowledge (AO1):
+ The impact of physical activity on the health of an individual with reference to heart disease, high blood pressure, cholesterol levels and strokes.
+ The impact of physical activity on the fitness of an individual in terms of stroke volume, heart rate and the cardiac output of trained/untrained individuals and during maximal/submaximal exercise.
+ Hormonal regulation of responses during physical activity and sport, with reference to anticipatory rise.
+ Neural regulation of responses in the sympathetic and parasympathetic systems, and the chemical regulation of responses with reference to carbon dioxide during physical activity and sport.
+ The roles of chemoreceptors, baroreceptors and proprioceptors in neural and chemical regulation of the heart during physical activity.
+ How hormonal, neural and chemical regulatory responses affect the cardiac conduction system and the redistribution of blood (vascular shunting) during exercise through vasoconstriction and vasodilation.
+ The transportation of oxygen and the roles of haemoglobin and myoglobin.

+ The oxyhaemoglobin dissociation curve and the Bohr shift.
+ The venous return mechanisms and their relationship with blood pressure (systolic and diastolic).
+ Starling's law of the heart and cardiovascular drift.
+ Arteriovenous oxygen difference (A-VO$_2$ diff), how it varies during exercise and between trained and untrained individuals, and how adaptations to body systems impact A-VO$_2$ diff.

AO2 marks will require application of this knowledge – for example, how exercise affects heart rate or blood flow, or application to aerobic events such as the triathlon.

AO3 marks are for analysis or evaluation. In this topic an AO3 response might involve an analysis of reasons why venous return changes during exercise, and the effects these changes have on performance.

Sometimes you might be required to apply (AO2) your knowledge of the cardiovascular system to another topic on the specification – for example, to explain how blood is redistributed in a cryotherapy chamber (see 4.3 Injury prevention and rehabilitation).

1.3 Respiratory system

The body needs a continuous supply of oxygen to produce energy. When we use oxygen to break down food to release energy, carbon dioxide is produced as a waste product and the body must remove this. Respiration, therefore, is the taking in of oxygen and the removal of carbon dioxide.

Lung volumes REVISED ○

You need to understand the following five lung volumes and the impact they have on physical activity and sport: tidal volume, minute ventilation, inspiratory reserve volume, expiratory reserve volume and residual volume.

Tidal volume

+ **Tidal volume** is the volume of air inspired or expired per breath.
+ At rest we inspire and expire approximately 0.5 litres of air. During exercise this increases to provide the muscles with more oxygen and to remove the extra carbon dioxide that is produced as a by-product of exercise.

> **Tidal volume** The volume of air breathed in or out per breath.

Minute ventilation

+ **Minute ventilation** is the volume of air inspired or expired per minute.
+ This can be calculated by multiplying the number of breaths taken per minute (approximately 12) by the tidal volume.

> **Minute ventilation** The volume of air inhaled or exhaled per minute.

$$\text{number of breaths (per min)} \times \text{tidal volume} = \text{minute ventilation}$$
$$12 \qquad\qquad \times \qquad 0.5 \qquad = \qquad 6 \text{ litres}$$

Changes in minute ventilation occur during different types of exercise. The more demanding the physical activity is, the more breathing increases to meet the extra oxygen demand. This is illustrated in Figure 1.7.

Figure 1.7 The respiratory response to various intensities of exercise

Inspiratory and expiratory reserve volume

+ At rest we still have the ability to breathe in and breathe out more air than just the tidal volume.
+ This extra amount of air inspired is the **inspiratory reserve volume (IRV)** and the extra amount expired is the **expiratory reserve volume (ERV)**.
+ Exercise will have an effect on these lung volumes.

Residual volume

+ **Residual volume** is the amount of air that remains in the lungs after maximal expiration.
+ We can never totally empty our lungs, even when we have exhaled as much as possible. This is because we need to keep the alveoli open so we can breathe effectively.

> **Inspiratory reserve volume (IRV)** The volume of air that can be forcibly inspired after a normal breath.
>
> **Expiratory reserve volume (ERV)** The volume of air that can be forcibly expired after a normal breath.
>
> **Residual volume** The amount of air that remains in the lungs after maximal expiration.

Lung volume types and using a spirometer

Table 1.2 summarises the five lung volumes you need, and identifies the changes that take place in these volumes during exercise.

Table 1.2 Lung volumes and changes

Lung volume or capacity	Definition	Changes during exercise
Tidal volume	Volume of air breathed in or out per breath	Increase
Inspiratory reserve volume	Volume of air that can be forcibly inspired after a normal breath	Decrease
Expiratory reserve volume	Volume of air that can be forcibly expired after a normal breath	Slight decrease
Residual volume	Volume of air that remains in the lungs after maximum expiration	Remains the same
Minute ventilation	Volume of air breathed in or out per minute	Large increase

Check your understanding and progress at **www.hoddereducation.co.uk/myrevisionnotes**

The volume of air we breathe in and out can be measured using a spirometer. An example of a spirometer trace is shown in Figure 1.8.

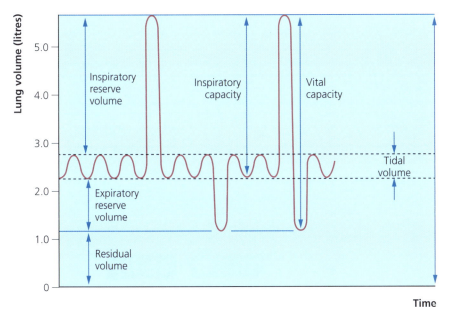

Figure 1.8 Spirometer trace of respiratory air

Exam tip

We all know that breathing increases during exercise, so it is an easy mistake to say that inspiratory and expiratory reserve volumes increase during exercise. In fact, they *decrease*.

Revision activity

Write out each of the lung volumes and definitions on separate pieces of paper and try to match each lung volume with its correct definition.

Now test yourself   TESTED ◯

1   What do you think will happen to a graphical representation of residual volume during exercise?

Answer on p. 260

Gas exchange systems at alveoli and muscles   REVISED ◯

+ Gaseous exchange is concerned with getting oxygen in air into the lungs so that it can diffuse into the blood and be transported to the cells of the body. It also involves the removal of carbon dioxide from the blood.
+ The terms diffusion and partial pressure are used when describing the gaseous exchange process. Quite simply, all gases exert a pressure. Oxygen makes up only a small part of air (approximately 21 per cent), so it therefore exerts a *partial* pressure.
+ Diffusion is the movement of gas molecules from an area of high concentration or partial pressure to an area of low concentration or partial pressure.
+ Since gases flow from an area of high pressure to an area of low pressure, it is important that as air moves from the alveoli to the blood and then to the muscle, the partial pressure of oxygen of each needs to be successively lower.

Gas exchange at the alveoli
The alveoli are responsible for the exchange of gases between the lungs and the blood, and their structure (Figure 1.9) is designed to help gaseous exchange.
+ Their walls are very thin (only one cell thick), which means there is a short diffusion pathway. This is because there are only two layers of cells between the air in the alveoli and the blood.
+ An extensive capillary network surrounds the alveoli, so they have an excellent blood supply.
+ They have a huge surface area because there are millions of alveoli in each lung, which allows for a greater uptake of oxygen.

Exam tip

Exam questions mentioning gas exchange require an explanation of the movement of both oxygen and carbon dioxide. Too often answers only mention one of these.

Gaseous exchange
Movement of oxygen from the air into the blood, and of carbon dioxide from the blood into the air.

Diffusion The movement of gas molecules from an area of high concentration or partial pressure to an area of low concentration or partial pressure.

Partial pressure The pressure exerted by an individual gas when it exists within a mixture of gases.

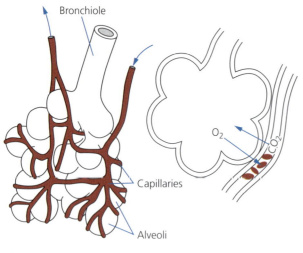

Figure 1.9 The structure of alveoli

Exam tip

The diffusion pathway of oxygen is: alveoli → blood → muscles.

+ The partial pressure of oxygen (pO_2) in the alveoli (100 mmHg) is higher than the partial pressure of oxygen in the capillary blood vessels (40 mmHg). This is because oxygen has been removed by the working muscles, so its concentration (and therefore its partial pressure) in the blood is lower.
+ The difference in partial pressure is referred to as the concentration/diffusion gradient. The bigger this gradient, the faster diffusion will be.
+ Oxygen will diffuse from the alveoli into the blood until the pressure is equal in both.
+ The movement of carbon dioxide occurs in the same way, but in the reverse order. This time the partial pressure of carbon dioxide in the blood entering the alveolar capillaries (45 mmHg) is higher than in the alveoli (40 mmHg), so carbon dioxide diffuses into the alveoli from the blood until the pressure is equal in both.

Concentration/diffusion gradient This explains how gases flow from an area of high concentration to an area of low concentration.

Exam tip

The diffusion pathway of carbon dioxide is: muscles → blood → alveoli.

Gas exchange at the muscles
+ The partial pressure of oxygen has to be lower in the tissues than in the blood for diffusion to occur.
+ In the capillary membranes surrounding the muscle, the partial pressure of oxygen is 40 mmHg, while it is 100 mmHg in the blood (Figure 1.10).
+ This lower partial pressure allows oxygen to diffuse from the blood into the muscle until equilibrium is reached.
+ Conversely, the partial pressure of carbon dioxide in the blood (40 mmHg) is lower than in the tissues (45 mmHg), so again diffusion occurs and carbon dioxide moves into the blood to be transported to the lungs.
+ Myoglobin stores oxygen in the muscle and has a higher affinity for oxygen than haemoglobin, and so pulls more oxygen into the muscle.

Making links

Gaseous exchange at the muscles links with knowledge of haemoglobin and myoglobin explained in the section on the vascular system.

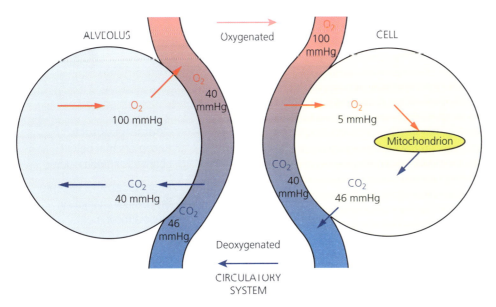

ALVEOLUS

Oxygenated

CELL

O_2 100 mmHg

O_2 100 mmHg

O_2 40 mmHg

O_2 5 mmHg

Mitochondrion

CO_2 40 mmHg

CO_2 40 mmHg

CO_2 46 mmHg

CO_2 46 mmHg

Deoxygenated

CIRCULATORY SYSTEM

Figure 1.10 Movement of O_2 and CO_2 in the body due to partial pressures

Now test yourself   TESTED ◯

3   Using Figure 1.10, explain how the gas exchange system operates at the muscles.

Answer on p. 260

Neural and chemical regulation of pulmonary ventilation

REVISED ◯

There are two factors involved in the regulation of pulmonary ventilation during exercise:

+ neural control
+ chemical control

+ The nervous system controls pulmonary ventilation automatically through two systems: sympathetic and parasympathetic.
+ Both of these cause opposite effects because their activating chemicals are different.
+ The sympathetic nervous system prepares your body for exercise, so it will increase how fast you breathe, whereas the parasympathetic nervous system will do the opposite and lower your breathing rate.
+ The respiratory centre located in the medulla of the brain controls the rate and depth of breathing, and uses both neural and chemical control.

An increased concentration of carbon dioxide in the blood stimulates the respiratory centre to increase respiratory rate. The respiratory centre has two main areas:

+ The inspiratory centre is responsible for inspiration and expiration.
+ The expiratory centre is inactive during quiet breathing (at rest) but during exercise it stimulates the expiratory muscles (sternocleidomastoid, scalenes, pectoralis minor) during exercise.

The inspiratory centre sends out nerve impulses via the phrenic nerve to the inspiratory muscles (diaphragm and external intercostals) to cause them to contract. This stimulation acts for approximately 2 seconds, and then the impulses stop and passive expiration occurs due to the elastic recoil of the lungs.

Pulmonary ventilation
The process of breathing.

Exam tip

Neural control involves the brain and the nervous system, while chemical control is concerned with blood acidity.

Making links

Remember that knowledge of the sympathetic and parasympathetic systems is also required for the heart, blood flow and the neuromuscular system.

Receptors involved in regulation of pulmonary ventilation

The respiratory centre responds mainly to changes in blood chemistry:

+ During exercise, blood acidity increases as a result of increases in the plasma concentration of carbon dioxide and in lactic acid production.
+ These changes are detected by chemoreceptors, which are found in the carotid artery and the aortic arch. These send impulses to the inspiratory centre to increase ventilation until the blood acidity has returned to normal.
+ To achieve this, the respiratory centre sends impulses down the phrenic nerve to stimulate more inspiratory muscles – namely, the sternocleidomastoid, scalenes and pectoralis minor.
+ As a result the rate and depth of breathing increase.
+ Proprioceptors detect an increase in muscle movement and provide feedback to the respiratory centre to increase breathing during exercise.
+ Baroreceptors detect a decrease in blood pressure in the aorta and carotid arteries, resulting in an increase in breathing rate.

Chemoreceptors Receptors that detect changes in blood acidity.

Proprioceptors Receptors that detect changes in muscle movement.

Baroreceptors Receptors that detect changes in blood pressure.

Exam tip

The order of neural/chemical control for inspiration during exercise is:

receptors → medulla oblongata → phrenic nerve → inspiratory muscles (diaphragm, external intercostals, sternocleidomastoid, scalenes and pectoralis minor)

The order of neural/chemical control for increased expiration during exercise is:

receptors → medulla oblongata → intercostal nerve → abdominals and internal intercostals

---

Now test yourself TESTED

4 Explain the roles of proprioceptors and baroreceptors in the regulation of pulmonary ventilation.

Answer on pp. 260–261

Impact of poor lifestyle choices on the respiratory system

Smoking affects oxygen transport because the carbon monoxide from cigarettes combines with haemoglobin in red blood cells much more readily than oxygen. This reduces the oxygen-carrying capacity of the blood, which increases breathlessness during exercise. Smoking can also cause the following:

+ irritation of the trachea and bronchi
+ reduced lung function and increased breathlessness caused by the swelling and narrowing of the bronchioles
+ damage to the cilia lining the airways from cigarette smoke, leading to a build-up of excess mucus in the lungs, which results in a 'smoker's cough' in an attempt to get rid of the mucus
+ reduction in the efficiency of gaseous exchange, which can increase the risk of COPD (chronic obstructive pulmonary disease)
+ reduction in the number of and/or damage to alveoli

Exam tip

Make sure that you can explain the impact of smoking on performance. For example, reduced oxygen transportation to the muscles will mean that an endurance performer will not function as well aerobically, so fatigue occurs more quickly.

Now test yourself TESTED

5 Identify one long-term effect of regular smoking on the structures of an endurance performer's respiratory system.

Answer on p. 261

Check your understanding and progress at www.hoddereducation.co.uk/myrevisionnotes

Exam practice

1 Explain how the gas-exchange system operates at the lungs. [4]
2 Explain the role of chemoreceptors in changing breathing rate during exercise. [4]
3 How does smoking affect oxygen transport? [2]
4 Identify what happens to the following lung volumes during exercise: tidal volume, inspiratory reserve volume. [2]
5 Why does residual volume remain the same? [1]
6 Using the values in Table 1.3, calculate minute ventilation during high-intensity exercise. [2]

Table 1.3

Exercise intensity	Tidal volume (litres)	Respiratory rate (breaths/ minute)
Low	1	20
High	2.5	36

Answers online

Knowledge and skills summary

This topic involves the following knowledge (AO1):

+ Residual volume, expiratory reserve volume, inspiratory reserve volume, tidal volume and minute ventilation, and the impact of physical activity and sport on these lung volumes.
+ Gaseous exchange of oxygen and carbon dioxide at alveoli and muscles, through the principles of diffusion and partial pressure.
+ Neural and chemical regulation of pulmonary ventilation during physical activity.
+ The role of chemoreceptors, proprioceptors and baroreceptors in the regulation of pulmonary ventilation during exercise.

+ The effects of poor lifestyle choices, such as smoking, on the respiratory system.

AO2 marks will require application of this knowledge – for example, how smoking can affect performance or how to calculate a lung volume such as tidal volume.

AO3 marks are for analysis or evaluation. In this topic an AO3 response might involve analysing the impact of increased minute ventilation on aerobic performance.

1.4 Neuromuscular system

The neuromuscular system involves the nervous system and muscles working together. When we exercise, the nervous system plays a crucial role in recruiting different muscle fibre types depending on the demands of the activity. It adjusts the strength of contraction and, with the use of sensory organs, can allow a muscle to stretch further via PNF (proprioceptive neuromuscular facilitation).

The nervous system

The sympathetic and parasympathetic systems are part of the peripheral nervous system. Their role is to transmit information from the brain to the parts of the body that need to adjust what they are doing, in order to prepare for exercise.

Making links

The sympathetic and parasympathetic systems are explained in more detail in 1.2 Cardiovascular system (p. 13).

Characteristics and functions of different muscle fibre types

There are three main types of muscle fibre:

+ slow twitch (type I)
+ fast oxidative glycolytic (type IIa)
+ fast glycolytic (type IIx).

Type I fibres are known as 'slow twitch' and type II fibres are known as 'fast twitch'. Our skeletal muscles contain a mixture of all three types of fibre, but not in equal proportions. This mix is mainly genetically determined.

Slow-twitch fibres (type I)

These fibres have a slower contraction speed than fast-twitch fibres and are better adapted to lower-intensity exercise, such as long-distance running. They produce most of their energy aerobically (using oxygen) and therefore have specific characteristics that allow them to use oxygen more effectively.

Fast-twitch fibres (type II)

These fibres have a much faster contraction speed and can generate a greater force of contraction. However, they also fatigue very quickly and are used for short, intense bursts of effort. They produce most of their energy anaerobically (without oxygen). There are two types of fast-twitch fibre:

+ **Type IIa fast oxidative glycolytic:** these are more resistant to fatigue and are used for events such as the 1500m in athletics, where a longer burst of energy is needed.
+ **Type IIx fast glycolytic:** these fatigue much more quickly than type IIa, and are used for highly explosive events such as the 100m in athletics, where a quick, short burst of energy is needed.

> **Exam tip**
>
> When giving a practical example, remember that slow-twitch fibres contract slower and do not fatigue quickly, so they tend to be used by endurance runners who exercise for long periods of time at low–medium intensity.

> **Now test yourself**   TESTED ⬤
>
> **1** Identify two sporting activities in which slow-twitch fibres are important.
>
> **Answer on p. 261**

Characteristics of slow-twitch and fast-twitch muscle fibres

All three fibre types have specific characteristics that allow them to perform their roles successfully. These can be found in the Table 1.4.

Table 1.4 Characteristics of slow-twitch and fast-twitch muscle fibres

Characteristic	Type I	Type IIa	Type IIx
Contraction speed (milliseconds)	Slow (110 ms)	Fast (50 ms)	Fast (50 ms)
Motor neurone size	Small	Large	Large
Motor neurone conduction capacity	Slow	Fast	Fast
Force produced	Low	High	High
Fatigability	Low	Medium	High
Mitochondrial density	High	Medium	Low
Myoglobin content	High	Medium	Low
Capillary density	High	Medium	Low
Aerobic capacity	Very high	Medium	Low
Anaerobic capacity	Low	High	Very high
Myosin ATPase/glycolytic enzyme activity	Low	High	Very high
Glycogen stores	Low	High	High
PC stores	Low	High	High

Each of the fibre type characteristics can be divided into two groups — functional characteristics or structural characteristics (Table 1.5). A functional characteristic is what the fibre does and a structural characteristic refers to the make-up of the fibre.

Table 1.5 Functional and structural characteristics of muscle fibres

Functional characteristics	Structural characteristics
✛ Contraction speed in m/sec	✛ Motor neurone size
✛ Motor neurone conduction capacity	✛ Mitochondrial density
✛ Force produced	✛ Myoglobin content
✛ Fatigability	✛ Capillary density
✛ Aerobic capacity	✛ PC stores
✛ Anaerobic capacity	✛ Glycogen stores
✛ Myosin ATPase/glycolytic enzyme activity	

Now test yourself   TESTED ⬤

2   Identify the type of fibre a football goalkeeper would use when jumping explosively to make a save.

3   Give three characteristics of this fibre type.

Answers on p. 261

Recruitment of muscle fibres   REVISED ⬤

Motor units

✛ A motor unit consists of a motor neurone and a group of muscle fibres.
✛ Only one type of muscle fibre can be found in one particular motor unit.
✛ Muscle fibres work with the nervous system so that a contraction can occur.
✛ The motor neurone transmits nerve impulses from the CNS to the muscle fibres.
✛ Each motor neurone has branches that end in the neuromuscular junction on the muscle fibre.

The all-or-none law

Once the motor neurone stimulates the muscle fibres either all of them contract or none of them contract. It is not possible for a motor unit to partially contract. This is called the all-or-none law.
✛ A minimum amount of stimulation, called the threshold, is required to start a contraction.
✛ If the sequence of impulses is equal to or more than the threshold then all the muscle fibres in a motor unit will contract.
✛ However, if the sequence of impulses is less than the threshold then no muscle action will occur.

How to increase the strength of contraction

A basketball player jumping up for a rebound needs to exert as much force as possible to gain the height needed to win the rebound. To increase the strength or force exerted by the quadriceps muscle to extend their knee as they jump, the following need to take place:

Wave summation

✛ The greater the frequency of stimuli, the greater the tension developed by the muscle. This is referred to as wave summation, where repeated activation of a motor neurone stimulating a given muscle fibre results in a greater force of contraction (Figure 1.11).
✛ Each time the nerve impulse reaches the muscle cell, calcium is released.

Exam tip

Read the exam question carefully. If the question is not specific and just asks for characteristics, your answer can include both structural and functional characteristics. However, mistakes occur when a question specifies either structural or functional characteristics.

Revision activity

Make a list of all the characteristics and then explain how they are suited to producing energy (ATP) aerobically and anaerobically. See 1.6 Energy systems for more on energy production.

Motor unit A motor neurone and muscle fibres.

Motor neurone A nerve cell that sends impulses from the brain and spinal cord to the muscles.

All or none law Where a sequence of impulses has to be of sufficient intensity to stimulate all of the muscle fibres in a motor unit in order for them to contract. If not, *none* of them contracts.

Wave summation Where there is a repeated nerve impulse with no time to relax, so a smooth, sustained contraction occurs rather than twitches.

+ In simple terms calcium needs to be present for a muscle to contract.
+ If there are repeated nerve impulses with no time to relax calcium will build up in the muscle cell.
+ This produces a forceful, sustained, smooth contraction, which is referred to as a tetanic contraction.

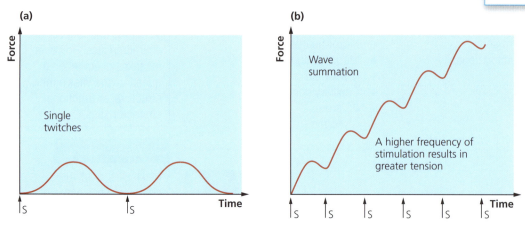

Figure 1.11 (a) Low-frequency stimuli; (b) high-frequency stimuli leading to increased tension

Spatial summation

+ Spatial summation occurs when impulses are received at the same time at different places on the neurone, which add up to fire the neurone.
+ It involves the recruitment of additional, bigger motor units and fast-twitch motor units to develop more force.
+ Activation of these motor units is staggered, which enables a sustained muscle contraction to be maintained, as some motor units are contracting while others are relaxing, thus delaying fatigue.

Spatial summation When the strength of a contraction changes by altering the number and size of the muscle's motor units.

Now test yourself | TESTED ⚪

4 Contraction of different types of muscle fibre involve the use of motor units. What do you understand by the term 'motor unit' and how are motor units involved in the process of spatial summation?

Answer on p. 261

Exam tip

Questions on motor units often ask how a performer can produce muscle contractions of varying strength.

Role of proprioceptors in PNF | REVISED ⚪

PNF stands for proprioceptive neuromuscular facilitation and is an advanced stretching technique. It is also considered to be one of the most effective forms of flexibility training for increasing the range of motion. There are a few different PNF techniques, but the most practical is CRAC.

CRAC Contract–relax–antagonist–contract

Making links

PNF is also covered in 4.2 Preparation and training methods in relation to maintaining physical activity and performance (p. 128).

Roles of muscle spindles and Golgi tendon organs

In PNF, muscle action has to be controlled in order for movement to be effective (Figure 1.12). There are several internal regulatory mechanisms that make this possible. Proprioceptors are sensory organs in the muscles, tendons and joints that inform the body of the extent of movement that has taken place. Muscle spindles and Golgi tendon organs are types of proprioceptor.

Figure 1.12 PNF in practice

Muscle spindles

+ Muscle spindles are very sensitive proprioceptors that lie between skeletal muscle fibres.
+ They are often called stretch receptors because they provide information (excitatory signals) to the central nervous system about how fast and how far a muscle is being stretched.
+ The central nervous system then sends an impulse back to the muscle telling it to contract, which triggers the stretch reflex.
+ This reflex action causes the muscle to contract to prevent overstretching, which reduces the risk of injury.

> **Muscle spindles**
> Proprioceptors that detect how far and how fast a muscle is being stretched, and produce the stretch reflex.

Golgi tendon organs

+ Golgi tendon organs are found between the muscle fibre and tendon and detect levels of tension in a muscle.
+ When the muscle is contracted isometrically in PNF they sense the increase in muscle tension.
+ They then send inhibitory signals to the brain to override the stretch reflex, which allows the antagonist muscle to relax and lengthen. This is known as autogenic inhibition.

> **Golgi tendon organs**
> Structures that detect levels of tension in a muscle.
>
> **Autogenic inhibition**
> Where there is a sudden relaxation of the muscle in response to high tension. The receptors involved in this process are Golgi tendon organs.

> **Now test yourself** TESTED ◯
>
> **5** Muscle spindles and Golgi tendon organs are types of proprioceptor. What is the role of proprioceptors?
>
> **Answer on p. 261**

> **Exam tip**
>
> Muscle spindles signal changes in the length of a muscle, while Golgi tendon organs signal information about the load or force being applied to the muscle.

> **Exam practice**
>
> **1** The training that elite performers undertake might include proprioceptive neuromuscular facilitation (PNF) stretching. Explain the role of the muscle spindle apparatus and Golgi tendon organs during PNF stretching. [5]
>
> **2** Describe the structural characteristics of the main muscle fibre type used by a triathlete. [4]
>
> **3** Analyse how the recruitment of muscle fibres can enable a 100 m sprinter to accelerate explosively at the start of the race. [8]
>
> **Answers online**

> **Knowledge and skills summary**
>
> This topic involves the following knowledge (AO1):
> + The characteristics and functions of the three fibre types – slow twitch (type I), fast oxidative glycolytic (type IIa) and fast glycolytic (type IIx) – for a variety of sporting activities.
> + The role of the sympathetic and parasympathetic nervous system.
> + The role of the two proprioceptors – muscle spindles and Golgi tendon organs – in PNF.
> + the recruitment of muscle fibres through an explanation of motor units, spatial summation, wave summation, all-or-none law and tetanic contraction.
>
> AO2 marks will require application of this knowledge – for example, looking at the demands of an activity when deciding on fibre type, or applying knowledge of motor units to explain how a maximal contraction can be achieved.
>
> AO3 marks are for analysis or evaluation – for example, analysing how the use of fast-twitch IIx fibres have an impact on performance.
>
> Sometimes you might be required to apply (AO2) your knowledge of fibre type to another topic – for example, 1.6 Energy systems.

1.5 Musculoskeletal system and analysis of movement

Types of joint and articulating bones

REVISED

Table 1.6 summarises joint types and the associated articulating bones.

Table 1.6 Joints and articulating bones

Joint	Joint type	Articulating bones
Ankle	Hinge	Talus, tibia, fibula
Knee	Hinge	Femur, tibia
Hip	Ball and socket	Pelvis, femur
Shoulder	Ball and socket	Scapula, humerus
Elbow	Hinge	Radius, ulna, humerus

> **Articulating bones** Bones that meet and move at a joint.

Planes and axes

+ Joint actions in the sagittal plane/transverse axis: flexion, extension/ hyperextension, plantarflexion and dorsiflexion occur in a sagittal plane about a transverse axis (Figure 1.13).
+ Joint actions in the frontal plane about a sagittal axis: abduction and adduction occur in a frontal plane about a sagittal axis (Figure 1.14).

> **Abduction** Movement away from the midline of the body.
>
> **Adduction** Movement towards the midline of the body.

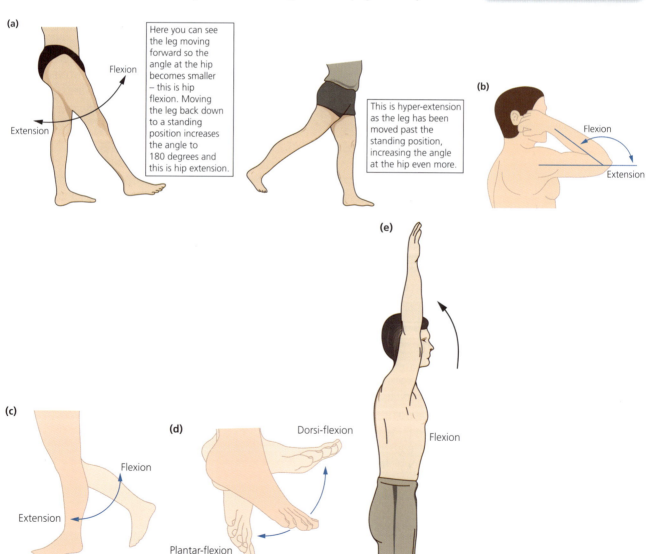

Figure 1.13 Joint actions in the frontal plane about a sagittal axis at the (a) hip, (b) elbow, (c) knee, (d) ankle and (e) shoulder

Check your understanding and progress at **www.hoddereducation.co.uk/myrevisionnotes**

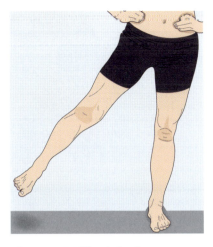

Figure 1.14 Hip abduction

✚ Joint actions in the transverse plane/longitudinal axis: horizontal adduction and horizontal abduction occur in the transverse plane about a longitudinal axis (Figure 1.15). These joint actions occur in the shoulder when the arm is held parallel to the ground – out at 90° to the body – and is either moved across the body (horizontal adduction) or away from the body (horizontal abduction).

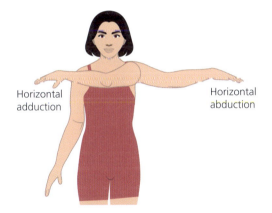

Horizontal adduction

Horizontal abduction

Figure 1.15 Horizontal adduction and horizontal abduction

Making links

Joint actions also need to be applied to levers (5.2 Levers) – for example, plantarflexion of the ankle is a second-class lever (p. 138).

Now test yourself   TESTED ○

1 Identify the joint actions occurring in the hip and shoulder as the performer moves from A to B in Figure 1.16.

A   B

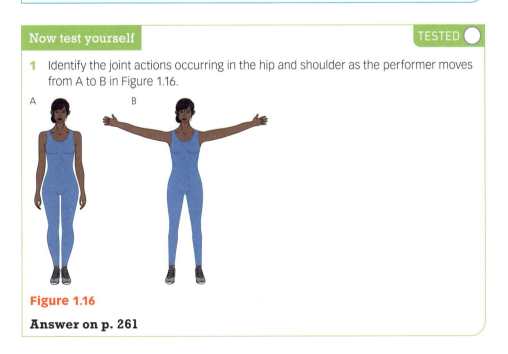

Figure 1.16

Answer on p. 261

Main agonists and antagonists

+ **Agonist** – the muscle that is responsible for the movement that is occurring.
+ **Antagonist** – the muscle that works in opposition to the agonist to help produce a coordinated movement.

You need to learn the main agonists and antagonists for each of the joint actions. These are identified in Table 1.7.

Table 1.7 Agonists and antagonists for joint actions

Joint action	Agonist	Antagonist
Elbow flexion	Biceps	Triceps
Elbow extension	Triceps	Biceps
Ankle plantarflexion	Gastrocnemius	Tibialis anterior
Ankle dorsiflexion	Tibialis anterior	Gastrocnemius
Knee flexion	Hamstrings	Quadriceps
Knee extension	Quadriceps	Hamstrings
Hip flexion	Iliopsoas or hip flexors	Gluteals
Hip extension/hyperextension	Gluteals	Hip flexors
Hip adduction	Adductors (adductor brevis/longus/magnus)	Gluteus medius and gluteus minimus
Hip abduction	Gluteus medius and gluteus minimus	Adductors (adductor brevis/longus/magnus)
Hip horizontal adduction	Adductors	Gluteus medius/minimus
Hip horizontal abduction	Gluteus medius/minimus	Adductors
Shoulder flexion	Anterior deltoid	Latissimus dorsi
Shoulder extension/hyperextension	Latissimus dorsi	Anterior deltoid
Shoulder horizontal abduction	Latissimus dorsi	Pectorals
Shoulder horizontal adduction	Pectorals	Latissimus dorsi
Shoulder adduction	Posterior deltoid/latissimus dorsi	Middle deltoid/supraspinatus
Shoulder abduction	Middle deltoid/supraspinatus	Posterior deltoid/latissimus dorsi

> **Revision activity**
>
> Write the names of all the agonists and antagonists on some sticky notes and place them on your body at the correct locations.

Types of muscular contraction

Isotonic

An isotonic contraction is when a muscle contracts to create movement.
+ **Concentric contraction** – when a muscle shortens under tension.
+ **Eccentric contraction** – when a muscle lengthens under tension.

> **Exam tip**
>
> Questions with a picture showing a performer moving their body weight or a free weight in the downward phase involve an eccentric contraction because the muscle is acting as a brake – for example, the triceps in the downward phase of a press-up.

> **Exam tip**
>
> Eccentric is the type of contraction most misunderstood. Remember, it is a contraction so the muscle cannot be relaxing, but it is lengthening under tension.

Isometric contraction

This is when a muscle can contract without actually lengthening or shortening, and the result is that no movement occurs – for example, the crucifix in gymnastics.

Now test yourself
TESTED ◯

2 Complete Table 1.8, showing a movement analysis for the (back leg) hip, knee and ankle action in the drive phase of running (Figure 1.17).

Table 1.8

Joint	Joint action	Plane and axis	Agonist	Type of contraction
Hip				
Knee				
Ankle				

Figure 1.17

Answer on p. 261

Exam practice

1 Figure 1.18 shows an overarm throw.

Figure 1.18

Using Figure 1.18, complete Table 1.9 to identify the joint actions, the names of the main agonists and the types of contraction taking place at the elbow and shoulder as the performer passes the ball. [6]

My Revision Notes: AQA A-level PE

Table 1.9

Joint	Joint action	Main agonist	Type of contraction
Elbow			
Shoulder			

2 Weightlifters need to ensure that they prepare physically and psychologically to perform in a competitive situation. Figure 1.19 shows a weightlifter who has moved into the squat position prior to attempting her lift.

Figure 1.19

Complete Table 1.10 to identify the joint action, main agonist and type of muscle contraction taking place at the knee and ankle joints as the weightlifter moves downwards from a standing position into the squat position. [6]

Table 1.10

Joint	Joint action	Agonist	Type of contraction
Knee			
Ankle			

3 Identify the plane and axis for abduction at the hip joint. [2]

Answers online

Knowledge and skills summary

This topic involves the following knowledge (AO1):
+ The type of joint and articulating bones for the ankle, knee, hip, elbow and shoulder.
+ The actions in these joints that occur in a sagittal plane/transverse axis as flexion, extension, hyperextension, plantarflexion and dorsiflexion.
+ Hip and shoulder abduction and adduction occur in a frontal plane about a sagittal axis.
+ Hip and shoulder horizontal adduction and horizontal abduction occur in a transverse plane about a longitudinal axis.
+ The main agonists and antagonists for the actions occurring at the ankle, knee, hip, elbow and shoulder.

+ The types of muscle contraction – isotonic (concentric, eccentric) and isometric.

AO2 marks will require application of this knowledge – for example, identifying the joint action in a movement.

AO3 marks are for analysis or evaluation. In this topic an AO3 response might involve analysing how the take-off leg in the long jump will flex more as the athlete sinks into the board to create momentum for an explosive take-off.

Sometimes you might be required to apply (AO2) your knowledge of the musculoskeletal system to another topic on the specification – for example, 5.2 Levers.

1.6 Energy systems

Energy transfer in the body

REVISED ●

In the body, the energy we use for muscle contractions comes from adenosine triphosphate (ATP), which is the only usable form of chemical energy in the body. The energy we derive from the foods that we eat, such as carbohydrates, is broken down to release energy that is used to form ATP (which consists of one molecule of adenosine and three (tri) phosphates).

The energy that is stored in ATP is released by breaking down the bonds that hold this compound together. Enzymes are used to break down compounds. In this instance, ATPase is the enzyme used to break down ATP, leaving adenosine diphosphate (ADP) and an inorganic phosphate (Pi) (Figure 1.20).

> **Adenosine triphosphate (ATP)** The only usable form of energy in the body.

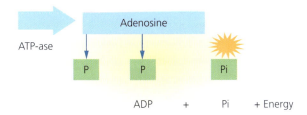

Figure 1.20 ATPase breaks down ATP to produce ADP + Pi + energy

The body has to constantly rebuild ATP by converting the ADP and Pi back into ATP. We can resynthesise ATP from three different types of chemical reaction in the muscle cells, which are fuelled by either food (carbohydrates, fats and protein) or a chemical called phosphocreatine, which is found in the muscles. The conversion of these fuels into energy takes place through one of three energy systems:
+ the aerobic energy system
+ the ATP–PC system
+ the anaerobic glycolytic system

The aerobic energy system

When exercise intensity is low and oxygen supply is high, for example when jogging, the aerobic system is the preferred energy pathway.

How it works to provide energy

The aerobic system has three stages as it works to provide energy: glycolysis, the Krebs cycle and the electron transport chain.

Stage 1: glycolysis

Glycolysis is the first stage and is anaerobic, so it takes place in the sarcoplasm of the muscle cell. Glycolysis is the breakdown of glucose into pyruvic acid. For every molecule of glucose undergoing glycolysis, a net of two molecules of ATP is formed.

> **Making links**
>
> Glycolysis takes place in the anaerobic glycolytic system (p. 37).

Before the pyruvic acid produced in glycolysis can enter the next stage (the Krebs cycle), it splits into two acetyl groups and is then carried into the Krebs cycle by coenzyme A.

Stage 2: the Krebs cycle
+ Acetyl coenzyme A diffuses into the matrix of the mitochondria and a complex cycle of reactions occurs in a process known as the Krebs cycle.

> **Glycolysis** The breakdown of glucose into pyruvic acid.
>
> **Krebs cycle** A series of cyclical chemical reactions that take place using oxygen in the matrix of the mitochondria.
>
> **Electron transport chain** A series of chemical reactions in the cristae of the mitochondria in which hydrogen is oxidised to water and 34 ATP are produced.
>
> **Sarcoplasm** The fluid that surrounds the nucleus of a muscle fibre – the site where anaerobic respiration takes place.

35

+ Here acetyl coenzyme A combines with oxaloacetic acid, forming citric acid.
+ Hydrogen is removed from the citric acid and the rearranged form of citric acid undergoes 'oxidative carboxylation', which simply means that carbon and hydrogen are given off.
+ The carbon forms carbon dioxide, which is transported to the lungs and breathed out.
+ The hydrogen is taken to the electron transport chain.
+ The reactions that occur result in the production of two molecules of ATP.

Beta oxidation

+ Fats can also enter the Krebs cycle. Stored fat is broken down into glycerol and free fatty acids for transporting by the blood.
+ These fatty acids then undergo a process called beta oxidation, whereby they are converted into acetyl coenzyme A, which is the entry molecule for the Krebs cycle.
+ From this point on, fat metabolism follows the same path as glycogen metabolism.
+ More ATP can be made from one molecule of fatty acids than from one molecule of glucose, which is why in long-duration, low-intensity exercise fatty acids will be the predominant energy source – but this does depend on the fitness of the performer.

> **Beta oxidation** A process in which fatty acids are broken down to generate acetyl-CoA, which enters the Krebs cycle.

Stage 3 Electron transport chain

+ Hydrogen is carried to the electron transport chain by hydrogen carriers.
+ This occurs in the cristae of the mitochondria.
+ The hydrogen splits into hydrogen ions and electrons, which are charged with potential energy.
+ The hydrogen ions are oxidised to form water, while the hydrogen electrons provide the energy to resynthesise ATP.
+ Throughout this process 34 molecules of ATP are formed.

> **Exam tip**
>
> As well as learning the key points of each energy system, make sure you can identify when the aerobic system is the predominant method of producing energy.

> **Now test yourself**   TESTED ⭕
>
> 1 Summarise the stages of the Krebs cycle.
>
> **Answer on p. 261**

> **Revision activity**
>
> Draw a diagram starting with glucose at the top and try to summarise all three stages of the aerobic system.

ATP–PC system

This is an energy system using phosphocreatine (PC) as its fuel. PC is an energy-rich phosphate compound found in the sarcoplasm of the muscles. It can be broken down quickly and easily to release energy to resynthesise ATP. Its rapid availability is important for 6–8 seconds of flat-out effort.

> **Phosphocreatine (PC)** An energy-rich phosphate compound found in the sarcoplasm of the muscles.

How it works to provide energy

The ATP–PC system is an anaerobic process and resynthesises ATP when the enzyme creatine kinase detects high levels of ADP. It breaks down the phosphocreatine in the muscles to phosphate and creatine, releasing energy:

phosphocreatine (PC) → phosphate (Pi) + creatine (C) + energy

This energy is then used to convert ADP to ATP in a coupled reaction:

energy → Pi + ADP → ATP

> **Exam tip**
>
> Exam questions often ask how energy is produced during a particular sporting activity. If the sporting example is a high-intensity activity lasting up to 8 seconds, then the main energy provider will be the ATP–PC system.

Now test yourself   TESTED

2   What are the key points you need to remember for the ATP–PC energy system?

Answer on p. 261

Anaerobic glycolytic system

+ The anaerobic glycolytic system provides energy for high-intensity activity for longer than the ATP–PC system.
+ However, how long this system lasts depends on the fitness of the individual and how high the intensity of the exercise is.
+ Working flat out to exhaustion will mean the system will last a much shorter time.
+ This is because the demand for energy is extremely high.
+ An elite athlete who has just run the 400m in under 45 seconds will not be able to run it again immediately at the same pace. However, by reducing the intensity a little the system can last longer – up to 2–3 minutes – because the demand for energy is slightly lower.

How it works to provide energy

+ When the PC stores are low the enzyme glycogen phosphorylase is activated to break down the glycogen into glucose, which is then further broken down to pyruvic acid by the enzyme phosphofructokinase.
+ This process is called anaerobic glycolysis and takes place in the sarcoplasm of the muscle cell where oxygen is not available.
+ Since this is an anaerobic process, the pyruvic acid is then further broken down into lactic acid by the enzyme lactate dehydrogenase (LDH).
+ During glycolysis, energy is released to allow ATP resynthesis.
+ The *net* result is that two molecules of ATP are produced for one molecule of glucose broken down (four moles of ATP are produced but two are used to provide energy for glycolysis itself).

> **Exam tip**
>
> The key points about glycolysis are:
> + breakdown of glucose to pyruvic acid
> + produces two molecules of ATP
> + during intense exercise, pyruvic acid converted into lactic acid

Energy continuum of physical activity   REVISED

The 'energy continuum' is a term used to describe which energy system is used for different types of physical activity and sport.
+ It refers to the contribution that the different energy systems make to the production of energy, depending on the intensity and duration of exercise.
+ The three energy systems do not work independently of one another.
+ They all contribute during all types of activity, but one of them will be the predominant energy provider.
+ The *intensity* and *duration* of the activity are the factors that decide which will be the main energy system in use (see Table 1.11).

> **Energy continuum** A term that describes which type of energy system is used for different types of physical activity and sport. The contribution of each system depends on the intensity and duration of exercise.

Table 1.11 The energy continuum

Duration of performance	Intensity	Energy supplied by
Less than 10 seconds	Very high	ATP–PC system
8–90 seconds	High to very high	ATP–PC and anaerobic glycolytic systems
90 seconds to 3 minutes	High	Anaerobic glycolytic and aerobic systems
3+ minutes	Low to medium	Aerobic system

37

Now test yourself TESTED ⬤

3 Decide on the intensity and duration of the following examples in a game of football, and then identify which energy system would be the predominant energy provider.

   a Short 10 m sprint into space to receive the ball.

   b Making a quick break in attack over the length of the pitch.

   c Jogging to keep in position.

Answer on p. 261

Exam tip

Do not explain all three energy systems if you are unsure which one(s) are relevant. This is not answering the question and marks could be lost.

The energy continuum is often explained in terms of thresholds. The ATP–PC/anaerobic glycolytic threshold is the point at which the ATP–PC energy system is exhausted and the anaerobic glycolytic system takes over. This is shown in Figure 1.21 at 10 seconds. The anaerobic glycolytic/aerobic threshold, shown in the graph at 3 minutes, is the point at which the anaerobic glycolytic system is exhausted and the aerobic system takes over.

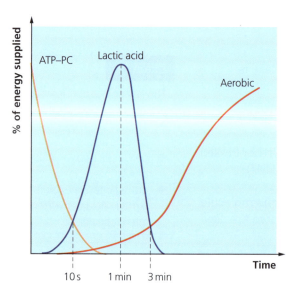

Figure 1.21 The energy continuum related to exercise duration

Differences in ATP generation

+ Slow-twitch fibres are recruited for low- to medium-intensity activity. They therefore use aerobic respiration to generate the required fuel for energy production.
+ Fast-twitch fibres on the other hand are recruited for high-intensity activities, such as sprinting, so anaerobic respiration is their main energy pathway (Table 1.12).

Exam tip

Slow-twitch fibres are aerobic and fast-twitch fibres are anaerobic.

Table 1.12 Summary of the differences in ATP generation between fast- and slow-twitch fibres

Slow-twitch (type I) fibres	Fast-twitch (type IIb) fibres
+ The main pathway for ATP production is via the aerobic system + This produces the maximum amount of ATP possible from each glucose molecule (up to 36 ATP) + Production is slow, but these fibres are more endurance based, so less likely to fatigue	+ The main pathway for ATP production is via the ATP–PC system and the anaerobic glycolytic energy system (during glycolysis) + ATP production in the absence of oxygen is not efficient – only two ATP produced per glucose molecule in glycolysis and one ATP molecule in the breakdown of phosphocreatine + Production of ATP this way is fast, but cannot last for long as these fibres have the least resistance to muscle fatigue

Energy transfer during short-duration/high-intensity exercise

During short-duration/high-intensity exercise, energy has to be produced rapidly. The aerobic system is too complicated to produce energy rapidly, so the body needs to rely on anaerobic respiration using the ATP–PC system and the anaerobic glycolytic system. However, these systems cannot produce energy for long periods of time.

Lactate accumulation

+ Lactate and lactic acid are not the same thing, but the terms are often used interchangeably.
+ Using the lactate anaerobic system produces the by-product lactic acid as a result of glycolysis.
+ The higher the intensity of exercise the more lactic acid is produced.
+ This lactic acid quickly breaks down, releasing hydrogen ions (H^+).
+ The remaining compound then combines with sodium ions (Na^+) or potassium ions (K^+) to form the salt lactate.
+ As lactate accumulates in the muscles, more hydrogen ions become present; it is the presence of hydrogen ions that increases acidity.
+ This slows down enzyme activity, which affects the breakdown of glycogen, causing muscle fatigue.
+ The lactate produced in the muscles diffuses into the blood, and blood lactate can be measured.

Lactate threshold and onset of blood lactate accumulation (OBLA)

+ As exercise intensity increases, the body moves from working aerobically to working anaerobically.
+ This crossing of the aerobic/anaerobic threshold is also known as the lactate threshold and is the point at which lactic acid accumulates rapidly in the blood (an increase of 2 millimoles per litre of blood above resting levels).
+ We are constantly producing small amounts of lactate due to red blood cell activity when working at low intensity, but the levels are low and the body deals with these effectively.
+ However, as the intensity of the exercise increases and the body is unable to produce enough oxygen to break down lactate, the levels of lactate build up/accumulate, and this is known as OBLA (onset of blood lactate accumulation).
+ OBLA and lactate threshold are simply different ways of measuring the same thing.
+ OBLA is the older term and lactate threshold is a more recent, American term.
+ At rest, approximately 1–2 millimoles per litre of lactate can be found in the blood. However, during intense exercise, levels of lactate will rise dramatically and as it starts to accumulate OBLA occurs.
+ This is usually when the concentration of lactate is around 4 mmol per litre.
+ Measuring OBLA gives an indication of endurance capacity.
+ Some individuals can work at higher levels of intensity than others before OBLA, and can delay when the threshold occurs.

> **Lactate threshold** The point at which lactic acid accumulates rapidly in the blood.
>
> **OBLA** The point at which lactate levels go above 4 millimoles/litre.

Lactate threshold is expressed as a percentage of VO_2 max:
+ As fitness increases the lactate threshold becomes delayed.
+ Average performers might have a lactate threshold that is 50–60 per cent of their VO_2 max, whereas elite performers might have a lactate threshold that is 70, 80 or even 90 per cent of their VO_2 max.
+ Training has a limited effect on VO_2 max because VO_2 max is largely determined genetically.

> **VO_2 max** The maximum amount of oxygen that can be utilised by the muscles per minute.

39

+ The big difference in performance comes from the delayed lactate threshold. When we exercise, we tend to work at or just below our lactate threshold. The fitter we are the higher our lactate threshold as a percentage of our VO_2 max, and hence the harder we can work.

Factors affecting the rate of lactate accumulation

+ **Exercise intensity** – the higher the exercise intensity the greater the demand for energy (ATP) and the faster OBLA occurs, because when glycogen is broken down anaerobically into pyruvic acid, lactic acid is formed.
+ **Muscle fibre type** – slow-twitch fibres produce less lactate than fast-twitch fibres. When slow-twitch fibres use glycogen as a fuel, due to the presence of oxygen, the glycogen can be broken down much more effectively and with little lactate production.
+ **VO_2 max of the performer** – the higher the VO_2 max the greater the delay in lactate accumulation.
+ **The respiratory exchange ratio** – this is described in more detail later in this chapter, but when the ratio has a value close to 1.0 glycogen becomes the preferred fuel and there is a greater chance of the accumulation of lactate.
+ **Fitness of the performer** – a person who trains regularly will be in a better position to delay OBLA because physiological adaptations occur in trained muscles. Increased numbers of mitochondria and levels of myoglobin, together with an increase in capillary density, improve the capacity for aerobic respiration and therefore avoid the use of the anaerobic glycolytic system.

Lactate-producing capacity and sprint/power performance

+ Elite sprinters and power athletes will have a much better anaerobic endurance than non-elite sprinters.
+ This is because their body has adapted to cope with higher levels of lactate.
+ In addition, through a process called buffering, they are able to increase the rate of lactate removal and consequently have lower lactate levels. Buffering works rather like a chemical 'sponge', mopping up the lactate molecules.
+ This means they are able to work at higher intensities for longer before fatigue sets in.
+ As well as being able to tolerate higher levels of lactate, the trained status of their working muscles will lead to adaptive responses. Mitochondria become more numerous and larger, alongside increases in associated oxidative enzymes, capillary density and myoglobin levels.

> **Buffering** A process that aids the removal of lactate and maintains acidity levels in the blood and muscle.

> **Exam tip**
>
> Make sure you can explain the impact of high levels of lactic acid/lactate on performance.

> **Now test yourself** TESTED ⬤
>
> 4 Outline three factors that affect the rate at which a performer accumulates lactate.
>
> **Answer on p. 261**

Energy transfer during long-duration/lower-intensity exercise

REVISED ⬤

Exercising for long periods of time at low intensity uses the *aerobic* system as the preferred method for producing energy.

Oxygen consumption during exercise

When we exercise, the body uses oxygen to produce energy (resynthesise ATP). Oxygen consumption is the amount of oxygen we use to produce ATP, and is usually referred to as VO_2.

> **Oxygen consumption** The amount of oxygen we use to produce ATP.

When we start to exercise, insufficient oxygen is distributed to the tissues for all the energy to be provided aerobically because it takes time for the body to respond to the increase in demand for oxygen. As a result, energy is provided anaerobically to satisfy the increase in demand for energy until the body can cope. This is referred to as submaximal oxygen deficit.

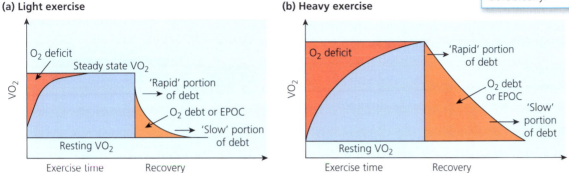

Figure 1.22 The difference between maximal and submaximal oxygen deficit

Maximal oxygen deficit is usually referred to as maximal accumulated oxygen deficit or MAOD. It gives an indication of anaerobic capacity. Figure 1.22 shows the difference between maximal and submaximal oxygen deficit.

Oxygen consumption during recovery

Recovery involves returning the body to its pre-exercise state. When a performer finishes exercise, oxygen consumption remains quite high in comparison at rest. This is because extra oxygen needs to be taken in and used to try to help the performer recover. This breathlessness after exercise is often referred to as excess post-exercise oxygen consumption (EPOC).

There are two main components to EPOC – the fast replenishment stage and slow replenishment stage.

The fast replenishment stage

+ The fast replenishment stage (also known as the alacticid component) uses the extra oxygen that is taken in during recovery to restore ATP and phosphocreatine and to resaturate myoglobin with oxygen.
+ Complete restoration of phosphocreatine takes up to 3 minutes, but 50 per cent of stores can be replenished after only 30 seconds, during which time approximately 3 litres of oxygen are consumed.
+ Myoglobin has a high affinity for oxygen. Oxygen that has diffused from the haemoglobin in the blood is stored in the sarcoplasm.
+ After exercise, oxygen stores in the myoglobin are limited.
+ The surplus of oxygen supplied through EPOC helps replenish these stores, taking up to 2 minutes and using approximately 0.5 litres of oxygen.

The slow replenishment stage

The oxygen consumed during the slow replenishment stage, also known as the lactacid component, has several functions, which are outlined below.

Removal of lactic acid

Lactic acid accumulates during exercise, and needs to be removed during recovery. Full recovery might take up to an hour or longer, depending on the intensity and duration of the exercise. Lactic acid can be removed in the following ways:
+ oxidation into carbon dioxide and water in the inactive muscles and organs, and used by the muscles as an energy source
+ transported in the blood to the liver, where it is converted to blood glucose and glycogen (Cori cycle)
+ converted into protein
+ removed in sweat and urine

Exam tip

Do not forget that the resaturation of myoglobin is part of the fast replenishment stage.

Revision activity

Summarise the key points of the fast replenishment stage.

+ Most of the lactic acid can be oxidised in mitochondria, so performing a cool-down can accelerate its removal because exercise keeps the metabolic rate of muscles high and keeps capillaries dilated, which means oxygen can be flushed through, removing the accumulated lactic acid.
+ The slow replenishment stage of recovery begins as soon as lactic acid appears in the muscle cells, and will continue using breathed oxygen until recovery is complete.
+ This can take up to 5 or 6 litres of oxygen in the first half hour of recovery, removing up to 50 per cent of the lactic acid.

Now test yourself   TESTED

5 Identify two ways in which lactic acid can be removed.

Answer on p. 261

> **Revision activity**
>
> Summarise the key points of the slow replenishment stage.

Maintenance of breathing and heart rates

Maintaining breathing and heart rates requires extra oxygen to provide the energy needed for the respiratory and heart muscles. This assists recovery because the extra oxygen is used to replenish ATP and phosphocreatine stores, resaturate the myoglobin and remove lactic acid, thereby returning the body to its pre-exercise state.

Glycogen replenishment

+ The replacement of glycogen stores depends on the type of exercise undertaken and when and how much carbohydrate is consumed following exercise.
+ It might take several days to complete the restoration of glycogen after a marathon. However, in less than an hour after short-duration, high-intensity exercise a significant amount of glycogen can be restored. Lactic acid is converted back to blood glucose and glycogen in the liver via the Cori cycle.
+ Eating a high-carbohydrate meal will accelerate glycogen restoration, as will eating within 1 hour following exercise.

There are two nutritional windows for optimal recovery after exercise. The first is 30 minutes after exercise, where both carbohydrates and proteins should be consumed in a 3:1 or 4:1 ratio. The second nutritional window is 1 to 3 hours after exercise, when a meal high in protein, carbohydrate and healthy fat should be consumed.

Increase in body temperature

When temperature remains high, respiratory rate rates will also remain high; this will help the performer take in more oxygen during recovery. However, extra oxygen (from the slow replenishment stage) is needed to fuel this increase in temperature until the body returns to normal.

> **Exam tip**
>
> Questions on EPOC often involve a description of the fast and slow replenishment stages.

Factors affecting VO₂ max/aerobic power   REVISED ⬤

The higher the VO_2 max the greater the endurance capacity of a performer. Consequently, this enables the performer to work at higher intensity for longer as they have more oxygen going to the muscles and can utilise this oxygen in the muscles more effectively and therefore delay OBLA. Figure 1.23 outlines the factors that can affect VO_2 max.

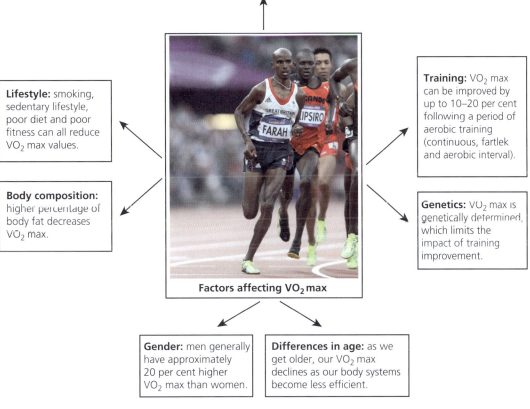

Physiological:
- increased maximum cardiac output
- increased stroke volume/ejection fraction/cardiac hypertrophy
- greater heart rate range
- less oxygen being used for heart muscle so more available to muscles
- increased levels of haemoglobin and red blood cell count
- increased stores of glycogen and triglycerides
- increased myoglobin content
- increased capillarisation around the muscles
- increased number and size of mitochondria
- increased surface area of alveoli
- increased lactate tolerance
- reduced body fat – VO_2 max decreases as the percentage of body fat increases
- slow-twitch hypertrophy

Lifestyle: smoking, sedentary lifestyle, poor diet and poor fitness can all reduce VO_2 max values.

Body composition: higher percentage of body fat decreases VO_2 max.

Training: VO_2 max can be improved by up to 10–20 per cent following a period of aerobic training (continuous, fartlek and aerobic interval).

Genetics: VO_2 max is genetically determined, which limits the impact of training improvement.

Factors affecting VO_2 max

Gender: men generally have approximately 20 per cent higher VO_2 max than women.

Differences in age: as we get older, our VO_2 max declines as our body systems become less efficient.

Figure 1.23 Factors affecting VO_2 max

Now test yourself

TESTED ⃝

6   What is the relationship between VO_2 max and lactate threshold?

Answer on p. 261

Measurements of energy expenditure

REVISED ⃝

Indirect calorimetry

+ Indirect calorimetry is a technique that provides an accurate estimate of energy expenditure through gas exchange.
+ It measures how much carbon dioxide is produced and how much oxygen is consumed both at rest and during aerobic exercise.
+ Calculating the gas volumes also enables us to find out the main substrate being used (fat or carbohydrate).
+ The accuracy of this test is very reliable because it gives a precise calculation of VO_2 and VO_2 max.

Exam tip

You will not need to calculate indirect calorimetry; you just need knowledge of the method itself.

43

Lactate sampling

+ This is an accurate and objective measure of the level of lactate in the blood.
+ It can also be used as a means of measuring exercise intensity (the higher the exercise intensity at which the lactate threshold occurs, the fitter the athlete is considered to be), to give an idea of level of fitness and to enable the performer to select relevant training zones.
+ Regular lactate testing provides a comparison from which the coach and performer can see whether improvement has occurred.
+ If test results increase, this should indicate that the performer has an increase in peak speed/power, increased time to exhaustion, improved heart rate recovery and a higher lactate threshold.

VO_2 max test

+ The most common test for evaluating VO_2 max is the multi-stage fitness test, more commonly called the 'bleep' test. Here the individual performs a 20-metre progressive shuttle run to a bleep, until they reach complete exhaustion. The level that is reached can be compared with a standard results table.
+ Other tests include the Harvard step test and the Cooper 12-minute run, but all of these only give an indication or prediction of VO_2 max.
+ A sports science laboratory can produce much more valid and reliable results using direct gas analysis. Tests using this method involve increasing intensities on a treadmill, cycle ergometer or rowing machine.

> **Direct gas analysis** A laboratory technique that measures the concentration of oxygen that is inspired and the concentration of carbon dioxide that is expired.
>
> **Cycle ergometer** A stationary bike that measures how much work is being performed.

> **Making links**
>
> Validity and reliability are discussed in detail in 4.2 Preparation and training methods (p. 122).

Respiratory exchange ratio

The respiratory exchange ratio (RER) is the ratio of carbon dioxide produced to oxygen consumed, and is used as a measure of exercise intensity. It calculates energy expenditure and provides information about the use of fats and carbohydrates during exercise.

> **RER** The ratio of carbon dioxide produced to oxygen consumed.

Calculating the RER will determine which energy sources are being oxidised and hence whether the performer is working aerobically or anaerobically:
+ A RER value close to 1 = performer using carbohydrates.
+ A RER value of approximately 0.7 = performer using fats
+ A RER value greater than 1 = anaerobic respiration, so more carbon dioxide is being produced than oxygen consumed.

Impact of specialist training methods on energy systems

REVISED

For your exam you need to understand the following training methods and how they impact on the different energy systems.

Altitude training

+ Altitude training is usually carried out at over 2500 metres above sea level, or in an environment that simulates high altitude, where the partial pressure of oxygen is lower.
+ This means that not as much oxygen can diffuse into the blood, so haemoglobin is not as fully saturated with oxygen, which results in a lower oxygen-carrying capacity of the blood.

+ Since less oxygen is therefore delivered to the working muscles, there is a reduction in aerobic performance and VO_2 max and a quicker onset of anaerobic respiration.

Table 1.13 lists the advantages and disadvantages of altitude training.

Table 1.13

Advantages	Disadvantages
+ Increase in the number of red blood cells + Increased concentration of haemoglobin + Increased blood viscosity + Increased capillarisation + Enhanced oxygen transport + Increased lactate tolerance	+ Expensive + Altitude sickness + Difficult to train due to the lack of oxygen + Detraining, because training intensity has to reduce when the performer first trains at altitude due to the decreased availability of oxygen + Benefits can be quickly lost on return to sea level + Psychological problems due to being away from home

> **Exam tip**
>
> Questions might want you to apply your knowledge of specialist training methods. For example, altitude training would be suitable for an endurance performer.

High-intensity interval training

Interval training can be used for both aerobic and anaerobic training. It is a form of training in which periods of work are interspersed with recovery periods.

+ High-intensity interval training (HIIT) involves short intervals of maximum-intensity exercise followed by a recovery interval of low to moderate intensity exercise – for example, 4 minutes of intense exercise made up of 8–20 seconds of maximum-effort work intervals, each followed by a 10-second recovery interval.
+ The work interval is anaerobic and the recovery is aerobic.
+ Pushing your body to the max during the work interval increases the number of calories you burn because it takes longer to recover from each work session.
+ HIIT therefore improves fat-burning potential, glucose metabolism and both aerobic and anaerobic endurance.

Plyometrics

Plyometrics training improves power and speed and involves high-intensity, explosive activities, such as hopping, bounding, depth jumping and medicine ball work using fast-twitch fibres. It works on the concept that muscles can generate more force if they have previously been stretched. This is frequently called the stretch-shortening cycle and consists of three phases:

> **Plyometrics** Repeated, rapid stretching and contracting of muscles to increase muscle power.

+ Phase 1 – the eccentric phase or preloading/prestretching phase. On landing, the muscle performs an eccentric contraction, where it lengthens under tension.
+ Phase 2 – the amortisation phase – is next and is the time between the eccentric and concentric muscle contractions. This time needs to be as short as possible, so the energy stored from the eccentric contraction is not lost. When an eccentric contraction occurs, a lot of the energy required to stretch or lengthen the muscle is lost as heat, but some of the energy can be stored and is then available for the subsequent concentric contraction.
+ Phase 3 – the concentric or muscle contraction phase – uses the stored energy to increase the force of the contraction.

Speed agility quickness (SAQ)

+ Speed refers to how fast a person can move over a specified distance or how quickly a body part can be put into motion.
+ Agility is the ability to move and position the body quickly and effectively while under control.

+ SAQ training aims to improve multidirectional movement through developing the neuromuscular system.
+ Drills include zig-zag runs and foot ladders. Often a ball is introduced so that passing occurs throughout the drill, making it more sport specific.
+ As SAQ training uses activities performed with maximum force at high speed, energy is provided anaerobically.

Now test yourself

TESTED ◯

7   How could SAQ training help a football player?

Answer on p. 261

Exam practice

1   Explain how energy is provided to allow an athlete to complete a hammer throw.   [3]

2   Gymnastic floor routines can last up to 90 seconds. Explain how the majority of energy is provided for this discipline during competition.   [6]

3   An athlete completes an interval training programme with short periods of high-intensity exercise followed by recovery periods lasting up to 30 seconds. What effect does this training programme have on their ATP and PC stores?   [3]

4   At the end of a team game, players might experience EPOC. Define EPOC and give the functions of the fast component of EPOC. Explain how these functions are achieved.   [4]

5   Evaluate how plyometric training can help a football player improve their level of performance.   [2]

6   Identify the three key processes involved in the aerobic energy system when glucose is used as the energy source.   [3]

Answers online

Knowledge and skills summary

This topic involves the following knowledge (AO1):
+ How the aerobic, ATP–PC and anaerobic glycolytic energy systems transfer energy (ATP) in the body.
+ During short-duration/high-intensity exercise the anaerobic glycolytic and ATP-PC systems are used.
+ During long-duration/low-intensity exercise the aerobic system is used.
+ An understanding of the energy continuum for different intensities and durations of physical activity.
+ Differences in ATP production depending on the fibre type used.
+ The effects of using the anaerobic glycolytic energy system through an explanation of lactate accumulation, lactate threshold and OBLA.
+ Oxygen consumption during exercise and recovery through oxygen deficit and EPOC.

+ The factors that affect VO_2 max.
+ The measurements of energy expenditure, to include indirect calorimetry, lactate sampling, VO_2 max test and respiratory exchange ratio.
+ The impact of altitude training, high-intensity interval training, plyometrics and speed agility quickness on the three energy systems.

AO2 marks will require application of this knowledge – for example, using the intensity and duration of an activity to decide on the predominant energy system in use.

AO3 marks are for analysis or evaluation. For this topic an AO3 response might involve an analysis of an energy system and its impact on performance, or how a high VO_2 max can aid the performance of an endurance performer.

2 Skill acquisition

2.1 Skill, skill continuums and transfer of skills

Characteristics of skill

REVISED

+ Aesthetically pleasing – the skill is good to watch.
+ Consistent – the skill repeatedly has a high success rate.
+ Efficient – the skill is produced with the least amount of energy and in the quickest time.
+ Fluent – the skill is performed smoothly, without stopping and starting.
+ Learned – the skill has been developed through practice.
+ Accurate – the skill is performed with precision.
+ Goal directed – there is a clear aim in mind.

> **Exam tip**
>
> Always address the command word in the question. If the command word is *describe*, make sure you do not just identify the characteristics of skilled performances.

> **Making links**
>
> The characteristics of a skilled performer will be demonstrated by a learner in the autonomous stage of learning. Autonomous performers are efficient and fluent in their movements, and are also pleasing to watch (pp. 55–56).

> **Exam tip**
>
> Use the mnemonic ACE FLAG to help you identify and describe the characteristics of skilled performance.

Skill continuums

REVISED

Every sporting action can be placed on a range of continuums, which can be used to classify the skill.

> **Exam tip**
>
> Ensure that you know the name of each end of the continuum, its description and a clear practical example to illustrate the classification. Do not give an example from the middle of the continuum.

Open and closed skills

Table 2.1 shows examples of open and closed skills.

Table 2.1

Open skills	Closed skills
The sporting environment/playing conditions around the pitch/court change while the skill is being performed. The performer must adapt and a high amount of decision making is involved.	The sporting environment/playing conditions are stable, enabling the performer to repeat the same movement pattern. There are few decisions to make.
Example: A chest pass in basketball/netball is an open skill because your teammates and opposition constantly move around the court as you prepare to pass the ball, and you change your pass height/weight/speed as a result.	*Example*: Performing a backwards roll in gymnastics is a closed skill because the environment does not change, and it can be performed repeatedly in the same manner.

> **Exam tip**
>
> Describing a skill classification is an AO1 skill. Giving an example is an AO2 skill, because the knowledge has been applied to a practical sporting example.

Gross and fine skills

Table 2.2 shows examples of gross and fine skills.

Table 2.2

Gross skills	Fine skills
The performer uses large muscle groups to perform the skill.	The performer uses small muscles to perform skills that require precision, accuracy and control.
Example: A sprint start is a gross skill, because the quadriceps and gluteals are used to drive out of the blocks.	*Example*: A pistol shot is a fine skill because it uses the muscles of the hand used to stabilise the gun for accuracy.

Self-paced and externally paced skills

Table 2.3 shows examples of self-paced and externally paced skills.

Table 2.3

Self-paced skills	Externally paced skills
The performer is in control of the speed and timing of the skill.	The performer must adapt to their environment because they have no control over the speed and timing of the skill. The performance is influenced by the sporting environment.
Example: The hammer throw is self-paced because the performer decides when to begin the rotations, and also dictates how quickly they spin.	*Example*: When *receiving* a hockey pass from a teammate, the performer reacts to the speed and direction of the incoming ball. This makes it an externally paced skill because the performer has no control over the speed of the incoming pass.

High- and low-organisation skills

Table 2.4 shows examples of high- and low-organisation skills.

Table 2.4

High-organisation skills	Low organisation skills
The skill is difficult to break down into its subroutines/parts due to the speed at which the action is performed. Whole practice is recommended for these skills (p. 51).	The skill can easily be broken down into its subroutines/parts. Subroutines can be practised in isolation.
Example: A sprint start is highly organised because it is performed rapidly, and is therefore hard to break down into subroutines.	*Example*: Back crawl in swimming has low organisation, because the subroutines, i.e. arm and leg actions, can be easily practised individually.

Simple and complex skills

Table 2.5 shows examples of simple and complex skills.

Table 2.5

Simple skills	Complex skills
The skill requires limited decision making.	There are several decisions to make before performing the skill.
Example: A forward roll is a simple skill because there is little information to process and few decisions to make when producing the action.	*Example*: A centre in rugby, running with the ball, takes into account the defenders' positions before deciding which teammate to pass to during attacking play. This is a complex skill because of the large number of decisions to make – including the height and speed of the pass – before the pass can be made.

Check your understanding and progress at **www.hoddereducation.co.uk/myrevisionnotes**

Discrete, serial and continuous skills

Table 2.6 shows examples of discrete, serial and continuous skills.

Table 2.6

Discrete skills	Serial skills	Continuous skills
The skill has a clear beginning and ending. It is one distinct action. *Example*: A pirouette in dance is discrete because there is an obvious start and finish.	A number of discrete skills are performed together sequentially, creating another skill. *Example*: The run-up, hop, step, jump and landing are linked and performed together as a triple jump. The individual skills are linked in a specific order, and therefore it is a serial skill.	The skill has no clear beginning or ending. The end subroutine of one skill becomes the beginning subroutine of the next. The movement is cyclical. *Example*: Cycling and swimming strokes are continuous because of their cyclical nature.

Now test yourself

TESTED ◯

1 In the context of skilful performers, describe what it means to be aesthetically pleasing and goal directed.

2 Using practical examples from invasion games to illustrate your answer, describe fluency and efficiency as demonstrated by skilful performers.

3 Give a definition of each of the 13 classifications.

Answers on p. 262

Revision activity

Draw six continuums like the one in Figure 2.1.

1 Label the extremes with the classifications.

2 Give a definition of each classification.

3 Describe the classification.

4 Give a practical example.

Remember that you will need to have three classifications on one of the continuums.

Figure 2.1

Exam tip

Remember to *justify* your answers to classification questions. Make sure that your examples are clear enough to illustrate each classification. In descriptions of low/high organisation, do not include details about governing body rules, officials, set playing areas etc., as this is a common mistake.

Transfer of learning

REVISED ◯

For your exam you need to be able to describe the four types of transfer, giving clear sporting examples to illustrate your answers. You must understand how the different types of transfer impact on the development of skills.

+ **Positive transfer** – learning a skill *facilitates* the learning of an additional skill. For example, learning to throw overarm *helps* when learning how to serve in volleyball.

+ **Negative transfer** – learning a skill *inhibits* the learning of an additional skill. For example, learning the forehand drive in tennis *hinders* the forehand clear in badminton.

> **Transfer** The effect that one skill has when learning and performing another skill.

+ **Zero transfer** – there are *no* similarities between the tasks, and therefore no effect on either skill. For example, learning to tackle in rugby has no effect on a tumble turn in swimming.
+ **Bilateral transfer** – learning and performing a skill *on one side of the body* is then transferred to the opposite side. For example, learning how to perform snooker shots with one hand and then transferring to the other.

Opportunities to highlight where positive transfer takes place should be sought out because these enable performers to develop a greater range of skills across sports. To encourage positive transfer, the coach should:
+ ensure that the performer has overlearned the first skill before introducing the second, more advanced skill
+ make the practice environment as close to a game situation as possible – for example, in a football free kick practice session, use real defenders instead of using free-kick mannequins
+ give praise/positive reinforcement when positive transfer takes place
+ avoid teaching skills close together that might appear the same but have a distinct difference – for example, tennis and badminton skills, as this increases the likelihood of negative transfer occurring

Now test yourself
TESTED ◯

4 Describe positive, negative, zero and bilateral transfer.

Answer on p. 262

Exam practice

1 Which of the following accurately describes the characteristics of a skilled performance? [1]
   A Consistent, genetic, aesthetically pleasing and goal directed
   B Consistent, genetic, long-lasting and goal directed
   C Consistent, learned, aesthetically pleasing and fluent
   D Consistent, learned, goal directed and enduring
2 Classify the triple jump on the following continua. Justify your answers. [4]
   a Gross/Fine
   b Open/Closed
   c Discrete/Serial/Continuous
   d Self-paced/Externally paced
3 Explain bilateral transfer, and give a sporting example to illustrate where this might take place. [2]

Answers online

Exam tip
A definition or description of the type of transfer is an AO1 skill. The application to a practical situation is an AO2 skill. Questions that ask you to explain the impact of transfer on skills include AO2 and AO3 marks.

Exam tip
Do not repeat words from the question in your answer. For example, negative transfer is when there is a negative effect on a skill. Use words such as 'hinders' or 'inhibits' to describe the impact of negative transfer.

Revision activity
Create a revision card for each type of transfer. On one side write the type and on the other side write the description and an example. Ask a friend to test you.

Knowledge and skills summary
This topic involves the following knowledge (AO1):
+ Identifying and describing the characteristics of skilful performers.
+ Using the six continua to classify skills in sport.
+ Describing the four types of transfer.

AO2 marks will require application of this knowledge – for example, supporting your classifications and justifications with clear sporting examples, and illustrating your understanding of transfer with clear examples.

AO3 marks are for analysis or evaluation. In this topic an AO3 response might involve analysing how transfer has an impact on skills as they are developed.

2.2 Impact of classification on practice

Methods of presenting practice

Table 2.7 outlines the methods of presenting practice.

Table 2.7

> **Grooved** Overlearned or practised to perfection.

Method	Choose this method when...	Advantages	Disadvantages	Use this method with
Whole The skill is presented in its *entirety* and not broken down into parts/subroutines	...the skill is: ✛ highly organised ✛ continuous/cyclic ✛ simple ✛ discrete ✛ fast/ballistic ✛ not dangerous ...the performer is: ✛ autonomous	Kinaesthesis is developed Fluency between subroutines is maintained Not time-consuming Creates a clear mental image Easily transferred into a full game situation Aids understanding of the entire skill	Not ideal for cognitive performers Can cause information overload Can cause fatigue The performer must be physically capable of producing the full skill	Golf swing Tennis serve Cycling Forward roll
Whole–part–whole The learner attempts the full skill, then one (or each) subroutine is practised in isolation before being integrated back into the entire skill	...the skill is: ✛ complex ✛ fast/ballistic ...the performer is: ✛ cognitive and is grooving individual parts ✛ autonomous and is concentrating on improving a specific weakness	Kinaesthesis is maintained in the whole Weak parts/subroutines can be improved Fluency between subroutines is maintained in the whole Confidence and motivation increase as success is seen in each part	Time-consuming Cannot use with highly organised skills Kinaesthesis/fluency can be negatively affected if the part is not integrated adequately and quickly	Front crawl (Whole) Introduce the full stroke; allow the performer to experience it entirely; note that arm action is weak (Part) Practise arm action in isolation with the aid of a pull buoy/floats until **grooved** (Whole) Practise the stroke as one again, now with improved arm action
Progressive part ('chaining') The first subroutine/part is taught and practised until perfected The rest of the parts are then added sequentially until the whole of the skill can be performed	...the skill is: ✛ low organisation ✛ serial ✛ complex ✛ dangerous ...the performer is: ✛ cognitive	Focusing on just one part of the skill reduces the chance of overload and fatigue Aids understanding of each part Confidence and motivation increase as success is seen in each part Danger is reduced	Very time-consuming Cannot use with highly organised skills Fluency between subroutines can be negatively affected Kinaesthesis/feel for whole skill not experienced until the very end	Triple jump Teach hop – practise until grooved Teach step – practise until grooved Practise hop and step together Teach jump – practise until grooved Practise hop, step and jump together

My Revision Notes: AQA A-level PE

Exam tip

Description of a method is an AO1 skill. Applying your knowledge to specific performers/skills or sporting example is an AO2 skill. You are accessing AO3 marks when giving advantages and disadvantages of a presentation or practice method, or if you are asked to analyse or evaluate.

Types of practice   REVISED ◯

Massed

Massed practice involves continuous practice without rest periods.

Choose this type when skills are:
+ discrete
+ closed
+ self-paced
+ simple

Choose it when performers are:
+ highly motivated
+ autonomous
+ physically fit

Advantages:
+ Grooves/overlearns the skills, so they become habitual
+ Motor programmes are formed
+ Improves fitness

Disadvantages:
+ Causes fatigue
+ Performer might not be physically capable of undertaking the practice
+ No time for feedback

Example: A badminton player attempting to perfect their short serve practises by continuously serving into a target area without rest, or a trampolinist continuously practises seat drops to make the skill habitual.

Distributed

Distributed practice involves practice with rest periods included.

Choose this type when skills are:
+ continuous
+ complex
+ serial
+ low organisation
+ dangerous/tiring
+ externally paced
+ open

Choose it when performers are:
+ cognitive
+ unfit
+ lacking motivation

Advantages:
+ More effective method than massed practice
+ Allows time for physical recovery
+ Allows time for mental practice
+ Coach can give feedback
+ Motivational

Disadvantages:
+ Time-consuming
+ Can cause negative transfer

Example: Distributed practice can be used by a steeplechaser. They run the race, followed by a rest period. During the rest period they will mentally rehearse their performance – visualising their stride pattern, and clearing the hurdles and water barriers.

Variable practice

Variable practice involves practising skills and drills in a constantly changing environment.

Choose this type when skills are:
+ open
+ externally paced
+ complex

Choose it when performers are:
+ cognitive
+ lacking motivation

Advantages:
+ Develops schema
+ Increases motivation
+ Performer gains experience in a range of situations
+ Positive transfer from training to game

Disadvantages:
+ Time-consuming
+ Can cause fatigue
+ Possibility of information overload
+ Can cause negative transfer

Example: Used in rugby, when practising a 3 v 2 attacking play. The performers will develop their passing technique and positional play, which can be directly transferred into a game situation.

> **Making links**
>
> Variable practice is the primary way to build schema (p. 71).

Mental practice

Mental practice involves going over the skill in your mind without moving.
+ Internal – seeing your performance from 'within' through your own eyes and being aware of your emotions.
+ External – seeing your performance from outside as a spectator.

Choose this type when skills are:
+ complex
+ serial

Choose it when performers are:
+ cognitive – to build a clear mental image of the basics of the skill
+ autonomous – to focus on key strategies/tactics

Advantages:
+ Produces a clear mental image
+ Performers can see themselves being successful
+ Can rehearse strategies/tactics
+ Increases confidence
+ Reduces anxiety
+ Muscles are stimulated
+ Reaction time improves

Disadvantages:
+ Difficult for cognitive performers to complete effectively
+ Mental image must be accurate
+ Difficult if environment is not quiet

Example: A triple jumper about to take their final jump in a competition might visualise the stages of the jump in their mind before beginning.

Now test yourself   TESTED ◯

3   What is variable practice and what are the advantages and disadvantages of using this method?

Answer on p. 262

Exam practice

1   With reference to shooting, describe how a basketballer or netballer might use mental practice.   [3]

Answer online

Making links

Questions will expect you to understand how the classification of a skill determines the methods of presentation and practice. For example, highly organised skills should be presented as a whole; open skills should be practised using the variable method.

Knowledge and skills summary

This topic involves the following knowledge (AO1):
+ How skills are presented using the various methods.
+ How practices are structured using the various methods.

AO2 marks will require application of this knowledge – for example, giving a clear practical example to illustrate how you would use each method; giving the most effective method to use with performers according to their experience; or giving the most effective method to use when learning and developing different skills.

AO3 marks are for analysis or evaluation. In this topic an AO3 response might involve analysing the advantages and disadvantages, or evaluating each method.

2.3 Principles and theories of learning and performance

Learning and feedback types   REVISED ◯

Making links

Questions frequently require you to describe which feedback method is used by each level of learner.

Exam tip

Do not confuse stages of learning with theories of learning. Read the questions very carefully.

Check your understanding and progress at **www.hoddereducation.co.uk/myrevisionnotes**

Stages of learning

1 The cognitive stage

Description:

+ The performer begins to create a clear mental image of what the skill is supposed to look like.
+ An accurate demonstration is necessary, which the performer will copy.
+ Mental rehearsal of the skill is required.
+ Many mistakes are made.
+ The performer uses trial-and-error learning to work out the correct method.
+ Movements appear uncoordinated and jerky.
+ The performer has to think about the skill: all their attention is placed on working out how to perform the main components of the skill.
+ Motor programmes are not yet formed.

Feedback:

+ The performer is reliant on extrinsic feedback from the coach to direct performance and highlight weaknesses.
+ Feedback should be positive, so the performer will persevere with the learning process.
+ Some knowledge of results can be used so that successful actions are repeated and unsuccessful actions are modified.

Example: A hockey player who is initially learning to dribble will be very slow. Their movements will be jerky and they will often lose control of the ball as a result of hitting it too hard. Their head will be down as they watch the ball intently. Since they do not yet know how it is supposed to feel, they rely on their coach for feedback. Their coach will give various demonstrations and the learner will watch and work out each subroutine. They should constantly mentally rehearse dribbling in this phase.

2 The associative stage

Description:

+ The performer must continue to practise.
+ The performer models their current actions with those of skilled athletes.
+ Some performers never progress out of this stage.
+ They become more proficient, making fewer mistakes.
+ Movement appears smoother and more coordinated.
+ The performer can begin to focus their attention on the finer aspects of the skill.
+ Motor programmes are developing and will be stored in the long-term memory.
+ Demonstrations, positive feedback and mental rehearsal are still required to aid learning.

Feedback:

+ The performer begins to develop kinaesthesis and uses intrinsic feedback to correct movement. They will know how the movement is supposed to feel.
+ Extrinsic feedback is still used to refine actions.
+ The performer begins to use of knowledge of performance.

Example: A gymnast on a beam will have practised and mastered the basic skills, and will now be able to execute more complex movements. They can now use intrinsic feedback, as they begin to become aware of how the movement should feel. They can now look up and forward rather than down at their feet.

3 The autonomous stage

Description:

+ Movements are fluent, efficient and have become habitual due to extensive practice.
+ Skills are executed automatically without consciously thinking about the subroutines.

+ Motor programmes are fully formed and stored in the long-term memory.
+ The performer can concentrate on fine detail, tactics and advanced strategies.
+ It is still important to practise and mentally rehearse to stay at this level.

Feedback:
+ The performer uses intrinsic feedback to correct their own mistakes by means of kinaesthesis.
+ Extrinsic feedback can be negative to aid error correction.
+ Use knowledge of performance to understand *why* the action was successful or unsuccessful.

Example: A basketball player will be able to dribble the ball fluently and consistently without having to look down at the ball. They are able to scan the court for passing options without concentrating on controlling the ball because it is being controlled automatically. They can correct errors they make immediately, without assistance from the coach.

Now test yourself TESTED ⭕

1 Give two characteristics of each stage of learning.
2 How does feedback differ when moving from the cognitive stage to the associative stage of learning?

Answers on pp. 262–263

Revision activity

Complete Table 2.8. Give a clear example from *your* sport in each stage.

Table 2.8

Name of stage	1	2	3
Characteristics			
Feedback used			
Example			

Learning plateaus

REVISED ⭕

The learning curve in Figure 2.2 illustrates the stages a performer goes through when learning a new closed skill.

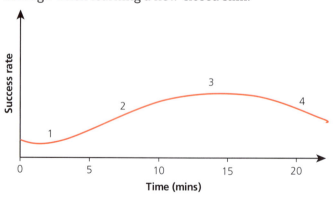

Figure 2.2 A typical learning curve showing the rate of improvement when attempting a closed skill over a 20-minute period

Stage 1 – the performer is in the cognitive phase of learning so their success rate will be low. They will be slow and jerky when performing. They are trying to work out the parts of the skill and are developing an understanding.

Stage 2 – as they practise there is a sharp increase in their success rate as they begin to grasp the skill. They enter the associative phase of learning and

Check your understanding and progress at **www.hoddereducation.co.uk/myrevisionnotes**

begin to look more fluid when performing. Motivation levels will be high as they recognise they are being successful.

Stage 3 – the performer reaches a plateau (Table 2.9), where they are no longer progressing with the skill. Performance levels are maintained with no further improvement shown.

Stage 4 – the performer has a dip in their success rate. There is a lack of motivation and they might be experiencing drive reduction. To remotivate them they will require a new task or challenge.

Table 2.9 The learning plateau – causes and solutions

Causes	Solutions
Loss of motivation/boredom	+ Set new tasks/challenges + Use variable practice + Offer tangible rewards
Mental/physical fatigue	Allow the performer to rest Use distributed practice
Have reached ability limit	Allow performer to compete against others of similar ability
Poor coaching	Try a variety of coaching methods Try an alternative coach
Incorrect goals set	Set goals using the SMARTER principle (pp. 181–182)

Now test yourself   TESTED ○

3   What are the main causes of the learning plateau? Give a solution for each.

Answer on p. 263

Revision activity

Draw the learning curve graph. Identify the key points on the curve and describe what is happening at each stage.

Cognitive theories: insight learning (Gestalt)   REVISED ○

+ Gestaltists believe that we learn skills through experiencing the whole task/skill rather than isolated parts/subroutines.
+ They believe that part learning is not effective and that by learning the skill as a whole, kinaesthesis and the flow of the skill is maintained, and the performer gains a greater understanding of the task they are faced with.
+ This is a cognitive theory, which suggests that the performer has to think about what to do, but using their experiences and prior knowledge to help with the situation in hand. They use their insight and adapt to the sporting situation they are faced with, even in completely new situations.
+ The coach might pose questions that the performers have to answer themselves. Insight learning allows performers to be creative and to develop their own strategies and tactics, without having to rely on the coach. This creates independent thinkers and is much better than being told what to do. Performers' intrinsic motivation will also improve as they know that they have successfully worked out what to do on their own.
+ For example, in a 2 v 1 situation in rugby, the attacking player who is the ball carrier evaluates the full situation and decides that the options are to pass, kick, take the tackle or dummy a pass and run for the try line. Remembering a previous match where they were successful, they decide once again to dummy. The full-back follows the dummy pass towards the second attacker, leaving space to run in the try.

Exam tip

Do not confuse cognitive theories of learning with the cognitive stage of learning.

Now test yourself   TESTED ○

4   Explain why Gestaltists believe that part learning is not as efficient as whole learning.

Answer on p. 263

Behaviourism: operant conditioning (Skinner)

REVISED ●

Learning happens by making and strengthening a link between a stimulus and a response. This is known as an S–R bond. Once this bond is made, it increases the likelihood of the desired response happening. S–R bonds are formed by using reinforcement. Skinner suggested that reinforced actions are strengthened and that incorrect actions can be weakened.

When learning skills using operant conditioning, the coach should apply the following:

+ Allow the performer to work using trial and error – for example, try various methods of serving in tennis.
+ Manipulate the environment to ensure that the successful/desired response occurs – for example, adapt the sporting environment by placing cones in the service box as a target for them to hit. Eventually the cones can be removed. Move them closer to the net to make the task easier to begin with. This ensures their success. Eventually they can be moved further back.
+ When a correct response is shown, offer a satisfier (e.g. positive reinforcement) so that the response will be repeated – for example, when they perform the serve correctly give them praise and positive reinforcement so that they will repeat the action.
+ When an incorrect response is shown, offer an annoyer (e.g. punishment) so that the response will not be repeated – for example, a lap of the court for every serve 'out'.

As a result of this, behaviour is shaped.

Positive reinforcement, negative reinforcement and punishment are used to shape behaviour and form S–R bonds.

+ Positive reinforcement is endorsing a performer's action when it is *correct*, so that they repeat that action in the future – for example, when a footballer defends a corner well the coach praises them, in the hope that they will repeat it in similar situations in the future.
+ Negative reinforcement is saying nothing when a *correct* action is shown, after a period of criticism about a performance – for example, a netball coach constantly criticises the GA for missing shots. When the GA scores a goal, the coach says nothing. The GA recognises that they have not been criticised, and repeats the correct shooting action.
+ Punishment is a method of reducing or eliminating undesirable actions. This can include extra training, substitution, fines or bans if necessary – for example, a basketball player is instructed to complete 'suicide runs' for being late for training.

> **Exam tip**
>
> Do not confuse negative reinforcement with negative feedback.

> **Now test yourself** TESTED ○
>
> 5 Define positive reinforcement, negative reinforcement and punishment.
>
> **Answer on p. 263**

Social learning: observational learning (Bandura)

REVISED ●

+ Bandura suggested that we learn by watching and replicating the actions of other 'model' performers, who we respect and admire.
+ These 'models' are known as significant others.
+ They might include our family members, coaches, teachers, peers or role models in the media.

> **Significant other** A person who is held in high esteem, such as a family member, friend, role model in the media or a coach/teacher.

Learners are more likely to copy:

+ significant others
+ models who have similar characteristics, for example age or gender
+ actions that are successful
+ actions that are reinforced

Bandura suggested that performers can learn new skills by engaging with the four key processes (Table 2.10).

Table 2.10 Four key processes

Model	Elements
1 Attention	+ The coach ensures that the performer concentrates on the model + The coach points out key cues in the demonstration + The model should be attractive (e.g. use a role model) + The performance should be accurate
2 Retention	+ The coach ensures the performer remembers the demonstration/mental image + The demonstration should be repeated + A clear mental image should be created through visualisation or mental rehearsal
3 Motor (re)production	+ The performer must be physically and mentally able to copy the model demonstration
4 Motivation	+ The performer must have the determination and drive to copy and learn the skill + The coach could generate this by offering praise or rewards
Matching performance	The performer can replicate the model

> **Now test yourself** TESTED ◯
>
> 6 Describe the attention and motor (re)production processes in Bandura's model.
>
> **Answer on p. 263**

Constructivism: social development theory (Vygotsky)

REVISED ◯

+ Vygotsky suggested that learning is a social process and that social interaction plays a key role in an individual's development.
+ In the sporting context this means that we learn skills from people around us who we interact with.
+ There are three key aspects to this theory.

1 Role of social interaction

+ Vygotsky suggests that social learning comes before development.
+ Initially we learn from other people on a social level. This is called **interpsychological learning**. For example, a performer begins to learn how to do a handstand by watching their older sibling performing and by receiving advice and feedback from more knowledgeable others (MKOs).
+ Next, the performer begins to think about how to do that handstand on their own, and constructs actions based on what they have learned from others. This is called **intrapsychological learning**.

2 More Knowledgeable Other

+ An MKO is a person, normally a coach or teacher, who has a greater understanding of the task than you do.
+ They give you technical advice and feedback on how to produce the skill. For example, the coach informs you where to place your hands in the handstand.
+ This might also be gained from online video clips/social media.

3 Zone of proximal development

+ There are three stages describing what the learner can do when assisted by the MKO:
    + The learner cannot perform the skill at this moment in time – for example, the gymnast cannot yet properly balance and hold a static handstand.
    + The performer can achieve with help from the MKO – for example, they can get up into the handstand position and balance if the coach uses manual guidance (p. 62) to support them. Scaffolding is used to allow learners to develop skills they will perform on their own in the future.
    + The performer can achieve independently without assistance – for example, they can get up into handstand position, and shuffle their hands when trying to achieve a balanced position.
+ Coaches should ensure that learners are provided with a range of experience in their zone of proximal development, as this will motivate and encourage them to advance their individual learning.

Now test yourself — TESTED

7 What is an MKO and why are they so important when learning skills in sport?

Answer on p. 263

Exam practice

1 Explain how Vygotsky's theory of social development applies to a footballer learning to shoot. [4]
2 Explain how a coach might use positive reinforcement to help a hockey goalkeeper learn to save penalty flicks. [2]

Answers online

Knowledge and skills summary

This topic involves the following knowledge (AO1):
+ Giving clear descriptions of the characteristics of the three stages of learning.
+ Drawing and fully labelling a graph showing a typical learning curve.
+ Giving reasons for the plateau.
+ Giving solutions to the plateau.
+ Explaining the key concepts of each of the four theories of learning.

AO2 marks will require application of this knowledge – for example, giving clear examples of each of the three stages of learning; explaining which types of feedback are most effective for each stage; or showing how skills can be learned by using the approach suggested in each of the theories.

AO3 marks are for analysis or evaluation. In this topic an AO3 response might involve demonstrating how the theories of learning impact on skill development.

2.4 Use of guidance and feedback

Purposes and types of feedback — REVISED

The purposes of feedback are to:
+ reinforce correct actions
+ correct errors
+ eliminate bad habits
+ act as a motivator
+ build confidence

Types of feedback are shown in Table 2.11.

Table 2.11 Types of feedback

Type of feedback	Description and uses
Knowledge of performance (KP)	Information about *why* the skill/action was successful/unsuccessful, including technique and quality of action
Knowledge of results (KR)	Information about whether or not the skill/action was successful (if so, repeat) or unsuccessful (if so, adjust next time)
Positive	Information about what was *correct*, so that it will be repeated in the future
Negative	Information about *incorrect actions*, so that they are not repeated and errors are corrected
Intrinsic	From *within* using kinaesthesis – used to 'feel' if the action was correct or not; can be positive or negative
Extrinsic	From an *outside* source – used to reinforce correct actions and correct errors; can be positive or negative

Now test yourself TESTED ○

1 Define and give an example of:
   a negative feedback
   b knowledge of results

Answer on p. 263

Exam tip

Remember, do not use the question word in your answer. For example, 'negative feedback is giving the performer negative information'. Describe what each type of feedback is.

Methods of guidance REVISED ○

There are four types of guidance used to assist the effective learning of skills: visual guidance (Table 2.12), verbal guidance (Table 2.13), manual guidance (Table 2.14) and mechanical guidance (Table 2.15).

Visual guidance

Table 2.12

Description	+ Any method where the performer sees the correct method to perform the skill + Could be a demonstration, coaching videos, clips on social media/websites or coaching manual + Effective for cognitive performers and should be readily used in this phase of learning + Performer should be given time to repeatedly practise and mentally rehearse following the demonstration + Performer should focus on the key aspects/coach should highlight key aspects of the skill + Coach can also change or modify the display – for example, placing a chalked square on the tennis court for the performer to aim for during their serves
Advantages	+ Illustrates exactly what a skill should look like + Helps to build a clear mental picture of how the skill should be performed + Used effectively in conjunction with verbal guidance + Highlights weaknesses
Disadvantages	+ Demonstration must be accurate + Performer must be able to match the demonstration given + Too much information given at once could induce overload
Example	A badminton coach introduces the overhead clear to the performers by demonstrating the technique, and by also showing them a video. The coach also chalks a circle in the back section of the court, which gives the performers a target to aim for.

Verbal guidance

Table 2.13

Description	+ The coach instructs, explains and directs the performer to the key points of the skill by telling them what to do and how to do it + Useful for more advanced performers, i.e. the autonomous stage of learning + Used to give tactical, strategic or technical information that a cognitive performer might not understand + Information should be kept brief and meaningful
Advantages	+ Can be given immediately during performance + Is useful for open skills where the performer needs to make decisions and quickly adapt + Used effectively in conjunction with visual guidance
Disadvantages	+ There might be a chance of information overload if too many instructions are given together + Lengthy explanations might cause the performer to lose concentration + Cognitive performers might not understand specific technical instructions
Example	A rugby coach instructs the performers to run a 'miss-pass' set play. This would be useless to cognitive performers who would not understand the terminology.

Manual guidance

Table 2.14

Description	The coach uses their body to physically support or manipulate the performer's body as a form of forced response
Advantages	+ Effective for cognitive performers + Useful in dangerous tasks because it improves safety during performance + Reduces fear/anxiety and therefore builds confidence + The whole skill can be attempted + Allows the performer to develop the kinaesthesis or feeling tone of the movement
Disadvantages	+ However, the performer might become reliant on the support/aid + It could create an incorrect kinaesthesis – the 'feeling' might not be correct + Bad habits might be instilled + Performer might become demotivated as they feel that they are not performing the skill by themselves + The physical contact or proximity of the coach might make the performer feel uncomfortable
Examples	During a vault, the coach would support the gymnast's back and assist them to travel over the vault. A golf coach might stand behind the performer and, with their hands on top of the performer's hands, force the performer through the golf drive.

Mechanical guidance

Table 2.15

Description	Any piece of equipment, apparatus or device used to aid and shape movement
Advantages	Same as manual guidance
Disadvantages	Same as the *first four* for manual guidance
Examples	A trampoline coach uses a rig and harness to teach the front somersault for the first time. The performer is able to experience the feeling of the whole movement safely. A swimming coach uses swimming floats/armbands with a young swimming group.

Now test yourself   TESTED ⬤

2 What are the advantages and disadvantages of verbal guidance?

Answer on p. 263

Check your understanding and progress at **www.hoddereducation.co.uk/myrevisionnotes**

Exam practice

1 Explain how a coach could utilise knowledge of performance feedback and visual guidance to assist a performer in the autonomous stage. Use examples to support your answers. [4]

Answer online

Knowledge and skills summary

This topic involves the following knowledge (AO1):

✚ Descriptions of the four types of guidance.
✚ Descriptions of the six types of feedback.
✚ Descriptions of how practices are structured.

AO2 marks will require application of this knowledge – for example, understanding the most effective methods of guidance and feedback to use with performers based on their experience; explaining the most effective methods of guidance and feedback to use when learning and developing different skill classifications.

AO3 marks are for analysis or evaluation. In this topic an AO3 response might involve analysing, evaluating or giving advantages and disadvantages of each method of guidance and feedback.

2.5 Memory models

2.5.1 Information-processing models

Information processing refers to the ways in which a performer is able to receive information from the sporting environment, rationalise the information and decide what to do with it, before putting it into action.

Stages of information processing

REVISED ◯

Information processing involves four main stages: input, decision making, output and feedback.

Input

✚ The senses (eyes – vision, ears – audition, proprioceptors, touch, balance and kinaesthesis) are used to gather cues from the sporting environment (display).
✚ The performer uses their perception to judge which of the environmental cues are required and which can be disregarded (the detection/comparison/recognition (DCR) process – see below).
✚ The cues are filtered into relevant and irrelevant cues by a process known as selective attention.
✚ The performer focuses on the relevant stimuli and ignores the irrelevant noise.

Selective attention
Focusing on the relevant information/cues in the sporting environment and disregarding the irrelevant.

Decision making

✚ A decision on what course of action to take is made. The memory system (pp. 66–68) is engaged and previous experiences are reflected on.
✚ The relevant motor programme is retrieved and sent to the muscles in readiness to produce the action.

Output

✚ The skill is produced.

Feedback

✚ The performer receives information about the action that they have produced. See pp. 60–61 for types of feedback that can be utilised.

2.5.2 Efficiency of information processing

Whiting's information-processing model

Whiting's information-processing model is outlined in Figure 2.3.

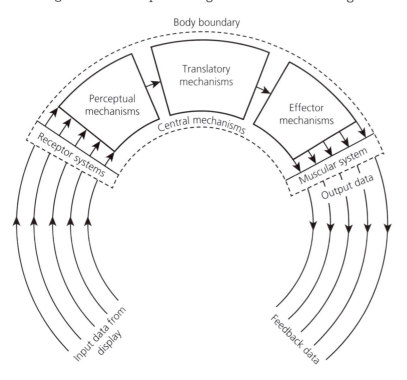

Figure 2.3 Whiting's information-processing model; Whiting 1969, *Acquiring Ball Skill*

Environment

This contains all the information required to perform the skill/action.

Display

This is the sporting environment and all the information contained in it. Some of this information will be relevant to the performer, some will be irrelevant. For example, a rugby player will have their teammates, opponents, ball, pitch markings, posts, referee, other officials, crowd, coach etc. in their display.

Sensory organs/receptor systems

We use three senses to receive the sensory information from the display. These are:

✚ vision – for example, seeing the ball and opponents
✚ audition – for example, hearing the shouts from the coach concerning tactics or the crowd calling 'offside'
✚ proprioception, which tells us about the position of our body

Proprioception consists of:

✚ touch – such as the feeling of equipment on the skin
✚ kinaesthesis – the internal muscle feeling that gives us information about whether the movement felt correct or not
✚ equilibrium – information about whether the body is balanced

Perceptual mechanism

A judgement is made regarding the incoming information received by the sense organs. Perception includes the DCR process:

+ Detection – cues are received.
+ Comparison – cues are compared with those already stored in the memory system.
+ Recognition – an understanding of what response is required based on the stored memories.

Selective attention occurs, which means that the relevant information – such as the ball, opponents and teammates – is focused on, whereas the irrelevant information – such as the crowd or the assistant referee – is filtered away. Only the relevant information is acted on, while the irrelevant information is disregarded.

Selective attention is important because it:

+ aids concentration
+ improves reaction time
+ filters out any distractions
+ controls arousal levels
+ reduces the chance of information overload in the STM (short-term memory).

For example, you detect a high ball through vision and judge the incoming speed of it travelling towards you. You compare it with memories stored and recognise that you have received a high ball before. Using selective attention you focus on the ball only and disregard the crowd etc. You now decide on a plan of action or an appropriate response – for example, I must turn sideways and jump to receive the high ball.

> **Short-term memory** The working memory where the motor programme is initiated.

Translatory mechanism

Using the information from the perceptual mechanism, a decision is then made on what action should be taken, with the help of previous experiences stored in the memory. The correct response is selected in the form of a motor programme and put into action – for example, select the motor programme for receiving a high ball.

Effector mechanism

Once the motor programme/plan of action is selected, this decision is put into action by sending impulses to the relevant working muscles to carry out the movement. For example, impulses are sent to the rectus femoris in the legs to prepare to jump for the ball and to the biceps brachii in the arms to get ready to receive the ball.

Muscular system

The muscles that are needed to catch the ball receive these impulses and are ready to catch. For example, the biceps brachii receive the impulse and begin to contract.

Output data

The movement/action is performed – for example, jump to receive the high ball.

Feedback data

Once the motor programme has been put into action, information about the movement is received. This could be **intrinsic** feedback. This is from within the performer using proprioception. For example, knowing that I have caught the ball correctly because it 'feels' right in my muscles. I know through touch that the ball is in my hands and I have landed on two feet, so I feel balanced. Or it could be **extrinsic** feedback from an outside source. For example, the coach shouts 'good jump, great catch', or the crowd cheers.

65

Now test yourself TESTED

1 What are the functions of the perceptual mechanism and the effector mechanism?

Answer on p. 263

Revision activity

Complete Table 2.16. Describe each part of Whiting's model and give an example from *your* sport.

Table 2.16

Aspect of model	Description	Example
Environment		
Display		
Sensory organs/receptor systems		
Perceptual mechanism		
Translatory mechanism		
Effector mechanism		
Muscular system		
Output data		
Feedback data		

The memory system

REVISED

The memory system is an integral part of information processing. It stores and retrieves information, makes comparisons with previous movement experiences, and selects which motor programme to retrieve in order to produce the movement.

Figure 2.4 illustrates one memory system suggested by Baddeley and Hitch (1978).

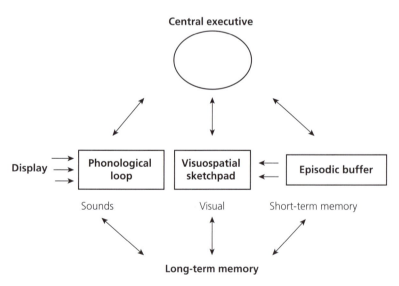

Figure 2.4 The working memory model

This model has a supervisory system called the **central executive** and three 'slave' systems. The central executive maintains overall control. It links with the long-term memory, focuses and switches attention if required, but has limited capacity. It identifies which information goes to which subsystem as they perform different functions.

✚ The **phonological loop** deals with auditory information. For example, it processes the call from your teammate. It is a temporary storage system,

Check your understanding and progress at **www.hoddereducation.co.uk/myrevisionnotes**

which creates a memory trace that is sent to the long-term memory (LTM) to trigger the motor programme. The memory trace will fade away if it is not rehearsed. For example, you repeatedly say out loud the moves in your ten-bounce trampoline routine so that you do not forget the order.

+ The **visuospatial sketchpad** holds visual and spatial information temporarily – for example, images of set plays and where you would be during the action. It also stores kinaesthetic information about how the movement feels.
+ The **episodic buffer** stores three/four chunks or 'episodes'. It allows different parts of the working memory system to talk to each other and produces sequences of information to send to the LTM, which initiates the motor programme. It also gathers perceptual information. For example, it gathers information about the flight of the ball as you receive a cross, the sound of the 'man on' call from the coach and how the limbs and muscles feel as you move to receive the pass.

Now test yourself TESTED ○

2 What are the functions of the central executive and episodic buffer?

Answer on pp. 263–264

Working and long-term memory

The functions and characteristics of components of the working memory model are as follows:

+ The working memory receives the relevant information that has been filtered away from the irrelevant by selective attention.
+ The working memory has a limited capacity; it can store 7 ± 2 items for up to approximately 30 seconds.
+ If a skill is practised/rehearsed, it can be transferred and stored in the long-term memory as a motor programme.
+ It produces a memory trace of the current skill, which is compared with information stored in the long-term memory.
+ The long-term memory then sends the motor programme to the working memory to use in the current sporting situation.
+ The long-term memory has an unlimited capacity and stores information for an unlimited time.
+ Once the LTM sends the motor programme to the working memory it initiates the motor programme.

Revision activity

Create a mind map for each of the following:
+ Central executive
+ Phonological loop
+ Visuospatial sketchpad
+ Episodic buffer

Ensuring effective storage

+ **Practice/rehearsal** – repetition overlearns or 'grooves' a skill. This will help to create a motor programme and enable it to be stored in the LTM.
+ **Linking/association with past experiences** – relating the new information to that already stored. For example, when learning to serve in tennis, link it to the basic overarm throw that the performer will have previously experienced. (See positive transfer, p. 49.)
+ Chunking – small groups of information should be put together and memorised as one. This expands the capacity of the working memory. For example, instead of learning a trampoline sequence as individual movements, the coach could 'chunk' three or four movements together.

Chunking Grouping information together to expand the capacity of the short-term memory.

67

However, coaches should avoid giving too much information because the working memory can easily become overloaded.

+ **Enjoyable/fun experiences** – if the learner has a positive experience that is presented to them in a new or distinctive way that they find interesting, they are more likely to remember the information.
+ **Meaningful** – information is more likely to be remembered if the learner understands its relevance to them and their performance. Coaches should explain explicitly to performers.
+ **Chaining** – information should be presented in an organised manner. For example, when learning a tumble sequence in gymnastics, the elements should be presented together to make it easy for the learner to remember.
+ **Mental rehearsal/imagery** – visualising the skill or going over it mentally enables learners to remember what is needed to perform the skill more easily. This is why demonstrations are imperative.
+ **Reinforcement/rewards** – if learners receive positive feedback or reinforcement, or are rewarded with praise after a correct response, they are more likely to remember the information.

Now test yourself TESTED ◯

3 What are the characteristics and functions of the working memory?

Answer on p. 264

Revision activity

Use the mnemonic below to help you to recall the strategies for ensuring **effective storage of information**:

Choose to
Make
Remembering
Easy –
Practising
Lots
Creates
Memories

Reaction, response and movement times   REVISED ◯

Key definitions

+ **Simple reaction time** is when there is one stimulus and one response. Reaction time will be very short. For example, in a swimming race, the stimulus is the starter signal and the only response is to dive in.
+ **Choice reaction time** is when there are several stimuli and several possible responses. Reaction time will be slower. For example, in football in open play, you might have several teammates calling for a pass, and several possible responses in terms of who you pass to, or the type of pass.
+ **Reaction time** is the time from the stimulus being presented, to the performer beginning to respond to it. It is the time from the onset of the stimulus to the onset of the response.
+ **Movement time** is the time from the beginning of the movement to the end of the movement. It is the time from the onset of the movement to the completion of the task
+ **Response time** is reaction time plus movement time. It is the time taken from the stimulus being presented to the end of the movement. It is the time from the onset of the stimulus to the completion of the task.

For example, in a 100-metre race:

+ Reaction time is the time from when the performer first hears the gun sound to when they begin to push on the blocks.

> **Exam tip**
>
> Remember that if reaction time or response time improves, the time is *decreased*.

Check your understanding and progress at **www.hoddereducation.co.uk/myrevisionnotes**

+ Movement time is the time from when the performer pushes on the blocks to when they cross the finish line.
+ Response time is both together – from when the performer first hears the gun sound, to when they cross the finish line.

Now test yourself
TESTED ◯

4 Define reaction time, movement time and response time.

Answer on p. 264

Hick's law

Hick's law describes the impact of choice reaction time on performance. It states that as the number of choices increases, so does the time it takes to react. In other words, the more choices there are, the slower the reaction time. This is illustrated in Figure 2.5.

Note that it is not a linear relationship. Reaction time does not increase proportionately with the number of choices.

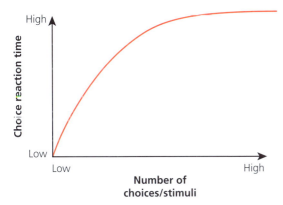

Figure 2.5 Hick's law

Single-channel hypothesis

According to the single-channel hypothesis, although we can detect many stimuli at once, we can only *process* one piece of information at a time (Figure 2.6). Any further stimuli must wait, because a 'bottleneck' occurs. If we are in the middle of processing one stimulus and a second arrives, it must wait until we have finished processing the first before it can be dealt with. The more stimuli presented, the slower the reaction time.

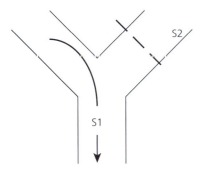

Figure 2.6 The single-channel hypothesis– only one stimulus can be processed at a time

Psychological refractory period

In the sporting arena, two or more stimuli can arrive in quick succession for processing. This causes a delay in processing and the performer might physically 'freeze' while they seek to clarify and process the correct stimuli.

Exam tip

Students often abbreviate this to PRP and therefore miss the mark. Make sure that you write it out fully. When asked for an example, use a dummy/feint because this is easiest. Make sure you use the same example throughout.

69

This delay in processing causes our reaction time to increase and is known as the psychological refractory period (Figure 2.7).

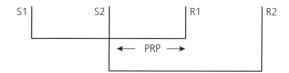

Figure 2.7 The psychological refractory period (PRP)

We can use this in sport to try to intentionally slow our opposition down. In rugby, for example, you might be approaching a defender with the ball in your hands and feign a pass to the left. This is the first stimulus and they begin moving in that direction. However, you decide to dummy and quickly run past them without releasing the pass. This is the second stimulus; however, they must process the first stimulus of the left pass. The time period where they might 'freeze' before changing direction (as the second stimulus has arrived before the first has been processed) is labelled the psychological refractory period.

Anticipation

REVISED

Anticipation can be:
+ **temporal** – this is predicting *when* the action will be performed. For example, in netball, a centre player hearing the whistle can assume that the wing attack will run into the centre third to receive the pass immediately.
+ **spatial** – this is predicting *what* action is going to be performed and *where*. For example, seeing a rugby player adjust their grip on the ball, you might predict they are going to kick over the top of the full-back rather than pass.

Strategies to improve response time

REVISED

+ **Practice** – the more you respond to a stimulus, the faster your reactions become.
+ **Selective attention** – if the performer focuses and concentrates just on the relevant information, reactions will be quicker.
+ **Mental rehearsal** – this is going over the performance in the mind. As discussed earlier (see practice), the muscles involved in the movement will be stimulated, and thus this is almost as good as physical practice.
+ **Experience** – participating in the activity gives you valuable insight and awareness of the stimuli being presented, meaning you can detect them more quickly and respond faster.
+ **Improve fitness levels** – the fitter you are, the quicker you can respond.
+ **Warm up** – if the body and mind are prepared, you can respond more quickly.
+ **Gain optimum arousal** – if you are at the peak of your arousal, you will respond more quickly.
+ **Detect cues early** – analyse your opponent's play – for example, body/limb position or line-out calls, to anticipate what they intend to do next.
+ **Try anticipation** – anticipation is predicting that a movement will happen before it occurs – for example, correctly judging that the centre player in netball will pass back to the wing defence from the centre pass because their body is slightly turned.

Now test yourself   TESTED

5 Define anticipation and explain the difference between temporal and spatial anticipation.

Answer on p. 264

Check your understanding and progress at **www.hoddereducation.co.uk/myrevisionnotes**

If a performer anticipates correctly, their response time will be very quick and they will have more time to perform the skill. However, if they anticipate incorrectly, response time can increase significantly, and the psychological refractory period might occur.

> **Revision activity**
>
> Write a list of questions and answers for Hick's law, the single-channel hypothesis and the psychological refractory period. Test a friend.

Schmidt's schema theory

REVISED ⦿

When playing sports like netball and basketball, we make several chest passes in a game, but it is highly unlikely that we make *exactly* the same pass twice. Each chest pass is unique in its speed, height, direction, force, and positions of teammates and opponents, but the basic movement pattern is the same.

Schmidt suggested that the brain is unable to store and retrieve every individual pass separately in the long-term memory. Instead he suggested we stored schema. A schema is a generalised motor programme that allows the performer to adapt their skills and transfer experiences of one skill to another. This accounts for why some performers seem to be effective in many sports. The performer might have taken their knowledge and skills from one sport, adapted them, and then transferred them into the current situation, even if they have never tried to play that sport/perform that specific skill before.

The parameters/considerations for every movement will be different – for example, environmental position, duration of movement, or muscles used to produce the action. Therefore, the performer's experiences draw together information within the schema from four areas, known as memory items, as shown in Table 2.17.

Table 2.17

Recall schema – stores information about and initiates the movement		
1 Initial conditions	This involves gathering information about whether you have been in this or a similar situation before Information about the environment and your body is collated	*Example*: I am a centre player in netball. I have the ball in my hands and I am on the edge of the shooting circle. The GS is unmarked to my left. I remember being in a similar situation before, both in training and previous games.
2 Response specification	Based on the initial conditions, you decide what movement to perform	*Example*: I decide that I will send a short, flat, fast pass to the GS, as they are quite near, before the defender recovers their position.
Recognition schema – controls and evaluates the movement		
3 Sensory consequences	This involves gathering information about the movement using intrinsic feedback or kinaesthesis	*Example*: As I pass the netball, I feel my elbows bend and I know that as the ball left my hands it felt correct. I placed enough power and height on the pass.
4 Response outcome	This involves gathering information concerning the result of the movement – was it successful or unsuccessful?	*Example*: The pass was successfully received by the GS, who went on to score a goal.

Developing schemas

✚ Ensure that practice is **variable** to build a range of experience.
✚ Ensure that practised skills are **transferable** from training to the game situation.
✚ Give **feedback** to continuously help to improve skills.
✚ Give **praise** and positive reinforcement.
✚ **Practise** a range of skills until they are well learned.

Now test yourself

TESTED

Now test yourself

TESTED

6   What are the functions of recall schema and recognition schema?

Answer on p. 264

Revision activity

Review the information on schema included in Table 2.17, and then cover it up. Complete Table 2.18 and then check your answers. Using a different-coloured pen, add any information that you missed out.

Table 2.18

R_____ schema		R_____ schema	
1		3	
2		4	
1	**2**	**3**	**4**
This gathers information… For example:	You now… For example:	This gathers information… For example:	This gathers information… For example:

Exam tip

Check the command word. For example, if you are asked to identify and describe, just stating 'chunking' might not be enough to gain the mark.

Questions are often asked on the ways to improve reaction/response time.

Exam practice

1   What is selective attention and how does it benefit the performer?   [4]

2   Explain how a player can improve their response time.   [4]

Answers online

Knowledge and skills summary

This topic involves the following knowledge (AO1):
+ Understanding the basic stages of information processing.
+ Understanding Whiting's model and all the associated terminology.
+ Explaining the functions and characteristics of Baddeley and Hitch's working memory model.
+ Identifying and describing methods to aid the storage of information.
+ Describing the importance of selective attention to the working memory.
+ Defining reaction time, movement time and response time.
+ Drawing and labelling Hick's law.
+ Explaining the functions of both recall and recognition schema, and their associated memory items.

+ Giving descriptions of temporal and spatial anticipation.

AO2 marks will require application of this knowledge – for example, explaining each section of the information processing or memory model and supporting your answer with the aid of a practical example; using practical examples to illustrate reaction time, movement time and response time (e.g. the sprint start); describing the psychological refractory period with a practical example; explaining each section of the schema using a practical example; describing the link with varied and realistic practices in the development of schema.

AO3 marks are for analysis or evaluation. In this topic an AO3 response might involve analysing the strategies to improve information processing, memory, reaction time and schema.

3 Sport and society

3.1 Emergence of globalisation of sport in the twenty-first century

3.1.1 Pre-industrial Britain – popular recreation (pre-1780)

Sport is often said to reflect the society of the time. This is certainly true of sport in pre-industrial Britain (i.e. pre-1780).

Characteristics of society   REVISED

Pre-industrial society had several characteristic features (sometimes referred to as 'sociocultural' factors in exam questions), including the following:
+ Communications and transport were limited, with life lived in a local area.
+ There was widespread illiteracy – the lower classes were uneducated, with little ability to read or write.
+ Harsh or even violent existences were the norm for the lower class (the upper class lived in luxury).
+ There was very limited free time for the lower class because work was based on the land; free time was dictated by the agricultural calendar/seasons.
+ Class divisions clearly existed; there was a two-tier divided society in existence (upper class and lower class) based on a feudal system.
+ Most of the population lived in rural areas.

> **Feudal system** Broadly defined, this was a way of structuring society around a relationship derived from the holding of land in exchange for service or labour.
>
> **Popular recreation** Sports and pastimes associated with the lower-class society in pre-industrial Britain.

Characteristics of popular recreation   REVISED

In the feudal society of pre-industrial Britain, certain sports were only played by the lower classes – for example, mob football.

Table 3.1 illustrates the links between other sociocultural features in pre-industrial Britain and popular recreation activities of the time.

> **Codification** The gradual organisation and defining of the rules – for the actual playing of a sport, as well as the conduct and behaviour of participants.

Table 3.1 Links between sociocultural features in pre-industrial Britain and popular recreation

Sociocultural features of pre-industrial Britain	Features of popular recreation
Limited transport/communications	**Local** – sport was restricted to local areas and played in the communities where people lived
Illiteracy common in lower class/largely uneducated; no NGBs (national governing bodies) had been formed at this time for lower-class sports	**Simple/basic rules**/lack of codification/limited organisation/locally set rules (e.g. no set space)
Harsh society	Sport was **violent/aggressive/unruly** in nature and male dominated, with gambling on the outcome
Seasonal structure/work linked to the agricultural calendar/very long working hours	Mob football was only played **occasionally**/annually/as part of a festival occasion (e.g. Holy days)
Pre-industrial revolution/pre-urban revolution – majority of population lived in the countryside/small villages in an agriculturally based society	Mob football was played in the **rural** areas where people lived, using the **natural resources** they had available (e.g. a pig's bladder as a ball)
Two-tier/feudal system	There was a clear division between activities played by the lower class (e.g. mob games) and upper class (e.g. real tennis)

73

Popular recreation activities, such as mob football, became increasingly unpopular with the local authorities as the nineteenth century progressed. They were eventually banned for a variety of reasons, including the following:

+ They were violent or unruly in nature and often associated with drunken behaviour, leading to injury or death in extreme cases.
+ They led to damage of property.
+ They involved gambling and alcohol consumption.

> ## Now test yourself   TESTED ⬤
>
> 1 Explain the characteristics of pre-industrial mob football.
> 2 Identify the characteristics of life in pre-industrial Britain.
> 3 Mob football was often linked to alcohol consumption and gambling. Identify other reasons why it was banned as the nineteenth century progressed.
>
> **Answers on p. 264**

> ## Making links
>
> In exam questions, you might be required to compare the characteristics of popular recreation in pre-industrial Britain with the characteristics of rational recreation in post-industrial Britain (p. 76).

Real tennis (also called 'royal tennis' or 'the sport of kings') was another activity played in pre-industrial Britain. However, it *did not* reflect the typical popular recreation characteristics of many activities at the time, and was more typical of rational recreation – i.e. it was a more structured, organised and civilised activity.

The characteristics of real tennis were reflective of upper-class life, and many reflected those of rational recreation (p. 76), including the following:

+ It was an exclusive activity, courtly and royal in nature, played by upper-class males of the two-tier society evident at the time (e.g. by Henry VIII, who had a real tennis court at Hampton Court).
+ The upper classes were educated and highly literate, so complex rules could be written down for the sport because those taking part could readily understand and apply them (i.e. it was codified).
+ The upper class played real tennis to a high moral code, so it lacked violence, and was instead played in a civilised manner, reflecting their society of the time, with opponents mutually respectful of one another.
+ With plenty of leisure time, the upper class were able to play real tennis on a regular basis, developing their skills/techniques to a high level in many cases.
+ It was played in expensive, purpose-built facilities, using expensive specialist equipment (e.g. racquets).
+ The upper class also had the ability to travel to play real tennis, so it was non-local in nature. Real tennis was a skilful game with difficult technical demands, which enabled the upper class to show their 'superiority' over the lower class. Wagering (i.e. betting) was common on the outcome of matches.

> ## Revision activity
>
> Summarise six characteristics of real tennis into a spider diagram to give you a visual image of key information that you can then apply to questions on the key features of real tennis.

It is important that you can compare and contrast the characteristics of mob football for the lower class with real tennis for the upper class, as in Table 3.2.

Exam tip

Exam questions on mob football characteristics with the command word 'explain' (AO2) require direct links between sociocultural factors and the characteristics of such an activity. You would need to say, for example, that mob football was violent and reflected a harsh and cruel society where violence was common (not just mob football was violent and aggressive). Say why.

Check your understanding and progress at **www.hoddereducation.co.uk/myrevisionnotes**

Table 3.2 A comparison of mob football and real tennis

Mob football	Characteristics of mob football compared with real tennis	Real tennis
Played by the lower classes	Participation	Played by the upper classes
Few/simple/locally agreed	Rules	Complex/written
Violent/unruly	Conduct	Non-violent/civilised
Occasional/annual/linked to festival occasions	When played	Regularly
Played in the natural environment, using available natural resources	Facilities/equipment	Played on purpose-built facilities, using specialist equipment

Now test yourself TESTED ◯

4 Identify the ways in which real tennis was different from most other popular recreation activities, such as mob football.
5 How did the availability of time influence the activities participated in by the lower class and upper class in pre-industrial Britain?

Answers on p. 264

Exam practice

1 Popular recreation was often cruel, violent and male dominated. Identify other characteristics of popular recreation activities, such as mob football. [3]
2 Why was mob football only played occasionally? [2]
3 Why did mob football have very basic rules that were locally set? [2]
4 Why could real tennis be played regularly to a complex set of written rules? [2]
5 Describe how transport, education and class affected the characteristics of pre-industrial sport. [3]

Answers online

Knowledge and skills summary

This topic involves the following knowledge (AO1):
✚ The characteristics of pre-industrial Britain section (i.e. how life was lived for the lower and upper classes during the period prior to 1780).
✚ The characteristics of mob football and real tennis.

AO2 marks will require application of this knowledge, for example, being able to explain which of these characteristics (sociocultural factors) influenced the sports and pastimes participated in by the upper class and lower class (i.e. by using the examples of real tennis for the upper class; mob football for the lower class).

AO3 marks are for analysis or evaluation. In this topic an AO3 response might involve an analysis of the characteristics of mob football and real tennis, linked to the sociocultural factors that existed at the time.

3.1.2 Industrial and post-industrial development of sport

In this section, the main focus is on how sport reflected a rapidly changing society as it moved from being an agriculturally/rurally based society to one that was dominated by factory life in a machine-based/urban environment.

As Britain changed into an industrially based society, sports and pastimes developed in different ways, reflecting such societal changes. The activities participated in were termed as 'rational recreation'. Rational suggests that a level of order, logic and structure began to be applied to sports such as football, lawn tennis and track and field athletics, reflecting a more ordered, industrially based society.

Characteristics of 'sport'/rational recreation

Rational recreation involved the post-industrial development of sport for the masses. This was characterised by features such as the following:

+ **Respectability** – sport was non-violent in nature and the emphasis was on sportsmanship/fair play.
+ **Played regionally/nationally/regularly** – sport was competitive, with winners and losers decided by competitions, which were played regionally, nationally and internationally. Watching Saturday afternoon football was particularly popular for the masses of working-class people in their time off work.
+ **Stringent administration and codification** – strict and complex written rules were set down by national governing bodies (NGBs) for the conduct of a sport across the whole country.
+ **Referees/officials** – neutral officials were present to enforce the newly developed rules in sporting contests.
+ **Purpose-built facilities** – sport took place on specially constructed grounds, pitches or tracks, often located around urban areas, with large populations to draw on for spectators (as there was less space available in urban areas).
+ **Skills/tactics based** – players had positional roles that they specialised in. Performers trained to improve their tactical awareness, as well as their techniques and fitness levels, to increase their chances of winning.

> **Revision activity**
>
> Draw a table comparing pre-industrial sociocultural factors relating to popular recreation with post-industrial factors relating to rational recreation.

Social and cultural influences on the development of rational recreation (1780–1900)

The Industrial Revolution

The Industrial Revolution was a key period in British history, which witnessed massive changes in the way people lived their lives. For example, it led to more of the population being concentrated in towns and cities working in factories, as opposed to living in the countryside and working off the land.

The influence of the Industrial Revolution on the development of rationalised sports and pastimes changed over the nineteenth century. During the first half of the nineteenth century, the initial effects were often **negative**, as outlined below:

+ **Migration of the lower classes into urban areas** – the search for work in the new factories being built led to a loss of space to play traditional mob games and overcrowding. There was no room for traditional mob games.
+ **Lack of leisure time** – the shift from 'seasonal' to 'machine' time, led to long, 12-hour working days, six days a week. The Sabbath (i.e. Sunday) was a religious observance 'day of rest'.
+ **Lack of income** – low wages and poverty were evident, with little spare income for leisure pursuits.
+ **Poor health** – associated with poor working and living conditions, pollution, and a lack of hygiene – meant little energy to play sport.
+ **Loss of rights** – restrictions were placed on mob games and blood sports by changes in criminal laws.
+ **Lack of public provision** – there was no access to private facilities or personal equipment for the lower classes.

> **Industrial Revolution**
> A period deemed to have occurred from the mid-eighteenth to the mid-nineteenth century that marked a change in Britain from a feudal, rural society into an industrialised, machine-based, capitalist society, controlled by a powerful urban middle class.

In the second half of the nineteenth century, some improvements had a **positive** effect, as outlined below:

+ **Health and hygiene** improved as a result of gradual improvements in living conditions and local council provision of public baths to improve cleanliness and help stop the spread of disease, enabling more energy and willingness to participate in sport.
+ There was a **gradual increase in wages and more time for sport** due to the Factory Acts, with Saturday half-days being provided to the workers (i.e. a gradual decrease in working hours).
+ Development of the **new middle class** (i.e. self-made entrepreneurs who took advantage of the new business opportunities available in the newly industrialised Britain). This changed ways of behaving and playing sport. It became more acceptable and respectable, and was played to a high moral code. The middle class developed strict rules, leagues and competitions. They provided facilities and public parks via their involvement in the local council, and offered more time off work and broken-time payments.
+ The influence of **ex-public schoolboys**, for example via industry and the Church.
+ The **values of** athleticism (i.e. physical endeavour with moral integrity – always trying hard and working to the best of your ability, but taking part in the spirit of fair play) spread to the lower classes.
+ Industrial patronage (i.e. kind factory owners becoming 'patrons of sport' for the working class by providing support for them to participate in various ways) led to provisions for recreation and sport. Factory teams were set up, sporting facilities were provided and excursions to the seaside were organised.
+ Improvements in **transport and communications** via the development of roads and steam trains influenced the distances spectators and players could travel, and allowed the establishment of leagues. Fixtures and results could be published in the papers of the time.
+ It **became cheaper to travel**, so participation in sport and the spectating of sport became more accessible.

Broken-time payments Financial payments made to factory workers/amateurs to compensate them for the time they had to take off work to compete.

Athleticism A fanatical devotion to sport involving high levels of physical endeavour and moral integrity.

Industrial patronage The setting up of factory teams by factory owners as a way of decreasing absenteeism and encouraging loyalty in the workforce.

Now test yourself

TESTED ⬤

6 Identify the ways in which the leisure opportunities for the working classes improved as a result of industrialisation.
7 How did industrial patronage encourage participation in sport/physical activity among the working class?

Answers on p. 264

Urbanisation

Urbanisation in the industrial period had a huge impact on the development of many of the sports we play today. Below is a summary of the key features of urbanisation that contributed to the development of sport in this period.

Urbanisation Large numbers of people migrating from rural areas into towns and cities, seeking regular work in the factories.

+ **Lack of space** – in cities, unlike the countryside, space was at a premium. This led to the development of purpose-built facilities to play sport (e.g. football grounds).
+ **Large working-class populations** – urbanisation meant a large working-class population that needed entertaining, resulting in mass spectator numbers at football and rugby matches for the first time.
+ **Loss of traditional sports** – many traditional working-class sports such as mob games were banned in a civilised urban society, so there was a need for new sports to emerge.
+ **Changes in working conditions** – initially, the working classes worked long hours in the factories, and had limited free time, income or energy to devote to sport. As this situation improved, sports attendance and participation among the working class went up.

Now test yourself TESTED

8 How did large numbers of people moving into towns and cities during the industrial revolution impact on how sport was played during this period?

Answer on p. 264

The transport revolution

The following is a summary of the key ways in which the development of the railways contributed to the development of sport in this period.

+ **Movement of teams/spectators** – the development of the **railways** and steam trains enabled faster and further travel for players and fans alike, leading to **nationwide fixtures** developing on a **regular** basis.
+ **Improved access to different parts of the country** – nationwide train travel enabled sport to develop from local to regional to national, with leagues forming, involving clubs from across the country (e.g. the Football League was formed in 1888, with 12 founder teams from the North/Midlands).
+ **Cheaper train travel** – train travel became relatively cheap and affordable with an Act making third-class travel cheaper, which led to the working classes following their teams home and away.
+ **Improved access to the countryside** – activities such as rambling became popular as rural areas became reachable and affordable via train travel.

Now test yourself TESTED

9 Identify the positive impact of developments in transport on sporting opportunities for the working classes.

Answer on pp. 264–265

Communications

+ Urban industrial society was associated with a gradual improvement in educational provision for the working class in the second half of the nineteenth century, which led to improvements in their reading and writing abilities.
+ **Rules** could therefore be developed as more people could understand them.
+ **Communication** (e.g. via newspapers) improved as society became more literate.
+ **Developments in the printed media** increased the **knowledge and awareness of sport** in a number of different ways – for example, by offering information on fixtures taking place involving local teams, or publishing the results of matches.
+ Printed publicity led to the **emergence of sporting heroes and role models** because people could read match reports and relate to their favourite players scoring goals or otherwise helping to win matches due to their high levels of skill.

Check your understanding and progress at **www.hoddereducation.co.uk/myrevisionnotes**

Now test yourself

TESTED

10 How did higher literacy levels in post-industrial Britain improve access to sport for the working class?

Answer on p. 265

Provision through factories

+ The factory system led to set working hours.
+ The working class experienced a reduction in their working week, such as the Saturday half day or the early closing movement.
+ Skilled manual workers were the first to gain additional time via the Saturday half day.
+ Worker's wages provided enough disposable income to pay the gate money entrance fee to watch Saturday afternoon football or rugby league.
+ Broken-time payments provided increased opportunities for working class factory workers to play football at a professional level.
+ Playing professional football was a more desirable job compared with the factory work alternative.

Making links

In exam questions you should be prepared to explain (AO2) the emergence of association football from mob football (p. 73), referring to the influence of various sociocultural factors, including industrialisation, urbanisation, provision through factories and improved transport/communications.

The influence of the Church

Changing views of the Church during Victorian times (i.e. the late nineteenth century) also helped to promote sport and recreation among local communities as their approval was given to rational recreation.

Reasons *why* the Church promoted sport included the following:
+ Sport **encouraged social control** (i.e. improved behaviour) through 'civilised' activities, diverting people away from 'less socially acceptable activities' such as drinking and gambling.
+ Church facilities, such as halls, provided venues for 'improving the morality' of the working classes through 'muscular Christianity'. Ex-public schoolboys promoted this muscular Christianity, which involved the clergy engaging their communities proactively by attempting to eradicate the excesses of working-class behaviour, such as gambling and drinking, in favour of more healthy and positive pursuits.
+ Sport was viewed as a good way of **promoting Christian values**. The development of the YMCA promoted the healthy body/healthy mind link. The clergy viewed sport as a good way to **increase church attendance** and help swell their congregations.
+ It **encouraged attendance at church**. Victorian vicars viewed the provision of sport as a good way of swelling their congregations on Sundays.

How the Church helped provide more opportunities for sporting involvement:
+ The approval and active involvement of the clergy gave encouragement to the working classes to participate in rationalised sporting activities such as association football.
+ The Church organised teams, set up clubs and arranged competitions. Many modern-day football clubs have their origins traceable to church organisations (e.g. Aston Villa via Villa Cross Methodist Church).
+ The Church provided sports facilities in their church halls and on their playing fields. A number of church groups formed, with sporting involvement a key part of their programmes of activities (e.g. the Boys' Brigade, the Scouts, the YMCA).

Exam tip

Make sure that you can identify (AO1), explain (AO2) and evaluate (AO3) the impact of sociocultural factors such as urbanisation and improved transport/communications on the increased opportunities these provided for the working class to participate in and watch sport.

The emergence of the middle classes

The key ways in which members of the middle class supported the development of sport were as follows:

+ **Codification** – the development of strict rules, as public school and university old boys played a key role in the formation of many national governing bodies (NGBs) of sport. They controlled sport and became key organisers via their administration experience, which enabled them to form and run clubs and NGBs – for example, the Football Association set up in 1863, the Rugby Football Union in 1871 and the Lawn Tennis Association in 1888. The middle class took prominent leadership roles in such organisations.
+ **Competitions** – the development of leagues and competitions via middle-class involvement in public schools, universities, clubs, NGBs, factory teams and church teams.
+ **Public provision** – the development of public facilities (e.g. parks and public baths) via middle-class philanthropists, factory owners, the Church, and the passing of government Acts in their roles as local politicians.
+ **Increased leisure time** – middle-class factory owners gradually gave their workers more leisure time (e.g. the Saturday half-day), which allowed more time to watch or participate in sport.
+ **Move to 'professionalism'** – the middle class helped in the development of early commercial/professional sport, for example by acting as agents or promoters in athletics or, in their role as factory owners, setting up factory teams and paying broken-time payments in football.

> **Philanthropists** Kind, generous, middle-class individuals who had a social conscience and were keen to try to provide for a better life among the working class.

The British Empire

Sport was seen as a good and powerful way of instilling moral values into people across the world, and of binding the various people of the Empire together. Young men (nineteenth-century public school boys and university old boys), educated to become leaders of the British Empire, spread the playing of sports in a number of ways:

+ As **teachers** they developed teams and taught traditional sporting values in schools throughout the Empire.
+ As **industrialists/factory owners** they set up teams and gave time off to play competitive sport nationally and internationally.
+ As **clergy** they developed church teams or became missionaries and took sport abroad (seen as good for social control or morality).
+ As **officers in the British army** they used sport within the armed services and spread sport throughout the Empire.
+ As **diplomats** they travelled the world and took sport with them (e.g. rugby and cricket).
+ They formed the **national governing bodies** of sport (e.g. the RFU), which codified sports and established leagues and competitions that eventually spread internationally as well as nationally.

> **British Empire** A worldwide system of dependencies that, over a timespan of some three centuries, were brought under the rule and administration of Great Britain.

Local authorities – public provision and its influence

Poor living conditions, disease and pollution were the side-effects of industrialisation. Local authorities and councils in the nineteenth century started to combat this by providing recreational and sporting activities and hygiene facilities for their local communities for a number of reasons:

+ To increase the health and fitness/personal hygiene of the working class.
+ To help gain prestige for the local area by providing public facilities (e.g. public parks).
+ To increase social control and civilise society, and to encourage middle-class values. The temperance movement wanted to keep the working class out of the pubs and away from alcohol
+ To improve the productivity of the workforce and raise the morale of the community.

Other specific actions included the following:

+ Increased provision was made for public bath houses, with first- and second-class facilities to reflect the prevalent social class system. Specifically, local authorities felt a civic responsibility to apply for grants to provide **public washing facilities** (e.g. via the Wash Houses Act of 1846).
+ **Plunge baths** were developed for **swimming/recreational use**.

> **Now test yourself**   TESTED ◯
>
> **13** Give reasons why local authorities in the nineteenth century started to provide recreational and sporting activities for their local communities.
>
> **Answer on p. 265**

Public schools/universities

Large numbers of middle-class schoolboys attended public schools in the nineteenth century. These schools played an important role in the promotion, organisation and spread of sports and games. Characteristics of public schools and the influences of these are shown in Table 3.3.

Table 3.3 The influence of public schools on sport

Characteristic	Influence on sport and games
Boarding	Plenty of time available so the pupils needed occupying in a positive way
Boys-only cohort	Energy and enthusiasm needed channelling into games
Families needed to pay fees	Money could go towards paying for facility development, equipment purchase, employment of staff etc.
Schools had large grounds	Space available to play sports/games competitions
Strict discipline	Harsh treatment prepared the boys for the rigours of competitive sport/physical nature of some of the games (e.g. rugby)

Public schools were important for sport for four distinct reasons:

+ Promotion and organisation of sports and games:
  + Public school reforms led by Thomas Arnold as Head of Rugby School promoted more regulated sports, which provided exercise and healthy competition. This included having sixth-form prefects involved in organisation.
  + These sixth-form prefects gained valuable organisational/leadership experience (e.g. of inter-house sport as part of a sports committee), which they could apply when they left. After university, these individuals played key roles in the formation of national governing bodies of sport.

Public provision Local council provision of facilities (e.g. sport/recreational) to allow the masses to participate.

Social class A term used to reflect social inequalities, i.e. where certain groups have more access to wealth, income and power than others. Factors that contribute to social class include a person's job, family background, education and income.

Exam tip

It is important to be aware of the Municipal Reform Act (1835) and of government provisions of funding for public facilities such as baths and parks, which eventually led to swimming as a sport for the working classes.

Public school A private, fee-paying secondary school, especially one for boarders.

Exam tip

For AO1 marks, make sure that you can identify the characteristics of public schools and, for AO2, explain how these characteristics influenced the development of team games.

81

+ Team games such as rugby union, football and cricket developed leadership qualities in public schoolboys – for example, teamwork and team loyalty. Being a captain in sport meant learning to give orders and leading by example – showing courage in the heat of the battle.
+ Promotion of ethics through sports and games:
  + Public schools emphasised high morality as a key value in their playing of sport/games – for example, fair play, sportsmanship and mutual respect for opponents and officials; self-discipline; taking part in sport was more important than winning, with no monetary prizes for winning.
  + Arnold helped develop the idea of 'muscular Christianity' which linked sport with being a Christian gentleman (i.e. high morals and positive ethics).
+ The 'cult' of athleticism — meaning, nature and impact:
  + The development of character through sport was referred to as 'the cult of athleticism' – a fanatical devotion to the playing of sport/team games.
  + The nature of this was a combination of physical endeavour (trying hard) with moral integrity (playing fairly/sportsmanship).
+ The spread and export of games and games ethic.

> **Making links**
>
> The ways in which nineteenth-century public schoolboys and university old boys influenced the development of sport in Britain and its spread through the British Empire are covered in the British Empire section (p. 80).

> **Now test yourself**　　　　　　　　　　　　　　**TESTED** ◯
>
> 14 Identify the characteristics of nineteenth-century public schools.
>
> **Answer on p. 265**

> **Exam tip**
>
> For AO2/AO3 marks, make sure that you can clearly describe and analyse how public schools influenced the promotion and organisation of sports and games, as well as how they influenced ethics/athleticism in Britain and across the world.

Development of national governing bodies

National governing bodies (NGBs) of sport emerged in the second half of the nineteenth century.

+ More teams and clubs were being formed as sports, such as football, became increasingly popular; these clubs needed an organisation to affiliate to/join with.
+ Clubs formed to control eligibility (i.e. who was allowed to play their sport) and maintain their power as middle-/upper-class amateurs for as long as possible. Maintenance of the 'amateur ideal' was important to the middle-class founders of NGBs (e.g. Clement Jackson and his associates at the AAA). They feared a 'win at all costs' mindset with increased deviance/breaking of the rules once money became involved. In addition, as the professionals improved, the middle class feared being beaten by their 'social inferiors'.
+ There was a need for codification – to standardise the rules across the country so that everyone played to the same set of national rules.
+ The clubs being formed required regular competitions against a range of teams, which could be organised by an NGB – for example, the FA and the FA Cup, and the Football League. The middle classes were keen to be involved – as public school old boys/university old boys themselves, they were skilled in organisation.

> **National governing body (NGB)** An organisation that has responsibility for managing its own particular sport (e.g. British Cycling).

> **Exam tip**
>
> Make sure that you are able identify the reasons for the emergence of NGBs in the second half of the nineteenth century in England (AO1), and then explain them (AO2).

> **Making links**
>
> For your exam you need to understand the role of public school/university old boys (pp. 81–82) in the formation of NGBs (p. 82), and why some NGBs tried to prevent professionals from competing in their sport – for example, due to the desire of the middle and upper classes to maintain control of sport.

Check your understanding and progress at **www.hoddereducation.co.uk/myrevisionnotes**

Amateurism and professionalism

Participation in sport over time has been viewed as being played according to two very different codes. First, there is the amateur code, which stresses sport purely for the sake of it. Second, there is the professional code, which places far more emphasis on winning (Table 3.4).

> **Exam tip**
>
> In modern times, amateurism is often taken to mean performing at a low level, but in the nineteenth century the opposite was true and the amateur sports performer was very much admired and respected.

> **Amateur** A person who plays sport for the love of it and receives no financial gain.
>
> **Professional** A person who plays sport for financial gain.

Table 3.4 A comparison of amateurism and professionalism

The gentleman amateur in nineteenth-century Britain	The working-class professional in nineteenth-century Britain
Came from a public school/university background (e.g. Repton and Oxford University)	Came from a state education background
Had high status in society and sport (upper and middle class); he was a politician and diplomat	Had a low status in society and sport (working class)
Had wealth and did not need 'financial compensation' to participate in sport	Had very little wealth, with limited income, and therefore needed 'financial compensation' to play sport – for example, broken-time payments emerged, which meant those in the working classes could eventually play sport and receive payments for doing so
Had plenty of free time available to participate in sport	Had very little free time available to participate in sport due to long working hours
Viewed sports participation as good for character building; training was frowned on as this would constitute professionalism	Viewed sport as a 'way out' of poverty; earning money from sport was seen as an avenue for social mobility
Played a lot of sports and was viewed as an 'all-rounder'; training was frowned on and he preferred to use his natural talents	Specialised in a single sport (e.g. association football); commitment to training to improve fitness and skill levels
Played sport to a high moral code with an emphasis on participation, fair play and an appreciation of the value of rule-regulated activity	Played sport with a lower level of morality, with an emphasis on winning, gamesmanship and cheating; viewed as 'corruptible' and open to bribes
Example: C. B. Fry, England international footballer and cricketer, and a world record holder in the long jump	*Example*: Jimmy Forrest, Blackburn Rovers, and the first professional to play for England (vs Wales) in 1884

Early twentieth-century amateurs

At the start of the twentieth century, amateurs maintained their prominence in sport, including their positions at the top of national governing bodies, which affected access for the working classes to amateur sports such as rugby union. The amateurs were therefore still the best performers, playing with high morality, and emphasising sportsmanship in their participation:
+ **High status** – they held a high status in both sport and society.
+ **Controllers of sport** – the middle and upper classes controlled sport, while excluding (e.g. financially) the working classes from 'amateur sports'.
+ **Top performers** – it was more likely that top performers would come from the middle or upper classes.
+ **Highly moral** – they had sufficient income and leisure time to play sport for the love of it, receiving no payment, and emphasised fair play and sportsmanship.

Modern-day 'amateurs'

As the twentieth century progressed, the amateurs began to lose some of their status and power in sport. Society slowly began to be based more on equality of opportunity, with achievements based more on merit and personal performance standards:

+ Modern-day 'amateurs' of the late twentieth and early twenty-first centuries tend to be of lower status (professionals now are of higher status).
+ Some high-level performers are still not professional (e.g. gymnasts).
+ There has been a blurring of amateur and professional distinctions, with less likelihood of exclusion; society has become more egalitarian (i.e. equal), with achievement based on merit.
+ Performance at the top level in most sports is now open to all.
+ Some amateurs receive finance to cover their expenses (e.g. for training) – for example, National Lottery and Sports Aid funding. It could be argued that this enables them to train as full-time athletes in modern-day sport, and they do not gain financially from this funding. But does this mean they are still amateurs?

'Positives' of modern-day 'amateurism'

The amateur code has continued in British sport in a number of ways:

+ Codes of amateurism are still evident in British sport, such as through fair play and sportsmanship.
+ Amateurism is still viewed positively and promoted through, for example, fair play awards in football, shaking of hands before and at the end of sporting contests, and the Olympics, with the Olympic ideal based on principles of amateurism.
+ Sports like rugby union maintained their amateurism until late into the twentieth century, and still have codes of conduct based on such principles, such as calling a referee 'Sir'.

Modern-day professionalism

Many factors are responsible for the growth of professional sport and the increased status of professional performers from the twentieth century through to the modern day:

+ All classes can compete; social class is no longer a barrier to participation. Social mobility is far more possible now than it was in nineteenth-century Britain. Social class is no longer a barrier to success.
+ People are now respected for their talents and efforts in reaching the top.
+ There are high rewards for professionals through media and sponsorship (e.g. footballers and tennis players).
+ Professionals have more time to train (i.e. many are full-time sports professionals), leading to higher standards of performance than among amateurs in the same sport.
+ Celebrity status, more media coverage and investment in sport have all led to vast increases in financial rewards available for performers, as large numbers of sports have become able to support professionals, for example in golf, tennis and football. Many professionals are very wealthy and can afford a luxury lifestyle. Such materialism is highly valued by many in modern-day society.
+ Positive role models act as motivators for others to achieve in professional sport.
+ Money invested in sports enables events and the sports themselves to operate and survive commercially; there has been a general increase in commercial sport and the sponsorship of sport.

Rationalisation and development of lawn tennis

REVISED

The middle classes aspired to be like the upper classes in society, who played real tennis (pp. 74–75). However, the middle classes were often excluded from the game, or could not play it, so they invented an alternative – lawn tennis:

Check your understanding and progress at **www.hoddereducation.co.uk/myrevisionnotes**

- Major Walter Clopton Wingfield patented a version of tennis on 23 February 1874.
- It had set rules and suited middle-class suburban housing, with lawned gardens, as appropriate venues for tennis courts.
- Walls and hedges ensured privacy from the lower classes, who were initially excluded from participation.
- By 1877, the All England Croquet Club had been renamed the All England Croquet and Lawn Tennis Club. The same year this version of tennis started being played at Wimbledon, alongside croquet.
- At this time, private tennis coaching clubs were founded across the country. The middle class had the organisational experience necessary to form their own clubs.
- The middle class had sufficient finance to purchase their own equipment. Wingfield sold a 'kit' as a portable product necessary to play the game of tennis. It cost five guineas (21 shillings or £1.05) and included a net, balls, racquets and poles for the net.
- Wingfield's kit also contained a rulebook, which helped standardise the game, with lawn tennis played to the same rules no matter where it was played.
- The game eventually spread to the working class via public parks, leading to public provision.

> **Lawn tennis** Originally called 'sphairistike' and played on an hourglass-shaped court, before its name and court shape were quickly replaced.

Lawn tennis was viewed as an important activity in the **emancipation of women**, with female participation first allowed in 1884, helping to overcome suppression and negative stereotypes.
- Positive female role models inspired participation – for example, Lottie Dod won five ladies' singles titles in the late nineteenth century.
- The game of lawn tennis aided women because it could be played in the seclusion and privacy of their own gardens.
- Women could play the game as a 'minimum-exercise activity', following a modest and reserved dress code, with their bodies fully covered by high-necked, long-sleeved dresses.
- As lawn tennis was 'not too vigorous', women were not expected to sweat, which was seen as unladylike.
- Both males and females played because it was seen as a good, civilised, 'social game' that all could enjoy, while improving their health at the same time.

Now test yourself TESTED ○

15 Identify the factors that led to tennis increasing women's participation in physical activity in the late nineteenth century.

Answer on p. 265

The Wenlock Olympian Games REVISED ○

- In 1850, the Wenlock Agricultural Reading Society (WARS) in Much Wenlock, Shropshire resolved to form a class called the **Olympian Class**, which was set up to promote moral, physical and intellectual improvements, especially in the lower-class people of Wenlock.
- The secretary of the 'class' and the driving force behind the Wenlock Olympian Games was Dr William Penny Brookes, who was inspired to create such an event because of his work as a doctor and surgeon in the town.
- Participation in outdoor recreation challenges was an important means of promoting improvement, with prizes offered for successful participants to encourage people to take part.
- At the first games held in October 1850, there was a mixture of athletics and traditional country sports, including football, cricket, running, the hurdles and cycling on penny farthings.

+ By 1867 the programme featured a range of early athletic events, many of which were later developed into track and field athletic events, for example the under-10 boys 60 yards; the under-14 boys 100 yards, a mile foot race, running high leap/long leap, putting the stone and hammer throwing.
+ Baron Pierre de Coubertin visited the Wenlock Olympian Society in 1890, which held a special festival in his honour. De Coubertin was inspired by Dr Brookes and went on to establish the International Olympic Committee (IOC) and reform the modern Olympic Games in Athens (1896).

> **Exam tip**
>
> Make sure that for the Wenlock Olympian Games you can identify (AO1) its original aims for the lower-class people of Wenlock.

> **Now test yourself** TESTED ○
>
> 16 Identify three aims of the Wenlock Olympian Games.
>
> **Answer on p. 265**

Rationalisation and development of track and field athletics   REVISED ●

+ Athletics events became popular in towns and cities, with purpose-built tracks and facilities in most major cities by the mid-nineteenth century.
+ Walking and running races took place over set distances on racecourses.
+ Large numbers of people attended athletics events, with up to 25,000 spectators at meetings as the nineteenth century progressed.
+ Wagering (risking a sum of money against someone else's on the basis of an unpredictable event) was common in athletics, as it was in its early days of pedestrianism/foot racing.
+ Class divisions were also evident as it became a 'rationalised' activity.
+ Upper- and middle-class amateurs ran for enjoyment or to test themselves, while the lower classes ran to make money and were deemed 'professionals'.

An 'exclusion clause' (excluding the working class/manual workers) attempted to separate modern athletics from the old professional/corrupt form.

+ In 1866, the Amateur Athletic Club (AAC) was formed by public school and ex-university men who were 'gentleman amateurs' and did not allow mechanics, artisans or labourers to join (i.e. they excluded the working classes from running for membership of the AAC).
+ They brought respectability to athletics, emphasising endeavour, fair play, courage and no wagering.
+ The Amateur Athletics Association (AAA), established on 24 April 1880, withdrew the exclusion clause and opened up the sport to everyone.
+ A professional became somebody who ran for money as opposed to someone from the working class.
+ However, track and field athletics was not deemed to be an acceptable activity for women because it was considered unladylike and without an appropriate dress code.
+ The Women's AAA was not founded until 1922, with female participants not allowed into any Olympic event until Amsterdam 1928. Even then, women were not allowed in some events that were seen as 'too strenuous', for example racing beyond 800 metres.

Rationalisation and development of association football   REVISED ●

A variety of reasons can be given to explain the growth and development of association football from the mid-nineteenth century through to the present day. In terms of the post-industrial revolution period through to the second half of the nineteenth century, these included the following:

+ **Urbanisation** – large numbers of people living in one place offered a large captive audience for football. The lack of space in urban areas led

Check your understanding and progress at www.hoddereducation.co.uk/myrevisionnotes

to purpose-built, specialist facilities for playing football, with terraces to house the high spectator demand.

+ **More free time/increased leisure time** – as workers spent less time in the factories, more time was available to them to watch and play sport. Saturday afternoon at 3 p.m. became the traditional time for 'association football' matches.

+ **More disposable income** – improved standards of living via higher wages gave the 'working class' enough money to pay entrance money and to fund transport to matches, as national fixtures began and football spread nationwide.

+ **Improved transport** – the development of trains, in particular, enabled fans to travel to watch away fixtures, and increased the regularity of matches, with the resultant need for organised leagues and cup competitions to be set up. The FA Cup was first played for in the 1871–72 season.

+ **Increased professionalism** – opportunities to play football professionally as a job gradually increased – for example, via broken-time payments, which enabled workers to get time off work to play football but still be paid their wage. Professional football, first recognised by the FA in 1885, was looked on as a desirable job because it was a chance for some to escape the factory system of work and the urban deprivation that accompanied it.

+ **Social-class links** – middle-class influence and approval gave association football more 'respectability', with its emphasis on high morality and sporting etiquette. This was challenged relatively quickly by the working class, who made it 'the people's game', with larger numbers both playing and watching association football, and the Football League commencing in 1888.

+ **Increased organisation** – football quickly became highly structured and standardised when in 1863 ex-public schoolboys set up the FA. National rules and codification meant the game was far more controlled, with less violence, which reflected an increasingly civilised society. Referees controlled the games to further improve the behaviour of the players. Football quickly expanded, with many teams being set up via factories and churches.

Now test yourself   TESTED

17 Identify two reasons why urbanisation played a key role in the development of association football.

Answer on p. 265

Making links

Make sure that you can link the impact of the sociocultural factors stated in the specification with the focus sports of association football (pp. 88–92), lawn tennis (pp. 92–93) and track and field athletics (pp. 93–94).

Exam tip

Organise your summary notes to aid your understanding of the development of football from pre-industrial times (i.e. mob football, pp. 73–75) to the public schools/ universities in the mid-nineteenth century (pp. 81–82) and its emergence as a rational recreation sporting activity in the late nineteenth century (p. 76).

Exam practice

1 Which of the following best describes a professional performer? [1]
   A One who plays sport for the love of it.
   B One who receives direct payment for their participation in sporting activities.
   C One who does not get paid for competing in sport.
   D One who plays sport while emphasising sportsmanship and fair play.

2 Explain two characteristics of lawn tennis in nineteenth-century Britain. [4]

3 Explain the impact of each of the following social and cultural factors on the development and spread of rational recreation during the nineteenth century. [6]
   a Urbanisation
   b Public provision
   c Communication

4 Explain why national governing bodies of sport emerged in the second half of the nineteenth century. [4]

5 What is meant by the 'cult of athleticism'? [1]

6 Identify three characteristics of early public schools and explain how each characteristic influenced the development of team games. [3]

7 Analyse the development of association football, from pre-industrial Britain, via nineteenth-century public schools, through to its development as a rational recreation activity. [8]

Answers online

Knowledge and skills summary

This topic involves the following knowledge (AO1):
+ The characteristics and impact on sport in industrial and post-industrial Britain of various sociocultural factors, including industrialisation, urbanisation, transport and communication, the British Empire, factory provision, churches, the development of local authorities, public schools/universities and the emergence of a three-tier class system.
+ The changing status of amateur and professional performers from the post-industrial period.
+ The characteristics and impact on sport of various sociocultural factors.
+ The changing role of women in sport during the industrial and post-industrial period.
+ The changing status of amateur and professional performers from the post-industrial period.

AO2 questions will ask for application of this knowledge – for example, explaining how these characteristics (i.e. sociocultural factors) influenced the sports and pastimes participated in by the middle class and lower class (e.g. lawn tennis for the middle class and association football for the working class); explaining the characteristics and impact on sport of various sociocultural factors; explaining why many national governing bodies emerged in England during the second half of the nineteenth century; explaining, with practical sporting examples (AO2), the changing role of women in sport during the industrial and post-industrial period.

AO3 marks are for analysis or evaluation. For this topic an AO3 response might involve an analysis of the impact on sport of various sociocultural factors.

3.1.3 Post-Second World War (1950 to present)

Development of modern-day association football

REVISED ●

Football became Britain's major sporting activity as the twentieth century progressed, with attendances and gate receipts soaring. However, the wages of the players did not reflect this increased income until later in the second half of the twentieth century, due to the setting of a 'maximum wage', which constrained earnings.

Check your understanding and progress at **www.hoddereducation.co.uk/myrevisionnotes**

- In 1900 the maximum wage was set at £4 a week and it was very slow to increase. £4 was seen as a wage of someone in a slightly higher-status working-class job like a foreman.
- A footballer's wages did not significantly increase until PFA chairman Jimmy Hill successfully fought for the abolition of the maximum wage in 1961, and Johnny Haynes became the first £100-a-week footballer.
- More recently in the late twentieth and twenty-first centuries, football has undergone a massive increase in commercialisation linked to far more media coverage through television and the internet.
- Top players such as Messi and Ronaldo are known the world over, with 'pop-star'/role-model status.
- Their salary scales have increased massively, with the Bosman ruling. This is a European Court of Justice decision made on 15 December 1995 concerning freedom of movement for workers. It allowed the free movement of labour in the European Union. It effectively allowed footballers within the EU to move at the end of their contract to another club without a transfer fee being paid, which gave 'freedom of contract' to players, and led to huge transfer fees being paid, particularly to a player who is 'out of contract'.

> **Bosman ruling** A ruling by the European Court of Justice, which gave professional football players the right to a free transfer at the end of their contract.

> **Now test yourself**
> TESTED ◯
>
> 18 How have professional footballers benefited from the Bosman ruling in the twenty-first century?
>
> **Answer on p. 265**

Emergence of elite female footballers

REVISED ◯

In the UK, football has become increasingly available to women. Key moments in the history of women's football in England are as follows:
- 1966 – England's successful hosting of the World Cup led to a resurgence of interest in women's football.
- 1969 – The Women's Football Association (WFA) was formed to promote the women's game at a national level, including the development of league structures.
- 1971 – The WFA organised the first national competition, the Mitre Trophy (now the Women's FA Cup); the FA's 50-year ban on women's football being played on league grounds was lifted.
- 1972 – The WFA launched an official England national team.
- 1991 – The WFA set up the Women's Premier League.
- 1993 – The FA began its direct involvement in women's football.
- 2001/02 – Premier League club Newport Ladies FC was the first to broadcast its match highlights via on-demand television.
- 2004 –The BBC broadcast the Women's FA Cup final to an audience of over 2 million.
- 2008–12 – The Women's Super League (WSL) was launched in 2011, initially as an eight-team summer competition. The television rights were sold to a pay-per-view channel, restricting its exposure and the additional sponsorship deals that would have been available if the coverage had been available via free-to-air (Digital Terrestrial Television) channels such as the BBC.
- 2012 – A Team GB women's team participated for the first time at the Olympics in London 2012.
- 2013–18 – The WSL announced a switch back to the winter season to move it in line with other leagues in Europe and to improve the chances of national team success, as well as increase attendances at games and participation in the sport at all levels.
- 2020 – The FA unveiled its new strategy for women's football (Table 3.5).

> **Digital Terrestrial Television (DTT)** The most common type of television service across the world. In the UK it is known as Freeview, and replaced the old analogue television service, which consisted of five channels. With Freeview you can get up to 70 free-to-air standard channels, 15 HD channels and around 30 radio services.

My Revision Notes: AQA A-level PE

+ **2021** – The FA announced that the Barclays FA WSL had signed the largest commercial broadcasting deal for women's football to date, for 3 years, starting in August with the BBC (18–22 matches a season) and Sky (35–44 matches a season). Women's football will benefit from the 'Sky treatment', which includes high-quality production, and detailed player/match analysis by well-known pundits.

'Inspiring Positive Change'

In 2020 the FA unveiled its latest strategy for women's football: 'Inspiring Positive Change' (2020–2024). It includes eight objectives (Table 3.5).

Table 3.5 The FA's Inspiring Positive Change objectives

Objective	Explanation
Equal access to 'early participation' in football	Pledge for equality of access to football for every primary school-aged girl via school PE and extracurricular provision, accessibility to external clubs and more
Equal access to 'development participation' in football	Pledge to provide access to every girl to participate and develop in football, from providing a purely fun experience, through to competitive opportunities and onto excellence levels
Develop a 'club player pathway'	Working with clubs, the aim is to develop an effective high-performance inclusive player-centred pathway to follow
Enhance elite domestic leagues and competitions	To create the best professional women's football leagues and competitions in the world (e.g. by attracting and developing world-class women footballers to play in the Barclays FA WSL and Vitality Women's FA Cup)
Achieve national competition success	To win a major international tournament by 2024 (e.g. the Euros in 2022 or the FIFA Women's World Cup in 2023)
Football for all	Recruit and support a diverse range of local leaders to organise football for their communities
Coaching	Support the development of top coaches who are representative of society at every level of the game (note: the report identified that of the 234,551 FA-qualified coaches, only 18,302 were female and 9% were from a BAME background)
Refereeing	Ensuring that every female referee receives bespoke learning and development opportunities at all levels to increase the number of female WSL officials (note: the report identified that of the 27,451 FA-qualified referees, only 1718 were female and 9.5% were from a BAME background)

Now test yourself   TESTED ⬭

19 Using Table 3.5, identify the inequalities that exist in terms of coaching and officiating for women in football.

Answer on p. 265

Sociocultural factors

Different sociocultural factors have led to an increase in opportunities for women to participate and progress through to elite level in activities such as football in modern-day society. These include the following:

+ **Equal opportunities** – more sports are generally available and socially acceptable to women, including football. The Sex Discrimination Act has led to less sexual discrimination in sport on the basis of gender. The war effort from women also led to the breaking down of myths and stereotypes about the physical capabilities of women.
+ **Increased media coverage of women's football** – Sky and the BBC took over broadcast from BT from the 2021/22 season, allowing a wider audience.
+ **More provision through school PE programmes** – in National Curriculum PE lessons as well as through extracurricular opportunities.
+ **Increased approval, encouragement and resource investment via the FA** – for example, the women's national teams at various levels are fully supported by the FA; the FA Cup Final was held at Wembley for the first time in 2015.

Check your understanding and progress at **www.hoddereducation.co.uk/myrevisionnotes**

- **More clubs are forming** – at local as well as professional levels (e.g. the WSL and Championship).
- **Increased participation via more funding into the game** – at grass roots level as well as elite level.
- **More free time** – as the traditional domestic responsibility role has decreased for women.

Now test yourself   TESTED ◯

20 Identify two ways in which increased media coverage of the WSL has impacted positively on women's football.

Answer on p. 265

Emergence of elite female officials in football   REVISED ◯

At the end of the twentieth century, very few female officials were progressing through to the Football League. The first female ever to officiate in the Football League and then Premier League, both times as an assistant referee, was Wendy Toms. Progress since this breakthrough has been slow.

The recruitment and retention of female officials in football has continued to face a number of barriers, including those identified and explained in Table 3.6.

Table 3.6 Barriers to recruiting female officials

Identification of barriers	Explanation of barriers
Stereotyping, sexism and hostile attitudes from male players; lack of adherence to FA Respect protocols	The relatively small number of female officials in the men's game (e.g. Sian Massey-Ellis) tend to receive sexist abuse, which might be off-putting to future participants
Lack of role models	Few female officials exist at elite level, while the majority work in the women's game, which currently receives far less media coverage and spectator interest
Lack of full-time opportunities/lack of sponsorship	Full-time opportunities for refereeing are restricted to higher-level men's football, with very few opportunities for women
Too many demands on time; lack of leisure time	Jobs/full-time employment and possible childcare responsibilities can limit the time available to devote to the demands of football officiating
Fewer opportunities/competitions to potentially officiate	There are fewer opportunities within the women's game due to the lower number of competitions

Various strategies are being used to try to challenge the barriers that exist, in an attempt to overcome the lack of female football officials. Table 3.7 identifies and explains such strategies before making a comment on their overall effectiveness.

Table 3.7 Strategies to overcome the lack of female football officials

Identification of strategies	Explanation of strategies
Increasing media coverage of women's football	More television coverage (e.g. by the BBC and Sky) creates more role models; over time, this creates mentors to advise on, encourage and support continued involvement as officials
Creation of a partnership in the elite women's game with Professional Game Match Officials Limited (PGMOL) to oversee the management of WSL and women's Championship officials, such as Stacey Pearson, Amy Fearn and Helen Conley	The partnership with PGMOL will enable the top officials in the women's game, including women, to access training and support, which officials (mainly male) receive in the Premier League and EFL
More sponsorship and full-time paid opportunities	As the WSL becomes increasingly commercial and professional in relation to players and officials (including women), working within it should become full-time/professional too

Table 3.7 *continued*

Identification of strategies	Explanation of strategies
Providing education to overcome stereotyping and sexism; use of laws to punish sexist behaviour and sex discrimination	Punishing and making examples of the individuals who make sexist comments towards female officials would show that it will not be tolerated
Use of social media to create supportive networks	Social media will provide support networks and information on officiating opportunities

Exam tip

If an extended question asks you to 'outline and evaluate' the barriers and solutions with regard to female football officiating, it is important that you identify (AO1) and explain (AO2) the barriers that exist against women becoming football officials. You also need to make sure that you identify (AO1), explain (AO2) and evaluate (AO3) the strategies that are being used to overcome the lack of female officials (i.e. are they working or not?). For evaluation, think of the first example on increasing media coverage. It can be effective if used to raise the profile of female officials because it gives young girls and women something to aspire to. But it could be less effective if there is negative media coverage of female officials (e.g. highlighting their mistakes).

Exam tip

Be prepared for exam questions linked to case study activities. These might require you to illustrate your knowledge and understanding of potential barriers and solutions to issues facing female participation as performers in football or as football officials.

Now test yourself   TESTED

21 Identify the barriers to women's involvement as officials in association football in England.

Answer on p. 265

The modern-day development of lawn tennis   REVISED

+ Modern-day tennis spread across the world, with tournaments in the USA, France and Australia taking place alongside Wimbledon as the four 'majors'.
+ Players soon realised that they could earn considerable amounts of money from their tennis skills. Professional tours and tournaments were established as early as the 1920s to enable them to do so.
+ However, the rest of tennis, including the four majors, remained strictly amateur, with professionals excluded from participation. It was not until 1968 that commercial pressures and rumours of some amateurs taking money illegally (colloquially known as 'shamateurism') led to the abandonment of the distinction between amateur and professional, inaugurating the open era, in which all players could compete in all tournaments.
+ With the beginning of the open era, the establishment of an international professional tennis circuit and revenues from the sale of television rights, the popularity of the game has spread worldwide and the sport has tried to shed its English, middle-class image.
+ Tennis in the UK is still perceived by many to be a middle-class preserve. This might be because it developed later than other sports, or it might be due to the fact that joining a tennis club has always appeared difficult or off-putting, for example with the requirement to stick to rigid dress codes. The image of the sport as a means to gather socially rather than as a competitive opportunity has been hard to shed.
+ The open era witnessed distinct inequalities in the amount of prize money offered to men and women. The 1968 Wimbledon Championship awarded £2000 to Rod Laver, the men's singles winner, with only £750 given to Billie Jean King, the women's champion.

Open era When professional tennis players were allowed to compete alongside amateurs and earn money.

Making links

Tennis, with its traditionally middle-class image, is a good activity to link with the section on social class (pp. 102–104).

Check your understanding and progress at **www.hoddereducation.co.uk/myrevisionnotes**

+ Representatives from the Women's Tennis Association (WTA), including Billie Jean King, fought for equal recognition and prize money, with equality achieved in 2007 at Wimbledon when both winners earned £700,000. By 2015 it had risen to £1,760,000 each for the respective men's and ladies' singles champions.

Emergence of elite female tennis players

The work of the WTA (which is now a global leader in women's professional sport) illustrates how tennis can be viewed as one of a few sports in which female professional performers have played a significant part.

+ As part of the battle fighting pay differentials in tennis tournaments such as Wimbledon, a number of women decided to create their own tour away from the men's. The WTA developed its own professional circuit in the late twentieth century, providing ground-breaking opportunities for women to play at the top level, eventually earning millions of pounds through tournament earnings and sponsorship deals – for example, Martina Navratilova and the Williams sisters (Venus and Serena).
+ Billie Jean King became the first female athlete to earn £100,000 in a single year, with Chris Evert generating over $1,000,000 in career earnings by the mid-1970s.
+ The WTA also stated that, in 2015, more than 2500 elite players competed for $129 million in prize money at the 55 WTA events and four Grand Slams available in tennis.
+ A lot of potential role models for girls, as well as large sponsorship deals, remain prevalent in the early twenty-first century, via the worldwide media coverage of women's elite tennis tournaments.

> **Now test yourself**   TESTED ○
>
> 22 Describe the role of Billie Jean King and the Women's Tennis Association in the development of women's tennis towards the end of the twentieth century.
>
> **Answer on p. 265**

Development of track and field athletics

+ As the twentieth century progressed, in the immediate post-Second World War period, UK interest in athletics was stimulated when the Olympics took place in London in 1948.
+ However, while the rest of the world found ways to get round the strict amateur rules of international athletics, Britain left its athletes to manage as best they could. 'Trust funds' were eventually established, which enabled athletes to safeguard their eligibility to take part in amateur competitions but still allowed them to receive financial rewards as an athlete.
+ The governing body for athletics kept control of the sport by insisting that all payments should be channelled or authorised by them. Payments from the fund for day-to-day living expenses were allowed and the balance became available to the athlete on retirement. Such arrangements enabled a group of male and female athletes to go around the world and compete in a programme of championships and grand prix events, with both appearance money as well as prize money for winning.
+ Today, there are no such trust funds because payments can be made directly to athletes and/or their agents within rules that were laid down by the International Amateur Athletics Association (IAAA), which is now called the **International Association of Athletics Federations (IAAF)**.
+ At the end of the twentieth century and into the early twenty-first century, the IAAF established and organised a number of major international

93

athletics competitions for male as well as female athletes to compete in and earn considerable amounts of money. For example, in 2010, a new global one-day competition structure headed by the **IAAF Diamond League** was unveiled. It involves 14 invitational track and field meetings in Asia, Europe, the Middle East and the USA. Large spectator numbers, both live and via global media coverage, ensure that athletes can generate healthy incomes via prize money and sponsorship deals, through large multinationals such as Nike and Adidas.

Making links

The sport of athletics is an example that can be linked with the earlier historical section on national governing bodies (p. 82) and the desire to control eligibility – i.e. allow professionals to compete in certain sports such as football (the FA), but not in others like athletics (the AAA).

Emergence of elite female athletes   REVISED

Treatment of women in athletics remained 'indifferent' at best through to the late twentieth century. Over the years, access to the full range of athletics events has been limited due to a number of factors:

+ False scientific/physiological claims about women – for example, the belief that long-distance running was harmful to women and would damage their fertility.
+ Beliefs on 'masculinity/femininity' leading to women being excluded from power events in athletics, such as the shot put and hammer throw.
+ A lack of media coverage and of female role models in athletics to aspire to.

Until very recently, such factors/beliefs impacted negatively on female involvement in the Olympics athletics programme:

+ Women were only allowed to compete in a limited number of athletics events until 1928 – 32 years after the modern Olympics began, and certain events remained inaccessible until very late in the twentieth century – for example, the marathon until 1984, the triple jump until 1996 and the hammer in 2000.
+ The recent Olympics in Rio (2016) and Tokyo (2020) were very similar in relation to the athletics programme of events for men and women, with the only events remaining different being the hurdles, race walking and the multi-events (decathlon/heptathlon).
+ Fortunately, the negative myths and stereotypes about the capabilities of elite-level female athletes are being successfully challenged, with competitions such as the Diamond League enabling female as well as male athletes to earn millions from their talents.

Now test yourself   TESTED

23 Identify the barriers to participation for women in elite athletic long-distance running (e.g. the marathon) and throwing events (e.g. the shot put).

Answer on pp. 265–266

The 'golden triangle'   REVISED

+ Sport, the media, business and sponsorship are all strongly interlinked and mutually dependent in what is known as the 'golden triangle' (Figure 3.1). Each element of the triangle relies on the others.

Check your understanding and progress at **www.hoddereducation.co.uk/myrevisionnotes**

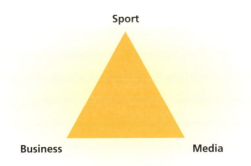

Figure 3.1 The 'golden triangle'

Media Organised means of communication by which large numbers of different people can be reached quickly.

Commercialisation Treating sport as a commodity, involving the buying and selling of assets, with the market force as the driving influence behind sport.

Sponsorship When a company pays for its products to be publicly displayed or advertised, usually in an attempt to increase the sales of their goods.

+ For instance, without media coverage, sports are less attractive to sponsors who want their business or product to be publicised to as many people as possible.
+ The media use sport to gain viewers, listeners and readers.
+ In turn, businesses and sponsors use the media to advertise their products and services, with organisations often paying substantial sums to sport and the media for advertisements.

Commercialisation, media and sponsorship

REVISED ◯

There is massive media interest in certain high-profile sports – for example, television companies pay huge amounts of money for the right to show a sporting event, such as football on Sky Sports and BT Sport, because sport has a positive image. Sponsorship deals then result from television exposure.

Merchandising too relates to media exposure – clothing and equipment companies such as Nike and Adidas have become strong rivals in sponsoring teams and individuals to aid their merchandising.

Characteristics of commercial sport

Commercial sport in association football, tennis and athletics has close links with the following:
+ **Professional sport** – it is high quality, with high skill levels.
+ **Sponsorship and business** – these go hand-in-hand.
+ **Entertainment** – watching sport is part of a mass-entertainment industry; viewing needs to fit into a relatively short timescale.
+ **Contracts** – for example, involving sales of merchandise and bidding for television rights.
+ **Athletes as commodities** – for example, as an asset to companies through product endorsement, which brings increased sales/profits; athletes become well-known role models.
+ **A wide level of media coverage** – there is interest in high-profile sports that are visually appealing and have high skill levels, well-matched competitions and simple, understandable rules.

> **Now test yourself** TESTED ◯
>
> **24** Identify the characteristics of a sport that make it attractive for television coverage.
>
> **Answer on p. 266**

Effects of commercialisation on sport

Some sports have changed as a result of commercial and media interests:

+ Rules and scoring systems have been changed or introduced to speed up the action and prevent spectator boredom – for example, the multiball system at football matches cuts down on time-wasting; cricket introduced 'The Hundred' in the summer of 2021, with fast-paced action and constant spectator involvement.
+ Breaks are extended/provided in play so that sponsors can advertise their products and services.
+ Competition formats have changed – for example, the Twenty20 and 'The Hundred' cricket formats are major revenue earners due to spectator, television and commercial interests.
+ Sports played by women receive less coverage, which can negatively affect participation and funding – there are fewer female role models and there is less money to reinvest into sport at grassroots and professional levels.
+ The increased use of technology through the media has led to a more personal experience for the viewer (e.g. HD coverage of sport).

The media

There are different types of media involved in covering sport. These include television, newspapers, radio, the internet and social media. Television can be viewed as the most powerful aspect of the media – the buying and selling of television broadcasting rights is a very important part of twenty-first century sport because it has 'gone global'.

Globalisation in sport is seen via the following:

+ The sponsorship of events (e.g. Coca-Cola as a 'universal sponsor').
+ The ways in which players are recruited to play for teams/compete in events in countries other than their own.
+ The spreading of different sports to 'new nations' – for example, the 1994 football World Cup was successfully hosted in the USA.
+ Increasing pressure on athletes to perform to their best. This might lead some to use illegal substances to maintain high performance levels and the accompanying rewards that success brings in a number of high-profile sports.

> **Globalisation** The process whereby nations are increasingly being linked together and people are becoming more interdependent via improvements in communication and travel.

> **Now test yourself**   TESTED ◯
>
> **25** Define 'globalisation of sport'.
>
> **Answer on p. 266**

> **Making links**
>
> Sport, sponsorship and the media form a possible synoptic exam question topic area. This is because they are included in the first section of the specification under the 'historical development of sport' as well as in second section – 'the impact of commercialisation on physical activity and sport and the relationship between sport and the media', which is covered later in this book (pp. 231–233).

The impact of social media on sport

REVISED ◯

Over the last few years, social media have changed the behaviour of both sports performers and fans at all levels.

+ More and more fans prefer getting their sports news from Twitter and Facebook rather than from television or national news websites.

+ Most top sports performers are heavily involved in social media, and creating much interest via their posts as opposed to other media channels, such as newspapers.
+ Twitter has made a number of high-profile purchases of sports broadcasting rights – for example, in the summer of 2016, signing deals to cover the 'big four US sports leagues' (i.e. the National Football League, Major League Baseball, the National Basketball Association and the National Hockey League).
+ In addition, YouTube is used by many athletes to help them achieve their goals (e.g. posting videos of edited highlights to attract university scholarships/coaches).

The power and reach available to sports performers via social media has changed sport at all levels:

+ It has enabled top-level sports performers to build up very large and engaged fan bases in a very short space of time. Social media have empowered athletes at every level to engage with a much wider audience than was possible a few years ago.
+ However, while this has some positives, a number of elite performers have found themselves in trouble for their postings on social media. Sports performers now need to be trained to understand the responsibilities and liabilities that go with global social media communication.

Now test yourself   TESTED

26 Identify four examples of sports broadcasting rights purchased by Twitter in 2016.

Answer on p. 266

Exam practice

1 What factors have been responsible for the advancement in opportunities for women in sport (e.g. in tennis, athletics or football) since the end of the Second World War? [5]

2 Describe the main factors responsible for the increased commercialisation of sports such as football in the twenty-first century. [5]

3 Define the 'golden triangle'. [2]

4 Define sponsorship. [2]

5 Explain the barriers to women officiating in association football. [3]

6 The FA's 'Inspiring Positive Change' initiative included the following data:
   + Total number of referees: 27,451
   + Total number of female referees: 1718

   While the number of female professional football players in England has increased significantly during the twenty-first century, the numbers of qualified full-time female football officials has remained at a relatively low level.

   Evaluate how effective the strategies being used have been in helping to overcome the barriers in place preventing women from becoming football officials. [15]

Answers online

This topic involves the following knowledge (AO1):

+ Barriers to participation as a performer in various sports, with a focus on the case study activities of football and athletics.
+ Barriers to participation as an official in football.
+ Strategies being used to overcome the barriers to participation as a performer and official in football.
+ Characteristics of commercial sport.
+ Different types of media involved in covering sport.

AO2 marks will require application of this knowledge – for example, explaining barriers to participation as a performer in various sports, with a focus on the case study activities of football and athletics; explaining barriers to participation as an official in football; explaining the various strategies being used to overcome the barriers to participation as a

performer and official in football; explaining the historical development and changing role of women in sport by providing relevant explanations and examples of the factors that have affected their emergence in modern-day elite sport, encouraging it in tennis, but discouraging it until relatively recently in athletics and football; explaining the impact of commercialisation on modern-day sport.

AO3 marks are for analysis or evaluation. In this topic an AO3 response might involve evaluating (e.g. with reference to data provided in a question introduction) the various strategies being used to overcome the barriers to participation as a performer and official in football, or an analysis of the impact of social media on twenty-first century sport.

3.2 The impact of sport on society and of society on sport

3.2.1 Sociological theory applied to equal opportunities

Key terms

REVISED

The specification requires you to know and be able to define a number of key sociological terms and to explain how they relate to equality of opportunity in sport.

Society

A human society is a group of people involved in persistent interpersonal relationships, often a large social grouping sharing the same geographical territory, and typically subject to the same political authority and dominant cultural expectations. A society can therefore be viewed as the sum total of all the relationships in a given space (e.g. within a specific country).

Success in sport on a global scale is often viewed as an important measure of the relative status of a society or nation in the world. For example, national identity and national pride are often achieved as a result of success at events such as the Olympics (e.g. in Britain, through Team GB's third position on the medal table at London 2012, second place at Rio 2016 and fourth position at Tokyo 2020, which was recognised with a homecoming concert at Wembley Arena televised on BBC1).

Socialisation

Socialisation is a lifelong process whereby members of a society learn its norms, values, ideas, practices and roles in order to take their place in that society. It can be divided into two main parts: primary and secondary socialisation.

Primary socialisation

+ This refers to socialisation during the early years of childhood, and which takes place mainly within the immediate family (the mother, father, brothers and sisters).

Society An organised group of people associated for some specific purpose or with a shared common interest.

National identity A person's sense of belonging to one state or to one nation. It is the sense of a nation as a cohesive whole, as represented by distinctive traditions, culture, language and politics.

National pride A feeling of attachment to one's homeland, and alliance with other citizens who share the same (i.e. patriotism).

Socialisation A lifelong process whereby members of a society learn its norms, values, ideas, practices and roles in order to take their place in that society.

Check your understanding and progress at **www.hoddereducation.co.uk/myrevisionnotes**

- A key process involved at this stage is the internalisation of a society's culture, whereby individuals absorb and accept its shared norms and values.
- The nature of living in a society is such that people are constantly communicating within a social group among family and close friends.
- Much of the early basic socialisation occurs as a young child, when families and early friends teach basic values and accepted behaviour patterns.
- Play is a good way to learn how to share, interact and practise becoming an adult.
- For many families, physical exercise provides a time when they come together, whether it be a shared involvement in an activity such as cycling, or a family commitment to one (or more) member of the family who has devoted themselves to regular involvement in sporting competition (e.g. at an athletics club).
- How active your parents/siblings are will have a big influence on your early views of sport/physical activity as well as the sports you watch or play.

> **Internalisation** The learning of values or attitudes that are incorporated within yourself.

Secondary socialisation
- This occurs during the later years (e.g. as teenagers) when the family is less involved and other 'agencies' are deliberately set up for the socialisation process and begin to exert more and more influence (e.g. peer groups, friends, schools).
- **School** is an important part of social development. For example, it can help with the socialisation process by teaching important moral skills, such as cooperation, teamwork and learning to take responsibility for one's own actions.

You also need to be aware of **gender socialisation**, which involves the learning of behaviour and attitudes historically considered appropriate for a given sex.
- 'Boys learn to be boys' and 'girls learn to be girls' via the many different 'agents of socialisation', including family, friends, school, college and the mass media.
- Participation in sport/physical activity can help create a 'social identity'. For example, gender socialisation can suggest the sports/activities that a male or female traditionally participates in (e.g. in athletics some girls/young women might avoid events requiring a lot of muscle power).

Note: As society has become more liberal and open, there has been a general tendency towards gender-neutral identity, with such gender stereotyping deemed less acceptable.

> **Exam tip**
>
> Make sure that you can apply your knowledge (AO1/AO2) of different types of socialisation to short-answer and extended questions linked to given sporting scenarios outlined in a question.

Now test yourself TESTED

1 Define the terms 'socialisation', 'primary socialisation' and 'secondary socialisation'.
2 Many people, organisations and institutions are involved in the socialisation process from the early childhood years into adulthood.

Look at the list of words below and identify the primary and secondary agents of socialisation.

Mother   Friends   Newspapers   Peer groups   Brother   Father
Social media   Secondary school teachers   Sister   Television

Answers on p. 266

Social processes

Social processes refer to some of the general and recurrent forms that social interaction might take – for example:
- Different forms of social interaction that reoccur and are the means by which culture and social organisations are either preserved or changed.
- Ways in which individuals and groups interact, adjust and readjust to establish relationships and patterns of behaviour on an ongoing basis.

Now test yourself

TESTED ○

3 Identify different types of social interaction that people regularly use to establish relationships and patterns of behaviour in an ongoing way.

Answer on p. 266

Social control

Social control is a concept that refers to the way in which people's thoughts, feelings, appearance and behaviour are regulated in social systems.

Society is made up of various institutions, with the family viewed as the most basic unit. These institutions work together for the benefit of society, undertaking a variety of 'social processes' to ensure socialisation into society, maintaining order and social control.

However, there are various social processes at work in society that act as constraints and potentially limit the opportunities to become involved in sport (e.g. historically, our society has been male dominated, with restrictions placed on women engaging in sport):

+ Nowadays, these constraints are less pronounced; however, milder forms of social control persist in the form of what is deemed by some to be 'gender-appropriate' behaviour. For example, mild disapproval from a parent might persuade girls/young women to limit their physical activity to what the parent views as 'respectable' and therefore 'socially acceptable'. So they might choose badminton over rugby or dance over boxing if under the influence of 'social control'.
+ Social control from peers or the media for women to look feminine and maintain a slim appearance could also rule out certain sports requiring muscular development, which is seen as 'unfeminine' (e.g. weightlifting and boxing).
+ Social pressures mean that sometimes women are made to feel guilty about leaving a young baby and therefore tend to give up previous active leisure pursuits once their child has been born.
+ A lack of free time compared with men and lower disposable income can also act as agents of social control, and decrease the opportunities for women to get involved in regular healthy sporting activity, as illustrated by recent data on sports participation. **Sport England's Active People Survey** (8Q3–9Q2) discovered that 40.6 per cent of men compared with 30.7 per cent of women took part in sport at least once a week.

Data on gender from the Active Lives Survey (2019/20) illustrate various patterns of behaviour in relation to sports participation:

+ Inactivity levels – although these are similar, women are still more likely to be inactive than men, with 26 per cent of women being inactive compared with 25 per cent of men.
+ Activity levels – men are more likely to be active than women; 65 per cent of men are active, compared with 61 per cent of women.
+ There are differences in the types of activity participated in, with women more likely to take part in fitness activities and walking for leisure, and less likely than men to involve themselves in general sporting activities (Sport England identifies team games, racquet sports etc. as general sporting activities).
+ The data confirm that some sports participation inequalities exist when comparing women with men.
+ It is difficult for any social group to bring about change without having a strong influence in the decision-making groups (e.g. local councils and national governing bodies).
+ In addition to gender inequalities, certain ethnic groups, such as Indians and Pakistanis, have faced constraints on their participation in sport. Some of these have been viewed as emerging from within the family

Social control A concept that refers to the way in which people's thoughts, feelings, appearance and behaviour are regulated in social systems.

Institution An established organisation founded for a religious, educational, professional or social purpose.

Social processes Forms of social interaction between individuals and groups that occur again and again.

Check your understanding and progress at **www.hoddereducation.co.uk/myrevisionnotes**

unit itself (e.g. via cultural norms valuing educational achievement over sporting participation, as well as restricting women's participation due to clothing restrictions).

Social change

Social change occurs when institutions readjust to meet new needs of groups in society. For example, leisure providers, such as local councils, are offering more crèche facilities to minimise the negative effects of childcare responsibilities and/or feelings of guilt at leaving young children while parents participate in sporting activity.

Social change can therefore be viewed as an alteration in the social order of a society. Sporting activities can be used in specialist programmes to try to bring about social change in a positive way.
+ Sport England launched 'This Girl Can' as a high-profile scheme to try to bring about social changes in the way women's participation in sport and physical activity is viewed.
+ 'Kick it Out' is a campaign designed to bring about social change by increasing awareness of racial issues in society. It uses positive role models, including high-profile sports performers, to educate individuals in society about appropriate behaviour, in an effort to reduce the incidence of racism in sport and society in general.

> **Social change** An alteration in the social order of a society, i.e. significant changes in social behaviours and/or cultural values over time, leading to long-term effects.

Now test yourself
TESTED ⚪

4 Define the term 'social change'.

Answer on p. 266

Social issues (causes and consequences of inequality)

Modern-day social issues lead to social inequality, which occurs when resources in a society are unevenly distributed among socially defined categories of people.
+ Sex and **gender-based prejudice** and **discrimination** (i.e. **sexism**) are major social issues that contribute to social inequality because they give rise to different role divisions, which ultimately lead to fewer women in positions of power and decision making, whether this be in the world of sport or more generally in political activities within society.
+ Women's participation in work has been increasing globally (e.g. in professional sport) but women still face wage differences compared with men's earnings, as well as differences in terms of political influence and their roles in most major religions.

These issues can result in:
+ a lack of confidence or low self-esteem
+ a lack of role models to aspire to as participants, coaches or leaders of sports organisations, or in other positions of responsibility
+ myths or stereotypes in some sections of society about the capabilities of women, minority ethnic groups and people with disabilities, which feeds into the above

As far as sport and physical activity are concerned, the **negative consequences** of such inequalities include lower participation rates in sport among a number of sections of society, including people with disabilities, women, those from minority ethnic groups, the unemployed and elderly people.

> **Social issues** Problems or conflicts that influence or affect a considerable number of people in society – for example, discrimination based on gender, disability or ethnic group, drug abuse and low activity patterns linked to obesity and health problems.
>
> **Inequality** The unfair situation in which resources or opportunities are distributed unevenly within a society

Now test yourself
TESTED ⚪

5 Identify three possible causes of inequality in sport that impact negatively on disadvantaged sections of society.

Answer on p. 266

Social structures and social stratification

Various social structures exist that have an impact (positive and negative) on an individual and their overall life chances.

When linked to participation in sport, the type of school you go to (e.g. state vs private) can affect the activities you get to try out, as well as the amount of time devoted to sport, the standard of teaching/coaching received to develop your talents, and the quality of facilities you train in.

Social stratification is a type of social inequality, and is the division of a society into different levels (i.e. strata) on the basis of a social characteristic such as wealth or social status. Social differences lead to a layering of society (i.e. upper, middle and lower classes), in which the relative possession or non-possession of a social characteristic, such as wealth or status, becomes the distributing principle for individuals within a system of unequal rewards.

Modern-day societies use individual wealth as a means of stratification, which gives individuals a relative social position. The importance of stratification is that those at the top of the system have greater access to resources than those at the bottom.

In some ways, participation in sport means participants can leave behind their 'normal lives' and adopt a 'new athletic identity' in a sporting context. This (temporarily) replaces the inequalities of everyday life with a situation in which all are equal. However, the idea that sport provides equality of opportunity can be viewed as problematic, because the very nature of sport emphasises competition and dominance.

The realities of the 'real world' and people's relative positions in the social class hierarchy do affect their involvement in sport. For example, disposable income can influence the type of activity participated in, the type of club joined, the equipment used and so on. Equestrian and other horse-related activities tend to be relatively expensive and require high income levels, which are linked to the upper class in society. Activities associated more with the middle class include rugby union and tennis, with rugby league and darts as more traditional lower-class pastimes.

The social stratification system continues to be visible in sport, with a number of sections or groups of society identified by Sport England as under-represented in terms of sports involvement. These include low-social-class groups and individuals with a disability.

When looking at the organisation and structure of society, it is clear that certain individuals and groups have traditionally held the positions of power. In the UK, those in such positions have tended to be white males from the middle classes.

This leads to the social stratification of society being reflected in sport, with a hierarchy evident, giving power and influence to those at the top. For many years, social-class-based variations in sports participation have been highlighted by research and data produced by Sport England.

Socioeconomic status

Socioeconomic status can be measured by education, occupation, income, and activity or inactivity levels.

Socioeconomic groups in society range from the highest groups (1–2 comprising high-earning professionals such as doctors and lawyers, who are most likely to be active/least likely to be inactive) down to the lowest groups (with group 8 most likely to be on state benefits, and including the long-term unemployed, who are most likely to be inactive and least likely to be active. Groups 6 and 7 comprise manual workers and lower-paid workers).

Social stratification A type of social inequality in which society is divided into different levels based on a social characteristic, such as wealth, social status or derived power.

Exam tip

The socioeconomic factors most likely to affect activity levels can be remembered as 'SOCIO' (Table 3.8). In general, low levels of motivation lead to low levels of participation and high levels of inactivity, while high levels of motivation lead to high levels of participation and low levels of inactivity.

Check your understanding and progress at **www.hoddereducation.co.uk/myrevisionnotes**

Table 3.8 Socioeconomic factors most likely to affect activity levels

Socioeconomic factors that are most likely to lead to high levels of inactivity	Socioeconomic factors that are most likely to lead to low levels of inactivity
S = Social support: Lack of social support/friendship groups to encourage activity (e.g. from family)	Peers/friendship groups more likely to encourage activity/discourage physical inactivity
O = Opportunities restricted/local area deprivation: Lack of access to facilities/quality facilities	Opportunities readily available – access to high-quality facilities to keep active in
C = Confidence/concerns about physical appearance: Low levels of self-esteem/confidence; negative self-image	High levels of self-esteem/confidence; positive self-image
I = Income levels: Low income levels/high costs of activity; reliant on benefits; limited money to pay the costs associated with participation in sport/physical activity (e.g. gym membership or travel costs)	High income levels enable participation costs to be easily met (e.g. gym memberships or golf club fees)
O = Overweight/associated health and wellbeing issues: Poor diet/associated health issues increase the likelihood of inactivity	Healthy diet and healthy lifestyle lead to low levels of inactivity

Social class and its impacts on sporting experiences

Evidence of the direct impact of social class on participation in sport can be found in Sport England's 'Active lives' data (2017/18). Those in the lowest socioeconomic groups are most likely to be inactive (33 per cent) and least likely to be active (54 per cent). For example, other data suggest that there are higher rates of participation in tennis among the highest socioeconomic groups.

+ While National Curriculum PE aims to offer all young people a broad and balanced programme, it is evident that some young people might be disadvantaged due to social inequality.
+ Children from low-income families tend to have poorer health than other children. Such poor levels of health might undermine their physical abilities and/or skill levels. Children from low-income families also have less money to spend on sports equipment, additional specialist coaching etc.
+ Schools themselves might magnify the social class differences. For example, public schools and state schools situated in more affluent areas often have better sports facilities than schools located in working-class areas (Table 3.9).

Table 3.9 The impact of social class on sporting experiences

	Impact of being 'working class' on sporting experiences	Impact of being 'upper class' on sporting experiences
As a child/teenager	+ Less access to sport/variety of sports + Unable to afford equipment, membership fees, coaching etc. to allow participation + Variable state school PE experiences might decrease access to quality sporting experiences (e.g. facilities/teaching), which can impact negatively on participation + Less understanding of the importance of physical activity + Might have limited time to participate if they have a part-time job or household chores (although this is not limited to the class of young person) + Might have more time for sport if it is viewed as an avenue of social mobility, and there is less expectation to perform well in education	+ Greater access to a wide variety of sports + Able to afford the equipment, membership fees etc. required to participate + A high-quality public school experience leads to increased access to sport and a higher-quality experience + Greater understanding of the importance of physical activity + Greater pressure to achieve academically (e.g. from parents and teachers) might decrease time for sport

Table 3.9 *continued*

	Impact of being 'working class' on sporting experiences	Impact of being 'upper class' on sporting experiences
As a lifelong participant – disposable income/social status can impact on participation in a positive/ negative way	+ Less access to as many sports might limit the level of continued participation due to negative experiences (e.g. poor facilities, low standard of equipment) + Less understanding of the importance of a healthy lifestyle decreases the likelihood of continued participation and increases the likelihood of a more sedentary lifestyle + However, some might be more likely to enjoy life-long participation because it provides additional income/escapism	+ Trying a wider variety of sports increases the chance of finding something they enjoy and continue to do + Better diet/more understanding of the importance of physical activity increases the likelihood of continued participation throughout life + However, some might be less likely to enjoy life-long participation due to pressures of a job or a lack of motivation

Possible solutions to participation issues

Participation in sport/physical activity can be increased among individuals from lower socioeconomic groups in society via:

+ increased publicity of opportunities available
+ making sure they are affordable/decrease costs/subsidise
+ provision of taster sessions (e.g. via local sports clubs and local authorities)
+ providing activities that motivate/appeal to such groups
+ investing in areas of social deprivation (e.g. via local authority, local council or Sport England)
+ schemes/initiatives via NGBs/Sport England (e.g. Street Games, Doorstep Sport)

> **Making links**
>
> There is a potential 'social class' link here with the change from a two-tier upper- and lower-class system in pre-industrial Britain (p. 73) to the emergence of the middle class and a three-tier system in the industrial/ post-industrial phase (p. 80).

> **Now test yourself** TESTED ○
>
> 6 Identify how participation in sport and other physical activity can be increased among individuals in the working class.
>
> **Answer on p. 266**

> **Revision activity**
>
> Create a table of the key sociological terms on the specification and their definitions so you are clear on their meanings.

Social action theory and its influence

REVISED ●

+ **Social action theory** was developed by the social theorist Max Weber. It looks at how people interact with one another by examining the cause-and-effect relationship of the social actions of people.
+ It suggests that sport is introduced and developed at a particular time through the relationships and social networks of people who share similar views. The links between these people and their social interdependence are the key ideas of such a theory.
+ Sports involvement and **progression** are therefore determined by the relationships between people based on the different amounts of power they have in society. The way these relationships are built up and why they change is an open-ended process.
+ Sport has therefore developed in a complex way alongside aspects of society, such as class structure, education and family. Social action theory stresses the fact that people can intervene in social processes and change them.

> **Social action theory** A way of viewing socialisation that emphasises the proactive role of people in shaping social life (i.e. social action).
>
> **Progression** The process of gradually developing towards a more advanced state.

Main features/concepts

Weber made some generalisations about different driving forces/types of motive for social action and identified four types of social action or motives, as identified and explained below:

Check your understanding and progress at **www.hoddereducation.co.uk/myrevisionnotes**

+ Traditional social action – actions are controlled by traditions, engrained social habits and long-standing beliefs. People engage in this type of action often unthinkingly – 'the way it has always been done' (e.g. taking up cycling or going to university, because this is what the family has always done).
+ Affective action – your actions are controlled by your emotional state. If you enjoy an activity, you are more likely to continue with it (e.g. you regularly go long-distance running because it makes you feel good or you simply enjoy doing it).
+ Value rational action – individuals take actions for self-gain, which are determined by a conscious belief in the inherent value of a type of behaviour. For example, undertaking regular exercise and a healthy diet to ensure positive health and wellbeing, going to church/mosque to ensure spiritual wellbeing.
+ Instrumentally rational action – individuals consider the most appropriate steps to take that will lead most effectively to achieving the set goal or desired result (e.g. volunteering as a sports coach to help get a job).

The interactionist approach

+ Social action theories are sometimes called 'interactionist theories'.
+ In sociology, the **interactionist approach** is the study of how individuals behave within a society. It is a theoretical perspective that stems from social processes – for example, cooperation and conflict, which occur when humans interact.
+ Interactionism works from the individual towards society and stresses the fact that it is people who have an active role in shaping society
+ The ways we communicate and interact (e.g. via language or gesture) are emphasised.
+ Although it is accepted that society does have some control over individuals, there is always the opportunity for some creative action. Through social interactions and the use of language, people negotiate the various social roles they are expected to play.

Social action theory/the interactionist approach views sport and physical activity as an essential, important part of a society's make-up. Sport can impact on the social and cultural fabric of society, and society can impact on sport. Ways in which sport can impact on society include the following:
+ By highlighting inequalities that exist between different social-class groups (e.g. via the types of sports participated in linked to wealth/upbringing).
+ By impacting on our ideas and beliefs concerning masculinity and femininity.
+ By impacting on our ideas and beliefs about race and ethnicity (e.g. negatively, through racist chanting at football matches aimed at players).
+ By impacting on our ideas about ability and disability (e.g. positively, through the achievements of Paralympic athletes such as Dame Sarah Storey).
+ By contributing to our sense of national pride and social integration (e.g. via media images of successful Team GB athletes winning and receiving their medals at the Olympics).
+ By targeting social problems, such as unemployment, crime, disengaged communities and inequalities. Sport can help increase understanding and appreciation of cultural differences and prejudices, limiting the social exclusion felt by minority groups in society. For example, schemes aimed at young people, such as Street Games/Doorstep Sport/Community Football Leagues, act as an incentive to integrate and interact with others without necessarily realising the wider concept of what they are doing. These also encourage a sense of belonging and increased self-worth.

Now test yourself TESTED

7 Outline the four types of social action identified by Weber's social action theory.

Answer on p. 266

105

Key terms relating to equality in sport

There are some key terms you need to understand when studying equal opportunities in sport and physical activity.

Embedded in British law, equal opportunities is a term used to emphasise inclusiveness and the importance of treating all people fairly and similarly, unhampered by artificial barriers, discrimination, prejudices or preferences.

Now test yourself   TESTED ◯

8 Define the term 'equal opportunities'.

Answer on p. 266

+ The explanation of equal opportunities given above identifies discrimination and prejudice as important factors that can determine whether equality of opportunity is present within a society or not.
+ In addition, negative stereotypes can adversely affect an individual's chances of taking part in certain types of sport (e.g. the idea that certain sports, such as boxing and rugby, are for men and not for women).
+ However, sport can also be used to break traditional gender stereotypes and ideologies of masculinity and femininity – for example, when women/girls take part in traditionally male sports, such as boxing, rugby and football (i.e. they participate in 'male-perceived sports').

Sport's interpretation of equal opportunities can be explained via reference to Sport England's equality and diversity policy, which involves a commitment to:
+ developing a culture that enables and values everyone's full involvement
+ creating an environment in which everyone has opportunities to play, compete, officiate, coach, volunteer and run community sport
+ overcoming potential barriers for those wishing to play sport, particularly if they are from groups that are currently under-represented in sport

Discrimination involves the unfair treatment of people based on a stereotype/prejudice, and can be divided into two types:
+ **overt discrimination** – visible/obvious (e.g. verbal racist abuse of a player)
+ **covert discrimination** – hidden/less obvious (e.g. non-selection of an individual as captain because of their ethnicity)

Now test yourself   TESTED ◯

9 The participation of people from minority ethnic groups in sport can be negatively affected by discrimination. Explain what is meant by the term 'discrimination'.

Answer on p. 266

Exam tip

Avoid giving general answers where questions are asking for specific examples/explanations of barriers to participation among a target group – for example, link gender to non-aggressive stereotypes that can negatively impact on the group's participation in a sport).

Equal opportunities
Treating people fairly; giving people the same chance (e.g. in relation to gender).

Discrimination The unfair treatment of a person or minority group; distinguishing and acting on prejudice (e.g. reduced access to clubs or coaches).

Prejudice An unfavourable opinion of an individual, often based on inadequate facts (e.g. lack of tolerance, dislike of people of a specific ethnicity, religion or culture), which can negatively affect the treatment of a performer from a minority ethnic group by a coach, for example.

Stereotyping A standardised image/belief shared by society; making simple generalisations about all members of a group, which allows others to categorise and treat them accordingly (e.g. negative stereotypes about women that negatively impact on their participation in sport in general and/or allow certain sports to be deemed 'inappropriate').

Exam tip

Avoid repeating words or phrases from the question. For example, if asked for a definition of equal opportunities, avoid using the word 'equal' and use an alternative such as 'the same'.

Barriers to participation

+ Sport England's data on sports participation has shown some improvements since it started surveys in 2005/06. This is currently presented in the Active Lives survey.
+ In figures published for November 2019 to November 2020, 61.4 per cent of adults were active (i.e. participating in at least 150 minutes of physical activity per week). Therefore 38.2 per cent were not active enough to meet the Sport England measure.

Check your understanding and progress at **www.hoddereducation.co.uk/myrevisionnotes**

It is therefore still important to be able to identify various **barriers** to participation for different sections of society that are under-represented in sport, as well as seeking to provide **solutions** to try to overcome these barriers (Table 3.10).

Table 3.10 General barriers to participation and possible solutions

Barriers	Solutions
Lack of time	Add physical activity to a daily routine (e.g. walk or ride to work/school)
Negative social influences; poor PE experiences	Invite family and friends to exercise with you; join a group where physical activity plays an important part (e.g. a youth club offering activities such as Duke of Edinburgh Award)
Lack of motivation	Invite a friend to exercise with you on a regular basis; join an exercise class
Lack of skill	Select activities requiring few or no skills (e.g. walking or jogging)
Lack of resources/costs of participation	Select activities that require few facilities/limited equipment (e.g. walking, jogging, skipping)
Family obligations/domestic responsibilities	Exercise with the children – go for a walk or swim

You will need to be aware of three main target groups, i.e. sections of society specifically targeted due to their relative lack of involvement in sport/physical activity.

The groups to focus on in terms of barriers to participation, along with various solutions to such barriers, are people with disabilities, individuals from minority ethnic groups and women/teenage girls.

Disability

People with disabilities generally have a low level of participation in sport. This can be illustrated using figures from Sport England's Active Lives – Adult survey (2019/20).
+ Those with a disability are almost twice as likely to be physically inactive (43 per cent) compared with those without a disability (23 per cent).
+ This inactivity inequality increases sharply as the number of impairments a person has increases (51 per cent for those with three or more impairments).

Disability can be physical, sensory or mental in nature, with all of these impairments potentially negatively affecting participation in sport in some way. Society continues to discriminate and impose barriers on the participation in physical activity of those with disability, as illustrated in the data above.
+ **Overt discrimination** is highly visible – for example, when there is verbal abuse aimed at individuals with a disability participating in sport.
+ **Covert discrimination** is harder to uncover – for example, when members of a sports club vote for their annual captain, and their negative stereotypes influence them in voting against a candidate with a disability.

Disability sport is sometimes participated in at the same time as able-bodied sport (i.e. it is **integrated**). Alternatively, disability sport can occur completely separately from able-bodied sport (i.e. when it is **segregated**).

Barriers
When analysing disability sports, common barriers that negatively affect participation include the following:
+ Negative self-image or lack of confidence.
+ Relatively low income levels, combined with high costs of participation, such as membership fees and transport costs.
+ Lack of access into and around facilities – for example, doorways are too narrow for wheelchair users, or there is a lack of ramps in and around the facility.
+ Lack of organised programmes.

+ Lower levels of media coverage and few role models to aspire to; lack of information available.
+ Lack of specialist coaches, clubs or competitions; lack of adapted/accessible equipment.
+ Myths/stereotypes about the capabilities of people with a disability; lower societal expectations; safety concerns – disability participation has traditionally been considered dangerous.

Solutions

Various solutions are being implemented to try to decrease the effects of such barriers for people with a disability, including the following:

+ Providing more opportunities for success; helping talented athletes reach the highest levels possible (e.g. the Paralympics).
+ Increased investment in disability sport – subsidising it and making it more affordable.
+ Providing transport to facilities; improved access into and around facilities (e.g. via local authority sport and leisure centres, using specialist architects when planning facilities so that they meet the needs of people with disabilities).
+ Improved technology (e.g. prosthetics and wheelchairs).
+ Increased media coverage, which is important in promoting role models to relate and aspire to.
+ Training of more specialist coaches; setting up more clubs for people with a disability to access.
+ Educating people on the myths/stereotypes about the capabilities of people with disabilities, and challenging inappropriate attitudes.
+ Designing activities specifically for individuals with disabilities, such as goalball, boccia for the visually impaired, or modifying existing activities to enable participation (e.g. wheelchair tennis and basketball).
+ Specialist organisations, such as the English Federation for Disability Sport (EFDS) and Sport England, working to support and coordinate the development of sporting opportunities for people with disabilities.

Now test yourself

TESTED

10 Define the terms overt discrimination and covert discrimination.

Answer on p. 266

Making links

There is a possible synoptic link here with Chapter 7: Sport and society and the role of technology in sport (p. 240). This includes the role of technology in physical activity in sport in relation to disability as an under-represented group in society – for example, knowledge of examples of advancements in technology (AO2) in helping to overcome participation barriers for individuals with disabilities.

Exam tip

When identifying barriers to participation in relation to disability, it is important to link coaching with a shortage of specially trained leaders/coaches, and to link activities with failure to modify them. In other words, link the points you are making with the specific target group being discussed.

Ethnicity

+ Britain aims to be a multicultural, multiracial and egalitarian (i.e. equal) society. Equal opportunities to participate in sport should exist for all ethnic groups in society. Such equality is not yet a reality due to many factors, including racism.
+ Racism is illegal but still exists in society (and therefore in sport, as a reflection of society) on the basis of someone's skin colour, language used or cultural observances.

Ethnic groups People who have racial, religious or linguistic traits in common.

Racism A set of beliefs or ideas based on the assumption that races have distinct hereditary characteristics that give some an intrinsic superiority over others; it might lead to physical or verbal abuse.

Check your understanding and progress at **www.hoddereducation.co.uk/myrevisionnotes**

+ Racism stems from prejudice linked with the power of one racial group in society over another. This can lead to discrimination, i.e. unfair treatment/acting on a prejudice – for example, exclusion of an individual from participation on the basis of their race/ethnicity.

Examples of racism in sport include the following:
+ Stacking – a term used as an illustration of possible racism in sport, particularly in relation to explaining the lack of team captains from minority ethnic groups. It is based on the stereotypical assumption that individuals from minority ethnic groups are more valued for their athletic prowess than for their decision-making or leadership capabilities.
+ Channelling – individuals from minority ethnic groups might also be channelled (i.e. pushed) away from certain sports into others, based on stereotypical assumptions about them – for example, people of an Indian or Pakistani descent channelled away from football and into cricket.

As a society it is important that we encourage diversity in sport and physical activity because it encourages social inclusion and better health, as well as improving standards of performance. However, there are still worrying statistics showing that ethnic diversity in sport and physical activity is not necessarily being achieved.

Recent research reported by Sports England suggests that more than 56 per cent of people from black and minority ethnic communities do not participate in sport or physical activity.

Causes
Possible causes of under-representation of ethnic groups in sport/physical activity include the following:
+ Conflict with religious/cultural observances (e.g. this is a particular concern with Muslim women).
+ A higher value placed on education as opposed to sporting participation; discouragement via family and friends.
+ Fear of racism, prejudice or discrimination.
+ Fewer role models to aspire to, particularly in coaching and managerial positions – for example, in football there are very few black footballers who break into and maintain management positions at Premier League or Football League clubs.
+ Fear of rejection/low levels of self-esteem.
+ Stereotyping/attempts at channelling people from minority ethnic groups into certain sports and away from others.
+ Language barriers might exist for some minority ethnic groups.

Note: Not all ethnic groups are the same; and not all ethnic groups will face precisely the same forms of discrimination and challenges.

Solutions
Possible solutions to the barriers facing people from minority ethnic groups in terms of participation in sport/physical activity include the following:
+ Training more coaches, teachers and sports leaders from minority ethnic groups, and educating them on the effects of stereotyping.
+ Ensuring that there is single-sex provision, to overcome any cultural barriers that might negatively impact on participation (e.g. for Muslim women).
+ Publicising and severely punishing any racist abuse (e.g. as exemplified by the FA, when the then Liverpool player Suarez racially abused his Manchester United counterpart, Evra).
+ Ensuring that provision in PE programmes is appropriate for all ethnic preferences (e.g. ensuring that kit rules and showering procedures are reflective of cultural norms).
+ Organising campaigns against racism in sport (e.g. Kick it Out is football's equality and inclusion scheme – see p. 101).

Race A categorisation of humans based on shared physical or social qualities into groups generally viewed as distinct within a given society.

Stacking The disproportionate concentration of people from minority ethnic groups in certain positions in a sports team, which tends to be based on the stereotype that they are more valuable for their physicality than for their decision-making and communication qualities.

Channelling When people from minority ethnic groups might be pushed into certain sports, and even certain positions within a team, based on stereotypical assumptions about them.

Making links

There is a possible synoptic link here with Chapter 6: Sport psychology (p. 161) and the changing attitudes section (p. 161), e.g. by cognitive dissonance and persuasive communication. This links with potential ways to overcome barriers to participation for under-represented groups in society.

In addition, lack of confidence/self-efficacy as a barrier to participation in under-represented groups could be linked with sport psychology and strategies to develop self-efficacy and confidence (pp. 186–187).

Now test yourself   TESTED

11 Identify barriers to sports participation that still exist for minority ethnic groups in twenty-first-century Britain.

Answer on p. 266

Under-representation of women in sport

Women should have the same opportunity as their male counterparts to participate and excel in their chosen sports. However, more men participate in sport than women, and fewer men than women are inactive. Sport England's Active Lives – Adult survey (May 2018 to May 2019) showed that there were 313,600 fewer women than men who were regularly active.

Exam tip

Equality of opportunity questions often use the command word 'discuss'. Be prepared to provide arguments *for and against* equality of opportunity.

Reasons

A variety of possible reasons (i.e. barriers) can be given to explain the continued under-representation of women in sport. They include the following:

+ Stereotypical myths are still evident in society – for example, the belief that women lack the aggression required for certain sports.
+ There is still less media coverage of women's sport compared with men's, with fewer attainable role models in sport for other women to aspire to.
+ Women in Sport identifies the pressure many women feel to be thin as opposed to being healthy. Many of the media promote a thin, decorative and passive ideal of the female body. Such an image is at odds with an 'active' body.
+ There are fewer sponsorship opportunities/opportunities to become full-time sports performers.
+ School PE programmes can have a negative impact – for example, rules on showering, kit styles and a lack of appealing activity options.
+ Lack of fitness, low levels of self-confidence and body image issues.
+ Lack of income, or reduced leisure time due to work, childcare and/or domestic responsibilities.
+ Women might be channelled into certain 'female-appropriate' sports, with fewer leagues, competitions or clubs available for women to be involved with.

Solutions

Possible solutions to gender inequality in sport include the following:

+ Introducing and enforcing laws that make sex discrimination unlawful in many spheres of life (e.g. the Sex Discrimination Act 1975).
+ Encouraging greater social acceptance of women having careers, with more disposable income, giving increased financial independence
+ Encouraging shared domestic/childcare responsibilities, creating more leisure time for women to devote to sport; improving childcare provision, which can also help to overcome the 'time barrier'.

Check your understanding and progress at **www.hoddereducation.co.uk/myrevisionnotes**

- Increasing media coverage of women's sport; giving women's international sport the recognition it deserves; providing more positive/attainable role models to aspire to.
- Increasing sponsorship attracted to women's sport.
- Providing education to refute the stereotypical myths; improving PE provision (e.g. via the WSFF's Changing the Game for Girls campaign).
- Providing more opportunities for women to join sports clubs/participate in the activities they enjoy.
- Making changing rooms/sports facilities as clean and attractive as possible.
- Use social media effectively – in modern-day society, social networking methods to link women playing sport can be used to create friendships with like-minded individuals and hopefully increase interest and enable the motivation to continue.
- Involve organisations such as Sport England, as well as specialist organisations, such as Women in Sport (formerly the WSFF).
- Use national success as a launchpad. For example, England's success at the 2019 FIFA World Cup helped fuel a growth in participation across all levels of the women's game.

Sociocultural explanations

In 2020, the FA reported that there were over 850,000 more committed female football participants since the 2019 FIFA World Cup in France, taking it to a total of 3.4 million. A number of sociocultural reasons can be given to explain this:

- Increased opportunities in society in general/increases in leisure time and disposable income.
- Increased media coverage of women's football, giving more female role models to identify with.
- More opportunities for girls to play football in school PE programmes.
- More football clubs to join in the area where they live.
- The rejection of stereotypes affecting female participation in contact activities such as football.
- More opportunities to play the game professionally in England (e.g. via formation of the FA).
- Creation of the Women's Super League (WSL) as part of the five-year FA strategy Game Changer, which was designed to build on the successes of the 2012 Olympics and 2015 World Cup to turn women's football into the second largest team sport in the country, behind only men's football, by 2018.

> **Making links**
>
> In your exam revision, make sure that you consider the changing role of women in sport over time and the barriers (and solutions to barriers) linked with a consideration of under-represented groups in sport/physical activity (e.g. based on gender).

> **Exam tip**
>
> In this section of the specification, it is important to develop your ability to understand and correctly interpret and analyse data and graphs relating to participation in physical activity and sport, and relate them to barriers or solutions at play, as appropriate.

Benefits of raising participation

 REVISED

Regular participation in physical activity and/or sport is an important part of a healthy lifestyle encouraged by society. Research commissioned by Sport England into the costs of physical inactivity showed that NHS providers in England spent more than £1 billion on treating people with diseases that could have been prevented if people were more physically active.

Long-term and ongoing health benefits include the following:

- Regular weight-bearing exercise increases bone density, which decreases the risk of osteoporosis in later life.
- Improved mental health/psychological wellbeing decreases the risk of anxiety and depression.

> **Exam tip**
>
> Make sure that you can show knowledge (AO1) and understanding (AO2) in answers linked to the specific benefits contained in the question set – i.e. health, fitness or social benefits.

111

+ Increased cardiovascular fitness can lead to reduced body weight, which decreases the risk of obesity, heart disease, stroke, type 2 diabetes and high blood pressure.
+ Increased joint flexibility as a result of regular stretching exercises reduces the risk of arthritis and maintains joint flexibility into later life.
+ The possibility of decreased risk of developing some cancers (e.g. colon and breast cancer).

Day-to-day health benefits include the following:
+ Improved posture, body shape and body tone as a result of a healthy weight.
+ Improved cardiovascular fitness, muscular strength and muscular endurance.
+ Improved flexibility, agility, balance and coordination.
+ Improved speed, power and reaction time.
+ Increased aerobic/cardiovascular endurance.
+ Fitness benefits for older people in particular make it easier to carry out daily tasks involving skills some younger people might take for granted.

Social health benefits include the following:
+ Team sports will improve communication and cooperative skills.
+ Increased ability to make friends with people of shared interests, and to be more approachable.

> **Making links**
>
> There is a potential synoptic link here with the applied anatomy and physiology section of the specification (pp. 9–10). This focuses on understanding the impact of physical activity and sport on the health and fitness of the individual, which can be linked with various fitness aspects (e.g. flexibility) as well as health problems (e.g. heart disease).

> **Now test yourself**   TESTED
>
> **12** Sport England estimates that taking part in regular sport can save millions of pounds on healthcare costs per annum. Identify the health benefits to society of raising participation in sport/physical activity.
>
> **Answer on p. 266**

Increasing participation at grass roots   REVISED

There is cooperation between Sport England and local and national partners aimed at increasing participation at grass-roots level and by under-represented groups in sport.

What Sport England does:
+ Awards funding – annual investment of National Lottery and public money to help increase numbers being active in society. Funds available for projects and organisations that help people to get active include the Strategic Facilities Fund and the Community Leisure Recovery Fund. Sport England also funds initiatives designed to decrease the ongoing impact of Covid-19.
+ Provides insight – via research into how different groups (more represented and less represented) can become active, and what prevents them from doing so, in order to address those issues.
+ Gathers data – via Active Lives surveys (e.g. Active Lives – Adult (16+) and Active Lives – Children and Young People (5–16) to help explore activity levels across England and understand what affects activity levels for specific population groups.

+ Provides advice/expertise – sharing knowledge to help people across the sport and activity sector in order to increase participation.
+ Tries to get more people active and tackle inactivity at national and local levels (e.g. national campaigns such as This Girl Can and We Are Undefeatable).
+ Uniting the Movement is their latest 10-year strategy (2021–2031), tackling five big issues/inequalities, in the following ways, with the aim to provide opportunities for people and communities who have traditionally been left behind, by removing the barriers to activity they face:
  + Recover and reinvent – to provide a relevant and sustainable network of organisations that provide sport and physical activity opportunities, in order to meet the demands of different people.
  + Connecting communities – to provide relevant local solutions aimed at tackling inactivity. For example, Active Calderdale worked with over 80 per cent of voluntary-sector organisations to find practical solutions to the challenges faced by people living in West Yorkshire.
  + Positive experiences for children and young people – to try to address inequalities that start from a young age by addressing these at the outset.
  + Connecting with health and wellbeing – to tackle the many and varied health problems that occur in society.
  + Active environments – to encourage formal and informal activity in places suited to the individuals/communities using them.

Local partners

+ Sport England places a key emphasis on **local delivery** in terms of meeting its objectives, and works with a range of local partners to try to ensure sport is accessible across every region in the country.
+ It funds a number of county sport partnerships (CSPs), which are now called Active Partnerships. These are spread across the country so that programmes can be delivered regionally/locally to meet specific local needs where these exist (Table 3.11).
+ CSPs/Active Partnerships work with a number of sport/physical activity providers, including local authorities, health organisations, national governing bodies, sports clubs and schools/education providers – all with a commitment to increasing participation across 'their network'. For example, in Oxfordshire the focus is on increasing physical activity among people in deprived areas, as well as among older and vulnerable people.

> **County Sport Partnerships (CSPs)**
> Now known as Active Partnerships, these comprise 43 national networks of local agencies spread across England, which are working together to increase numbers participating in sport and physical activity.

Table 3.11 How Sport England works with services provided by local partners (e.g. via CSPs/Active Partnerships) to increase participation and develop sport locally

Service provided by local partner	How it impacts on sport locally
Club development; creating better clubs	Leads to increased opportunities for more people to take part in sport
Coach/volunteer development; creating better coaches	Leads to improved standards of performance and the ability to cater for more participants
Communication and marketing	Allows local clubs to publicise the opportunities that are available to participants
Facility development; creating more and better facilities	New and improved facilities give more opportunities to participate in a higher-quality and more welcoming environment
Funding support	For local sports providers to pay for equipment, coaches etc. in order to increase participation
Education programmes	Increased awareness of the importance of health and fitness/physical activity
Equality campaigns	Working to increase participation among under-represented groups in society
Safeguarding	Allows clubs to provide safe, secure environments so that all participants feel comfortable
Strategic network	Organisations work in partnership with other organisations to increase participation

National partners

Sport England works with a number of national partners to contribute to the overall mission to create an active nation. These include the ten identified in Table 3.12. Some examples of ways in which each of these partners is helping to increase participation are also described.

Revision activity

Create a spider diagram identifying the key principles of Sport England's latest strategy.

Table 3.12 Sport England's national partners

Name of national partner	Explanation of their role in increasing participation in sport/physical activity
1 Child Protection in Sport Unit (CPSU)	Helps sports safeguard children and young people in and through sport (e.g. by helping facilities to develop responses, structures and systems for safeguarding).
2 Activity Alliance	The new name for the English Federation of Disability Sport, which is dedicated to increasing sport and physical activity among people with disabilities. It has an 'Inclusive Activity Programme' backed by National Lottery and Sport England funding. UK Coaching, Sport England and the Activity Alliance work together to provide individuals with disabilities with the best advice, training and pathways possible in order to increase physical activity.
3 Cricket Foundation	Delivers key programmes aimed at increasing opportunities for young people to play cricket (e.g. Chance to Shine Street). It allocates funding for grass-roots/youth development and has also developed a bank of resources for primary schools to help them deliver high-quality cricket sessions.
4 Football Foundation	A charity that directs £30 million into grass-roots sport in order to deliver a programme of new and improved community sport facilities in towns and cities across England. Its aim is to improve the quality and experience of playing sport, and to help increase participation/improve general skill levels.
5 Sporting Equals	An organisation that actively promotes greater involvement in sport and physical activity by all communities that are under-represented (e.g. the black and minority ethnic (BME) population. It advises and supports policy makers and delivery bodies in being inclusive for all under-represented groups. An example of a scheme it has introduced is the 'Making Equals' project, which aims to engage diverse young people through sport to break down barriers they face and empower them.
6 SportsAid	It works with NGBs to ensure that young, talented athletes are funded via cash awards during the early critical years of their careers, to ensure access to the best possible coaching and facilities. Its aim is to help young British sports performers who aspire to be Olympians and Paralympians.
7 Sports Coach UK/UK Coaching	Support is given to help recruit, develop and retain the coaches needed to increase participation in sport and help athletes reach their performance goals. This is achieved by improving coaching systems, providing research and developing learning and support for coaches.
8 Sport and Recreation Alliance	It provides advice, support and guidance to its members, including those who represent NGBs and County Sport Partnerships (CSPs), to help ensure the growth of the grass-roots sport and the recreation sector.
9 Street Games	A national sports charity that brings sport to the doorsteps of young people in disadvantaged communities (e.g. Doorstep Sport Clubs – youth sports clubs set up for young people in deprived areas of the country).
10 Women in Sport	Helps sports bodies to break down barriers and engage more women and girls in sport. It is the only organisation in the UK that researches sport from a female perspective. Working with NGBs such as British Athletics, the national introduction of the Parkrun has been highly successful in raising participation in women, as has been the development of a training online resource hub for CSPs.

Investment in national governing bodies (NGBs)

In June 2019, as part of its 'Building an Active Nation' strategy, Sport England awarded ten national governing bodies with £16 million to help keep people active in their sport or develop their sporting habit. The funding enabled investment for the selected sports/activities via the NGBs into clubs, coaches, facilities, equipment and 'new ways to play' (e.g. Swim England and Exercise Move and Dance UK).

Volleyball England, British Fencing and England Netball have also pledged to invest in supporting their talented/high-performance athletes so that they are able to fulfil their potential.

Check your understanding and progress at **www.hoddereducation.co.uk/myrevisionnotes**

Exam practice

1 Which one of the following best describes an agent of 'primary socialisation'? [1]

   A Brothers and sisters

   B Teachers

   C Sports coaches

   D Peer groups

2 Outline the impact social stratification can have on sporting participation in modern-day society. [4]

3 Using examples, explain what is meant by the following terms:

   a primary socialisation [1]

   b secondary socialisation [1]

4 Describe how participation in sport/physical activity can be increased among individuals from lower socioeconomic groups. [3]

5 Simone is a 21-year-old keen runner and member of a local athletics club, where she has competed in middle-distance races (i.e. 800 m and 1500 m) since her schooldays.

   Evaluate the impact of socialisation on Simone's choices and her current sporting involvement. [8]

6 Outline how Sport England works with its partners (CSPs) to develop sport locally. [2]

7 Table 3.13 contains data from the Sport England Active People survey. It shows the percentage of people in England taking part in physical activity at least once a week, according to their work status, over a 5-year period.

Table 3.13

Work status	2011/12	2012/13	2013/14	2014/15	2015/16
Full time	43.8%	44.2%	43.5%	43.6%	43.4%
Unemployed	29.8%	38.2%	27.9%	27.9%	27.1%

   Identify the barriers to participation for those at a socioeconomic disadvantage, and outline and evaluate possible solutions to overcome them. Refer to Table 3.13 in your answer. [15]

Answers online

Knowledge and skills summary

This topic involves the following knowledge (AO1):

+ Key terms relating to equality of opportunity in sport, such as socialisation, social processes, social issues, social structures/stratification and social action theory.
+ Different types of socialisation.
+ Key terms relating to equality of opportunity in sport, such as discrimination, stereotyping and prejudice.
+ Barriers/solutions to participation for under-represented groups in society.
+ Strategies being used to overcome the barriers to participation for under-represented groups in society.
+ The benefits of raising participation (i.e. health, fitness and social).
+ Identifying how Sport England is working in partnership, locally and nationally, to increase participation in sport among under-represented groups in society.

AO2 marks will require application of this knowledge – for example, explaining barriers/solutions to participation for under-represented groups in society; explaining strategies that are being used to overcome the barriers to participation for under-represented groups in society; explaining how Sport England is working in partnership, locally and nationally, to increase participation in sport among under-represented groups in society.

AO3 marks are for analysis or evaluation. In this topic, an AO3 response might involve evaluating barriers/solutions to participation for under-represented groups in society, or evaluating strategies that are used to overcome the barriers to participation for under-represented groups in society.

Sometimes you might be required to apply your knowledge of diet to another topic on the specification – for example, linking with sport and society and the role of technology in sport, including the role of technology in physical activity in sport in relation to people with disability as an under-represented group in society (e.g. knowledge of examples of advancements in technology that are helping to overcome participation barriers for individuals with disability).

4 Exercise physiology

4.1 Diet and nutrition and their effects

Exercise-related function of food classes

Carbohydrates

There are two types of carbohydrate.

+ **Simple carbohydrates** – the quickest source of energy, found in fruits, and easily digested by the body. They are also often found in processed foods and anything with refined sugar added.
+ **Complex carbohydrates** – found in nearly all plant-based foods, and usually take longer for the body to digest. They are most commonly found in bread, pasta, rice and vegetables.

Carbohydrates are the principal source of energy used by the body. They are also the main fuel for high-intensity or anaerobic work. Carbohydrate in food is digested and converted into glucose, and enters the bloodstream. The glucose is stored in the muscles and liver as glycogen, but these stores are limited, so regular refuelling is necessary.

> **Making links**
>
> The conversion of glycogen into glucose is discussed in more detail in relation to energy systems during anaerobic glycolysis (p. 35).

> **Exam tip**
>
> Carbohydrates are the principal source of energy for both low-intensity (aerobic) and high-intensity (anaerobic) exercise. They are the only food source that can be broken down anaerobically.

Fats

There are different types of fat.

Saturated fats

+ These can be found in both sweet and savoury foods, but most come from animal sources such as meat and dairy products.
+ Too much saturated fat leads to excessive weight gain, which will affect levels of stamina, limit flexibility, reduce speed and lead to health problems such as coronary heart disease, atherosclerosis, diabetes and high blood pressure.

> **Exam tip**
>
> Make sure that you can give practical examples of the effect of eating too much fat on performance. For example, a reduction in stamina means the performer will fatigue sooner, or decreased flexibility leads to an inefficient running action.

Cholesterol

+ Cholesterol is a type of fat found in the blood.
+ Too much saturated fat leads to high cholesterol levels.
+ Cholesterol is made predominantly in the liver and is carried by the blood as low-density lipoprotein (LDL) and high-density lipoprotein (HDL).
+ Too much LDL can lead to fatty deposits developing in the arteries, which can have a negative effect on blood flow.

Atherosclerosis This is where arteries become clogged with fatty substances.

LDL (low-density lipoprotein) Transports cholesterol in the blood to the tissues, and is classed as 'bad' cholesterol, because it is linked to an increased risk of heart disease.

HDL (high-density lipoprotein) Transports excess cholesterol in the blood back to the liver, where it is broken down. It is classed as 'good' cholesterol because it lowers the risk of developing heart disease.

- HDL takes cholesterol away from the parts of the body where it has accumulated to the liver, where it is disposed of.
- Exercising increases HDL and decreases LDL.

Making links

Cholesterol is also discussed in relation to the cardiovascular system (pp. 9–10).

Trans fats

Trans fats are a form of unsaturated fat that can be found naturally at low levels in meat and dairy products. They can also be made artificially as hydrogenated fats to allow food to have a longer shelf life. As with saturated fat, eating too much trans fat can lead to high levels of blood cholesterol, heart disease and diabetes.

However, not all fats are bad. Replacing saturated and trans fats with healthier unsaturated fats is important because fat is a major source of energy in the body.
- Fats are used for low-intensity, aerobic work such as jogging, and cannot be used for high-intensity exercise where oxygen is in limited supply, because they require oxygen to be broken down.
- Fats allow endurance athletes to meet the demands of training and competition as there is less chance of fatigue, so performance can be maintained for longer.
- Eating fats also spares glycogen stores, so these can be used in the closing stages of an event.
- Fats are also used for the absorption of fat-soluble vitamins A, D, E and K, maintaining bone density and reducing the risk of injuries such as stress fractures.

Exam tip

Fats are an energy source for long-duration, low-intensity exercise.

Making links

Stress fractures are discussed in relation to injury prevention and the rehabilitation of injury (p. 129).

Exam tip

Remember that fats cannot be used anaerobically – they require oxygen to be broken down.

Revision activity

Create a table to summarise the exercise-related roles of carbohydrates, fats and proteins.

Now test yourself TESTED ◯

1 Describe the importance of carbohydrates and fats for a games player.

Answer on p. 267

Proteins

- Proteins are a combination of many chemicals called amino acids.
- They are important for muscle growth and repair, and to make enzymes, hormones and haemoglobin.
- Proteins are a minor source of energy and tend to be used more by power athletes, who have a greater need to repair and develop muscle tissue.

Exam tip

Proteins are necessary for muscle growth and repair.

Vitamins

Vitamins keep us healthy with a good immune system. This allows a performer to train maximally and recover quickly. Table 4.1 lists the vitamins needed for your exam and summarises the exercise-related function of each.

Table 4.1 Sources and functions of vitamins

Vitamin	Source	Exercise-related functions
C (ascorbic acid)	Green vegetables and fruit	+ Protects cells and keeps them healthy + Required for the breakdown of carnitine, which is a molecule essential for the transport of fatty acids into the mitochondria (mitochondria convert food sources, such as fats, into energy in the body – therefore vitamin C is also indirectly responsible for this process) + Helps in the maintenance of bones, teeth, gums and connective tissue, such as ligaments
D	Most vitamin D is made by our body under the skin when it is exposed to sunlight; to a lesser extent it can come from oily fish and dairy produce	+ Has a role in the absorption of calcium, which keeps bones and teeth healthy + Helps with phosphocreatine recovery in the mitochondria
Vitamin B complex includes several important vitamins		
B1 (thiamin)	Yeast, egg, liver, wholegrain bread, nuts, red meat and cereals	+ Works with other B group vitamins to help break down and release energy from food + Keeps the nervous system healthy
B2 (riboflavin)	Dairy products, liver, vegetables, eggs, cereals and fruit	+ Works with other B group vitamins to help break down and release energy from food + Keeps the skin, eyes and nervous system healthy
B6	Meat, fish, eggs, bread, vegetables and cereals	+ Helps form haemoglobin + Helps the body to use and store energy from protein and carbohydrate in food
B12 (folate)	Red meat, dairy products and fish	+ Helps to make red blood cells, and keeps the nervous system healthy + Releases energy from food

Now test yourself   TESTED ◯

2   Explain the importance of vitamin B6 for an elite performer.

Answer on p. 267

Minerals

You need to know the importance of calcium, sodium and iron. Table 4.2 summarises their exercise-related function.

Table 4.2 The importance of minerals in the diet

Mineral	Exercise-related functions
Calcium	This is needed for strong bones and teeth, and is also necessary for efficient nerve and muscle contraction, which is important during exercise
Sodium	This helps regulate fluid levels in the body. However, too much sodium is linked to an increase in blood pressure, which can increase the risk of a stroke or heart attack
Iron	This helps in the formation of haemoglobin in red blood cells, which helps transport oxygen and therefore improves stamina; a lack of iron can lead to anaemia

Now test yourself   TESTED ◯

3   Explain the importance of calcium for a sports performer.

Answer on p. 267

Check your understanding and progress at **www.hoddereducation.co.uk/myrevisionnotes**

Fibre

+ Good sources of fibre are wholemeal bread and pasta, potatoes, nuts, seeds, fruit, vegetables and pulses.
+ Fibre is important during exercise because it can reduce the time it takes the body to break down food, which results in a slower, more sustained release of energy.
+ Dietary fibre causes bulk in the small intestine, helping to prevent constipation and aiding digestion.

Water

+ Water makes up to 60 per cent of a person's body weight, and is essential for good health.
+ It transports nutrients, hormones and waste products around the body, and is the main component of many cells, playing an important part in regulating body temperature.
+ When you take part in exercise energy is required and some of that energy is released as heat. Water will keep you from overheating. The evaporation of sweat helps to cool you down, but this means water is lost during this cooling down process. Therefore, it is important to replace water during exercise and remain hydrated.

A lack of water pre-, during or post-exercise can cause dehydration. This can result in:

+ increased blood viscosity, reducing blood flow to working muscles and the skin
+ reduced sweating to prevent water loss, which results in an increase in core temperature
+ muscle fatigue and headaches
+ reduction in the exchange of waste products/transportation of nutrients
+ increased heart rate, resulting in a lower cardiac output
+ decreased performance/decreased reaction time/decreased decision making

After exercise it is important to replace any fluids lost through sweating. Hypotonic drinks are low in carbohydrates and can quickly rehydrate during recovery. Hypertonic drinks contain higher levels of glucose and can replenish depleted glycogen stores as well as rehydrate.

> **Dehydration** A condition that occurs when the body is losing more fluid than it is taking in.

> **Exam tip**
>
> In an exam you might be asked to discuss or evaluate the importance of each of the food groups during exercise.

Effects of dietary supplements and manipulation

REVISED ○

Glycogen loading

Glycogen loading is a form of dietary manipulation to increase glycogen stores over and above those that can normally be stored (supercompensation). An increase in water intake will also aid glycogen storage. Glycogen loading is used by endurance performers, and there are three methods:

+ Method 1: 6 days before competition the performer eats a diet high in protein for 3 days and exercises at relatively high intensity to burn off any existing carbohydrate stores, followed by 3 days of a diet high in carbohydrates and some light training. The theory is that by totally depleting glycogen stores they can then be increased by up to two times the original amount (supercompensation) and can prevent a performer from 'hitting the wall'.
+ Method 2: 1 day before competition 3 minutes of high-intensity exercise opens a 'carbo window'. Replenishing glycogen stores during the first 20-minute window after exercise can enhance performance the next day. In the 20 minutes immediately after exercise the body is most able to restore lost glycogen. The 'carbo window' closes after 2 hours.

119

+ Method 3 – the non-depletion protocol: training intensity is reduced in the week before competition. Then 3 days before competition a high-carbohydrate diet is followed with low-intensity exercise.

Table 4.3 lists some positive and negative effects of glycogen loading.

Table 4.3 Effects of glycogen loading

Positive effects	Negative effects
+ Increased glycogen stores in the muscle, which can prevent hitting the wall and therefore allows the athlete to maintain levels of glycogen for energy production for longer + Delays fatigue for longer during performance + Increases endurance capacity, so a marathon runner, for example, can maintain a consistent pace for longer during a race	During the carbo-loading phase: + Water retention, which results in bloating and feelings of discomfort while performing + Weight increase caused by water retention can slow the performer down During the depletion phase: + Irritability + Can cause heavy legs and a feeling of lethargy, which can have a negative impact on training and race preparation

Creatine monohydrate

+ This is a supplement used to increase the amount of phosphocreatine stored in the muscles.
+ Phosphocreatine is used to fuel the ATP–PC system, which provides energy.
+ Increasing the amount of creatine in the muscles will allow this energy system to last longer. It can also help improve recovery times (Table 4.4).
+ Athletes in explosive events, such as sprints, jumps and throws, are likely to experience the most benefits as they can perform at higher intensity for longer.

> **Exam tip**
>
> Remember the ATP–PC system is an energy system that provides quick bursts of energy and is used for high intensity exercise but it can only last for up to 10 seconds.

Table 4.4 Effects of taking creatine monohydrate

Positive effects	Negative effects
+ Provides ATP (energy) + Increases the athlete's stores of phosphocreatine + Allows the ATP–PC system to last longer so a performer can work at a higher intensity for longer/improves anaerobic power + Improves muscle mass + Speeds up recovery time	+ Possible side effects are dehydration, muscle cramps, diarrhoea, water retention, bloating, vomiting and liver damage + Can be expensive to buy and supplementation might not be accessible to all + Mixed evidence on the benefits

Sodium bicarbonate

+ Sodium bicarbonate is an antacid. It can increase the buffering capacity of the blood, so it can neutralise the negative effects of lactic acid and hydrogen ions that are produced in the muscles during high-intensity activity (Table 4.5).
+ The concept behind drinking a solution of sodium bicarbonate or 'soda loading' is that it reduces the acidity within the muscle cells to delay fatigue, and allows the performer to continue exercise at a very high intensity for longer.

> **Lactic acid** A by-product of anaerobic respiration. As it accumulates, it causes fatigue.
>
> **Hydrogen ions** Responsible for the acidity of the blood.
>
> **Buffering** The ability of the blood to compensate for the build-up of lactic acid or hydrogen ions in order to maintain the pH level.

Table 4.5 Effects of taking sodium bicarbonate

Positive effects	Negative effects
+ Reduces acidity in the muscle cells + Delays fatigue + Increases the **buffering** capacity of the blood	+ Possible side effects, include vomiting, pain, cramping, diarrhoea, feeling bloated

Check your understanding and progress at www.hoddereducation.co.uk/myrevisionnotes

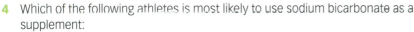

Now test yourself

> **Now test yourself**　　　　　　　　　　　TESTED ◯
>
> 4　Which of the following athletes is most likely to use sodium bicarbonate as a supplement:
> + 1500m runner
> + Long jumper
> + Hammer thrower
> + 100m sprinter
>
> **Answer on p. 267**

Caffeine

+ Caffeine is a naturally occurring stimulant, which can increase mental alertness and reduce fatigue. It is also thought to improve the mobilisation of fatty acids in the body, thereby sparing muscle glycogen stores.
+ It is used by endurance performers, who predominantly use the aerobic system since fats are the preferred fuel for low-intensity, long-endurance exercise (Table 4.6).
+ Caffeine can be found in coffee, tea, cola, chocolate, energy bars with caffeine and caffeinated gels.

> **Revision activity**
>
> Create your own table and summarise the positive and negative effects of glycogen loading, creatine, sodium bicarbonate and caffeine.

Table 4.6 Effects of taking caffeine

Positive effects	Negative effects
+ Stimulant/increased mental alertness + Reduces effects of fatigue + Allows fats to be used as energy source/delays use of glycogen stores + Improves decision making/improves reaction time + Might benefit aerobic performance/endurance athletes	+ Loss of fine control + Against rules of most sports if taken in large quantities + Possible side effects include dehydration, insomnia, muscle cramps, stomach cramps, vomiting, irregular heartbeat, diarrhoea

> **Exam practice**
>
> 1　Describe one method of glycogen loading and outline the benefits to a marathon runner.　　　　　　　　　　　　　　　　[5]
> 2　What are the problems an athlete will face if they dehydrate?　[4]
> 3　Explain why an elite performer might choose to take sodium bicarbonate.　[4]
> 4　Evaluate the importance of sodium in an athlete's diet.　　　[2]
> 5　Evaluate the use of creatine to improve a sprinter's performance in the 200m.　　　　　　　　　　　　　　　　　　[4]
>
> **Answers online**

> **Knowledge and skills summary**
>
> This topic involves the following knowledge (AO1):
> + The exercise-related functions of carbohydrate, fibre, fat (saturated fat, trans fat and cholesterol), protein, vitamins (C, D, B12, B-complex), minerals (sodium, iron, calcium) and water (hydration before, during and after physical activity).
> + The positive and negative effects of creatine, sodium bicarbonate, caffeine and glycogen loading on the performer.
>
> AO2 marks will require application of this knowledge, for example explaining how carbohydrates can help a games player, or the value of taking creatine for a power athlete.
>
> AO3 marks are for analysis or evaluation. In this topic an AO3 response might involve an analysis of fat intake for a particular performer, where you would discuss how fats can help performance but also analyse how eating the wrong fats can result in health problems, with examples.
>
> Sometimes you might be required to apply your knowledge of diet to another topic on the specification, for example explaining how creatine supplementation can help prolong the ATP–PC system (p. 36).

121

4.2 Preparation and training methods

Laboratory conditions and field tests

Quantitative and qualitative data

Quantitative data can be counted or measured, and given a numerical value.

Qualitative data are descriptive and expressed in terms of language rather than numbers.

When drawing conclusions from fitness testing, the results can be analysed quantitatively and qualitatively. Quantitative analysis compares the scores with those of other people or standardised tables, and qualitative analysis analyses the non-numerical data.

Objective

Objective data are based on facts, and are measurable. In fitness testing, objective tests will involve measurements, and are therefore more likely to be accurate.

Subjective

Subjective data are based on personal opinions, assumptions, interpretations and beliefs – for example, self-analysis, questionnaires, surveys, observation and interviews.

Validity

When testing a performer, it is important to ensure that the test is valid, and that it is set up in such a way as to produce reliable results. To assess the validity of a fitness test, the following questions are important:

+ Is the research method relevant, and does it do exactly what it sets out to do?
+ Is the test sport specific?

Reliability

Reliability means that a test produces results that are consistent and can be repeated with the same outcome. To ensure a test is reliable, the following considerations need to be taken into account:

+ The tester should be experienced.
+ Equipment should be standardised.
+ Sequencing of tests is important.
+ Repetition of tests should be possible to avoid human error.

> **Quantitative data** Data that can be measured (e.g. height) or counted (e.g. number of people).
>
> **Qualitative data** Descriptive information, perhaps relating to the way people think or feel.
>
> **Objective data** Data based on facts.

> **Exam tip**
>
> Quantity requires a number; quality requires a description of how or why.

> **Exam tip**
>
> Make sure you can give examples of fitness tests that use measurements – for example, the Wingate test or multi-stage fitness test.

> **Subjective data** Data based on opinions.
>
> **Validity** When the test actually measures what it sets out to do.
>
> **Reliability** The test can be repeated accurately.

> **Now test yourself** TESTED
>
> 1 When conducting field tests, data can be objective or subjective. What are objective data and subjective data?
>
> **Answer on p. 267**

> **Revision activity**
>
> Identify several fitness tests and try to decide on their validity and reliability.

Physiological effects and benefits of a warm-up and cool-down

Warm-up

The warm-up helps prepare the body for exercise and should always be carried out before the start of any training session.

Check your understanding and progress at www.hoddereducation.co.uk/myrevisionnotes

- The first stage of any warm-up is to perform some kind of cardiovascular exercise, such as jogging, gently increasing your heart rate.
- The second stage includes stretching/flexibility exercises especially with those joints and muscles that will be most active during the training session. The type of stretching used will depend on the activity.
- The third stage of a warm-up should involve the movement patterns that are to be carried out – for example, practising shooting in basketball or netball, or dribbling in hockey or football.

There are two types of stretching: static stretching and ballistic stretching.

Static stretching

- Static stretching is stretching while not moving and can be active or passive.
- Active static stretching involves the performer working on one joint, pushing it beyond its point of resistance, and lengthening the muscles and connective tissue surrounding it.
- Passive static stretching (Figure 4.1) is when a stretch occurs with the help of an external force, such as a partner or gravity or a wall.

> **Static stretching** When the muscle is held in a stationary position for 30 seconds or more.

Figure 4.1 A passive static stretch

Ballistic stretching

- Ballistic stretching involves performing a stretch with swinging or bouncing movements to push a body part even further.
- It is an effective form of stretching for fast, dynamic, explosive activities – for example, leg swings will mimic the action required by a long jumper and increase the range of movement at the hip.
- It is important that this type of stretching should only be performed by an individual who is extremely flexible, such as a gymnast or dancer, who will try to push their body beyond the limits of their range of movement, in contrast with a games player.

Whatever the stretch, it is important that it is started slowly, is sports specific and, if it is painful, the stretch is stopped. In addition, stretches should be balanced between agonists and antagonists; if the stretch is static, it should be held for approximately 30 seconds.

> **Ballistic stretching** Performing a stretch with swinging or bouncing movements, to push a body part even further.

> **Exam tip**
> Questions can ask you to discuss the suitability of a type of stretch for a particular performer.

> **Now test yourself**   TESTED ◯
> 2   Define static and ballistic stretching, and explain how to complete them safely.
> **Answer on p. 267**

Physiological effects and benefits

A warm-up can have the following physiological effects:
- It reduces the possibility of injury by increasing the elasticity of muscle tissue.
- The release of adrenaline will increase heart rate and dilate capillaries. This allows more oxygen to be delivered to the skeletal muscles.

+ Muscle temperature increases; this will first enable oxygen to dissociate more easily from haemoglobin and, second, allow for an increase in enzyme activity, making energy readily available through better chemical reactions.
+ An increase in the speed of nerve impulse conduction allows us to be more alert, improving reaction time.
+ It allows efficient movement at joints through an increased production of synovial fluid.
+ It allows for rehearsal of movement, so the performer is practising the same skills they use in their activity.
+ It facilitates mental rehearsal, stress or anxiety reduction, and psychological preparation.
+ It supplies an adequate blood flow to the heart, to increase its efficiency.

Cool-down

A cool-down takes place at the end of exercise. It consists of some form of light exercise to keep the heart rate elevated.

Physiological effects and benefits

A cool-down can have the following physiological effects:
+ It keeps the skeletal muscle pump working.
+ It maintains venous return.
+ Blood is prevented from pooling in the veins.
+ It limits the effect of DOMS (delayed onset of muscle soreness).
+ It removes lactic acid.

> **Revision activity**
>
> Use a mind map to identify the main stages of a warm-up, with an explanation of the benefits of performing each of these.

> **Exam tip**
>
> Questions on warm-up and cool-down usually ask for an explanation of either a warm-up or a cool-down, and the physiological benefits of performing them.

Principles of training

REVISED

For your exam you need to be able to identify the following principles of training, and apply them.

Specificity

Specificity is important to make sure the training you do is relevant for your chosen activity. You need to consider whether you are using the same energy system, muscle fibre type, skills and movements. The intensity and duration of the training should also be similar to your activity.

Progressive overload

This is where the performer gradually trains harder throughout their training programme as their body adapts. A performer who wishes to improve their power, for example, will be lifting heavier weights at the end of their training programme compared with the start. This is because the muscles will be overloaded every few weeks as the amount of weight lifted is increased. It is important to not overload too much too soon. Doing it more gradually will reduce the risk of injury.

Reversibility

This is often referred to as detraining. If training stops, then the adaptations that have occurred as a result of the training programme deteriorate.

Recovery

Rest days are needed to allow the body to recover from training. Research suggests that the 3:1 ratio should be used where the performer trains hard for 3 days and then rests for 1 day.

> **Exam tip**
>
> Remember 'SPORR' for the principles of training:
>
> **S**pecificity
> **P**rogression
> **O**verload
> **R**eversibility
> **R**ecovery

FITT principles

REVISED ○

To improve performance it is important to apply the FITT principles:

+ F stands for **frequency**, so you need to increase the number of training sessions, increase the work period or number of sets and decrease the number of rest periods.
+ I is **intensity**, so to improve you must train harder. To implement this you might use heart rate/Borg scale/1 rep max to help.
+ T is the **time** spent training, so this needs to gradually increase and rest periods to decrease.
+ T stands for the **type** of exercise. Using different forms of exercise maintains motivation but the type chosen needs to be relevant to your chosen activity. For example, if an improvement in stamina is the aim of a training programme there are different types of training that can be used to maintain motivation, such as continuous training, circuit training and fartlek training. However, if you are a games player you need to make sure that these types of training involve running (as opposed to cycling), so you are exercising your muscles in a similar way to how you use them in the game.

Application of principles of periodisation

REVISED ○

Elite performers need to programme their training year very carefully so they can improve performance but also reduce the risk of injury. Periodisation is a key term when planning a training programme. It involves dividing the year into blocks or sections where specific training occurs.

> **Periodisation** Dividing the training year into specific sections for a specific purpose.

Periodisation is divided into three cycles: macro cycle, meso cycle and micro cycle.

Macro cycle

A macro cycle is the 'big' period, which involves long-term planning. In rugby it might be the length of the season, while for an athlete it could be 4 years as they build up to the Olympics. A macro cycle is made up of three distinct periods:

> **Macro cycle** A long-term planning form of periodisation.

+ The preparation period involves general conditioning and the development of fitness levels.
+ The competition period is where the performer refines skills and techniques as well as maintaining fitness levels.
+ The transition period is the rest and recovery stage. This phase allows the athlete to recharge physically and mentally, and ensures an injury-free start to the forthcoming season.

Meso cycle

A meso cycle is usually a 4–12 week period of training with a particular focus. A sprinter, for example, will focus on power, reaction time and speed, whereas an endurance performer will focus more on strength endurance and cardiorespiratory endurance.

> **Meso cycle** Usually a 4–12 week period of training, with a particular focus, such as power.

125

Micro cycle

A micro cycle refers to 1 week or a few days of training, which is repeated throughout the length of the meso cycle.

Micro cycle Planning for a week, a few days or an individual training session.

> **Now test yourself** TESTED ⬤
>
> 5   Explain what is meant by macro cycle, meso cycle and micro cycle.
>
> **Answer on p. 267**

Exam tip

Questions can ask you to analyse how a specific performer would have used macro, meso and micro cycles to achieve a world-class performance.

Tapering and peaking

+ Tapering is where there is a reduction in the volume of training prior to a major competition. This usually occurs a few days beforehand, but can depend on the event or type of competition.
+ It can help to avoid overtraining, reducing the likelihood of injury and reversibility.
+ Planning and organising training in this way prepares the athlete both physically and mentally for the big event, enabling both physical and psychological rest, which allows peaking to occur.

Tapering Reducing the volume and/or intensity of training prior to competition.

Peaking Planning and organising training so that the performer is at their peak, both physically and mentally, for a major competition.

Training methods to improve physical fitness and health

REVISED ⬤

Continuous training

+ Continuous training works on developing aerobic endurance.
+ It involves working at 60–80 per cent of maximum heart rate for 30 minutes or longer, without rest intervals.
+ Activities include jogging, swimming and cycling.
+ As a result, improvements in the cardiovascular and respiratory systems take place, which increase the ability to take up, transport and use oxygen more effectively.

Fartlek training

+ The word 'fartlek' is Swedish, and means speed-play.
+ It is a combination of different training types (continuous and interval).
+ The intensity is varied to stress both the aerobic energy system, due to its continuous nature, and the anaerobic energy systems through high-intensity bursts of exercise.
+ This is a much more demanding type of training, which matches the varying intensity demands of a sport and will improve an individual's stamina and recovery times.

HIIT/interval training

Interval training is predominantly used by elite athletes to improve anaerobic power. It is a form of training in which periods or intervals of high-intensity work are followed with recovery periods. This method of training is very versatile because it can be adapted to suit a variety of anaerobic needs.

When planning an interval training session, it is important to take the following into account:

+ duration of the work interval
+ intensity or speed of the work interval
+ duration of the recovery period
+ number of work intervals and recovery periods

> **Making links**
>
> HIIT links with energy systems (pp. 35–37).

Circuit training

+ In circuit training the athlete performs a series of exercises at a set of stations (Figure 4.2).
+ When planning a circuit, it is important to decide on the number and variety of stations, the number of repetitions or time spent at each station, and the length of the rest interval.
+ The resistance used is the athlete's body weight, and the layout of each exercise should ensure that the same body part is not exercised continuously, to allow for recovery.
+ A circuit can be designed to cover any aspect of fitness, but tends to be used for muscular endurance.

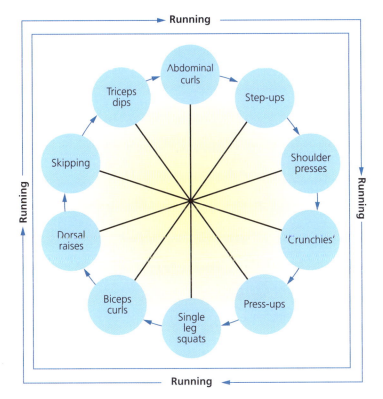

Figure 4.2 An example of a circuit

Weight training

+ Weight training can be used to develop power, muscular endurance and help reduce injury.
+ It involves doing a series of resistance exercises using free weights or fixed weight machines, which are described in terms of sets and repetitions.
+ A repetition is the number of times you do a particular weight exercise, while a set is the number of cycles of repetitions that you do. For example, a performer might squat ten times; this means they have done one set of ten repetitions.
+ The number of sets and repetitions that are performed and the amount of weight lifted will depend on the type of strength being improved.
+ Before a programme can be designed, it is important to determine the maximum amount of weight that a performer can lift with one repetition (1 rep max).
+ If increased power is the goal, it will be necessary to lift heavy weights with low repetitions.
+ If muscular endurance is the goal, it will be necessary to perform more repetitions of lighter weights – for example, three sets of ten repetitions at approximately 50 per cent of 1 rep max.

The choice of exercise should relate to the muscle groups used in sport – both the agonists and antagonists (specificity). The exercises are usually classed into four groups:

Sets The number of cycles of repetitions (reps).

Repetitions The number of times you do an exercise (often referred to as reps).

1 rep max (1RM) The maximum amount a performer can lift in one repetition.

My Revision Notes: AQA A-level PE

+ shoulders and arms (e.g. bench press, curls, pull downs)
+ trunk and back (e.g. sit-ups, back hyperextensions)
+ legs (e.g. squats, calf raise, leg press)
+ all-body exercises (e.g. power clean, snatch, dead lift)

Proprioceptive neuromuscular facilitation

+ Proprioceptive neuromuscular facilitation (PNF) is an advanced stretching technique to improve range of movement.
+ Increasing flexibility can improve performance – for example, a hurdler will improve stride length and therefore generate more power, and a tennis player will have a greater reach when playing a shot.

> **Making links**
>
> How PNF works is covered in the section on the neuromuscular system (pp. 28–29).

> **Exam tip**
>
> Do not forget about the health benefits of these training methods for a sedentary adult:
> + Increase in cardiovascular fitness will allow everyday tasks to be completed with ease.
> + Increase in strength will mean less stress placed on the body when lifting heavy objects.
> + Increase in muscular endurance will reduce fatigue.
> + Improved body composition means less weight to carry, and therefore performing tasks is easier.
> + Social advantages/good for mental health.

> **Now test yourself**   TESTED ⚪
>
> 6 Which methods of training could be used to improve (a) muscular endurance and (b) anaerobic power?
>
> **Answer on p. 267**

> **Exam practice**
>
> 1 Explain how frequency and intensity can be applied to a training programme. [4]
> 2 Describe the main parts of a cool-down that should end a session and the benefits of that cool-down. [5]
> 3 Explain how tapering can help prepare an athlete for competition. [2]
>
> **Answers online**

> **Exam tip**
>
> Questions might ask you to explain how weight training can improve performance – for example, improving strength and power can help a rugby player tackle with more force.

> **Exam tip**
>
> Questions can ask how PNF could improve performance.

> **Knowledge and skills summary**
>
> This topic involves the following knowledge (AO1):
> + An understanding of the terms 'quantitative', 'qualitative', 'objective', 'subjective', 'validity' and 'reliability' for laboratory conditions and field tests.
> + The physiological benefits of a warm-up and cool-down.
> + The principles of training as SPORR and FITT.
> + Application of the principles of periodisation.
> + How interval, continuous, fartlek, circuits, weights and PNF training can improve physical fitness and health.
>
> AO2 marks will require application of this knowledge – for example, giving practical examples explaining how the
>
> macro, meso and micro cycles in periodisation can be used to improve performance, or practical examples of how one of the training methods can improve performance in a team game.
>
> AO3 marks are for analysis or evaluation – for example, analysing the suitability of a training method for a particular performer.
>
> Sometimes you might be required to apply your knowledge of training to another topic on the specification – for example, explaining the impact of specialist training methods on energy systems (pp. 35–37).

4.3 Injury prevention and rehabilitation

Types of injury

There are two types of sports injury: acute and chronic.

✚ An acute injury occurs suddenly during exercise or competition – for example, a sprained ankle or torn ligament. Pain is felt straight away and is often severe.

✚ A chronic injury occurs after playing sport or exercise for a long time. This type of injury develops slowly and can last a long time, and is often ignored by performers, which makes the injury worse, causing more problems.

Acute injuries

You need to know about fractures, dislocations, strains and sprains.

✚ **Fracture** involves a break or a crack in a bone. Bone can fracture in different ways:
  ✚ A simple or closed fracture is a clean break to a bone that does not penetrate the skin or damage any surrounding tissue.
  ✚ A compound or open fracture is when the soft tissue or skin has been damaged. This is more serious, as there is a higher risk of infection.

✚ **Dislocation** happens when the ends of bones are forced out of position. It occurs at joints and is very painful.

✚ **Strain** – often called a 'pulled' or 'torn' muscle – occurs when muscle fibres are stretched too far and tear.

✚ **Sprain** occurs to ligaments (strong bands of tissue around joints that join bone to bone) when they are stretched too far or tear.

Chronic injuries

You need to know about Achilles tendonitis, stress fractures and tennis elbow.

✚ **Achilles tendonitis** – pain and inflammation of the Achilles tendon. The Achilles tendon is located at the back of the ankle and is the largest tendon in the body. It connects the gastrocnemius to the heel bone, and is used for walking, running and jumping, so when we do a lot of regular activity it can be prone to tendonitis.

✚ **Stress fractures** are most common in the weight-bearing bones of the legs, often when there is an increase in the amount of exercise, or the intensity of an activity rises too quickly. They happen when muscles become fatigued and so are no longer able to absorb the added shock of exercise. The fatigued muscle eventually transfers the stress overload to the bone, and the result is a tiny crack called a stress fracture. The area becomes tender and swollen.

✚ **Tennis elbow** occurs in the muscles attached to the elbow that are used to straighten the wrist. The muscles and tendons become inflamed, and tiny tears occur on the outside of the elbow. The area becomes very sore and tender. Any activity that places repeated stress on the elbow through overuse of the muscles and tendons of the forearm can cause tennis elbow. As the name suggests, this injury often occurs in tennis.

Injury prevention, rehabilitation and recovery

Injury prevention methods

You need to know how screening, protective equipment, warm-up, flexibility training, taping and bracing are used in injury prevention.

Acute injury Sudden injury caused by a specific impact or traumatic event, where a sharp pain is felt immediately.

Chronic injury A slowly developing injury that can last a long time. Often referred to as an overuse injury.

Exam tip

Remember the difference between a strain and a sprain. Strains occur in muscles, and sprains occur in ligaments.

Revision activity

Give some sporting examples of when each of the acute injuries described above could occur.

Screening

Sports screening involves a series of tests that can be used to help identify those at risk of complications from exercise, prepare performers for their sport, enhance performance and reduce injury. It can be used to detect a problem early before any symptoms occur.

+ Screening can be used to identify a current or past injury.
+ It can highlight any muscle imbalances or assess any posture weaknesses in the musculoskeletal system.
+ Screening can also save lives – for example, many young elite performers have CRY (cardio risk in the young) heart screening.
+ It can also identify a suitable rehabilitation programme.
+ However, screening can have disadvantages. Some screening tests are not 100 per cent accurate, and might miss a problem (false negative) or can identify a problem that does not exist (false positive). It can also increase anxiety when an athlete finds out they have a health problem or are more susceptible to injury.

Now test yourself
TESTED ◯

1 Evaluate the importance of screening.

Answer on p. 267

Protective equipment

Wearing the correct protective equipment can help reduce injuries in sport. This equipment needs to fit correctly and follow national governing body (NGB) regulations. In football, for example, ankle and shin pads are worn to prevent injury.

Making links

The warm-up is also an injury prevention method, and is discussed in detail under preparation and training methods (pp. 122–124).

Revision activity

Many games players wear protective clothing to prevent injury. Choose five games and identify what protective clothing can be worn.

Flexibility training

Flexibility training should involve the joints and muscles that will be most active during the activity.

+ Active stretching occurs when a stretched position is held by contraction of an agonist muscle. An example is lifting your leg up and holding it in position. The tension in the hip flexors caused by holding the leg up in the air (Figure 4.3) helps to relax the antagonist muscles being stretched (gluteals).
+ Passive stretching is when a stretch occurs with the help of an external force, such as another part of your body, a partner or a wall.
+ Static stretching is when the muscle is held in a stationary position for 10 seconds or more.
+ Ballistic stretching involves performing a stretch with swinging or bouncing movements to push a body part even further, and should be performed by an individual who is extremely flexible, such as a gymnast or a dancer.

Figure 4.3 Active stretching

Now test yourself
TESTED ◯

2 Describe the different types of flexibility training that can be used to prevent injury.

Answer on p. 267

Taping and bracing

+ Taping a weak joint can help with support and stability, in order to reduce the risk of injury.
+ Taping can also be used on muscle. Kinesiology tape is used on muscles because it is more elastic than the tape used on joints. It is applied directly to the skin to provide controlled support, because it expands as the muscle contracts.
+ Bracing is much more substantial than taping, and often involves hinged supports. It is used to give extra stability to muscles and joints that are weak or have been previously injured.

Injury rehabilitation methods

Proprioceptive training

Proprioceptive training uses hopping, jumping and balancing exercises to restore lost proprioception and teach the body to control the position of an injured joint subconsciously. Sprained ankles are a common sporting injury, and proprioceptive exercises are done on a balance board for rehabilitation.

Strength training

+ Strength training allows the injured performer to strengthen weaker muscles to prevent injuries reoccurring, and uses a resistance of some kind.
+ This resistance can be weight machines or free weights, body weight or the use of thera-bands.
+ Thera-bands are good in the early stages of injury because they offer a range of resistances.
+ Body weight exercises put less stress on the body, because the performer is only required to hold their own body weight, so this method is also good in the early stages of injury.
+ Fixed-weight machines provide the performer with a lot of control, which allows them to focus on improving strength, but the range of motion generated by the machines can be limited.
+ Free weights are most beneficial in the later stages of injury rehabilitation, where more control is needed and varying degrees of weight can be used to build up to full strength.

> **Exam tip**
>
> Proprioceptive training and strength training are easily accessible rehabilitation methods.

Hyperbaric chambers

+ The aim of a hyperbaric chamber is to reduce the recovery time for an injury.
+ The chamber is pressurised rather like an aeroplane (in some chambers a mask is worn) and there is 100 per cent pure oxygen.
+ The pressure increases the amount of oxygen that can be breathed in, and this means more oxygen can be diffused to the injured area.
+ The excess oxygen dissolves into the blood plasma, where it can reduce swelling and both stimulate white blood cell activity and increase the blood supply at the injury site.
+ Many of the top rugby union, cricket and football teams use hyperbaric chambers.

Cryotherapy

Cryotherapy is the use of cold temperatures to treat injuries. For common sporting injuries, such as muscle strains, treatment is simply RICE, which involves the use of ice. This has an analgesic effect and can limit pain and swelling by decreasing blood flow to the injured area.

Hydrotherapy

Hydrotherapy takes place in warm water and is used to improve blood circulation, relieve pain and relax muscles. Typically, hydrotherapy pools are heated to approximately 35–37°C, which increases blood circulation. The

> **Cryotherapy** The use of cold temperatures to treat an injury.
>
> **RICE** Rest, ice, compression, elevation.
>
> **Hydrotherapy** The use of water to treat injuries.

131

buoyancy provided by the water helps to support the body weight so that there is less load on joints, allowing for more exercise than is permitted on land.

Exam tip

Hyperbaric chambers, cryotherapy and hydrotherapy are rehabilitation methods that have limited access. It is mostly elite performers who have the opportunity to use them.

> **Now test yourself**   TESTED ◯
>
> 3 How can hydrotherapy help sports rehabilitation?
>
> **Answer on p. 267**

Methods of recovery after exercise

Compression garments

Compression garments have been used in medicine for a long time to try to improve blood circulation and prevent medical problems such as deep-vein thrombosis (DVT) occurring.

Massage

Sports massage is a popular form of treatment that can prevent or relieve soft tissue injuries. The benefits of sport massage include:

+ increased blood flow to soft tissue, so more oxygen and nutrients can pass through to help repair any damage
+ removal of lactic acid
+ stretching of soft tissue to relieve tension and pressure
+ breakdown of scar tissue which, if not removed, can lead to mobility problems in muscles, tendons and ligaments

Soft tissue Includes tendons, ligaments, muscles, nerves and blood vessels.

Foam rollers

Foam rollers can be used as part of self-massage. They can release tension and tightness in a muscle as well as between the muscles and the fascia. They can be used to prevent injury and improve mobility.

Fascia A layer of fibrous connective tissue that surrounds the muscle or group of muscles.

Cold therapy

+ As a method of recovery, cold therapy is useful after intense exercise, where it can target any minor aches and pains.
+ Cooling the surface of the skin using ice gives pain relief, and causes vasoconstriction of the blood vessels, which decreases blood flow and reduces any bleeding or swelling.
+ A decrease in swelling enables the muscle to have more movement.
+ Ice can also reduce muscle spasms by decreasing motor activity, because the speed of the nerve impulse slows down in cold conditions.
+ **Ice baths** and cryotherapy are popular methods of cold therapy.
+ After a gruelling training session or match, sports performers get into an ice bath for 5–10 minutes.
+ The cold water causes the blood vessels to tighten (vasoconstriction) and therefore reduces blood flow to the area.
+ On leaving the bath, the legs fill up with new blood (vasodilation) that invigorates the muscles with oxygen, to help the cells function better.
+ The blood that leaves the legs takes away with it the lactic acid that has built up during the activity.
+ **Cryotherapy** can also help with recovery from exercise.
+ Many sportspeople now use whole-body cryotherapy (WBC) to aid their recovery – it targets the whole body and not just a particular muscle.
+ This is still a relatively new practice, but WBC is a much quicker alternative to ice baths and, according to participants, more pleasant.

> **Now test yourself**   TESTED ◯
>
> 4 Explain the use of an ice bath as a method of recovery from exercise.
>
> **Answer on p. 267**

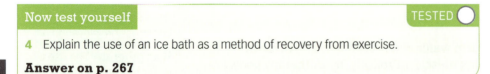

Check your understanding and progress at **www.hoddereducation.co.uk/myrevisionnotes**

Importance of sleep and nutrition for improved recovery

- Deep sleep is important for muscle recovery.
- The deepest part of sleep is the third stage of non-REM sleep.
- Here brain waves are at their slowest and blood flow is directed away from the brain towards the muscles to restore energy.
- If sleep is too short then the time for repair is cut short.
- Most elite athletes have a minimum of 8–9 hours' sleep each night, but your body will tell you if you need more.
- Not having enough sleep results in fatigue and will there reduce performance – for example, it will be more difficult to concentrate and make the correct decisions.
- A lack of sleep can also have a detrimental effect on motivation levels.
- Nutrition is also crucial for recovery after exercise.
- During exercise, muscle glycogen stores decrease, so they need to be replenished when exercise is finished.
- Research shows that replenishing glycogen stores during the first 20-minute window after exercise can enhance performance the next day. In the 20 minutes immediately after exercise the body is most able to restore lost glycogen.

> **Non-REM sleep (NREM)**
> Sleep with no rapid eye movement. It consists of three stages of sleep, which get progressively deeper.

Making links

The importance of glycogen is also studied with diet and nutrition (pp. 116–121) and energy systems (pp. 35–37).

Now test yourself

TESTED ◯

5   Why is sleep important for improved recovery?

Answer on p. 267

Exam practice

1   The use of ice baths and cryotherapy can aid recovery. Analyse which of these methods you think is the most effective, and give reasons why. [4]

2   Explain why an elite performer might suffer from Achilles tendonitis. [3]

3   Explain how hyperbaric chambers can aid injury rehabilitation. [4]

4   What is the difference between an acute and a chronic injury? [2]

Answers online

Knowledge and skills summary

This topic involves the following knowledge (AO1):
- Acute and chronic injuries.
- Injury prevention methods – screening, protective equipment, warm-up, flexibility training, taping and bracing.
- Rehabilitation methods – proprioceptive training, strength training, hydrotherapy, hyperbaric chambers, cryotherapy and hydrotherapy.
- Recovery methods – compression garments, massage/ foam rollers, cold therapy, ice baths and cryotherapy.
- The importance of sleep and nutrition for improved recovery.

AO2 marks will require application of this knowledge – for example, using strength training as a rehabilitation method, giving a practical example such as using dumbbells for a shoulder press to help an athlete recover from a shoulder injury.

AO3 marks are for analysis or evaluation – for example, analysing the suitability and impact of a particular rehabilitation method.

Sometimes you might be required to apply your knowledge of injury prevention and rehabilitation to another topic on the specification – for example, preparation and training (pp. 122–128).

5 Biomechanical movement

5.1 Biomechanical principles

Biomechanical principles involve an understanding of how motion (movement) and forces can be applied to performance in physical activity and sport.

Newton's laws of motion applied to sport

REVISED

+ **Linear motion** is motion in a straight or curved line, with all body parts moving the same distance at the same speed in the same direction.
+ A 100-metres athlete will travel with linear motion in a straight line during their race, while a 200-metres athlete will travel with linear motion in a curved line when running the bend.

> **Linear motion** Motion in a straight or curved line, with all body parts moving at the same speed in the same direction.

Newton's first law of motion

Newton's first law (the law of inertia) states:

> 'Every body continues in its state of rest or motion in a straight line, unless compelled to change that state by external forces exerted on it.'

+ In simple terms, a force is required to change the state of motion.
+ If a body changes its state of motion, it starts, stops, accelerates, decelerates or changes direction.
+ In the high jump, for example, the athlete runs horizontally towards the bar and then changes their state of motion at take-off, when they travel vertically to try to clear the bar.

> **Newton's first law** A force is required to change the state of motion.

Newton's second law of motion

Newton's second law (the law of acceleration) states:

> 'The rate of change of momentum of a body (or the acceleration for a body of constant mass) is proportional to the force causing it, and the change that takes place is in the direction in which the force acts.'

+ In simple terms, this law means that the magnitude (size) and direction of the force applied to a body determines the magnitude and direction of the **acceleration** of a body, when the mass stays the same.
+ The acceleration is directly proportional to the force causing the change.
+ The following equation is often used to calculate the size of a force:

    force = mass × acceleration ($F = ma$)

To provide the acceleration at the start of a sprint race an athlete will have to apply a large force internally with their gluteals, quadriceps and gastrocnemius as they drive forward. Similarly, a tennis player will exert a large force on the ball with the racquet so that it travels over the net in the direction in which the force has been applied.

> **Newton's second law** The magnitude (size) and direction of the force determines the magnitude and direction of the acceleration when the mass remains constant.
>
> **Acceleration** Rate of change of velocity.

Newton's third law of motion

Newton's third law (the law of action and reaction) states:

> 'To every action (force) there is an equal and opposite reaction (force).'

+ This law describes what happens when two bodies (or objects) exert forces on one another.
+ Action and reaction are equal and opposite, and always occur in pairs.

> **Newton's third law** For every action force there is an equal and opposite reaction force.

Check your understanding and progress at **www.hoddereducation.co.uk/myrevisionnotes**

- Action acts on one of the bodies, and the reaction to this action acts on the other body.
- At a sprint start, the athlete *pushes back on the blocks* as hard as possible (the action), and the blocks *push forward* on the athlete (the reaction) – providing forward acceleration on the athlete.

Exam tip

Make sure you know which law is which. Exam questions might ask for a specific law or laws – for example, 'Using Newton's first and second laws…'.

Revision activity

Give examples of how each of the laws can be applied to a sport of your choice.

Making links

An explanation of how Newton's laws can help perform an explosive movement successfully can be linked to the recruitment of fast-twitch fibres.

Now test yourself   TESTED ⚪

1 During a race, a swimmer has to dive off the starting blocks as quickly as possible. Using Newton's first and second laws of motion, explain how the swimmer dives off the starting blocks.

Answer on p. 268

Exam tip

Most questions on Newton's third law involve a ground reaction force exerted on a performer, which is equal and opposite to the muscular force applied by the performer on the ground.

Make sure you include the words 'equal' and 'opposite' when you are defining Newton's third law.

Definitions, equations and units of example scalars

REVISED ⚪

Many different measurements are used in linear motion, but for your exam you only need to study three scalar quantities: speed, distance and mass. A scalar quantity is when measurements are described in terms of just their size or magnitude. Direction is not taken into account.

Scalar quantity A quantity that has size only.

Exam tip

You have to be familiar with three scalar quantities: speed, distance and mass.

Speed
Speed can be defined as the rate of change of position, and can be calculated as follows:

$$\text{speed in metres per second (m s}^{-1}\text{)} = \frac{\text{distance covered in metres (m)}}{\text{time taken in seconds (s)}}$$

Distance
Distance is the length of the path a body follows when moving from one position to another. For example, a 200-metres runner who has just completed a race has run a distance of 200 metres. Distance is also a scalar quantity because it just measures size.

$$\text{distance} = \text{speed (m s}^{-1}\text{)} \times \text{time (s)}$$

Figure 5.1 Triangle for calculating speed and distance

Exam tip

An easy way to calculate speed and distance is to use the triangle in Figure 5.1.

From this triangle you can see that: speed = distance/time, distance = speed × time, and time = distance/speed.

When calculating speed and distance, it is important that the units used correspond with each other. If the question gives the distance in kilometres and the time in hours, then the measurement of speed should be calculated as $km\,h^{-1}$.

Speed and distance can also be used in graphs along with time (Figure 5.2).

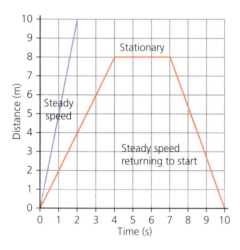

Figure 5.2 A distance/time graph

This graph shows that when a performer is stationary the line on the graph is horizontal. Running at a steady speed in a straight line means the line on the graph remains straight but is now angled. The steeper the line is, the faster the speed of the performer. The runner represented by the blue line is running faster than the runner represented by the red line.

Centre of mass

REVISED ◯

Mass is the quantity of matter the body possesses, and is measured in kilograms (kg).

+ The centre of mass is the point in the body at which the force of gravity can be thought to act.
+ The human body is an irregular shape, so the centre of mass cannot be identified easily. In addition, the body is constantly moving, so the centre of mass will change as a result – for example, raising your arms in the air raises your centre of mass to keep the body balanced (Figure 5.3).

> **Mass** The quantity of matter a body has.
>
> **Centre of mass** The point from which the whole mass appears to act, or the point in the body at which the force of gravity can be thought to act.

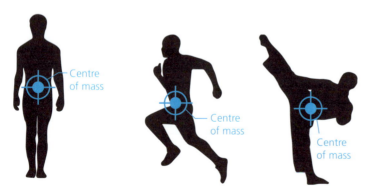

Figure 5.3 The centre of mass

- In general, the centre of mass for someone adopting a standing position is around the hip region, but it differs according to gender. Males have more weight concentrated in their shoulders and upper body, so their centre of mass is slightly higher than in females, who have more body weight concentrated at their hips.

Factors affecting stability

All sports require good balance. To increase your stability, the following mechanical principles need to be considered:

- The height of the centre of mass – lowering the centre of mass will increase stability.
- The position of the line of gravity – this should be central over the base of support, to increase stability.
- Area of the support base – the more contact points, the larger the base of support becomes and the more stable the body becomes. For example, a headstand has more contact points than a handstand, so is a more balanced position.
- Mass of the performer – often the greater the mass, the more stability there is because of increased inertia.

Now test yourself
TESTED

3 How can you increase your stability in a game of football?

Answer on p. 268

Exam practice

1 Using Newton's three laws of motion, explain how a high jumper takes off from the ground. [6].
2 Calculate the distance covered if a football player runs at a speed of $9\,m\,s^{-1}$ for 15 seconds towards the ball. [2]
3 Calculate the time taken to run the 800 m at an average speed of $8\,m\,s^{-1}$. [2]

Answers online

Knowledge and skills summary

This topic involves the following knowledge (AO1):
- Newton's three laws of linear motion applied to sporting movements.
- The scalars mass, speed and distance, giving equations and units of measurement.
- Centre of mass and the factors affecting stability.

AO2 marks will require application of this knowledge – for example, applying the factors that affect stability to a particular body position.

AO3 marks are for analysis or evaluation – for example, analysing how Newton's laws of motion can produce an explosive movement.

Sometimes you might be required to apply your knowledge of this topic to another topic on the specification – for example, linking Newton's laws with the recruitment of fast-twitch motor units (neuromuscular system, p. 28).

5.2 Levers

- A lever consists of three main components: a pivot (**fulcrum**); the weight to be moved (**resistance**); and a source of energy (**effort** or **force**).
- In the body, the skeleton forms a system of levers that allow us to move.
- The bones act as the levers, the joints are the fulcrums, the effort is provided by the muscle and the resistance is the weight of the body part that is being moved (often against the force of gravity).

Classification of levers

There are three types of lever – first, second and third – and the classification of each depends on the position of the fulcrum, resistance and effort in relation to each other.

First-class lever

In first-class levers the fulcrum is located between the effort and the resistance (Figure 5.4). There are two examples of this type of lever in the body – the movement of the head and neck during flexion and extension, and extension of the elbow.

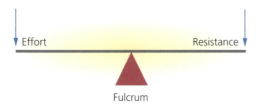

Figure 5.4 First-class lever

Second-class lever

In second-class levers the resistance lies between the fulcrum and the effort (Figure 5.5). There is only one example of this lever in the body, and that is plantarflexion of the ankle.

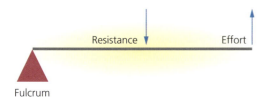

Figure 5.5 Second-class lever

Third-class lever

Third-class levers can be found in all the other joints of the body, where the effort lies between the fulcrum and the resistance (Figure 5.6). Some examples are hip, knee and elbow flexion.

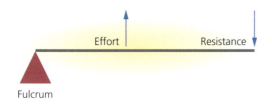

Figure 5.6 Third-class lever

> **Revision activity**
>
> Remember the rhyme **FRE 123**, where 123 is the type of lever and FRE refers to the element that is in the middle. So, for example, F for fulcrum is the first letter, so when the fulcrum is in the middle it is a first-class lever.

> **Exam tip**
>
> If you are asked to classify and label a lever, make sure you do not abbreviate. For example, use the label 'effort' and not the letter 'E'.

> **Making links**
>
> You need to be able to link lever systems with joint actions (pp. 30–31).

> **Now test yourself**   TESTED
>
> 1 Name and sketch the lever system that operates during flexion of the neck.
>
> **Answer on p. 268**

Check your understanding and progress at **www.hoddereducation.co.uk/myrevisionnotes**

Mechanical advantage and disadvantage

A lever can have a mechanical advantage or disadvantage. This depends on the length of the effort arm and the resistance arm. The effort arm is the name given to the shortest perpendicular distance between the fulcrum and the application of effort. The resistance arm is the shortest perpendicular distance between the fulcrum and the resistance (Figure 5.7).

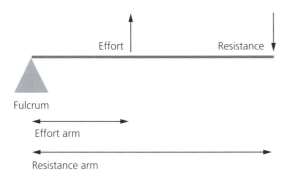

Figure 5.7 The effort/force arm and the resistance arm

Mechanical advantage occurs when the force arm is longer than the resistance arm. This means that the lever system can move a large load over a short distance, and requires little effort. However, it has a small range of movement, and it is difficult to generate speed and distance.

Mechanical disadvantage occurs when the resistance arm is longer than the effort arm. This means that the lever system cannot move as heavy a load, but can do it faster. It also has a large range of movement (Table 5.1).

> **Mechanical advantage**
> Where the effort arm is longer than the resistance arm.
>
> **Mechanical disadvantage** Where the resistance arm is longer than the effort arm.

Table 5.1 Examples of mechanical advantage/disadvantage

Type of lever	Mechanical advantage	Mechanical disadvantage
Second class: Gastrocnemius in plantarflexion of the ankle	Can generate much larger forces Has to lift the whole body weight	Slow, with a limited range of movement
First class: Triceps in extension of the elbow **Third class:** Biceps in flexion of the elbow	Large range of movement, and any resistance can be moved quickly	Cannot apply much force to move an object

Exam practice

1 Name and sketch the lever system that operates during flexion of the elbow joint. [3]

2 What do you understand by the terms 'mechanical advantage' and 'mechanical disadvantage'? [3]

3 Analyse how the lever system at the ankle achieves an effective drive off the blocks in sprinting. [4]

Answers online

Knowledge and skills summary

This topic involves the following knowledge (AO1):
+ The three classes of lever, and examples of their use in the body during physical activity and sport.
+ The mechanical advantage and disadvantage of each class of lever.

AO2 marks will require application of this knowledge – for example, giving practical examples of lever systems for particular joint actions, such as extension of the elbow as a first-class lever.

AO3 marks are for analysis or evaluation – for example, analysing the effectiveness of a lever system in a specific sporting example.

Sometimes you might be required to apply your knowledge of training to another topic on the specification – for example, the musculoskeletal system (pp. 30–34).

5.3 Linear motion

Forces acting on a performer

A force changes a body's state of motion. Forces can be internal or external.

+ An **internal force** is applied when our skeletal muscles contract – for example, the force generated as the quadriceps contract concentrically to extend the knee in a jump.
+ An **external force** comes from outside the body – for example, friction, air resistance and weight. Gravity is also an external force, and is often described in terms of weight as weight is the gravitational force that the Earth exerts on a body to pull the body downwards.

You need to be able to identify and apply the following external forces that act on a sports performer.

Weight and gravity

+ Weight is a gravitational force that the Earth exerts on a body, pulling it towards the centre of the Earth, or effectively downwards.
+ The greater the mass of the individual, the greater the weight force pulling the body downwards.
+ Weight is equal to the mass of the body multiplied by the acceleration of a body due to gravity.

Friction

There are two types of frictional force – static and sliding. Static frictional force occurs before an object starts to slide. When friction acts between two surfaces that are moving relative to one another, sliding friction occurs.

Friction acts in opposition to motion. This is often confusing, but try to remember that friction resists the slipping and/or sliding motion of two surfaces. When a runner's foot lands on the ground, the foot is stationary on the ground. The direction of the frictional force changes as the body moves over the foot. When the foot is in front of the body, the frictional force is backwards, to stop it moving forwards over the ground. When the foot is behind, the frictional force is forwards to stop the foot moving backwards. An arrow is therefore drawn in the opposite direction to this slipping.

Friction can be affected by the following factors:

+ The surface characteristics of the two bodies in contact. Think of a 100-metres sprinter who wears running spikes. These help to increase friction as the spikes make contact with the track, and therefore minimise slipping.
+ The temperature of the two surfaces in contact. In curling, for example, the ice is swept in front of the curling stone. The sweeping action slightly raises the surface temperature of the ice, which reduces the friction between the stone and ice, allowing the stone to travel further.
+ The mass of the objects that are sliding. A larger mass results in greater friction.

Air resistance

Air resistance opposes the motion of a body travelling through the air, and depends on the following:

+ The velocity of the moving body – the faster the performer moves, the greater the air resistance.
+ The cross-sectional area of the moving body – the larger the cross-sectional area, the greater the air resistance. For example, think of the Tour de France and how the competitors crouch low over the handlebars, rather than sit upright (Figure 5.8).

> **Exam tip**
>
> Weight and reaction are vertical forces.
>
> Do not confuse weight and mass. Weight is a measure of the amount of downwards force that gravity exerts on an object. Mass is the quantity of matter the body possesses.

> **Exam tip**
>
> Friction occurs when two or more bodies are in contact with one another.

Check your understanding and progress at **www.hoddereducation.co.uk/myrevisionnotes**

Figure 5.8 Cyclists minimise their air resistance so that they go faster

✦ The shape and the surface characteristics of a moving body – a streamlined shape results in less resistance, as does a smooth surface. For example, most elite swimmers shave off all body hair or wear half/full body swimsuits, so they create a smooth surface. Those who do not shave their head wear a swimming cap instead.

Air resistance is sometimes referred to as 'drag' – although this term is most commonly used when describing resistance in water. Compare running in water with running on land. There is a much greater drag force in water due to its greater density.

Now test yourself   TESTED ⬤

1 Identify and explain the external vertical force acting on a long jumper as they travel through the air after take-off.

Answer on p. 268

Exam tip

Two forces that can act horizontally are air resistance and friction.

Forces on the performer during linear motion

Forces are vectors. How they act on a performer can be shown using an arrow on a free-body diagram. The position, direction and length of the arrow are important, and need to be drawn accurately (Figure 5.9).

Exam tip

When you draw a force, make sure you give your arrow a point of application (correct starting point), direction (with the arrowhead) and size (shown by the length of the arrow).

Length of arrow = magnitude/size

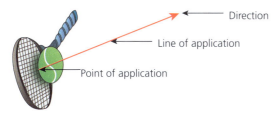

Direction

Line of application

Point of application

Figure 5.9 Vectors

141

Weight/gravity (W), friction (F) and air resistance (AR) can all be drawn as shown in Figure 5.10.

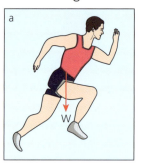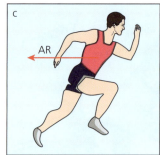

Figure 5.10 Free body diagrams

The length of the arrow drawn reflects the magnitude or size of the force – the longer the arrow, the bigger the size of the force (Figure 5.11).

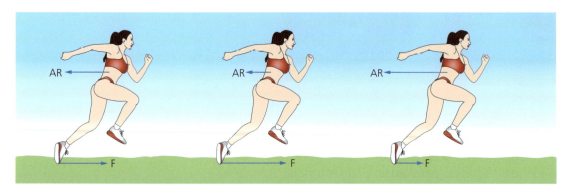

Figure 5.11 From left to right: F = AR, so the performer is travelling at a constant velocity, F > AR shows acceleration, and F < AR shows deceleration

+ The effects of internal and external forces can be represented as a vector diagram.
+ In the high jump, the performer uses a large internal muscular force from the leg muscles to create a big action force to achieve as much vertical displacement (height) as possible.
+ The relationship between the amount of vertical force and horizontal force provided by the muscles will lean towards the vertical component (V).
+ The resultant forces for the high jumper can be drawn as a vector diagram (Figure 5.12).
+ The small horizontal force and the large vertical force provided by the muscles have a resultant force with a high trajectory (close to the vertical).
+ A long jumper, however, is trying to achieve as much horizontal distance as possible. This means there will be a greater contribution to the overall force from the horizontal component (H), as outlined in Figure 5.13.

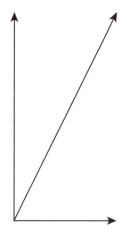

Figure 5.12 A vector diagram showing the resultant forces for the high jump.

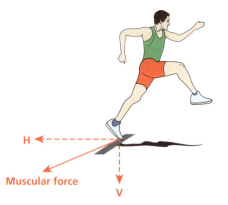

Figure 5.13 The forces exerted by the performer's leg muscles on the ground, when performing a long jump

Check your understanding and progress at **www.hoddereducation.co.uk/myrevisionnotes**

✚ As a result of the application of these forces, the resultant forces for the long jumper can be drawn as a vector diagram (Figure 5.14).

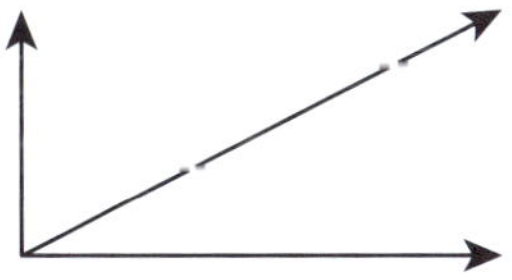

Definitions, equations and units of vectors and scalars

REVISED ⬤

There are several vector quantities used in linear motion. These are measurements described in terms of magnitude (size) and direction – weight, acceleration, displacement, velocity and momentum.

Figure 5.14 A vector diagram showing the resultant forces for the long jump.

> **Vector quantity** A measurement described in terms of both size and direction.

> **Exam tip**
>
> Remember, you also need to have knowledge of the three scalar quantities: speed, distance and mass.

You need to be able to give definitions, units of measurement and, where relevant, equations for the scalars and vectors shown in Table 5.2.

Table 5.2 Scalars and vectors

Measurement		Definition	Unit of measurement	How to calculate (if relevant)
Scalar	Mass	Mass is the quality of matter the body possesses	Kilograms (kg)	–
	Distance	Distance is measured in metres and is the path a body takes as it moves from the starting to the finishing position	Metres (m)	–
	Speed	Speed is a measurement of the body's movement per unit of time, with no reference to direction	Metres per second (m s^{-1})	$\text{speed (m s}^{-1}) = \dfrac{\text{distance covered (m)}}{\text{time taken (s)}}$
Vector	Weight	Weight is the gravitational force exerted on an object	Newtons (N)	weight (N) = mass (kg) × gravitational field strength (N kg^{-1})
	Displacement	Displacement is the shortest route in a straight line between the starting and finishing position	Metres (m)	–
	Velocity	Velocity is the rate of change of displacement	Metres per second (m s^{-1})	$\text{velocity (m s}^{-1}) = \dfrac{\text{displacement (m)}}{\text{time taken (s)}}$
	Acceleration	Acceleration is the rate of change of velocity	Metres per second per second (m s^{-2})	$\text{acceleration (m s}^{-2}) = \dfrac{\text{change in velocity (m s}^{-1})}{\text{time taken (s)}}$
	Momentum	Momentum is the product of the mass and velocity of an object	kg m s^{-1}	momentum (kg m s^{-1}) = mass (kg) × velocity (m s^{-1})

> **Now test yourself**
>
> TESTED ⬤
>
> 2 Calculate the momentum of a forward in rugby who has a mass of 110 kg and a velocity of 10 m s^{-1}.
>
> **Answer on p. 268**

Graphs of motion

You need to be able to plot, label and interpret biomechanical graphs and diagrams.

Distance/time graph

Distance/time graphs (Figure 5.15) show the distance travelled over a period of time.

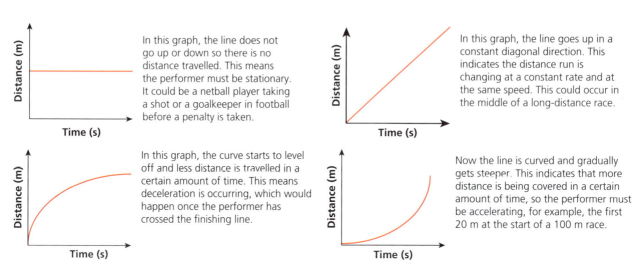

In this graph, the line does not go up or down so there is no distance travelled. This means the performer must be stationary. It could be a netball player taking a shot or a goalkeeper in football before a penalty is taken.

In this graph, the line goes up in a constant diagonal direction. This indicates the distance run is changing at a constant rate and at the same speed. This could occur in the middle of a long-distance race.

In this graph, the curve starts to level off and less distance is travelled in a certain amount of time. This means deceleration is occurring, which would happen once the performer has crossed the finishing line.

Now the line is curved and gradually gets steeper. This indicates that more distance is being covered in a certain amount of time, so the performer must be accelerating, for example, the first 20 m at the start of a 100 m race.

Figure 5.15 Distance/time graphs

The gradient of a graph

The gradient of a graph is a measure of the slope of the graph (Figure 5.16). This is determined by:

$$\text{gradient} = \frac{\text{change in the quantity on the } y \text{ or vertical axis}}{\text{change in the quantity on the } x \text{ or horizontal axis}}$$

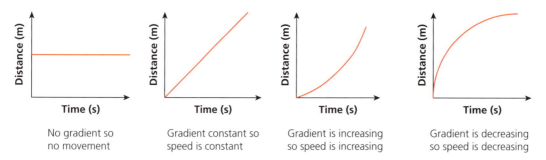

No gradient so no movement

Gradient constant so speed is constant

Gradient is increasing so speed is increasing

Gradient is decreasing so speed is decreasing

Figure 5.16 The gradient of a distance/time graph represents the speed of the movement

Velocity/time graphs and speed/time graphs

A velocity/time graph can be both positive and negative, but a speed/time graph will only be positive. The shape of the velocity/time graph will represent the same pattern of motion as the shape of a speed/time graph. These graphs indicate the velocity or speed of a performer or object per unit of time (Figure 5.17). The gradient of the graph will help you to decide whether the performer is travelling at a constant velocity, accelerating or decelerating.

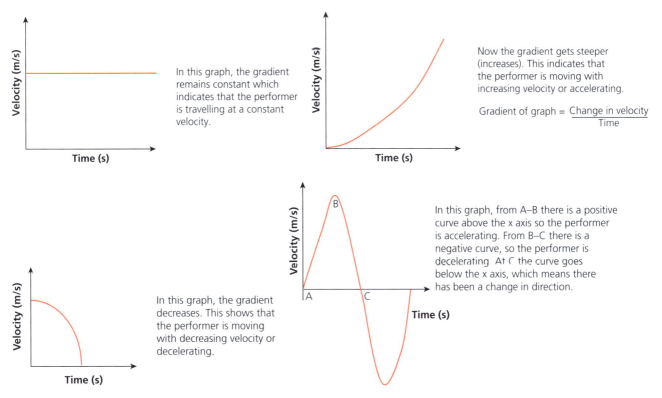

Figure 5.17 Velocity/time graphs showing constant velocity, increasing velocity, decreasing velocity and a more complex pattern of motion

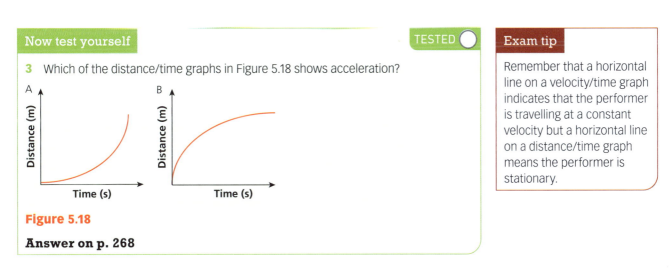

Now test yourself   TESTED ○

3   Which of the distance/time graphs in Figure 5.18 shows acceleration?

Figure 5.18

Answer on p. 268

Exam tip

Remember that a horizontal line on a velocity/time graph indicates that the performer is travelling at a constant velocity but a horizontal line on a distance/time graph means the performer is stationary.

Relationship between impulse momentum   REVISED ○

Impulse

+ **Impulse** is the time it takes a force to be applied to an object or body. It can be calculated as force × time, and is measured in newton seconds (Ns).
+ An increase in impulse will result in an increase in the change of momentum, which causes a large change in velocity.
+ Therefore, impulse is equivalent to a change in the momentum of a body as a result of a force acting on it.

Impulse The time it takes a force to be applied to an object or body, given by force × time.

Using impulse to increase momentum can be achieved through increasing the amount of:

+ muscular force that is applied
+ time over which a force is applied – for example, following through with the arm in a throw

145

Using impulse to decrease the momentum of an object or body occurs by increasing the time over which forces act on them. In any activity that involves a landing action, such as a gymnast dismounting from the parallel bars, flexion of the hip, knee and plantar flexion of the ankle occurs, which extends the time of the force on the ground (how long the feet are in contact with the mat) and therefore allows the gymnast to control the landing while reducing the chance of injury.

Interpretation of force/time graphs

+ Impulse is represented by an area under a force/time graph.
+ The graphs in Figure 5.19 show various stages of a 100-metre sprint.
+ In the 100-metre sprint, impulse is only concerned with horizontal forces.
+ As the sprinter's foot lands on the ground, the muscles contract and a force is applied to the ground (action force) and the ground reaction force then acts on the foot, which allows the athlete to accelerate forwards.
+ The action of the foot in contact with the ground is referred to as a single footfall.
+ It is important to note that in running/sprinting, negative impulse occurs first when the foot lands to provide a braking action; then, positive impulse occurs as the foot takes off for acceleration.

> **Exam tip**
>
> For your exam you need to be able to interpret the relationship between impulse and increasing and decreasing momentum in a force/time graph.

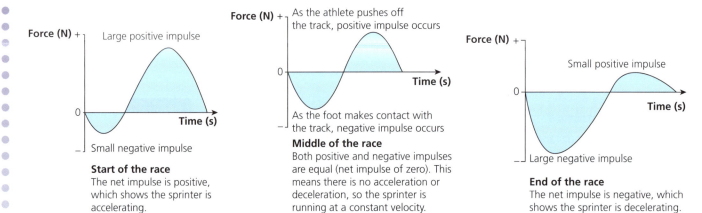

Figure 5.19 Force/time graphs to show various stages of a 100-metre sprint

---

Now test yourself · TESTED ⬤

4 Define impulse and state the units of measurement.

Answer on p. 268

Exam practice

1 When accelerating along the track at the beginning of a 100-metre race, a sprinter generates a large impulse. Sketch and label a graph to show the typical impulse generated by the sprinter at this stage of the race. [4]

2 Give two horizontal forces acting on a 200-metres sprinter. [2]

3 Sketch a vector diagram to represent the differing resultant forces for a long-jumper, and explain your answer. [3]

4 How would you calculate velocity? [1]

Answers online

5.4 Angular motion

Angular motion is movement around a fixed point or axis, such as a somersault, throwing a discus or moving around the high bar in gymnastics. It occurs when a force is applied outside the centre of mass. An off-centre force is referred to as an eccentric force.

> **Angular motion** The motion of a body about a fixed point or axis.

Application of Newton's laws to angular motion

REVISED ○

We can relate Newton's laws to angular motion by changing the terminology.

Newton's first law

+ A rotating body will continue in its state of angular motion unless an external force (torque) is exerted on it.
+ In practice, think of an ice skater spinning in the air. They will continue to spin until they land. Here the ground exerts an external force (torque), which changes their state of angular momentum.

> **Torque** A rotational force.

Newton's second law

+ The rate of change of angular momentum of a body is proportional to the force (torque) causing it and the change that takes place in the direction in which the force (torque) acts.
+ In practice, leaning forwards from a diving board will create more angular momentum than standing straight.

Newton's third law

+ When a force (torque) is applied by one body to another, the second body will exert an equal and opposite force (torque) on the other body.
+ In practice, performing the hang technique in the long jump exerts an equal and opposite force. As the long jumper brings their legs forwards and upwards (action) the arms come forwards and downwards (reaction).

> ### Making links
>
> You need to be able to apply Newton's laws of motion to both linear motion (biomechanical principles, pp. 134–135) and angular motion.

147

Now test yourself   TESTED ◯

1   Explain Newton's second law of motion in relation to a dancer spinning.

Answer on p. 268

Revision activity

Choose a somersault, cartwheel or other rotational movement and try to apply all of Newton's laws to it.

Definitions and units for angular motion

REVISED ◯

You need to be able to define and give a unit of measurement for each of the measurements in Table 5.3.

Table 5.3

Measurement of angular motion	Definition	Units and equation
Angular displacement	The smallest change in angle between the starting and finishing points	Measured in radians (1 radian = 57.3 degrees)
Angular velocity	The rate at which a body rotates about an axis	Measured in radians per second $$(\text{rads s}^{-1}) = \frac{\text{angular displacement (rad)}}{\text{time taken (s)}}$$
Angular acceleration	The rate of change of angular velocity over time	Measured in radians per second squared $$(\text{rads s}^{-2}) = \frac{\text{change in angular velocity (rad s}^{-1})}{\text{time taken (s)}}$$

Now test yourself   TESTED ◯

2   How is angular velocity calculated?

Answer on p. 268

Conservation of angular momentum and moment of inertia

REVISED ◯

Angular momentum (L) depends on the moment of inertia (I) and angular velocity (ω). When angular momentum is constant, these two are inversely proportional; if moment of inertia increases, angular velocity decreases (and vice versa).

✚ Inertia is a resistance to change in motion, so moment of inertia is the resistance of a body to angular motion (rotation). This depends on the mass of the body and the distribution of mass around the axis of rotation.

✚ The greater the mass, the greater the resistance to change, and therefore the greater the moment of inertia. For example, a medicine ball is more difficult to roll along the ground than a tennis ball.

✚ The closer the mass is to the axis of rotation, the easier it is to turn, so the moment of inertia is low.

✚ Increasing the distance of the distribution of mass from the axis of rotation will increase the moment of inertia, for example, a somersault in a straight position has a higher moment of inertia than the tucked somersault because in the straight position the distribution of the diver's mass is further away from the axis of rotation (Figure 5.20).

Exam tip

angular momentum $(L) = I\omega$

Moment of inertia The resistance of a body to having its speed of rotation about an axis altered by the application of a turning force.

Figure 5.20 Tucked and open somersaults

+ Angular momentum stays constant unless an external torque (force) acts on it (Newton's first law).
+ When an ice skater executes a spin, for example, there is almost no change in their angular momentum until they use their blades to slow the spin down.
+ A figure skater can also manipulate their moment of inertia to increase or decrease the speed of the spin (angular velocity).
+ At the start of the spin, the arms and leg are stretched out (Figure 5.21). This increases their distance from the axis of rotation, resulting in a large moment of inertia and a large angular momentum to start the spin (decrease in angular velocity).
+ When the figure skater brings their arms and legs back in line with the rest of their body (Figure 5.22), the distance of these body parts to the axis of rotation decreases significantly.
+ This reduces the moment of inertia, meaning that angular velocity has to increase, as the angular momentum remains constant. The result is a very fast spin.

Figure 5.21 The start of a spin

Exam tip

Questions often ask you to explain how the speed of rotation can be altered or controlled. To answer this, you need to know the relationship between angular momentum, moment of inertia and angular velocity.

Exam practice

1 Explain how a gymnast can alter the speed of rotation during flight. [6]
2 Explain Newton's first law of motion in relation to a dancer spinning. [2]
3 Define angular displacement and give the unit of measurement. [2]

Answers online

Figure 5.22 Increasing angular velocity during a spin

Knowledge and skills summary

This topic involves the following knowledge (AO1):
+ Application of Newton's laws to angular motion.
+ Definitions and units of measurement for angular motion, angular acceleration, angular displacement and angular velocity.
+ How angular momentum can be conserved during flight, using moment of inertia and its effect on angular velocity.

AO2 marks will require application of this knowledge – for example, applying moment of inertia to a skater spinning or a diver performing a somersault.

AO3 marks are for analysis or evaluation – for example, analysing how the angular analogues of Newton's laws of motion affect rotational movement.

Sometimes you might be required to apply your knowledge of this topic to another topic on the specification – for example, linking the application of Newton's laws of angular motion to the recruitment of fast-twitch motor units (neuromuscular system, pp. 27–28).

149

5.5 Projectile motion

+ Projectile motion refers to the movement of either an object or the human body as it travels through the air.
+ In sport, as soon as a ball is released in a kick, hit or throw, it becomes a projectile.
+ The human body acts as a projectile in a variety of sporting situations, such as the long jump and gymnastic vault.

Horizontal displacement of projectiles

REVISED

Three factors determine the horizontal displacement of a projectile:
+ angle of release
+ speed of release
+ height of release

> **Horizontal displacement**
> The shortest distance from the starting point to the finishing point in a line parallel to the ground.

Angle of release

+ To ensure that an object or person travels as far as possible, the angle of release is important, whether this is the angle the object leaves a performer's hand or the angle at which a performer takes off.
+ The optimum angle of release is dependent on release height and landing height.
+ When both the release height and the landing height are equal, the optimum angle of release is 45° (ignoring wind resistance). This would be the case for a long jumper, who takes off from the ground and lands on the ground.
+ If the release height is below the landing height, the optimum angle of release needs to be greater than 45°. Shooting in basketball highlights this, if we assume the ring is the landing height, as the ring is above the release height.
+ If the release height is above the landing height, the optimum angle of release needs to be less than 45°. This can be seen in the flight path of the shot put, where the hand is the point of release, which is higher than the landing point (ground).

Speed of release

+ The greater the release velocity of a projectile, the greater the horizontal displacement.
+ In the shot put the speed across the circle ensures that the shot leaves the hand at maximum velocity, so that a greater horizontal displacement can be achieved.

Height of release

+ A greater release height also results in an increase in horizontal displacement.
+ The force of gravity is constantly acting on the mass of a shot put.
+ This therefore means that, technically, the shot putter should try to release the shot at the highest point possible above the ground to gain maximum horizontal displacement.

Now test yourself   TESTED ◯

1 Identify the three factors that affect the distance a shot travels.
Answer on p. 268

Check your understanding and progress at **www.hoddereducation.co.uk/myrevisionnotes**

Factors affecting flight paths of projectiles

➕ Weight (gravity) and air resistance are two forces that affect projectiles while they are in the air.

➕ These two factors are crucial in deciding whether a projectile has a flight path that is a true parabola or a distorted parabola.

➕ A parabola is a uniform curve that is symmetrical about its highest point (i.e. with matching left and right sides).

➕ Projectiles with a large weight and smooth profile have a small air resistance force and follow a true parabolic flight path. A good example is the shot put.

➕ Figure 5.23 shows the forces acting on the flight path of a shot put at the start, middle and end of flight.

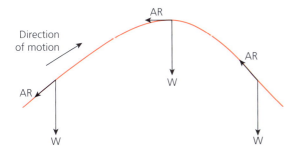

Figure 5.23 A parabolic flight path of a shot put

➕ As the shot has a large mass, there is a longer weight arrow.

➕ The longer the flight path, the longer air resistance can affect a projectile and have a greater influence.

➕ In projectiles with a lighter mass the effects of air resistance result in a flight path that deviates from a true parabola to a distorted parabola.

➕ The badminton shuttlecock is a good example of this.

➕ Figure 5.24 shows the forces acting on the flight path of a shuttlecock.

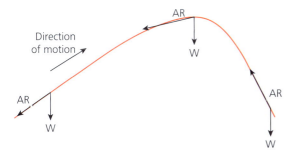

Figure 5.24 A non-parabolic flight path of a shuttlecock

➕ Compared with the shot put, the shuttlecock has a lighter mass and an unusual shape that increases its air resistance. In a serve the shuttle starts off with a high velocity – provided by the force of the racquet. As the shuttle continues its flight path it slows down and the effect of air resistance reduces.

> **Revision activity**
>
> Choose projectiles from five different sports and see if you can identify their flight path, and explain why they follow this flight path.

> **Making links**
>
> Forces are also discussed in relation to linear motion (p. 140).

Vector components of parabolic flight

➕ A shot follows a parabolic flight path.

➕ As it is released at an angle to the horizontal, its initial velocity has a horizontal component and a vertical component.

➕ These two components can be represented by vectors.

➕ A vector is drawn as an arrow and it has magnitude (size) and direction.

➕ Drawing a bigger arrow means there is more magnitude while a smaller arrow means less magnitude.

> **Horizontal component**
> The horizontal motion of an object.
>
> **Vertical component** The upward motion of an object.

2 Draw two vectors – one to represent the horizontal component and one for the vertical component.

Answer on p. 268

+ Figure 5.25 shows both the horizontal and vertical vectors on the flight of a shot put as it follows a parabolic flight path:

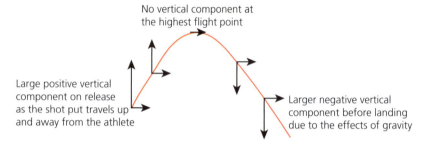

No vertical component at the highest flight point

Large positive vertical component on release as the shot put travels up and away from the athlete

Larger negative vertical component before landing due to the effects of gravity

Figure 5.25 The forces acting on the flight path of a shot put

+ Here the vertical component can only be affected by gravity, which is why the vertical component decreases during flight.
+ Air resistance is negligible, so both the horizontal and vertical components are unaffected by air resistance.
+ This means the horizontal component remains constant throughout the flight.
+ It is also possible to add the horizontal and vertical vectors together to get a resultant vector. This shows the true flight path of the shot (Figure 5.26).

Exam tip

The release point of the shot is drawn higher than the landing point, while the horizontal component arrow stays the same at each stage of the flight.

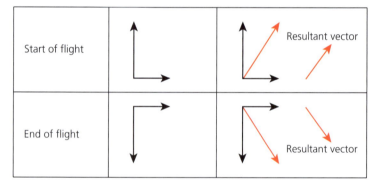

| Start of flight | | Resultant vector |
| End of flight | | Resultant vector |

Figure 5.26 The true flight path of the shot put

Exam practice

1 Elite football players use their feet to overcome the forces acting on the football so that it can travel long distances. Describe how the impact of the foot, weight and air resistance affect the velocity and acceleration of a football, and give the main factors that limit the distance the football can travel. [6]

2 In a game of badminton the performer hits the shuttle into the air and it then becomes a projectile. Explain how the various forces act to affect the badminton shuttle *during* its flight. [3]

3 Draw a diagram to show the flight path of a shot put. On your diagram label and explain the changing vertical and horizontal vectors at the following points:
+ the point of release
+ the highest point of flight
+ the point immediately before landing [6]

4 Identify two forces that affect a projectile while it is in the air. [2]

Answers online

Check your understanding and progress at **www.hoddereducation.co.uk/myrevisionnotes**

Knowledge and skills summary

This topic involves the following knowledge (AO1):

+ Angle of release, speed of release and height of release as the factors that affect the horizontal displacement of projectiles.
+ The factors affecting flight paths of the shot put and badminton shuttlecock.
+ The vector components of parabolic flight.

AO2 marks will require application of this knowledge – for example, drawing the horizontal and vertical vectors on the flight of a shot put as it follows a parabolic flight path.

AO3 marks are for analysis or evaluation – for example, analysing how an athlete can maximise horizontal displacement.

Sometimes you might be required to link your knowledge of this topic to another topic on the specification – for example, explaining the effect of weight and air resistance (also discussed in relation to linear motion) on the flight path of the shot put and shuttlecock.

5.6 Fluid mechanics

+ Fluid mechanics is the study of fluids and how forces affect them.
+ You need to be able to explain how a variety of sports can be affected by their fluid environment.
+ Fluid dynamics is a branch of fluid mechanics.
+ Drag and lift are dynamic fluid forces. These two forces have an effect in a variety of sports, including cycling, sprinting and swimming.
+ Any projectile, such as a ball, discus or javelin, will experience a drag and lift force.

Drag force

Drag is the resistance force caused by the motion of a body travelling through a fluid, slowing it down.

+ A drag force acts opposite to the direction of motion, and therefore has a negative effect on velocity.
+ A drag force results from friction with the particles of the fluid the body is travelling through. Air resistance equals drag.

There are two different types of drag:

+ Surface drag relates to friction between the surface of an object and the fluid environment. It is sometimes called 'skin drag'. Swimmers wear specialised, smooth clothing and shave off body hair from their limbs and torso to reduce surface drag.
+ Form drag relates to the impact of the fluid environment on an object. It is sometimes referred to as 'shape drag'. The forces affecting the leading edge of an object increase form drag, while the forces affecting the trailing edge reduce form drag. Form drag relates to streamlining – a swimmer, for example, has to create the thinnest and straightest form as they move through the water. A large form drag also offers less turbulent air for anything that is following, i.e. slipstream (Figure 5.27). In cycling, for example, a cyclist will use another rider's slipstream (also known as 'drafting').

Drag force A force that acts in opposition to motion.

Surface drag The resistance that occurs from friction between the surface of a body and the fluid through which it is moving.

Form drag The resistance caused by an object's shape as it moves through a fluid.

Streamlining Shaping a body so it can move effectively and quickly through a fluid.

Second rider requires less energy   Air passes around first rider

Figure 5.27 Slipstreaming in cycling

+ As the wind hits the front cyclist it goes around the sides, and the cyclist behind uses the air pocket that has been created.
+ For it to work, the second cyclist has to ride very close to the bike in front (approximately 15–30 cm) and can save up to 30 per cent more energy as a result.

Factors that reduce and increase drag

 REVISED

The velocity of the moving body

+ The greater the velocity of a body through a fluid, the greater the drag force.
+ A racing car, sprinter or cyclist, for example, will experience greater air resistance in their competition, which increases drag.
+ Consequently, in a sport that is very quick it is important to reduce the effects of drag. This is done by streamlining the body as much as possible.

The cross-sectional area of a moving body

+ A large cross-sectional area increases drag.
+ In some sports, reducing the effects of drag is crucial to ensure success.
+ For example, in the Tour de France the competitors reduce their cross-sectional area by crouching low over the handlebars, rather than sitting upright.
+ Similarly, speed skiers reduce the effects of drag by also crouching low. This will allow them to travel faster.

The shape and surface characteristics of a moving body

+ A more streamlined, aerodynamic shape reduces drag.
+ Sports scientists are regularly trialling drag-resistant clothing to achieve marginal gains in speed to give competitors the edge over their opposition.
+ Speed skiers have helmets that extend to the shoulders to give them a more streamlined position, while their special form-fitting suits and aerodynamic boots are also streamlined.
+ In cycling, clothing with ridges and an aerodynamic helmet with air ducts have recently been designed to try to reduce the effects of drag even more.
+ The shape and surface characteristics of a badminton shuttlecock result in a much larger drag force from air resistance. The shuttlecock has an unusual shape involving feathers, and it is also very light. The larger drag force from air resistance means that it loses speed quickly.

> **Exam tip**
>
> Make sure that you can give examples from different sports of where shape and surface characteristics can either increase or decrease drag.

> **Revision activity**
>
> Think of some other examples in sport where the shape and surface characteristics of a moving body can increase or decrease drag.

> **Making links**
>
> This topic is also discussed in relation to linear motion (p. 140).

> **Now test yourself** TESTED
>
> 1 Distinguish between surface drag and form drag, giving examples from sport.
> 2 Explain how fluid mechanics can be applied to improve sporting performance in cycling through advancements in equipment and technique.
>
> **Answers on p. 268**

The Bernoulli principle

+ When the discus is thrown, it experiences an upward lift force during flight. A lift force enables the discus to stay in the air for longer, therefore increasing the horizontal distance it travels.
+ Lift is achieved when different air pressures act on an object. Air that travels faster has a lower pressure than air that travels slower. This is known as Bernoulli's principle (Figure 5.28).

Upward lift force

+ When a projectile such as the discus is released, the angle of attack is important.
+ The angle of attack changes the flow of air around the discus, so the air that travels over the top of the discus has to travel a longer distance than the air underneath.
+ This results in the air above the discus travelling at a faster velocity, which therefore creates a lower pressure.
+ The air that travels below the discus has less distance to cover and so travels at a slower velocity, which therefore creates a higher pressure.
+ This higher pressure below the discus creates an upward lift force and allows the discus to stay in the air for longer, resulting in a greater horizontal distance.
+ If the angle of attack is too great, then lift is reduced and drag increases, causing the discus to stall.
+ The optimum angle of attack that produces the best lift for the discus is anything between 25° and 40°.

> **Lift force** The force that causes a body to move perpendicular to the direction of travel.
>
> **Bernoulli principle** Where air molecules exert less pressure the faster they travel, and more pressure when they travel slower.
>
> **Angle of attack** The tilt of a projectile relative to the air flow.

> **Exam tip**
>
> If the angle of attack is too great, then too much drag will result.

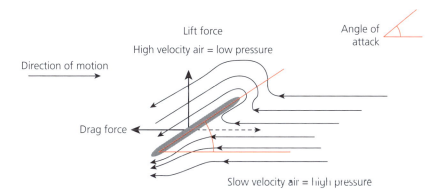

Figure 5.28 The Bernoulli principle producing an upward lift force on the discus

Downward lift force

+ A lift force does not always have to work in an upward direction.
+ Bernoulli's principle can also be used to describe a downward lift force, such as that required by racing cars, cyclists and speed skiers.
+ The car, bike and skis need to be pushed down into the ground so that a greater frictional force is created.
+ In a Formula 1 sports car, for example, the spoiler is angled so that the lift force can act in a downward direction to push the car into the track (Figure 5.29).
+ This happens because the air that travels over the top of the car travels a shorter distance than the air underneath due to the angle of the spoiler.
+ As a result, the air above the car travels at a slower velocity and a higher pressure.
+ This creates a downward force and therefore a greater frictional force, so the tyres maintain a firm grip on the track as the car travels at high speed and around corners.

> **Exam tip**
>
> The shape and angle of the rear spoiler of a racing car result in the force created by Bernoulli's principle acting in a downward direction.

Figure 5.29 A downward lift force is caused by the shape and angle of the rear spoiler

+ Similarly, with the cyclist, the low, streamlined body position over the handlebars means that the air that travels over the top of the cyclist has to travel a shorter distance than the air underneath.
+ This results in the air above the cyclist travelling at a slower velocity, which therefore creates a higher pressure.
+ This higher pressure above the cyclist creates a downward lift force and allows the tyres of the bike to maintain a firm grip on the track.
+ Speed skiers need to stay in contact with the ice for faster speed because more downward-acting lift means more force, which melts the ice for a better friction-free surface.

Now test yourself　　　　　　　　　　　　　　　　TESTED ◯

3　Identify whether there is an upward or downward lift force acting on the following: discus, racing car, cyclist and speed skier.

Answer on p. 268

Exam practice

1　Explain what would happen if the angle of attack for the discus was too high. [2]
2　Identify and explain three factors that can increase or decrease drag. [3]
3　Describe how a racing car makes use of a downward lift force. [4]
4　Identify how a cyclist reduces their cross-sectional area and the effect this has on their speed. [2]

Answers online

Knowledge and skills summary

This topic involves the following knowledge (AO1):
+ What is meant by dynamic fluid force and its relationship to drag and lift.
+ The factors that reduce and increase drag in sport.
+ Bernoulli's principle in relation to an upward lift force for the discus throw and a downward lift force for speed skiers, cyclists and racing cars.

AO2 marks will require application of this knowledge – for example, explaining the principles of lift in relation to the discus, a racing car, a cyclist and a speed skier.

AO3 marks are for analysis or evaluation – for example, analysing the impact of reducing drag to maximise speed.

Sometimes you might be required to apply your knowledge of this topic to another topic on the specification – for example, analysing the factors that affect drag and explaining how air resistance acts on the performer during linear motion (pp. 140–141).

Check your understanding and progress at **www.hoddereducation.co.uk/myrevisionnotes**

6 Sport psychology

6.1 Psychological factors that can influence an individual in physical activities

6.1.1 Aspects of personality

Some psychologists argue that personality characteristics are innate; others argue that they are learned.

> **Personality** The unique, psychological, temperamental features of an individual.

Nature versus nurture

REVISED ●

Trait perspective
Trait theorists include Eysenck, Cattell and Girdano.
+ A performer is born with their personality.
+ Personality is determined genetically.
+ Extroverts will show their outgoing personalities both on and off the field of play.
+ Introverts will always be reserved.
+ Personality characteristics will most likely be shown in all situations.
+ Personality and behaviour can be predicted.
+ Personality will be stable and enduring.
+ Personality does not change and is permanent.
+ Trait theory does not consider any effects of environmental learning.
+ It does not accept that personality cannot be predicted.
+ It does not accept that individuals might consciously decide to structure their own personality.

For example, a netballer who is calm and controlled would always show these characteristics even when playing against an opponent who is continually making contact. The coach would be confident that the player would not lash out in retaliation, despite the contact.

Social learning perspective
Social learning theorists include Bandura (see theories of learning, pp. 57–60).
+ Personality is not innate.
+ It is learned from our experiences.
+ It changes according to the situation.
+ Personality and behaviour cannot be predicted.
+ Performers observe and copy the behaviour and personality of significant others.
+ These include parents, peers, coaches and role models in the media.
+ Socialisation also plays an important part (see attitudes, p. 160).
+ Successful and reinforced behaviours are more likely to be imitated.
+ Performers are more likely to copy the behaviour/personality of those who share similar characteristics, such as gender, age and ability levels.

> **Significant others** People who performers hold in high esteem, including family, coaches, teachers, peers and role models in the media.
>
> **Socialisation** A lifelong process whereby members of a society learn its norms, values, ideas, practices and roles in order to take their place in that society.

157

For example, your tennis coach constantly praises your teammate for showing determination and controlled emotions during matches. You decide to copy their behaviour to gain the same reinforcement.

The opposing views of trait and social learning approaches give rise to the nature vs nurture debate – i.e. are we born with our personality traits (nature) or do we in fact learn them as we go (social learning/nurture)?

Now test yourself   TESTED ◯

1   What are the differences between the trait and social learning approaches?
2   According to the social learning perspective, when is personality more likely to be copied?

Answers on p. 268

Interactionist perspective   REVISED ◯

+ The interactionist perspective states that personality is made of traits plus the influence of what you have learned from your environmental experiences.
+ Trait and social learning approaches are both deemed relevant and are therefore combined.
+ We can predict personality and behaviour in a specific situation.
+ A performer will adapt to the situation they find themselves in, even behaving differently from how they normally would.

Lewin suggested that an individual's personality is produced when both their natural predispositions and the experiences they have combine in a specific situation. His equation to describe this is $B = f(P \times E)$, meaning behaviour is a function of an individual's personality traits and the environment.

For example, a generally introverted rhythmic gymnast is ordinarily reserved, but has learned to adapt when performing, and displays more assertive, extroverted characteristics during a competition to appeal to the judges.

Hollander suggested that there are three aspects to an individual's personality (Figure 6.1).

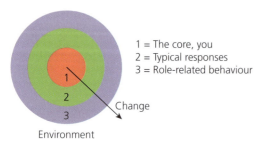

1 = The core, you
2 = Typical responses
3 = Role-related behaviour

Figure 6.1 The Hollander model

Hollander believed that personality could be represented by three concentric rings, with the innermost ring being the most difficult to penetrate.
1   The core is the real you and what your true beliefs and values are. It does not change – it is the stable aspects of your personality. Often this is kept hidden.
2   Typical responses describe how individuals usually respond.
3   Role-related behaviour is how an individual responds in a specific environment. This might be uncharacteristic behaviour. It is the most unstable aspect of your personality. It does not necessarily reflect the psychological core.

Now test yourself

TESTED ○

3   What is the equation used to describe the interactionist approach?
4   What are the three parts of Hollander's model?

Answers on p. 268

Making links

Trait, social learning and interactionist perspectives are also relevant to theories of leadership (p. 187) and aggression (p. 168).

Using the interactionist perspective to improve performance

+ If a coach understands their players' innate personalities and how they would 'normally' respond in specific situations, they can use this to their advantage – for example, understanding that a centre forward with an aggressive personality is likely to retaliate when fouled.
+ The coach might therefore substitute them if they observe that their level of aggression is increasing due to the centre back continually sliding in late. The coach can try to *adapt* the responses of this player by offering cognitive and somatic strategies (p. 170) to reduce their stress and therefore levels of aggression.
+ This might form part of training sessions in which demanding situations are created to generate a negative response from the player, who is then given the opportunity to use the strategies. In future, when they are fouled, they will respond differently from their instinctive response. The player has learned to act in a more controlled way.
+ If the player has a role of responsibility in the team, they will recognise that they are a role model and therefore cannot react angrily.

Revision activity

In pairs, have the nature versus nurture debate. Take an approach each – either trait or social learning.

Exam tip

Ensure that you use the correct terminology. Your example should relate specifically to personality – trait, social learning and interactionist perspectives are also seen in leadership and aggression, and therefore your example must be clear.

If the question asks for a practical example, you must give one.

Exam practice

1   With reference to the interactionist approach, explain why a rugby player might react differently when being high-tackled in two separate games.

Answer online

Knowledge and skills summary

This topic involves the following knowledge (AO1):
+ Explanations of the trait, social learning and interactionist perspectives of personality.

AO2 marks will require application of this knowledge – for example, applying the theoretical concept to a sporting

example. This can relate to a specific skill, performer or situation.

AO3 marks are for analysis or evaluation. In this topic an AO3 response might involve analysing the strengths/ weaknesses of trait or social learning perspectives, i.e. the nature versus nurture debate.

159

6.1.2 Attitudes

An attitude describes an individual's predisposition to believe, feel and act towards an attitude object. Attitude objects are the focus on which the attitude is directed, and can include other people, places, situations and items. Attitudes, while usually deep rooted, are not permanent and can be changed.

Attitude formation

REVISED

Attitudes can be positive or negative, and are developed through experiences rather than being innate. They often begin to develop at an early age, and can be formed by the following:

+ **Past experiences** – winning matches or titles, for example, is an enjoyable experience and can lead to the individual developing a positive attitude. As a result, the individual might develop a strong perception of their own ability, which increases their confidence. A bad experience, such as losing or being injured, might lead to a negative attitude. The performer might have low self-confidence and a poor perception of their ability. This might manifest itself in the performer developing a negative attitude towards physical activity as a whole. They might develop learned helplessness.

> **Learned helplessness**
> The feeling that failure is inevitable.

+ **Socialisation** – this describes how an individual wishes to fit in with the cultural norms surrounding them. If it is the norm for your friendship group or family to participate regularly and have positive attitudes towards physical activity, then you will conform to fit in. For example, they might all play for a team or attend the gym on a regular basis, and therefore you do the same because you do not want to feel left out. However, if it is the norm for your peers/family not to participate and to hold negative attitudes, you will adopt these to be consistent with the people around you.
+ **Social learning** – imitating the attitudes of significant others – for example, parents, teachers and peers. If your parents/friends have a positive attitude towards a particular sporting activity, it is likely that you will copy them, especially if you are reinforced or praised for doing so. Conversely, if they hold negative attitudes and your parents/friends abstain from participating, it is likely that you will copy the same attitude and behaviour.
+ **Media** – high-profile role models in the media often display positive attitudes and, as we regard them highly, we are likely to adopt their positive attitude towards being active.

The triadic model

REVISED

The **triadic model** suggests that an attitude is made up of three components. For example, an individual might show a positive attitude towards squash in the following way:

+ **Cognitive** – beliefs/thoughts – for example, 'I *believe/think* that I can be a successful squash player'.
+ **Affective** – emotions/feelings – for example, 'I *enjoy* playing squash and feel energised after each training session'.
+ **Behavioural** – actions/responses – for example, 'I *have 1–2–1 training twice a week and compete on the club's squash ladder*'.

Attitudes, however, are inconsistent. A performer might believe that attending the gym is good for them and really enjoy it when they go, but might not actually attend due to lack of time or motivation. Beliefs do not always correspond with behaviour, and sometimes all three aspects of a person's attitude might be negative.

Now test yourself   TESTED

5 How would a performer demonstrate a positive attitude towards pre-season training?

6 What are the three components of the triadic model?

Answers on pp. 268–269

Changing attitudes   REVISED

It is important to be able to change the negative attitude of an individual. Some general strategies include:

+ ensuring **positive, successful experiences**
+ **praising** positive attitudes/behaviour
+ **punishing** negative attitudes/behaviour – for example, substitution/bans
+ using positive **role models** to highlight positive attitudes

Coaches might also try **persuasive communication**, particularly by significant others who encourage you to change your mind to take on board their more positive point of view. If you have a deep-seated, negative attitude, realistically you are only likely to want to change if a significant other or an expert is asking you to. They have to give a very clear message about why you should change your attitude, and you have to understand what they are saying. They might enlist the help of your peers to support their view. This strategy is very difficult to get right. Ultimately, the individual must *want* to change.

An alternative strategy is **cognitive dissonance**. When an individual's attitude components all match, whether positively or negatively, they are in a state of **cognitive consonance**. Their beliefs, feelings and actions are in harmony and the individual's attitude will remain. To change the attitude, you can create cognitive dissonance. Dissonance is caused by generating unease inside the individual. This unease is created by changing one or more of the negative attitude components into a positive, thus causing the individual to question their attitude and change it into a positive one.

Table 6.1 illustrates these ideas with the negative attitude of one individual towards attending the local gym. Using any of the strategies in the right-hand column can cause dissonance/unease and therefore instigate an attitude change.

Table 6.1 Changing attitudes

Strategy	Negative attitude	Change by:
Cognitive	I think that going to the gym is a waste of time	Educating – preferably by a significant other Highlight the idea that attending the gym can make you healthy – it creates muscle tone, improves appearance and reduces the risk of disease
Affective	I hate going to the gym	Ensuring a positive, varied experience Make it fun/enjoyable Ensure that they are successful
Behavioural	I do not go to the gym	Persuasive communication – preferably by an expert Praise them in order to reinforce their behaviour, so they continue to go to the gym

Revision activity

Find a picture of a sportsperson who, in your view, has demonstrated a negative attitude. Make a poster with their face in the middle and write down the cognitive, affective and behavioural ways this negative attitude was shown. In a different colour pen, write down how you would change their negative attitude, with reference to cognitive dissonance theory.

Knowledge and skills summary

This topic involves the following knowledge (AO1):
+ A definition of an attitude.
+ The components of the triadic model.

AO2 marks will require application of this knowledge – for example, applying practical examples to each of the three components of the triadic model demonstrating

either a positive or negative attitude, and explaining how persuasive communication and cognitive dissonance can be used to change attitudes.

AO3 marks are for analysis or evaluation. In this topic an AO3 response might involve analysing the effects of a negative attitude on participation.

6.1.3 Arousal

Theories of arousal

REVISED

Arousal is the level of somatic or cognitive stimulation that gets us ready to perform. Being aroused to the correct level and being motivated are important in sport.

Drive theory

+ As arousal increases, so does performance quality – linearly (Figure 6.2).
+ Performance (P) is a function of drive (D) multiplied by habit (H): $P = f(D \times H)$.
+ At high arousal, the performer reverts to their dominant response. This is a well-learned skill that the performer will use under competitive pressure.
+ If the performer is in the autonomous phase of learning, their dominant response is likely to be correct. Performance levels are therefore high.
+ If the performer is in the cognitive phase of learning, their dominant response is likely to be incorrect. Performance levels are therefore low.
+ This theory does not account for elite performers deteriorating under pressure.

Somatic Relating to the body.

Cognitive Relating to the mind.

Dominant response A well-learned skill that the performer will use under competitive pressure.

Exam tip

There are *three* graphs related to arousal. Students often confuse them, so revise each one thoroughly.

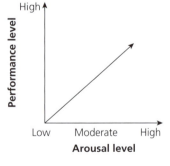

Figure 6.2 Drive theory

Inverted-U theory

This is a more practical theory because it accounts for how different performers, personality types and skills can be performed with equal amounts of success. However, it does not account for the dramatic decrease in performance seen by some elite performers once they have exceeded their optimum level of arousal.
+ As arousal increases, so does performance quality – up to an optimum point at moderate arousal (Figure 6.3).

162

Check your understanding and progress at **www.hoddereducation.co.uk/myrevisionnotes**

- After this, performance quality decreases as a result of over-arousal.
- Under- and over-arousal can both be detrimental to performance.

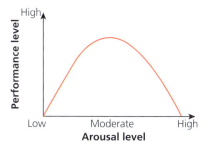

Figure 6.3 Inverted-U theory, showing how increased arousal affects performance

Inverted-U theory for performers and skills

Not all performers and skills operate efficiently at a moderate level of arousal. Some performers and skills cannot tolerate much arousal. Others might only perform at their best at higher levels.

Optimum performance occurs at *lower* levels of arousal (shown by the green curve in Figure 6.4) in situations involving:

- **novice/cognitive** performers
- **fine skills** that require a high level of precision and control
- **complex skills**, where several decisions are made
- introverts, who already have a high resting level of adrenaline

> **Introvert** A performer who is reserved and avoids social situations.

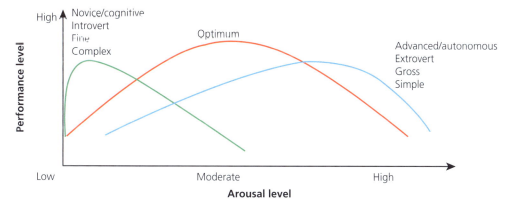

Figure 6.4 Adaptations to the inverted-U theory, showing how the task and the performer can affect the optimal level of arousal for best performance

This graph suggests that optimum performance occurs at *higher* levels of arousal in situations involving:

- **advanced/autonomous** performers
- **gross skills**, where precision and control are not needed
- **simple skills**, with few decisions to make
- extroverts, who have a low resting level of adrenaline and who strive for 'exciting' situations

> **Extrovert** A performer who is outgoing and likes social situations.

Now test yourself   TESTED ◯

7   What is the optimal level of arousal when performing a pistol shot?
8   What is the optimal level of arousal for a complex skill?
9   What is the optimal level of arousal for a simple skill?

Answers on p. 269

Catastrophe theory

This theory accounts for the sudden drop in performance once the optimum has been exceeded (Figure 6.5). It illustrates why there is a total 'catastrophe' for some performers, including the elite.

This theory is multidimensional. It considers the effects of both cognitive and somatic anxiety.

+ As arousal increases so does performance quality up to an optimum point at moderate arousal, as shown by the inverted-U theory.
+ There is then a dramatic decrease in performance as a result of high cognitive anxiety combined with high somatic anxiety.
+ The body and the mind have become over-aroused, causing an immediate and catastrophic decline in performance.
+ The effects can be reversed by performing relaxation techniques – for example, deep breathing exercises or progressive muscle relaxation.
+ The performer can then continue to play, providing they have reached a level of relaxation below the point of catastrophe.

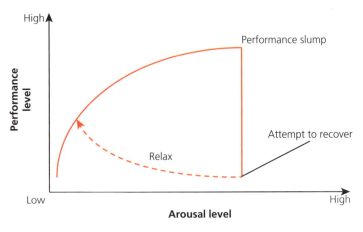

Figure 6.5 Catastrophe theory

Now test yourself   TESTED ◯

10 What causes a 'catastrophe' and what happens as a result?

Answer on p. 269

Hanin's zone of optimum functioning

The 'zone' is a mental state that autonomous performers normally only experience once or twice in their entire sporting career, when everything is 'perfect' (Figure 6.6). Characteristics of the zone include:

+ performing at optimum arousal levels
+ feeling completely calm
+ complete attentional control – fully concentrated on the task
+ performing on 'autopilot' – some performers have no memory of it
+ feeling completely confident that success is inevitable
+ performing smoothly, efficiently and effortlessly

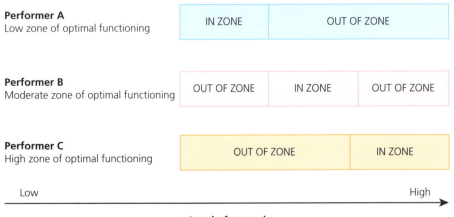

Figure 6.6 The zone of optimal functioning

Check your understanding and progress at **www.hoddereducation.co.uk/myrevisionnotes**

✚ A more recent theory by Hanin suggests that optimum performance is reached during a band or zone, not at a single point as described by the inverted-U theory.

✚ Performer A enters the zone, achieving best performance at low levels of arousal.

✚ Performer B is in the zone at moderate levels of arousal.

✚ Performer C enters the zone at high levels of arousal.

✚ Individuals have a variety of strategies to get them into the zone. These include somatic and cognitive strategies.

Peak flow experience

REVISED ⬤

Peak flow describes the ultimate positive psychological state for a performer. It is very rare and intense. The performer is fully concentrated on the task, has absolute control over their actions, which seem effortless, and might feel an 'out-of-body' experience that they have difficulty in remembering.

Peak flow happens to a performer when:
✚ the level of challenge they are presented with matches their skill level
✚ they have a clear goal
✚ they have the correct attentional style (see p. 192)
✚ they have a positive attitude before and during the performance
✚ they have control of their arousal levels

It is very difficult to achieve peak flow. If a performer is presented with a challenge that is perceived as too high for them, it will result in anxiety. For example, a novice skier attempting a black piste will undoubtedly feel nervous. If the task is too easy for their level of skill, they will become bored. For example, a club-level high jumper would find it very monotonous while their classmates were being taught the basics. An apathetic view would be taken by a performer who has a low skill level and is presented with an easy task.

To achieve peak flow, performers should be given a task that is realistic and yet challenges them at an appropriate level. They then enter the most rewarding psychological and physical state.

Now test yourself

TESTED ⬤

11 Give three characteristics of being in 'the zone'.

12 How will a performer feel if they achieve peak flow?

Answers on p. 269

Revision activity

This section is heavy on theory. Read the chapter out loud and record yourself using a voice recorder. Listen to it repeatedly.

Making links

This topic links with the classification of skills, personality types and stages of learning.

Exam practice

1 Explain how over-arousal can affect performance, with reference to catastrophe theory. [4]

Answer online

6.1.4 Anxiety

Anxiety affects performance negatively. It is caused by a performer's perception that their ability is not good enough.

> **Perception** How environmental information is judged, understood and interpreted by the performer.

Types of anxiety

REVISED

+ **Cognitive** anxiety – mental symptoms of anxiety – for example, worrying, irrational thoughts, confusion, learned helplessness.
+ **Somatic** anxiety – physiological symptoms of anxiety – for example, increased heart rate, blood pressure, increased sweat levels, muscle tension.
+ **Competitive trait** anxiety – the performer has a natural tendency to become anxious in all sporting situations. They have a genetic predisposition (trait anxiety) – for example, a skier thinks that they will fall when attempting to ski down any piste, regardless of whether it is black, red or blue.
+ **Competitive state** anxiety – the performer is only anxious in specific sporting situations and often in high-pressure moments. It can be caused by negative past experiences – for example, a footballer experiences worry and heightened blood pressure when taking a penalty because they have missed one before.

Causes of anxiety

Causes of anxiety include:
+ task importance (e.g. playing in a final)
+ losing/fear of failing
+ perceived inaccuracy of the official's decisions
+ being fouled
+ injury/fear of being injured
+ lack of self-confidence/efficacy
+ audience effects (e.g. an abusive crowd)
+ evaluation apprehension

Both cognitive and somatic anxiety often occur together in sport. To achieve maximal performance the athlete should experience *low* levels of *cognitive* anxiety. They should not be worried about performing. As described in the inverted-U theory, performers should have *moderate* levels of *somatic* anxiety because this produces the best performance. Low levels mean that the performer is not stimulated enough, while high levels mean there is an excessive level of adrenaline in the body, increasing the likelihood of the somatic symptoms occurring and therefore reducing performance levels.

Check your understanding and progress at **www.hoddereducation.co.uk/myrevisionnotes**

Measuring anxiety

Anxiety can be measured using questionnaires, observation and physiological methods, such as heart rate monitors and measuring sweat levels.

Questionnaires

+ Self-report questionnaires are often used to measure anxiety. Martens' **sport competition anxiety test** (SCAT) was devised specifically to measure anxiety in sporting situations. Performers answer statements rating their level of anxiousness. Coaches and psychologists can therefore evaluate which performers need help with managing anxiety.
+ The **state–trait anxiety inventory** (STAI) is a questionnaire test that distinguishes between specific state and trait anxiety. Performers score themselves on a scale of 1–4 in each of 40 questions, which measure feelings of nervousness, worry, apprehension and tension based on the performer's current feelings (state) and their general feelings (trait).
+ The **competitive state anxiety inventory-2** (CSAI-2) was developed to measure cognitive and somatic anxiety and self-confidence in competitive situations. Performers rate themselves on a four-point scale as to how they are feeling now in 27 statements. Usually this is given out on more than one occasion leading up to an event, i.e. in the week before, day before, then hour before, as this will indicate the level and type of anxiety experienced, and when.
+ Questionnaires are cheap and efficient. A lot of information can be gathered in a short period of time. However, the performer might not answer truthfully; they might not understand the question being asked; and the responses that are given can be affected by environmental factors – for example, the time of day the questionnaire is being completed.

Observation

Observation is a real-life method in which the performer's behaviour is analysed before, during and after play. However, it is very subjective. Each observer will perceive the situation differently. It is also time consuming. The observers will need to be aware of the performer's 'normal' anxiety levels so they can see the changes, if any, during competitive situations. Also, the performer will change their behaviour as soon as they realise they are being observed.

Physiological measures

Physiological measures generate factual data on somatic responses such as heart rate and blood pressure levels. These measures can be taken immediately during performance. However, they involve the performer wearing a monitor that might restrict their movements; the equipment could be expensive; and the performer realises they are being monitored, which will cause a physiological response and therefore an inaccurate reading.

> **Now test yourself** TESTED
>
> **15** What are the advantages and disadvantages of using observation as a way of measuring anxiety?
>
> **Answer on p. 269**

> **Revision activity**
>
> Try out each of the cognitive and somatic strategies.

6.1 Psychological factors that can influence an individual in physical activities

Knowledge and skills summary

This topic involves the following knowledge (AO1):
+ Definitions of somatic, cognitive, competitive trait and competitive state anxiety.
+ Descriptions of how anxiety is measured by questionnaires, observation and physiological testing.
+ The advantages and disadvantages of each method.

AO2 marks will require application of this knowledge – for example, practical examples of somatic, cognitive, competitive trait and competitive state anxiety.

AO3 marks are for analysis or evaluation. In this topic an AO3 response might involve an analysis of the methods used to measure anxiety.

6.1.5 Aggression

Aggression or assertion?

REVISED

Aggression is when an individual *purposefully* harms or injures their opponent. It is outside of the rules, hostile and reactive – for example, a rugby league player angrily punching an opponent when getting up to play the ball.

Assertion is often confused with aggression. This is when an individual plays hard, but within the rules, perhaps using more effort than usual, but there is no intention to harm the opposition. A very strong, quick bowl at the batter in cricket or a crunching but fair tackle in rugby union are both examples of assertive play.

There are many causes of aggression. These include:
+ playing badly
+ feeling that teammates are not trying
+ disagreement with officials' decisions
+ provocation by the opponent/crowd
+ importance of the game (e.g. semi-final/final)
+ local derby
+ religious/cultural reasons (e.g. Celtic 'versus' Rangers)
+ contact sport, and therefore expected (e.g. ice hockey or Gaelic football)
+ naturally aggressive personality
+ social learning
+ over-arousal

Aggression An emotional response (involving anger) to an individual perceived as an enemy or a frustrating rival; an intent to harm outside the laws of the game.

Assertion Hard but fair play. More effort than normal may be exerted, but there is no intention to harm.

Exam tip

Definitions of aggression and assertion are sometimes unclear – make sure you know the difference.

Exam tip

Make sure that you give a range of answers. For example, playing badly or losing might appear under the same mark scheme point and can only be credited once.

Theories of aggression

REVISED

Instinct theory
+ Humans have a natural trait or predisposition to be aggressive.
+ It is genetically determined/we are born with it.
+ We have a natural tendency to defend ourselves and, in sport, our territory.
+ Instinct theorists believe that, inevitably, aggression builds up within us.
+ With enough provocation we will react aggressively.
+ Once the aggressive act occurs, there is a **cathartic** effect.
+ Aggression is released, and we feel calmer.

Catharsis The release of emotions, including aggression.

168

This theory has the following drawbacks:

+ It does not consider the effect of environmental/social learning on aggression.
+ Individuals often experience increased aggression during sporting competition, rather than it having a cathartic effect.
+ The instinct approach suggests that, as humans, we are all genetically determined to behave aggressively. This is not true. Some people never act aggressively.

Now test yourself TESTED ◯

16 What is catharsis?

Answer on p. 269

Frustration–aggression hypothesis

+ A performer has a drive to achieve a goal.
+ If stopped from achieving that goal, they experience frustration.
+ Frustration always leads to an aggressive response.
+ If the aggressive act is successful, catharsis occurs.
+ Frustration and aggression are reduced.
+ If aggression is not released, frustration builds.
+ This results in further aggression.

For example, a basketball player is dribbling and running towards the basket. They are fouled and their goal has been blocked. They feel frustrated, which leads them to push their opponent. This will have a cathartic effect, reducing frustration and aggression. However, if they are then unable to release their aggression due to the presence of the officials, more frustration builds, and the performer is likely to retaliate at a later point in the match.

This theory does not account for:

+ performers who experience frustration and aggression even when goals have not been blocked
+ performers who have their goals blocked and experience frustration but do not react aggressively

Aggressive cue hypothesis (Berkowitz)

Berkowitz updated the frustration–aggression hypothesis as follows:

+ When a goal is blocked, arousal levels increase.
+ The performer experiences frustration.
+ This leads to them being *ready* for an aggressive act, rather than aggression being inevitable.
+ An aggressive act will only happen if learned **cues** or triggers are present.

For example, aggressive objects such as bats and clubs or aggressive contact sports such as rugby and ice hockey are more likely to produce aggressive responses. A footballer who has been praised by their coach for aggressive, dangerous tackles might learn that this is a positive behaviour, and the coach acts as a cue to be aggressive in future matches.

Social learning theory

+ This theory opposes the trait approach to aggression, and is based on the work of Bandura.
+ Aggression is learned by watching and copying the behaviour of **significant others**.
+ If an aggressive act is reinforced or is successful, it is more likely to be copied.
+ Aggression is more likely to be copied if the model shares similar characteristics with the performer.
+ Performers might also become aggressive due to **socialisation**.

For example:

+ A young rugby player watches their idol high tackle an opponent. The crowd cheers and the opponent is prevented from scoring a try. As this aggressive act is reinforced and successful, the young player copies this behaviour in their next match.
+ A footballer observes many teammates shouting abuse and acting aggressively towards the referee as they disagree with a penalty call. The individual joins in to fit in with the teammates.

This theory does not take into account any genetic explanations as to why aggression might happen. For example, it will discount the trait approach even though studies have shown that there might be an aggressive/angry gene in humans.

> **Now test yourself** TESTED ⬤
>
> 17 According to the aggressive cue hypothesis, when will an aggressive act occur?
>
> **Answer on p. 269**

Strategies to control aggression REVISED ⬤

Players can use cognitive and somatic techniques. Cognitive techniques (p. 191) include:

+ mental rehearsal
+ imagery
+ visualisation
+ selective attention
+ negative thought-stopping
+ positive self-talk

Somatic techniques (p. 191) include:

+ relaxation techniques
+ deep breathing
+ biofeedback
+ counting to ten
+ walking away
+ mantra
+ displacing/channelling aggressive feelings by playing hard (e.g. kicking the ball harder)

Coaches can:

+ praise non-aggressive acts
+ highlight non-aggressive role models
+ punish aggression (e.g. substitution/fines)
+ use peer pressure to remind each other that aggression is unacceptable
+ set process and performance goals rather than product goals
+ ensure their own behaviour is not aggressive
+ give the performer responsibility within the team
+ ensure the performer understands their specific role

> **Now test yourself** TESTED ⬤
>
> 18 Name three cognitive and three somatic strategies to combat aggression.
>
> **Answer on p. 269**

> **Revision activity**
>
> Take an A3 sheet of paper, divide it into four and in each quadrant make a bullet point list for each of the four main theories of aggression.

> **Exam practice**
>
> 1 What strategies can a coach use to eliminate aggressive actions? [5]
>
> **Answer online**

Check your understanding and progress at **www.hoddereducation.co.uk/myrevisionnotes**

6.1.6 Motivation

Motivation is an individual's *drive* that inspires them to perform in sport.

> **Motivation** The drive/desire/need to achieve a goal.

Types of motivation

REVISED

Extrinsic motivation

Extrinsic motivation is anything received from an outside source. It could be tangible, such as money, trophies or medals, or intangible, such as praise from the coach or crowd.

This type of motivation attracts performers to the sport to begin with, and is therefore a useful strategy for cognitive performers. It raises their confidence and increases participation.

However, this should be used sparingly, especially with young performers, as they might begin to only perform for the rewards – losing enjoyment and the satisfaction gained from performing. Ultimately, for these performers, withdrawing extrinsic rewards can lead to total withdrawal from participation.

Intrinsic motivation

This comes from the performers themselves. They participate for the 'love' of the sport, self-satisfaction and the pride of achieving their own goals. Developing their health and fitness might be the driving factor. This could be someone learning to somersault on a trampoline, for their own gratification, or a javelin thrower attempting to throw a personal best.

This type of motivation will maintain participation for a longer period of time than extrinsic motivational methods. Therefore coaches should try to encourage performers to set personal goals and try to generate intrinsic motivation whenever possible.

Make sure you use the correct terminology – intrinsic and extrinsic not internal and external.

> **Exam tip**
>
> Ensure that you can describe each type of motivation and give clear examples.

Now test yourself

TESTED

19 What is the difference between extrinsic and intrinsic motivation?
20 Give two examples of extrinsic motivation and two examples of intrinsic motivation.

Answers on p. 269

Motivational strategies

REVISED

A range of strategies should be used to maintain drive in all performers:
+ Tangible, extrinsic rewards will initially attract them, and should be given periodically – for example, certificates, medals, player of the match award.
+ Intangible extrinsic rewards will increase the confidence of the performer – for example, praise, positive reinforcement.

171

- Make the activity fun/enjoyable.
- Set easily achievable tasks to ensure success.
- Use positive role models/significant others that they can identify with, to help motivate.
- Highlight the health and fitness benefits of participation.
- Use variable practice.
- Generate intrinsic motivation through performance goals – for example, beating a PB time in 100 metres.
- Continually set new, challenging goals, just within their reach.
- Punish lack of motivation.
- Use peer group pressure.

Exam practice

1 Which of the following is an example of intrinsic motivation? [1]
  A Receiving a trophy for being voted 'players' player'.
  B Praise from your coach for having an excellent serving technique.
  C Pride in achieving a personal best in the long jump.
  D Receiving money for winning a golf tournament.

2 Evaluate the effectiveness of intrinsic motivation. [4]

Answers online

Knowledge and skills summary

This topic involves the following knowledge (AO1):
- Definitions of intrinisic, extrinsic, tangible and intangible motivation.

AO2 marks will require application of this knowledge – for example, practical examples of each type of motivation or suggesting which types of motivation are relevant to performers in the three stages of learning.

AO3 marks are for analysis or evaluation. In this topic an AO3 response might ask you to evaluate the various types of motivation, giving advantages and disadvantages.

6.1.7 Achievement motivation theory

Atkinson's model

REVISED ◯

Atkinson suggested that in demanding situations performers will exhibit either need to achieve (**NACH**) or need to avoid failure (**NAF**) characteristics (Table 6.2). This is based on both their personality and the situational factors in hand. It can be defined as *the drive to succeed minus the fear of failure*.

Avoidance behaviour
Steering clear of situations where evaluation might take place, i.e. competitive situations.

Approach behaviour
Having the competitive drive to persist and achieve success.

Table 6.2 NACH and NAF characteristics

NACH performer	NAF performer
+ Exhibits **approach behaviour**	+ Exhibits **avoidance behaviour**
+ Has high self-efficacy/confidence	+ Has low self-efficacy/confidence
+ Enjoys competition and challenges	+ Dislikes competition and challenges
+ Will take risks	+ Will take the easy option
+ Sticks with the task until it is complete	+ Gives in easily, especially if failing
+ Regards failure as a step to success	+ Does not welcome feedback
+ Welcomes feedback as they use it to improve	+ Might experience learned helplessness
+ Takes personal responsibility for the outcome	+ Attributes failure internally (see attribution, pp. 182–183)
+ Attributes success internally (see attribution, pp. 182–183)	+ Dislikes performing in front of an audience
+ Likes an audience when performing	

Situational characteristics:	Situational characteristics:

+ Very competitive – likes tasks with:
   + a low probability of success, i.e. a challenging task
   + a high incentive, i.e. will be extremely proud to have achieved their goal
	+ Is not competitive – likes tasks with:
	   + a high probability of success, i.e. an easy task
	   + a low incentive, i.e. little satisfaction in achieving their goal

Example: a snowboarder decides to take the risky black run rather than the easier blue run down the mountain, knowing that they are likely to fall over, but sees it as a challenge	*Example*: a mid-table squash player prefers to play opponents from the bottom of the table rather than those closer in ranking, as then they are more likely to win

Now test yourself

TESTED ◯

21 What types of competitive situation would a NACH performer prefer?

22 Give three characteristics of a performer who has a need to avoid failure.

Answers on p. 269

Achievement goal theory

REVISED ◯

This theory suggests that every performer will have their own perception of what achievement means to them and what being successful looks like. In specific situations or tasks, individuals can set either outcome-oriented goals or task-oriented goals.

Outcome-oriented goals are set with the specific aim to beat and show superiority over others – for example, to win a 5000 metres race. If a performer continually achieves their goal, then motivation and confidence will be high. However, it is unrealistic to expect victory in every sporting encounter and therefore being defeated might reduce confidence.

Task-oriented goals do not seek to show a person's ability against others. The aim is to master a skill or to improve on your own performance. The process is more important than the outcome – for example, to master a somersault on the trampoline or achieve a personal best distance in the hammer throw. Regardless of the result in the hammer competition, the task-oriented goal can be achieved.

To generate approach behaviours:
+ Ensure success by setting achievable goals.
+ Raise confidence by giving positive reinforcement, praise and rewards.
+ Highlight successful role models who have comparable characteristics.
+ Credit internal reasons (e.g. ability, for success).

Revision activity

Create two mind maps – one for NACH and one for NAF. Include personality and situational characteristics.

Exam practice

1 What are the personality characteristics of a performer with a need to avoid failure (NAF) profile? How would a coach develop a need to achieve (NACH) attitude in this performer?   [6]

Answer online

Knowledge and skills summary

This topic involves the following knowledge (AO1):
+ The personality and situational characteristics of NACH and NAF performers.
+ Incentive value and probability of success.
+ The different types of goal in relation to achievement goal theory.

AO2 marks will require application of this knowledge – for example, giving practical examples of each of the above and also of incentive value and probability of success, and suggesting ways to increase approach behaviour in performers.

AO3 marks are for analysis or evaluation. In this topic an AO3 response might require you to analyse why players might have responded differently in different situations – that is, why some exhibit NACH characteristics and some exhibit NAF characteristics.

6.1.8 Social facilitation

Social facilitation and inhibition

Performers react differently to being observed while participating. Some enjoy performing with an audience and as a result their performance improves. This is known as social facilitation and might well motivate performers. However, some dislike performing with an audience and their performance worsens when being observed. This is known as social inhibition. These performers might find it stressful to perform with an audience, and many lose motivation because they cannot deal with the pressure.

Zajonc's model

Zajonc suggested that four types of 'others' might be present during performance (Figure 6.7).

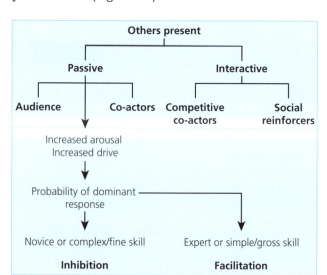

Figure 6.7 The Zajonc model

Passive others

Passive others do not interact with the performer, but have an effect simply by being present. These include the following:

+ **Audience** – do not speak, but just watch – for example, a television audience/silent observers during a tee-off in golf; a scout turning up unannounced to observe you performing. Their mere presence might make you feel anxious and can affect your performance.
+ **Co-actors** – perform the same task at the same time, but are not competing against you – for example, seeing another cyclist in front of you makes you speed up to overtake them. Although you win nothing by doing so, their presence has made you cycle faster.

Interactive others

Interactive others communicate directly with the performer and include the following:

+ **Competitive co-actors** – the opposition – for example, other swimmers in a race who are in direct rivalry with the performer.
+ **Social reinforcers** – the coach/crowd – for example, the spectators at a football match cheer and applaud, but might also shout abuse at performers. They give you the motivation to improve.

Audience effects

Even when passive others such as an audience are present, the main effect on the performer is that they will experience increased arousal levels.

> **Social facilitation** The positive effects experienced by a performer while in the presence of an audience.
>
> **Social inhibition** The negative effects experienced by a performer while in the presence of an audience.

Check your understanding and progress at **www.hoddereducation.co.uk/myrevisionnotes**

The presence of an audience has the same varied effects on performance depending on the skill classification and the performer's level of experience.

Performance will be *facilitated* if:

+ the performer is an **expert**, because they are used to performing in front of an audience
+ they are performing a **simple skill**, which requires limited decision making/information processing
+ they are performing a **gross skill** of large muscle group movements that does not require precision/accuracy

In the above circumstances, the performer will be able to cope with the additional arousal caused by the presence of the audience, and their performance will improve.

However, performance will be *inhibited* if:

+ the performer is a **novice**, because they find performing in front of an audience intimidating
+ they are performing a **complex skill**, because this requires several decisions to be made and a lot of information processing, which might not be performed successfully at high arousal
+ they are performing a **fine skill**, because it requires precision and accuracy, which is difficult to maintain at high arousal

In the above circumstances, the performer cannot cope with the extra arousal, which means their performance will deteriorate.

> **Now test yourself**   TESTED ◯
>
> 23 According to Zajonc, what are the four types of 'others'?
> 24 According to Zajonc, what effect would an audience have on a cognitive performer?
>
> **Answers on p. 269**

> **Making links**
>
> This section links to the classification of skills (pp. 47–48) and stages of learning (p. 55).

Dominant response

Drive theory (p. 162) explains the linear relationship between drive and performance. There is a strong link between drive theory and Zajonc's model. At heightened levels of arousal, performers revert to their **dominant response**. This is a well-learned skill that the performer will use when under competitive pressure. If the performer is an expert, they will have overlearned motor programmes stored in their long-term memory and their dominant response is likely to be performed correctly. Therefore, performance will be facilitated. As described earlier, if the response is gross or simple, it will be enhanced.

However, if the performer is a novice, they have not yet grooved their responses. By being under competitive pressure and in the presence of an audience, their performance will be inhibited. Fine or complex skills will deteriorate.

Evaluation apprehension   REVISED ◯

Evaluation apprehension is the fear of being judged. The performer might not be being judged, but if they *perceive* that they are then this will have an effect on their performance. Other factors causing evaluation apprehension include the following:

+ If the audience is **knowledgeable** you will be increasingly nervous – for example, if a scout is watching.
+ If **significant others**, such as parents/peers, are present – positive and negative effects are seen based on the task/performers, as described above.
+ If the audience is **supportive/abusive**, performance will be facilitated/inhibited.
+ If the performer naturally has **high trait anxiety** (p. 166), they will be inhibited by an audience.
+ If the performer has **low self-efficacy** (p. 185) they don't believe in their ability and will be inhibited.

Strategies to combat social inhibition

REVISED

+ Familiarisation training – allow an audience to watch you training/play crowd noise during training.
+ Increase self-efficacy.
+ Practise skills until they are grooved.
+ Use selective attention to improve focus/concentration – block out the crowd and concentrate on the relevant stimuli, such as the ball/opposition.

Use other cognitive strategies such as:
+ mental rehearsal – going over the performance in your mind will maintain focus and lower arousal levels
+ imagery
+ positive self-talk
+ negative thought-stopping

In addition, the coach could:
+ decrease the importance of the task
+ offer encouragement, positive reinforcement and praise to the performer to support them
+ slowly introduce evaluation in training

Now test yourself

TESTED

25 Give two cognitive and two somatic strategies to combat social inhibition.

Answer on p. 269

Making links

This section links to classification of skills (pp. 47–48), stages of learning (p. 55) and stress management (p. 190).

Exam practice

1 What strategies can a performer use to combat the effects of social inhibition? [5]

Answer online

Knowledge and skills summary

This topic involves the following knowledge (AO1):
+ All parts of Zajonc's model.
+ Definition of evaluation apprehension.
+ Strategies to combat social inhibition.

AO2 marks will require application of this knowledge – for example, giving practical examples of passive others and interactive others, suggesting causes of evaluation apprehension, and explaining how a range of strategies could eliminate the adverse effects of social facilitation and social inhibition.

AO3 marks are for analysis or evaluation. In this topic an AO3 response might require you to analyse the impact of the presence of an audience.

Check your understanding and progress at **www.hoddereducation.co.uk/myrevisionnotes**

6.1.9 Group dynamics

Group formation

REVISED

A group is two or more people who:
+ **interact** with each other, i.e. they communicate
+ share a **common goal**, i.e. they have the same aim
+ have **mutual awareness**, i.e. they influence and depend on each other
+ have a **collective identity**, e.g. a specific kit that makes them feel that they belong

Tuckman's model

Tuckman suggested that there are four stages that a group goes through in order to begin working together effectively (Table 6.3). The time it takes per team will vary depending on the experience of the players and the size of the group.

Table 6.3 Tuckman's model

1 Forming	2 Storming	3 Norming	4 Performing
+ Group members initially get together + Roles and responsibilities are unclear + Members start to work together + Members decide if they fit in with the team	+ Many teams fail at this stage because there is conflict + Relationships can be strained + Competition for positions/roles + Boundaries are pushed – positions of authority are challenged + Goal is unclear or questioned	+ Conflicts are resolved + Goal is clarified + Greater commitment to achieving goal + Authority figures respected + Appreciation of teammates' strengths + Group cohesion develops – both task and social	+ Players interact effectively + Full commitment to achieving team goals + Individual roles and responsibilities are completely understood

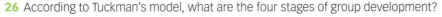

Now test yourself

TESTED

26 According to Tuckman's model, what are the four stages of group development?

27 What are the components of a group?

Answers on pp. 269–270

Cohesion

REVISED

A cohesive team has unity and a structure, and all members pull together to reach their shared aim. The more cohesive a team is, the more successful it will be, and the more successful the team is, the more cohesive it becomes.

There are two types of cohesiveness shown within a group. The most effective groups show both:
+ **Task cohesion** – group members work in unity to meet a common aim. They might not socialise away from the team and might not share views. However, to achieve their potential in the sporting arena they come together and can get good results. This is important in interactive sports, for example football and volleyball, where the team members must cooperate, work together and rely on each other's timing and coordination to achieve.
+ **Social cohesion** – group members get along and feel attached to others. They communicate and support each other in and outside of the sporting arena. This is important in more coactive sports, where you perform individually but your effort contributes to the whole team's performance, such as the Davis Cup in tennis or in a swimming team.

Task and social cohesion are reasons for being attracted to the group. Perhaps the other members share your goal of wanting to win, but also your friends might be part of the team, which also makes you want to join. Also, you *integrate* within the group to work effectively with others to achieve your goal and to attempt to get along socially with the other members.

Carron suggested that there are four factors or antecedents that affect task and social cohesion (Figure 6.8). These factors can bring a team together, making the team more effective, stable and satisfied. They include the following:

+ **Personal** – the level of motivation shown, how satisfied you feel within the group and if you share individual characteristics such as age, gender or ability.
+ **Environmental** – whether a player has a contract or scholarship; their location or age, and the size of the group.
+ **Leadership** – the leadership style, and the relationships between the leader and group members.
+ **Team** – the stability of the group, common experiences in victory and defeat, and a common will to win.

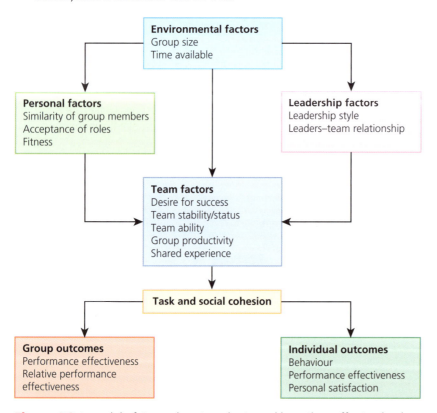

Figure 6.8 A model of Carron's antecedents and how they affect cohesion

Now test yourself　　　　　　　　　　　　　　TESTED ⬤

28 What are task cohesion and social cohesion?

29 List Carron's antecedents.

Answers on p. 270

Revision activity

Use the mnemonic 'PELT' to help you remember Carron's antecedents.

Steiner's model of group performance

 REVISED ⬤

Steiner proposed that the results of group effort could be based on an equation that sums up the influences on cohesion:

> actual productivity = potential productivity – losses due to faulty processes

+ **Actual productivity** – the team's level of achievement on a specific task – for example, a netball team reaching the semi-final of a cup competition.

Check your understanding and progress at **www.hoddereducation.co.uk/myrevisionnotes**

- **Potential productivity** – the team's best possible level of achievement when it is cohesive – for example, 'the netball team could have won the cup competition'.
- **Losses due to faulty processes** – the things that go wrong, including the coordination and motivation problems the team faces. These losses reduce the level of cohesion and therefore lower the actual productivity. For example, 'the arousal and motivation levels of some team members were lower than expected and therefore we did not reach/win the cup final'.

Steiner suggested that teams face many problems that affect their productivity, including:
- coordination problems, such as team members failing to communicate properly with each other, resulting in poor timing and set plays breaking down
- a lack of understanding of their role in the team
- a lack of understanding of tactics or strategies set by the coach
- the Ringelmann effect
- motivation losses, such as team members withdrawing effort when training and/or playing
- social loafing

The Ringelmann effect

REVISED

- The Ringelmann effect and social loafing are both faulty processes that have a detrimental effect on the cohesiveness and attainment of a team.
- The Ringelmann effect was suggested after a tug-of-war experiment showed that eight participants failed to pull eight times as hard as a single participant. Ringelmann's study therefore found that as the number of people in the group increases, so the level of performance of each individual in the group decreases.
- For example, a rugby union player performs much better when playing in a seven-a-side tournament than when playing in a full 15-a-side game.
- It was suggested that the reduction in performance in the tug-of-war was due to the lack of coordination, i.e. they were not all pulling on the rope in unison. However, follow-up studies showed that it might be due to a reduction in motivation rather than a loss of coordination.

Social loafing

REVISED

Social loafing is when a performer lowers the level of effort they contribute to the team. This happens when they believe that they are not a valued member of the group and their input is not noticed, so they stop trying. If the coach does not praise you when you feel you have played well, you will eventually give up. Other factors that might cause performers to loaf include the following:
- No clear role within the group – for example, being unsure of their position within the team.
- Low self-efficacy/confidence – for example, believing that they are not good enough. They might be experiencing learned helplessness.
- Their teammates are not trying, so they also stop putting in effort – for example, the winger fails to chase a ball that goes into touch, so you think 'why should I bother?'.
- The coach and/or captain are poor leaders. They do not encourage the performers and/or use weak strategies.
- Experiencing high levels of trait/state anxiety.
- Carrying an injury – for example, the performer twisted an ankle in training, and therefore decides not to bother reaching to return wide serves in tennis.
- Experiencing social inhibition as a result of an offensive crowd.

Strategies to enhance team performance

By raising cohesiveness, making individuals feel valued, and reducing faulty processes – for example, social loafing within a team – the coach can improve individual and whole-team performance. Methods include the following:

+ Highlighting individual performances – for example, giving statistics (shots on target, tackles, assists etc.).
+ Giving specific roles/responsibilities within the team.
+ Developing social cohesion – for example, team-building exercises, tours, or encouraging friendship.
+ Praising/rewarding cohesive behaviour – for example, giving encouragement when they work as a team.
+ Raising individuals' confidence levels.
+ Encouraging group identity – for example, having a set kit.
+ Effective leadership that matches the preferred style of the group.
+ Selecting players who work well together rather than individual 'stars'.
+ Setting achievable process/performance goals rather than product team goals.
+ Continually emphasising the team goal.
+ Selecting players who are less likely to exhibit social loafing.
+ Punishing social loafing.
+ Grooving set plays/completing many sessions of coordination practice.
+ Training with an audience present.

Now test yourself
TESTED

30 What is Steiner's model of group productivity?

31 What are faulty processes?

Answers on p. 270

Revision activity

Complete Table 6.4.

Table 6.4

Reason for social loafing	Strategy to overcome
	Coach ensures everyone understands their position and responsibilities
Injured	
	Remind them of past successes and praise them
Experiencing social inhibition	
	Performer tries mental rehearsals and breathing control

Exam practice

1 What is social loafing? Suggest reasons why some performers might experience this. [5]

Answer online

Knowledge and skills summary

This topic involves the following knowledge (AO1):

+ Giving a definition of a group or team.
+ Describing Steiner's model, Tuckman's model, the Ringelmann effect and social loafing.
+ Causes of the Ringelmann effect and social loafing, and what a coach can do to try to eliminate these from happening.

AO2 marks will require application of this knowledge – for example, giving practical examples of each of the above, describing the components of a cohesive team and giving strategies to increase cohesion.

AO3 marks are for analysis or evaluation. In this topic an AO3 response might require you to evaluate the effectiveness of a team or analyse the faulty processes that a team might experience.

Check your understanding and progress at **www.hoddereducation.co.uk/myrevisionnotes**

6.1.10 Importance of goal setting

Psychological research has shown that setting goals has a positive effect on performance. Generally, performers who set goals are more committed, maintain participation and are more task persistent.

Benefits of types of goal setting

REVISED

The benefits of setting goals (Figure 6.9) include:

+ giving the performer an aim or focus
+ increasing motivation when the goal is accomplished
+ increasing confidence levels
+ controlling arousal/anxiety levels
+ focusing efforts in training and game situations

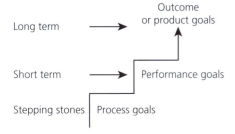

Figure 6.9 Goal-setting summary

+ **Task-oriented goals** do not seek to show a person's ability against others. The aim is to master a skill or to improve on your own performance. The process is more important than the outcome – for example, to achieve a personal best time in a 10 km race. Regardless of the place the performer comes in the race, their goal can be achieved.
+ **Process goals** are relatively short-term goals set to improve technique. For example, a speed skater aims to improve their cross-over technique.
+ **Performance goals** are intermediate goals, often set against yourself to improve performance from last time – for example, to get a faster time than in the last competition.
+ **Outcome (product) goals** are long-term goals reached after extensive work (Figure 6.9). They are often set against others and are based on the outcome – for example, to win the short-track junior championships.

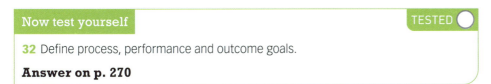

Now test yourself

TESTED

32 Define process, performance and outcome goals.

Answer on p. 270

Principles of effective goal setting

REVISED

When setting goals, the SMARTER principle should be followed (Table 6.5).

Table 6.5 The SMARTER principle

	Explanation	Example
Specific	The goal must be clear and exact; it should reflect a performer's individual playing position or event	A full-back in rugby aims to improve the number of high ball catches successfully completed in the 22-metre area by 5%
Measurable	The goal must be quantifiable so that progress can be assessed	A GA in netball aims to achieve an 80% shot success rate
Achievable	The performer must be able to achieve their goal within the time frame set	You and your coach both decide to reduce your 400 m time by 2 seconds

Table 6.5 continued

	Explanation	Example
Realistic	The goal must be within the performer's reach from where they are now to ensure sustained effort and motivation; if the target set is insurmountable, it might cause distress/anxiety	Aim to run 10 km in under 55 minutes in the road race in 12 months' time
Time phased	A set period must be stated clearly in order for progress to be tracked and to sustain motivation	Perform a PB time in the 100 m freestyle by the end of next month
Evaluate	The performer and coach should gauge whether or not the goal was achieved and the reasons for any progress made – positive or negative; the effective strategies can then be used when setting future goals	Coach and performer check times and realise that the performer did not manage to reduce their PB 100 m time by 0.5 seconds within the given time frame; the coach realises that more time should have been allocated to improving the sprint start
Re-do	The performer should repeat their efforts for any goals that have not been met; following the evaluation the coach and/or performer might decide to adjust the goal to ensure success	The performer and coach decide to adjust the goal to reduce their PB 100 m time by 0.3 seconds, and will spend more training time focused on the sprint start

Revision activity

Using each component of the SMARTER principle, set goals in your sport.

Making links

Understand that goal setting is an important part of mental preparation, and is important in developing confidence, concentration and emotional control.

Exam tip

You should appreciate that goals do not always have to be 'to win', as this might cause stress on the performer.

Exam practice

1 What are the benefits of goal setting? [4]

Answer online

Knowledge and skills summary

This topic involves the following knowledge (AO1):
+ Describing the types of goal and the SMARTER principle.

AO2 marks will require application of this knowledge – for example, giving practical examples of the different types of goal.

AO3 marks are for analysis or evaluation. In this topic an AO3 response might require you to evaluate the effectiveness of setting the various types of goal.

6.1.11 Attribution theory

Weiner's model

REVISED

Attribution theory tells us how individuals explain their behaviour. In a sporting context, performers use attributions to offer reasons for when they win or play well, or reasons for why they lose or play badly.

Weiner suggested that four key attributions lie on two dimensions (Figure 6.10).

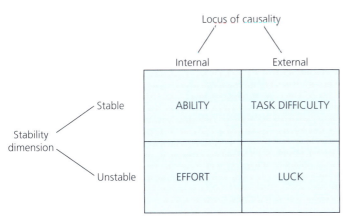

Figure 6.10 Weiner model of attribution

* The locus of causality describes where the performer places the reason for the win/loss:
  * **Internal** – within the performer's control – for example, the amount of *natural ability* they possess or the amount of *effort* they put in to training.
  * **External** – out of the performer's control and under the control of the environment – for example, the *task difficulty* is the level of opposition they face; or *luck*, which relates to the decisions made by the officials or environmental factors, such as an unlucky ball bounce.
* The stability dimension describes how fixed the attributions are:
  * **Stable** – the reason is relatively permanent – for example, the *ability* (internal, stable) of the performer remains the same over a long period of time, as does the *task difficulty* (external, stable), which is the ability of the opposition.
  * **Unstable** or **very changeable** – this change could be from week to week or even within minutes in a fixture – for example, the *effort* (internal, unstable) shown to chase down a ball might be higher when winning at the beginning of the match than the effort shown towards the end of the same match when losing. *Luck* (external, unstable) is also very changeable – for example, the tennis ball hitting the top of the net and bouncing either on your side or the opposition's side is down to luck.

> **Locus of causality** Where the performer places the reason for winning or losing. Can be internal or external.
>
> **Stability dimension** How fixed the attributions are. Stable attributions are relatively permanent, whereas unstable attributions are highly changeable.

Now test yourself — TESTED ◯

33 Describe the locus of causality and the stability dimension.

Answer on p. 270

Link between attribution, task persistence and motivation

REVISED ◯

* Attributions can be used to ensure that even when individuals or teams lose, they keep trying to improve and do not just give up.
* The locus of causality tells us that we have control of, for example, effort, and therefore if we put more effort into training sessions we might well be victorious in the future.
* Similarly, if we attribute success to high ability or to the amount of effort we put into a match, then we might well achieve success in a similar task in the future.
* In addition, the stability dimension tells us that things can change – for example, a 50/50 decision went against us today, but in future fixtures, with a different official, the decision could go the other way.
* Attributing in this way can help performers to understand the need to practise, persevere and stay motivated – to be task persistent.

Performers and coaches should attribute the reasons for winning internally to ability and effort (rather than externally to luck), and failure should be attributed externally rather than internally to ability. This is known as self-serving bias. This will raise self-efficacy and self-esteem, and increase the likelihood of an individual continuing to participate.

Self-serving bias
Attributing the reason for winning internally and for failure externally.

Learned helplessness

REVISED

Learned helplessness develops when performers attribute failure internally to stable reasons – for example, I lost the swimming race as I simply haven't got the stamina (ability). They believe that no matter what they do or how hard they try, they are destined to fail and therefore are not persistent. This can be either *general*, relating to all sports (for example, I cannot play any sport) or *specific*, relating to one skill in sport (for example, I can't take penalty flicks in hockey as I will miss) or to a single sport (for example, I cannot play badminton). This usually occurs when performers have low self-confidence due to past failings and so they completely withdraw their effort and stop participating. It might be due to having unrealistic goals set by the coach. Learned helpless performers share similar characteristics with NAF performers and if their attributions remain unchanged, it is likely that they will not participate in sporting activity, as they have such low self-esteem relating to sport.

Learned helplessness
A performer's belief that failure is inevitable.

Now test yourself

TESTED

34 What are the causes of learned helplessness?

Answer on p. 270

Strategies to avoid learned helplessness

To reduce the effects of learned helplessness, the performer should change their negative attributions into positive ones. This process is known as **attribution retraining**. The performer's perception of why they have failed is altered – they now routinely attribute success to external factors, such as luck, or to controllable factors such as effort, which they know they can improve on. Success is attributed internally to ability; the performer knows that they have what is necessary to repeat the victory in the future.

In addition to this, the coach can:

+ set realistic/achievable process and/or performance goals
+ raise self-efficacy by using Bandura's model
+ highlight previous quality performances
+ give positive reinforcement and encouragement

Revision activity

Make a list of the reasons why you have won/ lost fixtures before. Use Weiner's model and categorise them as ability, effort, task difficulty or luck.

Exam practice

1 What is learned helplessness, and what can a coach do to combat the effects of it? [5]

Answer online

Knowledge and skills summary

This topic involves the following knowledge (AO1):

+ Labelling and describing all aspects of Weiner's model.
+ Explaining the locus of causality and the stability dimension.
+ Explaining the link between the attributions given by a performer, how task persistent they are and their level of motivation.

AO2 marks will require application of this knowledge – for example, giving practical examples of each aspect of

Weiner's model and self-serving bias, general and specific learned helplessness, and attributional retraining, and describing the strategies coaches can employ to avoid learned helplessness in their performers.

AO3 marks are for analysis or evaluation. In this topic an AO3 response might ask you to evaluate the effectiveness of using each of the attributions when teams have either (a) won or (b) lost.

6.1.12 Self-efficacy and confidence

As a performer you might be generally confident in all sports. This is known as **trait sports confidence**, which relates to a performer's natural confidence levels – for example, they are a generally confident performer and will show this in all sporting situations. However, some performers are only confident in specific tasks, sports or situations. This is known as **state sports confidence** or self-efficacy, and is linked directly to positive past experiences – for example, they are confident that they will score because they have kicked many conversions successfully before.

> **Self-efficacy** Describes the amount of confidence you have in a particular sporting situation.

Bandura's self-efficacy theory

REVISED

Self-efficacy is specific rather than general, and varies in different circumstances. Bandura suggested that four factors can influence the level of self-efficacy shown by a performer. By addressing these factors, coaches/teachers can raise the performer's self-esteem, resulting in a more positive, successful performance and increased task persistence.

> **Exam tip**
>
> Read the question carefully. Students often write about Bandura's social learning theory when the question is asking about self-efficacy. Bandura has a range of theories – check which one the question is referring to.

For example, a young gymnast is experiencing fear when asked to perform on a full-height beam. To increase her self-efficacy, the coach should use the four factors described in Table 6.6.

Table 6.6 Applying Bandura's four factors to increase self-efficacy

Performance accomplishments	Vicarious experiences	Verbal persuasion	Emotional arousal
Self-efficacy is affected by past experiences; therefore, the coach should remind performers of past successes in similar situations For example, remind the gymnast that she was brilliant on the lower beam and that she did not fall off; the width of the beam is the same, so she is equally unlikely to fall	The coach should ask for a performer who shares characteristics with the gymnast (e.g. ability, gender, age) to show that it is possible for them to achieve also, thereby increasing self-efficacy For example, ask a gymnast of similar age and standard to perform on the beam; the young gymnast will feel 'if she can do it, so can I'	Giving praise and positive reinforcement increases self-efficacy; significant others should be used to enhance this For example, the performer's coach and friends persuade the gymnast that they believe she can perform well on the beam	The coach should show the performer how to cope with and control their arousal levels – this might include both cognitive and somatic strategies; often they *perceive* they are unable to meet the demands of the task For example, the coach tells the gymnast to use mental rehearsal to go over the moves on the beam in her mind before mounting; this will allow her to focus and lower her arousal levels

Vealey's model

REVISED

Athletes who have high sports confidence in one sporting situation will feel more confident in their ability to succeed in others.

Vealey suggested that the performer will undertake the task (objective sporting situation), such as taking a conversion in rugby, with a certain amount of the following (Figure 6.11):
+ Trait sports confidence (SC–trait) – their natural, *innate* confidence levels – for example, they are a generally confident performer in a range of sports.

+ State sports confidence (SC–state) – their level of confidence in this situation (self-efficacy) is often based on past experience – for example, they are confident that they will score as they have kicked many conversions before.

+ Competitiveness orientation – how driven the performer is and the types of *goal* they might have set themselves. For example, the kicker is very motivated to succeed and has set the performance goal of successfully kicking 90 per cent of their conversion attempts.

The performer produces the response (for example, attempts the conversion) and considers the subjective outcomes. If they perceive the outcome as being a positive result (for example, they successfully kick the conversion), then the level of general SC–trait and specific SC–state will increase. This will further the chances of **approach behaviour** being shown in other situations. A successful attempt will also increase the level of competitiveness orientation shown by the performer. For example, the kicker becomes even more motivated and sets a new goal of 95 per cent success rate. A negative outcome will lower trait and state confidence, along with competitiveness, and might lead to future avoidance behaviour and an inactive lifestyle.

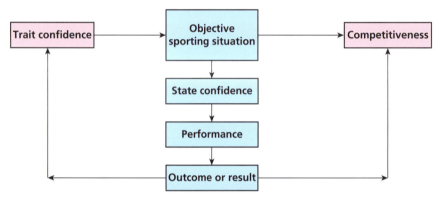

Figure 6.11 Vealey's model of sports confidence

Exam tip

If you find it difficult to explain Vealey's model, try using the example of a penalty in football, and work your way through the boxes, describing each as you go.

Now test yourself   TESTED ◯

35 Define SC–trait, SC–state and competitiveness orientation.

36 What are the four components of Bandura's self-efficacy model?

Answers on p. 270

Home-field advantage

REVISED ◯

Home-field advantage suggests that performers usually perform better when playing at home because they have many supporters present and are familiar with the venue. This keeps the level of uncertainty, and therefore arousal, low. The influence of the home crowd and familiar venue can increase confidence – often more home games are won than away fixtures. The larger and more supportive the crowd is, the greater the effect on the performer's confidence. If the audience is very close to the playing area, home-field advantage is even more important. In basketball, for example, seating is very close to the court.

However, there can be some negative effects, which can reduce confidence. This might happen during the later stages of a competition, when the home crowds expect a win. If the team is losing the home crowd can become hostile. The pressure might be extremely high and can cause social inhibition.

Strategies to develop high levels of self-efficacy

REVISED ◯

A coach can use all aspects of Bandura's model:

+ Point out when the performer succeeded previously.

Check your understanding and progress at **www.hoddereducation.co.uk/myrevisionnotes**

- Ask one of their peers to demonstrate the skill to show them that they can do it too.
- Give praise and positive reinforcement.
- Use cognitive and somatic strategies to control their arousal and anxiety levels.
- Allow success in training, then gradually increase the difficulty of the task.
- Set achievable process and performance goals.
- Attribute success internally.

Exam practice

1. Using Bandura's model, explain how a coach could increase self-efficacy by using performance accomplishments and vicarious experiences. Give practical examples to illustrate your answer. [4]

Answer online

Revision activity

Use the abbreviations PA, VE, VP, EA (Table 6.6) to help you to remember Bandura's model of self-efficacy. Think of a skill in your sport and describe how you would use each part of the model to raise the self-efficacy of a young performer trying to groove the skill.

Knowledge and skills summary

This topic involves the following knowledge (AO1):
- Defininitions of self-efficacy, self-confidence and self-esteem.
- Describing the components of Bandura's and Vealey's models.

AO2 marks will require application of this knowledge – for example, giving practical examples of Bandura's and Vealey's models, and how to raise the self-esteem of individuals and/or teams.

AO3 marks are for analysis or evaluation. In this topic an AO3 response might ask you to evaluate the effectiveness of Bandura's or Vealey's model, or to analyse how sports confidence can affect participation in sport.

6.1.13 Leadership

Characteristics of effective leaders

REVISED

Effective leaders are often *ambitious*, have a *clear vision* or *goal* and have the ability to *motivate* others to achieve that goal.

Leaders often show other characteristics, including being:
- effective communicators
- charismatic
- knowledgeable about the sport/skilful
- empathetic
- confident
- flexible

Exam tip

A question on the qualities of a good leader is an easy starter, so make sure you can give a range of answers.

Prescribed and emergent leaders

REVISED

Prescribed leaders are chosen from outside the group. For example, national governing bodies appoint national team managers. They often bring new ideas to the group, but can cause disagreements if the group members are opposed to the appointment.

Emergent leaders are selected from within the existing group, often because they are nominated by the other group members. For example, a Sunday league football team votes the previous season's 'players' player' as the new captain. There is already a high level of respect for this person, but as they have had the same experiences as the other team members, they might not be able to bring any new strategies to enable the team to progress.

Prescribed leader Chosen from outside the group.

Emergent leader Chosen from within the group.

Now test yourself

TESTED

37 List five characteristics of an effective leader.

38 What is the difference between an emergent leader and a prescribed leader?

Answers on p. 270

Styles of leadership

Three styles of leadership are outlined in Table 6.7.

Table 6.7 Styles of leadership

Autocratic/task-oriented	Democratic/social-oriented	Laissez-faire
+ Dictatorial in style + Only interested in ensuring the task is fulfilled + Sole decision maker + Use in dangerous situations + Use with large groups + Use if time is limited + Use with hostile groups + Use with cognitive performers	+ Interested in ensuring that relationships are developed within the group + Group members are involved in making decisions + Use with small groups + Use if plenty of time available + Use with friendly groups + Use with advanced performers	+ Leader is more of a 'figurehead' than an active leader; they take a hands-off approach + Group members make all the decisions + Useful if a problem-solving approach is required + Only effective with advanced performers
Example: a basketball coach calls a time out towards the end of a match and instructs the players to run a specific set play in the remaining seconds	*Example*: a doubles tennis coach spends time with the players discussing which strategies are best to use in their upcoming fixture	*Example*: a football manager allows the team to decide which skills/drills to work on during their training sessions

Now test yourself TESTED ●

39 What type of leadership style would be most appropriate when teaching a novice group of rock climbers?

Answer on p. 270

Theories of leadership

Fiedler's contingency model

Fiedler suggested an interactionist approach, in which an effective leader will match their style with the situation they are faced with. One of two leadership styles should be adopted:

+ A **task-oriented leader** is mainly concerned with achieving the goals that are set and takes a pragmatic approach to getting things done. They are very direct and authoritarian. This style should be used in both most- and least-favourable situations.
+ A **person-oriented leader** focuses on developing harmony and good relationships within the group. They are open to suggestions and take more of a democratic approach. This style should be used in moderately favourable situations.

The favourableness of the situation dictates which leadership style should be adopted in the following way:

+ In the **most-favourable** situations, the leader is in a strong position of authority and has the respect of the group; the members have good relationships with each other, and the task is clear. For example, a team that has played together for several years under the same captain and whose members have good relationships with one another might have a number of set plays rehearsed. When the captain calls the play, they are all aware of what should happen and complete the move immediately. In this situation, a task-oriented approach would work best to complete the task effectively.
+ In the **least-favourable** situations, the leader has no power or respect from the group; there might be infighting in the group and hostility towards the leader, with the task being unclear. For example, an unpopular caretaker manager is placed in charge of a team. The team members might not show the new leader any respect. The new leader is unclear as to what is needed

to motivate the team and what strategies to employ. In this situation, a task-oriented approach would also need to be used.

+ In **moderately favourable** situations, the leader would choose a person-oriented style which allows other team members to contribute to the decision-making process. The leader would have some power/respect, there would be some good relationships and parts of the task would be clear. For example, two new players join your netball team. The whole team discusses which positions are best for them.

Task-oriented leadership is used effectively with cognitive performers, with large groups, when time is limited and in dangerous situations.

Person-oriented leadership is used effectively with advanced performers, with smaller groups, with large amounts of time and when tasks are not dangerous.

Chelladurai's multidimensional model of leadership

Chelladurai suggests that in order to ensure group satisfaction and high levels of performance, leaders must be able to adapt their leadership style. He suggests that leaders get the best from their teams if the leadership style 'fits' the situation and with what the team needs.

Leaders should consider three factors before adopting a specific leadership style (Figure 6.12):

+ **Situation**, such as the strength of the opponents, or if there is any danger involved. For example, learning to trampoline is dangerous and requires an autocratic approach.
+ **Leaders** themselves, in terms of their ability, personality and preferred leadership style. For example, the leader is highly experienced and prefers to use an autocratic style.
+ **Group**, in terms of their ability levels, and the relationships with each other and with the leader. For example, the group members are cognitive performers, and therefore need to be given direct instructions about how to perform moves on the trampoline bed.

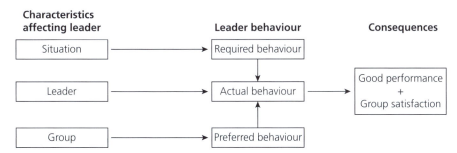

Figure 6.12 Chelladurai's model of leadership

The leadership style is also affected by the following:

+ **Required behaviour**, or what the situation demands – a dangerous task, such as trampolining, would require an autocratic rather than a democratic approach to maintain safety levels.
+ **Actual behaviour**, or what style and approach the leader decides to take in a given situation. This is based on factors such as their own ability. For example, the leader considers all the factors and decides to adopt an autocratic style of leadership.
+ **Preferred behaviour** or what style of leadership the team members would like best, based on their own experiences and characteristics such as ability. For example, the group likes the autocratic approach because they find that they develop their basic skills and can therefore move onto more difficult skills quickly.

Once these factors have been considered, the leader must try to balance their style of leadership with each of these to gain the highest level of performance

> **Revision activity**
>
> Many students find the Chelladurai model difficult. Try to explain the model by working backwards through it, describing each box and what it means. Use the same example at each stage.

189

and satisfaction from the group. The more the leader's actual behaviour matches what the group wants and what the situation needs (known as **congruence**), the better the performance will be. In the trampolining example, the leader decides to use the autocratic style. Since this matches what the group likes and what the situation needs, there is a greater chance that the group will be satisfied and performance will be high.

Now test yourself TESTED ◯

40 In terms of the situation, group and leader, what should be taken into consideration before beginning to lead a group?

Answer on p. 270

Exam practice

1 Fiedler states that the favourableness of the situation dictates which leadership style should be used. What are the characteristics of an unfavourable situation, and what style of leadership does Fiedler suggest should be used here? [5]

Answer online

Exam tip

When giving practical examples, with clear descriptions and examples of the various leadership styles, it is not enough to simply say 'e.g. José Mourinho', because this tells you nothing about the way he leads.

Knowledge and skills summary

This topic involves the following knowledge (AO1):
+ The qualities of a good leader.
+ The characteristics of the various leadership styles.
+ Distinguishing between emergent and prescribed leaders.

AO2 marks will require application of this knowledge – for example, giving practical examples with clear descriptions,

giving examples of the various leadership styles, or explaining Fiedler or Chelladurai's models, with clear examples throughout.

AO3 marks are for analysis or evaluation. In this topic an AO3 response might require you to evaluate whether leaders are born or made, with reference to theories, or to evaluate the various theories of leadership.

6.1.14 Stress management

+ Unlike anxiety, stress is not always negative. Individuals react differently; one person's stressor might be another person's motivator.
+ In eustress, the performer rises to the challenge they are faced with, feels confident and is motivated to complete the task. Performance can be facilitated.
+ In distress, the performer finds the stressor threatening and difficult to cope with. Performance can be inhibited.

Exam tip

Make sure you are familiar with the key terms in this section.

There might be **cognitive** or **somatic** responses to stressors:
+ Cognitive effects of stress – psychological responses to stressful situations – for example, anxiety, irrational/negative thoughts, reduced concentration/attentional narrowing and poor decision making.
+ Somatic effects of stress – physiological responses to stressful situations – for example, increases in heart rate, blood pressure, sweating, adrenaline production and muscle tension.

Stress An individual's physical response that prepares the body for action when a threat is perceived.

Stressor The *cause* of the stress response – for example, playing in an important competitive situation (final or semi-final), sustaining an injury, being fouled/injured, the perception that you are playing badly/feel that you are letting the team down, fatigue or the weather/conditions.

Eustress A positive response to a stressful situation.

Distress A negative response to a stressful situation.

Now test yourself TESTED ◯

41 What is the difference between eustress and distress?

Answer on p. 270

Stress management techniques

Somatic strategies

+ **Biofeedback** – using equipment (e.g. heart rate monitors reading bpm) generates physiological data. The data can show which sporting situations cause the most stress and which strategies are the most effective for them (e.g. heart rate will reduce). These strategies are very effective but are time consuming. Using equipment during performance can distract athletes and increase anxiety levels, because they are aware they are being monitored.
+ **Progressive muscular relaxation** – concentrating on each muscle group in turn. By tensing, holding and then relaxing each group, the performer begins to relax.
+ **Breathing control** – by controlling and concentrating on the rate and depth of breathing, the performer becomes less distracted and is able to focus on the task.
+ **Centring** – used alongside controlled breathing, this is useful during breaks in performance, i.e. during time-outs or at the end of a tennis set. Concentrate fully on your body (often the centre, i.e. your belly-button region) and breathe in. As you breathe out, chant a word or phrase reflecting how you wish to perform – strong, focused, calm etc. By doing this, you maintain focus on yourself and any negative thoughts are disregarded.
+ **Warm-up** – traditionally a warm-up focuses on preparing the body through a session that includes CV work, stretching and sport-specific skills and drills. However, the psychological importance of the warm-up should not be underestimated. It controls arousal, and allows the performer to achieve a state of readiness, fully concentrate using selective attention, and adopt the correct attentional style. A warm-up reduces the chance of attending to incorrect environmental cues, and therefore reduces stress and anxiety. Cognitive strategies (e.g. imagery) should form part of the warm-up, to mentally review skills and tactics.

Cognitive strategies

+ **Psychological skills training** – describes an individualised programme that regularly and methodically utilises a range of mental training strategies. This will be tailor-made for the performer and will take into consideration their specific sport and position within the sport as well as their current psychological condition. As a result, athletes are more successful and demonstrate increased confidence and motivation, improved focus and lower stress.
+ **Mental rehearsal** – go over the performance in your mind before the action begins, e.g. seeing all the subroutines of the triple jump without moving.
+ **Visualisation** – when you perform a skill successfully in training, you lock in the mental image of it. This is then re-lived in the competitive situation. It can be internal (e.g. visualising a successful smash shot and how it 'feels' kinaesthetically) or external (e.g. visualising your successful slam dunk as if by a spectator on television).
+ **Imagery** – recalling a successful previous performance, using all the senses including kinaesthesis to recreate the feeling of success, e.g. remembering how the serve felt when you hit an ace. This can also be internal or external.
+ **Positive self-talk** – verbally reminding yourself of the key points of the movement and telling yourself that you can achieve. For example, a rugby league player taking a conversion will talk himself through the run-up, contact and follow-through. He will tell himself that he can take the points. He might also have a 'mantra' or saying that he continually repeats.
+ **Negative thought-stopping** – often used with above. A tennis player whose first serve is letting them down begins to think, 'I can't hit one in', should replace that thought with, 'I can and I will hit the next one in.'
+ **Attentional control and cue utilisation** – **Easterbrook's cue utilisation hypothesis** links a performer's ability to sustain focus on the correct cues in the environment with their level of arousal. At low levels the performer

is not stimulated enough and takes in a large number of environmental cues. They are unable to distinguish what the relevant cues are and can become confused, reducing performance levels. At high levels, the performer takes in a very small number of cues as they are excessively stimulated and might begin to panic. The correct cues are missed, again reducing performance levels. At moderate levels of arousal, the performer filters out the irrelevant cues and focuses only on the relevant cues required. This lowers the level of stress that the performer is experiencing and allows them to complete the task to the highest level.

Nideffer's model of attentional focus

Nideffer suggested that different activities require different types of attentional focus. For example, invasion games often require a broad focus, whereas net/wall games often require a narrower style. Performers are required to apply a variety of attentional styles, with the best athletes being able to switch from one style to another. Having attentional focus and the correct attentional style will reduce the level of stress experienced by the performer, and therefore performance is improved.

There are two dimensions of focus:
+ **Broad–narrow** – how many cues are being focused on. Broad involves many cues, while narrow involves one or two.
+ **Internal–external** – where the focus is being placed. Internal involves the thoughts and feelings of the performer themselves; external involves a focus on environmental cues.

Four attentional styles arise from this:
+ **Broad–internal** – many cues concerning the performer themselves – for example, a footballer planning their team strategies/next set piece.
+ **Narrow–internal** – one or two cues concerning the performers themselves; often used to calm nerves – for example, a swimmer mentally rehearsing the sound of the starter signal and subsequent dive into the pool.
+ **Broad–external** – many cues in the environment – for example, a centre player in netball focusing on the many teammates who they might pass to.
+ **Narrow–external** – one or two cues in the environment – for example, a basketballer focusing on the net during a free throw.

Revision activity

Guess the strategy! Write each strategy on a post-it note. Place them face down and shuffle. With a partner, take it in turns to select one and stick it to your forehead without looking at it. Your partner has to describe the strategy to you without naming it.

Now test yourself   TESTED ◯

42 Describe the two dimensions of focus according to Nideffer.

Answer on p. 270

Exam practice

1   Define mental rehearsal, and give a practical example of how a team player might utilise it.   [2]
2   Define progressive muscular relaxation, and give a practical example of how an individual performer might utilise it.   [2]

Answer online

Knowledge and skills summary

This topic involves the following knowledge (AO1):
+ Explaining the terms stress and stressor.
+ Describing the cognitive and somatic techniques used.

AO2 marks will require application of this knowledge – for example, giving practical examples of performers utilising the cognitive and somatic methods.

AO3 marks are for analysis or evaluation. In this topic an AO3 response might require you to evaluate the use of the cognitive and somatic methods.

7 Sport and society and the role of technology in physical activity and sport

7.1 Concepts of physical activity and sport

When observing or watching people taking part in physical activity, you might notice a number of different features (i.e. characteristics). For example, at one end of the 'continuum', there might be a relaxed/fun atmosphere evident, as opposed to a more serious attitude when watching top sports performers.

> **Characteristics** Key features used to identify a particular concept (e.g. fun/enjoyment in physical recreation or a serious attitude in sport).

The sporting development continuum

REVISED

Different forms of physical activity can be viewed on a sporting development continuum.

+ The 'foundation level' is the first introduction to physical activity/sport (for example, at grass-roots level in primary school PE programmes).
+ This is followed by the 'participation level', with its emphasis on fun, socialising and developing friendships; participating in a recreational, relaxed manner.
+ More dedicated, focused individuals can reach the 'performance level', where there is a commitment to regular involvement in sport and the emphasis is on winning.

> **Sporting development continuum** Participation in various forms of physical activity at various stages of development. For example, the grass-roots 'foundation stage' in primary school PE or 'participation stage' involvement as an adult in physical recreation.

Characteristics and functions of physical recreation

REVISED

Physical recreation can be defined as 'the active aspect of leisure'. Leisure time is free time, which can be spent actively or passively.

The following list summarises some characteristics commonly associated with physical recreation:

+ It is fun, enjoyable, non-serious and informal in nature, so winning is not important; taking part is the main motive for participation.
+ It is physically energetic, i.e. it involves effort being applied into physical activity.
+ Participating is a matter of 'choice'; it is voluntary and up to you whether you take part or not in the free time you have available.
+ It tends to involve adults at the participation level of the sporting development continuum.
+ It is flexible in nature, so how long you take part for and the rules being followed can be adjusted by participants as they wish.
+ It is self-officiated/self-regulated (i.e. any decisions during activities are made by the participants themselves).

> **Participation level** An emphasis on taking part recreationally, with enjoyment as a key motivator to participate.

Check your understanding and progress at www.hoddereducation.co.uk/myrevisionnotes

Now test yourself

TESTED ◯

1 Identify the characteristics of physical recreation.
2 Define the term sports development continuum.
3 Complete Table 7.1.

Table 7.1

Stage/level of sports development continuum	Definition	Example (i.e. link to concept)
	First introduction to physical activity	Primary school PE
Participation level	Relaxed, fun participation in physical activity	
Performance level		Sport

Answers on p. 270

Making links

The participation level of the continuum (i.e. physical recreation) can be linked to positive ethics in participation in physical activity (i.e. the emphasis is on taking part).

Functions

The functions of physical recreation can be examined in terms of positive outcomes for individuals, as well as how a society can benefit if more people increase their physical activity levels and recreation.

In terms of the individual:
+ Regular participation in physical recreation increases an individual's health and fitness, and helps in the development of physical skills (e.g. improvement of a golf swing).
+ It provides individuals with a challenge, which, if they overcome it, will lead to a sense of achievement and increased levels of self-esteem and self-confidence.
+ Recreation can provide a chance to refresh oneself and it can act as a stress relief from work, while helping individuals to relax.
+ Involvement in physical recreation can help people to socialise and meet up with friends (e.g. as members of a regular circuit training class at a leisure centre).
+ As recreation takes place in a relaxed atmosphere, it provides people with a sense of fun and enjoyment.
+ For many, it helps ensure participation in physical activity for as many years as possible, well into later life, because the emphasis is on taking part at your own level and pace, rather than trying to beat others.

> **Exam tip**
>
> If questions are set on the functions of physical recreation for an *individual*, make sure you clearly link them to key benefits of physical activity at an *individual* level rather than a *societal* one (e.g. increased health and fitness of the individual, as opposed to less strain on the NHS for society).

Now test yourself

TESTED ◯

4 Explain the benefits to society of increasing participation in physical recreation.

Answer on p. 271

> **Exam tip**
>
> When applying knowledge/explaining the benefits of physical recreation to society (AO2), it is important to ensure relevant key points are linked together (for example, increased health and fitness results in less strain on the NHS).

Characteristics and functions of sport

REVISED ◯

Sport can be viewed as a serious and/or competitive experience, and can be identified by a number of key features (characteristics), including the following:

> **Revision activity**
>
> Draw a table with two columns linking the benefits of physical recreation to (1) the individual directly and (2) to society.

- It is highly structured and has set rules/strict rules (e.g. set time limits; set boundaries).
- It involves use of specialist equipment/set kit.
- Officials are present who are trained or appointed by national governing bodies to enforce the rules.
- Strategies and tactics are involved to try to outwit opponents and win.
- Rewards are received as a result of success. These can be extrinsic rewards, such as medals or trophies, or intrinsic rewards, such as gaining personal satisfaction from your performance.
- High skill levels/high levels of prowess are visible in sporting performance.
- High levels of commitment and/or strict training are involved to maintain and improve fitness and skill levels.
- It is serious and competitive (i.e. winning is important).

> **Making links**
>
> Characteristics of sport can be linked to rational recreation in post-industrial sport (p. 76).

> **Making links**
>
> Make sure that you can identify the key characteristics of recreation and sport (AO1), link and apply them to relevant sporting examples (AO2), and analyse how experiencing recreation and sport might impact on performance (AO3).

> **Exam tip**
>
> Remember that stating the 'characteristics' of sport (AO1) is different from stating the benefits of sport (AO1) (i.e. not improved health and fitness, decreased crime etc.)

> **Now test yourself** TESTED
>
> 5 Sport has an emphasis on winning, with high rewards at stake at the elite level. Identify other characteristics of sport.
> 6 List three types of extrinsic reward an individual might receive as a result of sporting success.
>
> **Answers on p. 271**

> **Exam tip**
>
> Remember the key characterics of SPORT as follows:
> - **S**erious/competitive – 'win at all costs' attitude or sportsmanship (how?)
> - **P**rowess – high skill levels, particularly among professionals (who?)
> - **O**rganised – sport has rules/regulations (how?)
> - **R**ewards – available for winning (extrinsic) and intrinsic satisfaction (why?)
> - **T**ime and space restrictions apply (when/where?)

Functions

Taking part in sport has several important functions for individuals, as well as society in general. These are similar in some respects to the functions of physical recreation.

For **individuals**:

- Sport can help improve their health and fitness and physical skill levels. Self-confidence often increases due to skill improvement and success, which can lead to a feel-good factor for participants.
- Sport often provides increased social opportunities – for example, the chance to communicate, socialise and work as part of a team, and make friends at sports clubs.
- Participation in sport can help develop positive sporting morals and attitudes, such as fair play and sportsmanship, which can influence a person's general behaviour and keep them out of trouble via a positive use of their free time.

For **society**:

The benefits of sports participation for society can be remembered as three 'S' factors and three 'E' factors:

+ **S** – Strain on the NHS is reduced because levels of obesity and other health issues decline.
+ **S** – Social control is increased because individuals make more positive use of free time.
+ **S** – Social integration is increased, along with community cohesion/morale, via increased participation in sport by different socioeconomic and ethnic groups.
+ **E** – Employment opportunities increase (e.g. through employment as sports coaches, fitness trainers etc.).
+ **E** – Economic benefits result as people pay to participate and spend money on new equipment and the latest fashionable kit on the market.
+ **E** – Equality of opportunity via 'sports participation' for all.

Revision activity

Draw a spider diagram of the 'S' and 'E' factors, identifying the benefits of sports participation for a society.

Now test yourself   TESTED ◯

7   Many people take part in sport to increase their health and fitness. Identify the functions of taking part in sport for an individual.

Answer on p. 271

Characteristics and functions of PE   REVISED ●

The National Curriculum for Physical Education (PE) was introduced following the 1988 Education Reform Act. It has been reviewed and modified slightly since, but essentially its key characteristics and aims have remained broadly similar. The **key characteristics of PE** can be summarised as follows:

+ It is compulsory.
+ It involves formally taught lessons.
+ It has four key stages as part of the National Curriculum from ages 5 to 16.
+ It begins at primary school 'foundation level'.
+ Teachers are in charge and deliver lessons.
+ Lessons are pre-planned; it is highly structured.
+ It is in school time.

Functions

PE has a variety of different functions, including the following:

+ The development of health and fitness, as well as positive attitudes, which hopefully lead to healthy lifestyles being continued when PE is no longer compulsory. Ultimately, PE is about encouraging lifelong participation and trying to create a sporting habit for life after pupils finish compulsory PE at the age of 16.
+ PE provides opportunities for increased participation in a variety of activities, developing and improving a range of physical skills and competencies.
+ The development of personal and social skills is an important aim of PE (for example, teamwork, communication, leadership, cooperation). PE also aims to develop positive sporting ethics, such as morality, fair play and sportsmanship.
+ Cognitively, PE can help improve problem solving, decision making and creativity (for example, developing a new sequence in dance or gymnastics). PE also aims to help students to develop skills of self-analysis, as well as learning to recognise strengths and weaknesses in performance and where improvements have occurred.

Exam tip

It is important to identify a variety of functions of PE (AO1) as well as link them to relevant examples (AO2).

Figure 7.1 Objectives of National Curriculum PE

National Curriculum PE (Figure 7.1) includes the opportunity to participate in outdoor and adventurous activities (OAA) as outdoor education (Figure 7.2). Such activities provide the opportunity for pupils to overcome fears, face personal challenges and experience an adrenaline rush.

> **Outdoor education**
> Activities that take place in the natural environment and utilise nature/ geographical resources, such as mountains, rivers, and lakes.

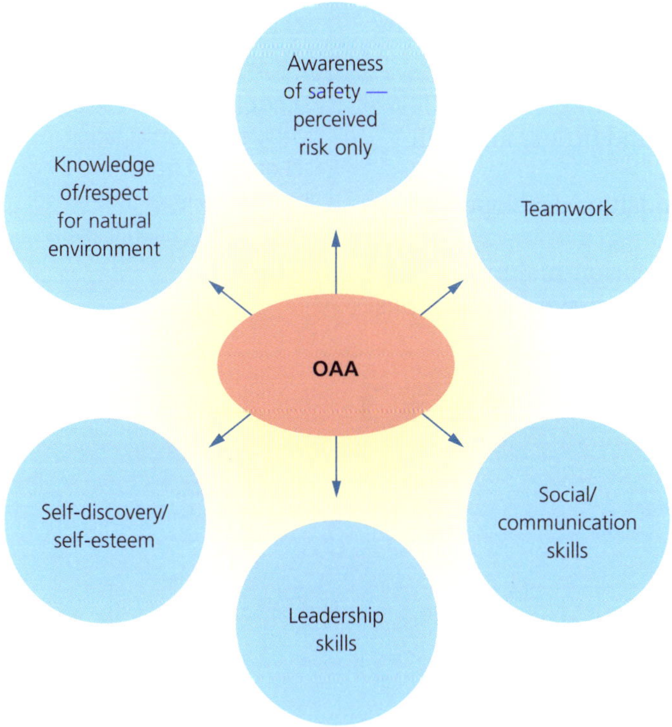

Figure 7.2 Benefits of OAA as outdoor education

The functions of outdoor education for young people include the following:

✚ It helps children learn to appreciate and engage with the natural environment, as well as increase its conservation. While in the natural environment, they are learning to develop new physical and survival skills (e.g. abseiling, climbing), which can result in increased self-esteem. Outdoor education activities such as climbing are physically challenging, so they result in increased levels of health and fitness.

✚ Working with others is a key feature of outdoor education activities, so increased cooperation, and an improvement in social skills and leadership skills often result.

197

+ Mentally, there are different functions to outdoor education, including learning how to deal with a challenging situation, while allowing the pupil to learn how to perceive risk, as well as learning to get excited by participation in activities such as abseiling and climbing. Improved cognitive and decision-making skills can also be gained by the students as a result of outdoor education participation.

> **Perceived risk** A sense of danger and adventure stimulated by challenge facing beginners or inexperienced performers in a safe environment, with danger minimised via stringent safety measures (e.g. wearing a harness when climbing).

Now test yourself   TESTED ◯

8 Identify two positive sporting ethics PE aims to develop in young children.

9 OAA forms part of a school's overall PE programme. Identify the benefits of participating in OAA (e.g. climbing).

10 List two different outdoor education activities that could be undertaken on or in mountains.

Answers on p. 271

Characteristics and aims of school sport   REVISED ◯

School sport is different from PE because it mostly occurs in extracurricular time as a choice for children attending school.

+ School sport is competitive and has been promoted as important by governments, with the introduction of initiatives such as School Sport Partnerships and School Games.

+ Schools sometimes use sports coaches to help increase the range of extracurricular sporting opportunities available to pupils, as well as using their specialisms to develop pupils' talents to the full.

> **School Sport Partnerships** The creation of increased opportunities for school sport via junior/primary schools working together with secondary schools and further education providers.
>
> **School Games** An initiative to increase participation in school sport from intra-/interschool level through to county and national levels.

Benefits to participating in school sport include the following:

+ Physical – increased activity levels improve health and fitness and skill levels, which can increase a child's self-esteem.

+ Socially, new groups can be formed, and new friendships developed, via extracurricular involvement in school sport.

+ Improved cognitive skills can result in increased decision-making capabilities, as well as an improvement in academic achievement if pupils become more motivated to attend and achieve at school.

Now test yourself   TESTED ◯

11 Identify two characteristics of school sport.

Answer on p. 271

Making links

The functions of various concepts can be linked to the health benefits of increasing physical activity and sport in the sport and society section (pp. 111–112).

Having considered the concepts of physical activity and sport mainly in isolation, it is also important to consider how they compare and contrast in a variety of different ways (i.e. their similarities and differences).

Similarities and differences   REVISED ◯

Physical recreation and sport

Sport and recreation are *similar* in that they both involve physical activity, which helps increase health and fitness. They can be performed in a person's free time as voluntary activities, with individuals gaining intrinsic benefits as a result of participating – for example, achieving a sense of personal satisfaction as a result of reaching goals.

Check your understanding and progress at **www.hoddereducation.co.uk/myrevisionnotes**

Sport and recreation have a number of *differences*, including those identified in Table 7.2.

Table 7.2 Physical recreation compared with sport

Physical recreation	Sport
Available to all/voluntary/choice	More selective/obligatory/for some, an occupation
Emphasis on taking part/participation focus	Emphasis on winning/serious/competitive
Limited/varied effort/commitment required	Involves a high level of effort/commitment (e.g. to train for a specific event/competition)
Rules can be modified (e.g. timings, numbers involved)	Set rules apply
Self-officiated/self-regulated	External officials enforce rules
Mainly intrinsic rewards	Extrinsic rewards available for success (e.g. winning trophies/medals)
Varied skill/fitness levels	Higher skill/fitness levels
Basic equipment and clothing used or worn	High-tech equipment and clothing used or worn

Physical recreation and PE

Physical recreation and physical education are *similar* in that they both develop physical skills and are energetic, so have health-and-fitness benefits. They can both be enjoyable and fun to participate in, so have intrinsic benefits.

The *differences* between physical recreation and PE are summarised in Table 7.3, directly comparing key features of these two concepts of physical activity.

Table 7.3 Physical recreation compared with PE

Physical recreation	PE
Voluntary/choice	Compulsory
In a person's free time	In school time
Informal/relaxed	Formal teaching and learning
Participants control activity themselves; self-regulated	Teacher in charge
Participation level	Foundation level at primary school
Simple/limited organisational structure	Highly structured

Now test yourself   TESTED ◯

12 Identify the similarities and differences between PE and physical recreation.

Answer on p. 271

PE and school sport

As mentioned above, the overall concept of PE can be experienced in different ways. A direct comparison can be made between PE as a compulsory National Curriculum subject and school sport as a choice for young people, as illustrated in Table 7.4.

Table 7.4 National Curriculum PE compared with school sport

National Curriculum PE	School sport
In lesson time; curriculum time	In free time; extracurricular
Compulsory	Element of choice; voluntary involvement
For all	For the chosen few; elitist
Emphasis on taking part	Emphasis on winning; competitive
Teacher-led	Coaches involved
Wide variety of activities experienced	Specialisms develop

Now test yourself   TESTED ◯

13 Identify the differences between school sport and National Curriculum PE.

Answer on p. 271

School sport remains an extracurricular activity for pupils. This has several *advantages*:

✚ It allows the ethos of PE to dominate/an educational focus is maintained within school sport provision.
✚ It allows individual choice for both teachers and pupils, who are under no pressure to involve themselves/participate if they do not want to.
✚ Schools can cater for those who are interested in competitive sport via provision of a range of sporting opportunities to develop and improve their talents.
✚ School sport is relatively easy to access/cheaper to access than joining a sports club.

School sport remaining as an extracurricular activity also has some *disadvantages*:

✚ If optional as an extracurricular activity, it does not necessarily reach the maximum number of pupils, and some talented individuals might miss out; it might be viewed as 'elitist' if only a minority of pupils stay behind at school/compete for the school at weekends.
✚ It relies heavily on teacher goodwill; teachers might sometimes opt out due to other pressures on their time (e.g. attendance at staff meetings).
✚ School sporting facilities might not be used to their full capacity.

Now test yourself   TESTED ◯

14 Identify three disadvantages of school sport remaining as an extracurricular activity.

Answer on p. 271

Exam practice

1 Explain the potential benefits to society of increasing participation in sport and physical recreation. [4]

2 Outline the functions of National Curriculum PE in schools today. [4]

3 Modern-day sport performers face high levels of pressure to succeed, which sometimes has a negative effect on their behaviour.

Explain why there are fewer acts of negative behaviour during physical recreation compared with sport. [5]

4 State three characteristics of National Curriculum PE. [3]

5 Identify two characteristics of physical recreation. [2]

6 Explain how three characteristics of sport are evident in a game of lawn tennis. [3]

7 Which of the following is not a characteristic of PE? [1]

  A Optional
  B Compulsory
  C Formally taught
  D Delivered in timetabled lessons

8 How does swimming teaching in lessons meet the functions of PE? [3]

9 Abbie plays table tennis with her friends at the school table tennis club lunchtime sessions. She is also a member of her local table tennis club where she plays in the local league every weekend.

Check your understanding and progress at **www.hoddereducation.co.uk/myrevisionnotes**

Compare Abbie's experience of table tennis as recreation and her experience of table tennis as sport, and analyse how these experiences might impact on her performance. [8]

10 Sport England's Active Lives – Adult survey data show us how many people engage at least twice in 28 days in different activities as recreation and sport, to help increase our understanding of their contribution to overall levels of activity.

Describe the trends in adult activity patterns illustrated by the data in Table 7.5. [4]

Table 7.5

Activity	May 2017/18	May 2018/19
Walking for leisure	19.2 million	19.7 million
Fitness activities	13.4 million	13.8 million
Cycling for leisure and sport	6.2 million	6.3 million
Team sports	3.2 million	3.2 million
Adventure sports	2.7 million	3.3 million
Racquet sports	2.2 million	2.1 million

Answers online

> **Exam tip**
>
> It is worth familiarising yourself with Sport England Active Lives statistics and how they are applied/used to illustrate participation patterns in recreation and sport (AO2).

Knowledge and skills summary

This topic involves the following knowledge (AO1):

+ Characteristics and functions of recreation, sport, PE and school sport, for the individual and society in general.
+ Key characteristics of recreation and sport.

AO2 marks will require application of this knowledge – for example:

+ Understanding and application of the characteristics and functions of recreation, sport, PE and school sport, and awareness of similarities and differences.

+ Linking the characteristics of sport to the development of rational recreation in post-industrial Britain.
+ Linking the functions of recreation, sport, PE and school sport to the health benefits of raising participation in physical activity and sport.

AO3 marks are for analysis or evaluation – for example, analysing how experiencing recreation and sport might impact on performance.

7.2 Development of elite performers in sport

Factors required to support progression

REVISED ⬤

The personal, social and cultural factors required to support progression from talent identification to elite performance are considered here.

Personal factors

It is important that all young, talented athletes in the UK can fulfil their sporting potential and have in place all they need to support and develop their talents. When considering the factors necessary to progress through to the elite performance level, a useful way to start is to identify some key personal qualities (for example, physical/psychological) which are viewed as important in talented athletes.

Below is a summary of key personal factors and qualities necessary to develop as an elite performer:

+ Commitment, dedication and self-discipline.
+ Determination to succeed, as well as being single-minded and mentally tough and focused.

> **Elite** The best, highest level sports performers at 'excellence' level.
>
> **Personal qualities** The attributes and personality characteristics of an individual person.

- Highly motivated/self-motivated with the desire to achieve/clearly set goals to achieve.
- Willing to self-sacrifice in order to succeed.
- High pain tolerance/resilience/perseverance/patience.
- High levels of self-confidence and self-efficacy.
- Highly skilled physically and/or naturally talented.
- High level of physical fitness (e.g. sport endurance for distance runners).
- Good communicators.

> **Now test yourself** TESTED ◯
>
> 1 Identify the psychological qualities you feel are necessary for an individual to develop as an elite performer.
>
> **Answer on p. 271**

Social and cultural factors

A wide range of social and cultural factors can influence the progression of a young talented individual through to elite performance level, including the following:

- The support of friends and family when starting out in sport and trying to progress. Having friends and family present in the crowd at sports events to support and encourage is viewed as very important, both socially and emotionally.
- The financial resources of a family can be important in an individual's development because money is required to pay for specialist equipment, travelling expenses, specialist coaching and medical support. (This is sometimes referred to as the 'bank of Mum and Dad'.) An important social and cultural influence on performer progression is therefore an individual's socioeconomic status.

> **Socioeconomic status**
> An individual's position in the social structure, which depends on their job, level of income and area they live in.

The social and cultural factors necessary to develop as an elite performer can be summarised as follows:

- Highly supportive family/high socioeconomic status.
- Evidence of equal opportunities and anti-discrimination practices within a sport, and setting of equity targets.
- High-quality, supportive educational provision/clear links to clubs.
- Structured levels of competition to progress through.
- High levels of media coverage and role models to aspire to.

> **Exam tip**
>
> For AO1 make sure that you can identify the personal factors that individuals require to develop as elite performers, as well as the different support systems and structures needed to support progression through to excellence level.

> **Now test yourself** TESTED ◯
>
> 2 Identify the sociocultural factors that encourage the development of elite performers and improve the chance of UK athletes winning medals at the Olympics.
>
> **Answer on pp. 271–272**

Organisations providing support and progression

REVISED ◯

The specification focuses on three organisations as being particularly important when considering talent identification and elite performer progression:

- UK Sport
- the English Institute of Sport (as an example of a national institute of sport)
- the national governing bodies (NGBs) of sport

> **Talent identification** The multidisciplinary screening of athletes to identify those with the potential for world-class success.

UK Sport

UK Sport has a single focus on developing high-performance sport in the UK. Its work is aimed at developing and implementing various strategies to increase sporting excellence in this country. Its primary role is to strategically invest and distribute National Lottery funding for elite performer development to maximise the performance of UK athletes in the Olympic and Paralympic Games.

It does this via two main channels. The first is to provide funding to NGBs, which enables them to operate a World Class Programme (p. 207), covering all funded summer and winter Olympic and Paralympic sports. The second channel provides funding directly to athletes via an Athlete Performance Award, which contributes to their living and sporting costs once they have reached elite performance level. The role and purpose of UK Sport in supporting progression through to elite performance are summarised in Table 7.6.

Table 7.6 The strategy of UK Sport

UK Sport strategy	Explanation of strategy
It works on an overall strategy to increase sporting excellence in the UK – for example, through funding/financial decisions It invests/distributes National Lottery money for elite performer development in Olympic and Paralympic sports	For example, it funds: ✦ World Class Performance Programmes via NGBs ✦ athletes directly, to cover living and sporting costs via the Athlete Performance Award scheme (up to £28,000 a year) ✦ BOA preparation camps prior to the Olympics (e.g. Keio University and Yokahama International Pool as part of a multi-sport preparation camp prior to Tokyo 2020) It grants funds to the EIS
Development of world-class coaches/elite-level coaches	For example, via the UK Sport World Class Coaching Strategy, which aims to deliver targeted and innovative programmes to aid the development/work of world-class coaches (e.g. the Elite programme)
Lead agency overseeing the running of Talent ID	This is part of a range of campaigns that have been operating successfully over the years to support various developmental stages (e.g. Talent Search to Talent Confirmation) to ensure the best athletes are recruited and developed across a range of Olympic and Paralympic sports (Talent ID) Others include: ✦ #DiscoverYourGold, prior to Tokyo 2020 ✦ From Home 2 The Games, prior to Paris 2024
Lead agency in providing performance lifestyle advice/support	Gives mentor advice/help with time management, budgets, educational demands etc.
Development and management of the UK's international sporting relationships It also works to attract major international events to the UK (e.g. via the Gold Events series)	For example, via the International Voice Programme (works with NGBs to build positive relations with their international counterparts, i.e. their international federations)
Cooperative, coordinated approach to work with other organisations involved in elite performer development, and to promote ethical behaviour at the highest level (e.g. Win Clean)	For example, EIS/NGB/National Lottery
Performance Innovation (formerly Research and Innovation)	Partners include BAE Systems as a technology partner (e.g. with British cycling)

National institutes of sport

+ In England, there is the English Institute of Sport (EIS), with bases in, for example, Bath and Loughborough.
+ The EIS is a subsidiary of, and wholly owned by, UK Sport. The EIS receives a grant of £40 million over 4 years from UK Sport, and generates its own income by providing services to NGBs, such as performance analysis and sports medicine.
+ The EIS is UK Sport's science, medicine and technology arm, which acts as the team behind many of Team GB's most successful Olympians and Paralympians. Its job is to increase the probability of a potential elite athlete being successful by providing a range of different services to improve their health, fitness, training and preparation.
+ In terms of such sporting services, the EIS operates World Class Performance environments via nine high-performance centres, as well as numerous other training bases across England. Its partner sites include the Team GB Intensive Rehabilitation Unit at Bisham Abbey, as well as Holme Pierrepont National Water Sports Centre in Nottingham.
+ Its staff work with high-level coaches and NGB performance directors to help improve the performance of their best athletes, by delivering a range of services to enable them to optimise training programmes and maximise performance in competition.

Table 7.7 summarises the role and purpose of the EIS as an example of a national institute of sport.

Table 7.7 The strategy of the EIS

EIS strategy	Explanation of strategy
Offers a range of sport support services to NGBs to develop elite performers	Services include sports science, physiotherapy, diet and nutrition, biomechanics, performance analysis, psychology, technology and medical support (e.g. physiotherapy/rehab for injuries)
Provides performance lifestyle advice and personalised support to athletes on the World Class Programme	For example, mentor support relating to time management (e.g. demands of elite sport and education), dealing with the media, balancing family and work life, budgeting
Provides top-quality/world-class facilities and the best coaches to develop elite performers to their full potential	For example, high-quality performance environments to train in, physiology labs, medical and physiotherapy facilities, performance analysis suites and elite-level coaches
Hosts venues for Talent ID assessments and Talent Confirmation etc.	Home to the UK Talent Team, which operates a system to help deliver ongoing success by developing pathways to identify and nurture talent (e.g. via talent recruitment and confirmation campaigns)
Performance innovation and research innovation	Researches how technology and engineering can be used to develop kit/equipment to give athletes an edge (e.g. marginal gains in cycling)

Now test yourself   TESTED ◯

5   The home nations of England, Northern Ireland, Scotland and Wales all have national institutes of sport. Describe how these national institutes are aiding the development of the UK's elite athletes.

6   Identify three roles of EIS Performance Lifestyle Advisors in supporting elite-level athletes.

Answers on p. 272

National governing bodies of sport

Making links

You should be aware of the possible synoptic link between the reasons for the development of NGBs in nineteenth-century sport and society (p. 82) and the modern-day role of NGBs in elite performer development.

National governing bodies (NGBs) can help ensure the development of elite performers in a number of ways, as outlined in Table 7.8.

Table 7.8 The strategy of NGBs

NGB strategy	Explanation of strategy
Introduce schemes and campaigns to develop elite performers to their full potential	For example, elite performer development to win medals in international sporting competitions
	They liaise/work with organisations involved in elite performer development, such as UK Sport/EIS
Development of effective Talent ID schemes to maintain the talent factory in their sport	For example, via the use of regional scouts/schemes specific to the demands of their sport
Decide on allocation of UK Sport lottery funding to athletes in their sport	For example, via World Class Programme funding/Athlete Performance Awards
Development of top-level coaches in their sport	Provide a developmental coaching structure through to a very high level in the sport they are responsible for
Provide developmental training squads	Different levels are provided, with progressive levels of competition to progress through
Provide support services to elite performers	For example, via links with EIS centres/payment to the EIS for various support services (e.g. performance lifestyle advice, performance innovation, sport science support)

Now test yourself   TESTED ◯

7   Identify ways in which a national governing body can help to ensure the development of elite performers.

Answer on p. 272

National sports institute support services   REVISED ◯

Working in partnership, UK Sport, the national institutes of sport (e.g. the EIS) and national governing bodies (NGBs) of sport are committed to systematically unearthing sporting talent with the necessary potential and mindset to win medals and world titles. This is done through talent identification programmes.

Various reasons for using talent identification programmes can be put forward by such organisations, including the following:

✦   It means all potential performers can be screened.

✦   Performers can be directed to the sports most suited to their talents.

+ The development process can be accelerated as a result of the information gained.
+ Efficient use can be made of available funding for Talent ID schemes.
+ The chances of producing medallists are improved.
+ They provide a coordinated approach between organisations such as NGBs, the EIS and UK Sport.

Possible disadvantages of talent identification programmes include the following:
+ They might miss late developers.
+ They require high levels of funding.
+ They require large numbers to be tested to be of use.
+ There are no guarantees of success.
+ Many sports are in competition for the same talent pool; high-profile sports might attract more performers or the best performers.

Now test yourself   TESTED ◯

8 Give three reasons why Talent ID programmes are important in the pursuit of more medals for Team GB.

Answer on p. 272

The EIS is one of the national institutes of sport that provide support services to help ensure talent development. Its Performance Pathway Team works with UK Sport to support the World Class Programme in identifying and developing talented athletes by providing them with the necessary support services to ensure their progress. The team at the EIS has identified a number of areas of support as important for the identification and development of talent:

+ **Pathway Frontline Technical Solutions** – these are designed to meet the specific needs of each sport when identifying and developing talent (e.g. to design talent recruitment and confirmation programmes for different sports, such as the UK Athletics Futures programme).
+ **Pathway Education** – this provides educational opportunities for development coaches covering a variety of topics linked to elite performer development.
+ **Pathway Analytics** – this gives sports the ability to provide meaningful measurements of the effectiveness of their performance pathways by using a range of diagnostic tools; they can also take a 'Performance Pathway Health Check'.
+ **Performance Pathway Health Check (PHC)** – the PHC is an important diagnostic tool, supporting summer and winter Olympic and Paralympic sports. It provides a review of current systems and practices for supporting the development of potential medal winners in any given sport. It includes a review of the sport's long-term vision and strategy for elite development, as well as a consideration of the coaching and training environments a sport has in place to develop elite performers.
+ **Pathway Strategy** – this is designed to assist sports to develop and put in place a clear progressive pathway from Podium Foundations level to Podium level in their sport.

The ultimate aim of support services provided by national institutes of sport, such as the EIS, is to identify new athletes with clear sporting potential, and help them to progress onto the World Class system and successfully represent Great Britain in major international sporting events.

Performance Pathway Team A combination of EIS and UK Sport expertise used to identify and develop world-class talent.

Exam tip

For AO1 and AO2, make sure that you have the knowledge to enable you to identify and explain the reasons for and against talent identification programmes. For AO3, make sure that you can analyse and evaluate the effectiveness of talent identification programmes in the UK.

Revision activity

Draw a spider diagram identifying and describing the key roles of NGBs, UK Sport and national institutes of sport in developing elite performers in Britain.

World Class Performance Programme

It can take athletes many years to develop the necessary high-level skills and competitive maturity required to be successful at the top level of international sport. UK Sport has therefore adopted a funding philosophy that reflects potentially long journeys to the top, investing around £100 million annually into elite-level sport.

✚ This funding philosophy is called 'no compromise' and bases its decisions on performances at major sporting competitions. UK Sport has adopted this approach to raise standards/performance levels among Team GB athletes.

✚ It is designed to make the best use of the funding available to elite sport by investing in athletes/sports deemed to have the best chance of success (i.e. it is directed to potential medal winners).

✚ Such an approach has increased Team GB medal chances, and helps justify the large National Lottery investment in elite sport.

The World Class Performance Programme (WCPP) operates at two distinct levels that make up the World Class Pathway. It covers all funded summer and winter Olympic and Paralympic sports. The two levels are:

✚ **Podium** – designed to support athletes with realistic medal-winning capabilities at the next Olympics/Paralympics (i.e. a maximum of 4 years away from the podium).

✚ **Podium Potential** (previously known as Development) – designed to support athletes whose performances suggest they have realistic medal-winning capabilities at subsequent Olympic/Paralympic Games (i.e. a maximum of 8 years away from the podium).

Beneath Podium Potential is the **Talent** level, which provides funding and support to identify and confirm athletes who have the potential to progress to the World Class Pathway.

> **Exam tip**
>
> For AO1 marks you need to be able to identify the different levels of the WCPP. For AO2, you need to be able to explain the World Class Performance Programme. You should use the correct terms to identify the different levels of the pathway (AO1) before providing clear and correct explanations of the levels to distinguish between them (AO2).

Gold Event Series

UK Sport is the lead agency attempting to ensure that the UK successfully bids to host and stage major sporting events.

It has a flagship programme called the Gold Event Series, which has been working hard to bring 100 targeted major international sporting events to the UK during the 10 years it is operating (i.e. from 2013 to 2023). Successful bids were made to host the World Gymnastics Championships (Liverpool; October–November 2022), the Canoe Slalom World Championships (London; September 2023) and the Trampoline World Championships (Birmingham; November 2023).

✚ The Gold Event Series focuses mainly on attracting World Championships, European Championships and premium world circuit events to the UK.

✚ Prior to developing event bids, UK Sport works with the sport and host location, helping them to draw up a detailed business plan and giving a budget to work to.

✚ When UK Sport agrees a financial award to support an event bid, it continues to work with the NGB involved to develop and support its planning and delivery of the actual event.

✚ Ultimately, UK Sport has a number of objectives it aims to achieve as a result of staging major international sporting events in the UK, including:
  ✚ supporting high-performance success
  ✚ creating high-profile opportunities for people to engage in sport
  ✚ using and demonstrating the legacy of London 2012 and Glasgow 2014
  ✚ driving positive economic and social impacts for the UK

Now test yourself   TESTED ◯

9 Identify the key objectives UK Sport aims to achieve through its Gold Event Series.

Answer on p. 272

Talent identification and development

UK Sport is a lead agency in running talent identification programmes with national institutes of sport, such as the EIS, acting as host venues. The coordinated work of the EIS with UK Sport in supporting talent identification and development is described above. Additional information contained here focuses more on UK Sport's specific roles when looking to discover sporting talent of the future.

+ UK Sport has a clearly defined mission to drive forward Olympic and Paralympic Performance Pathways, which help to ensure continued success at future Games events.
+ Its Performance Pathway team supports World Class Programmes to identify and develop talented athletes and construct the necessary support systems needed to help ensure success. Frontline Technical Solutions are provided via the Pathways Team, looking to create a 'talent profile' that is capable of predicting future Olympic and Paralympic potential.
+ It is also involved in possible positive transfer of sporting talent from one sport to another, following in the footsteps of dual Olympic medal winner Rebecca Romero, who successfully switched from rowing to cycling.
+ The Performance Pathway team also provides specialist knowledge for Olympic and Paralympic talent and development managers and coaches on the issues they face in identifying and developing future generations of elite performers.
+ UK Sport's educational work involves creating a unique learning programme for talent development managers and coaches nominated into the WCPP by their NGB. It draws on best practice in developing excellence in those from many areas of life other than sport, including astronauts, junior surgeons and musicians, to try to learn from 'gold-standard' examples of how to create successful opportunities to progress for elite performers.
+ **Pathway Analytics** enables sports to measure and benchmark the effectiveness of their performance pathway using a Talent Health Check, which is delivered every 4 years by the Performance Pathway team. It discusses topics such as junior to senior transition, as well as retention and attrition rates of athletes on the pathway. Overall, UK Sport looks to develop and implement a clearly defined pathway, vision and strategy, from foundation through to podium level.

UK Sport's talent recruitment and confirmation programmes involve a number of different phases. Campaigns start with a 'talent search', which can involve the general public and/or the sports community. Interested athletes are invited to submit an application form to UK Sport for it to consider, with successful applicants invited to Phase 1 testing, hosted at venues around the home nations. Phase 1 involves performing a range of different fitness and skill tests linked to the sport. Results from these influence progression onto Phases 2 and 3, which further assess an athlete's suitability for a sport via medical screening, performance lifestyle workshops and psychological/behavioural assessments.

Following these assessment phases, selected athletes then embark on a 6–12-month 'confirmation phase', where they are totally immersed into the sport's training environment, with exposure to a carefully constructed developmental experience. Rates of progression are tracked to see if individuals are suitable for the sport and potential funding on their WCPP.

UK Sport also operates a World Class Talent Transfer initiative for athletes exiting an Olympic or Paralympic World Class Programme who are interested in exploring their possible potential to achieve elite-level performance in another sport.

The latest talent ID initiative put in place by UK Sport to discover future Olympic and Paralympic stars is 'From Home 2 The Games' (www.uksport.gov.uk/news/2021/06/02/from-home-2-the-games).

Answer on p. 272

Now test yourself   TESTED ◯

10 What role does pathway analytics play in the talent identification process?

Answer on p. 272

Exam practice

1 UK Sport plays a key role in coordinating talent identification programmes to help achieve its aim of developing elite performers.

Outline and explain the characteristics of an effective talent identification programme. [4]

2 Discuss the use of talent identification programmes in the UK to support the development of elite performers. [6]

3 Large numbers of Team GB athletes who were successful in Tokyo 2020 were supported by UK Sport National Lottery funding. Justify the decision to allocate this funding based on performances at major competitions. [6]

4 Which of the following organisations is responsible for the Gold Events Series? [1]
   A EIS
   B UK Sport
   C Sport England
   D British Gymnastics

5 Identify three personal qualities necessary for elite performer development. [3]

6 Outline two possible disadvantages of using talent ID programmes. [2]

7 Explain 'World Class Podium' as part of the World Class Performance Pathway. [2]

Answers online

Knowledge and skills summary

This topic involves the following knowledge (AO1):
+ Identification of the factors required to support progression from talent identification to elite performance.
+ Strategies that UK Sport, national institutes of sport (e.g. the EIS) and NGBs have in place to support elite performer development in the UK.
+ Reasons for and against talent identification programmes.
+ Different levels of the World Class Performance Programme (WCPP).
+ Key features of UK Sport's programmes supporting elite performer development in the UK, including the World

Class Performance Programme, the Gold Event Series and Talent Identification and Development.

AO2 marks will require application of this knowledge – for example, explaining the reasons for and against talent identification programmes; explaining the different levels of the WCPP.

AO3 marks are for analysis or evaluation – for example, analysing or evaluating the effectiveness of talent identification programmes in the UK; analysing or evaluating the relative success of organisations such as UK Sport and NGBs in achieving Olympic/Paralympic sporting success.

7.3 Ethics in sport

Amateurism

REVISED ●

Amateurism was a nineteenth-century code or ideal of sporting ethics that developed among upper and then middle classes during the Victorian era.

In the nineteenth century, elite sport was dominated by the upper and middle classes, who had high status in sport as well as in society. Upper- and middle-class amateurs held a higher status than professionals at the time.

In modern-day British sport, amateurism is still evident:

+ Fair play/sportsmanship is still viewed positively, encouraged and promoted in various ways – for example, the Fair Play Awards in football, shaking of hands prior to and at the end of sporting contests, and through the Olympics, with the Olympic ideal based on principles of amateurism.
+ Some sports maintained their amateurism until late into the twentieth century and still have codes of conduct based on such principles – for example, rugby union players calling a referee 'Sir' and shaking hands at the end of a match/applauding the opposition off the field of play.

> **Amateurism** Participation in sport for the love of it, receiving no financial gain; it is based on the concept of athleticism (i.e. physical endeavour with moral integrity).

> **Making links**
>
> Ethical principles associated with amateurism can be traced back, and therefore linked to, sport and society (pp. 83–84), which includes the role of the public schools in promoting fair play in sport.

The Olympic oath

REVISED ●

Originally written by Baron de Coubertin, the founder of the modern Olympics, the Olympic oath was first taken at the 1920 summer Olympics in Antwerp. It comprises promises made by one athlete (as a representative of all of the participating competitors), one coach (as a representative of all coaches) and one judge (as a representative of the Olympic officials), who commit to impartiality at the opening ceremony of each Olympics.

The current oath of the athlete reads as follows:

```
We promise to take part in these Olympic Games,
respecting and abiding by the rules and in the spirit
of fair play, inclusion and equality. Together we
stand in solidarity and commit ourselves to sport
without doping, without cheating, without any form of
discrimination.
```

You could argue that it is still relevant in modern-day sport because:

+ The Olympics are still viewed by large numbers of people as a festival of sport, with fair play and sportsmanship very much in evidence.
+ Amateurism is still encouraged, with no prize money or appearance fees paid by the IOC.

However, there are unfortunately many examples of doping and positive drugs tests at Olympic Games (e.g. Ben Johnson at the Seoul Olympics in 1988). Some argue that this leaves the relevance of the Olympic oath in question. Ben Johnson is thought to have sparked a significant increase in drugs testing and a tightening up of procedures and practices, following his positive test for drugs the day after winning the 100 metres gold medal, breaking the world record in the process.

In addition, with professional athletes now allowed to compete in the Games, more examples of 'win-at-all-costs' behaviour and stretching of the rules to

Check your understanding and progress at **www.hoddereducation.co.uk/myrevisionnotes**

their absolute limit are occurring in Olympic sport, which further questions respect of, and adherence to, the oath (e.g. Russian athletes during the London 2012 Olympics).

The impartiality of Olympic judges has also been the subject of a formal enquiry by Richard McLaren following Rio 2016. He discovered that a system was used to manipulate the outcome of boxing matches, which resulted in some unfair decisions being given. All 36 boxing judges and referees from Rio 2016 were banned from officiating at the 2020 Tokyo Olympics.

> **Exam tip**
>
> For AO2 and AO3 it is important to develop knowledge and understanding of discussions/evaluations concerning the continued relevance of ethics, such as the Olympic oath in relation to the Olympics in the twenty-first century.

Sportsmanship

REVISED ◯

Sportsmanship involves playing by the unwritten rules to a high code of ethics.

Fairness, maintaining self-control and treating others fairly are all positive virtues associated with sportsmanship. It also involves maintaining high levels of etiquette to ensure fair play is clearly evident in a sporting contest. It therefore involves playing the game in a positive spirit, with respect shown for opponents and officials alike.

Examples of sportsmanship at elite level include the following:
+ Professional footballers returning the ball to the opposition when it has been kicked out of play to allow an injured player to have treatment.
+ Cricketers 'walking' before being given out when they know they have made contact with bat on ball and it has been caught.
+ Professional sports performers sometimes showing 'good grace' when returning to play at former clubs and not celebrating the scoring of a goal or try as a mark of respect to their old football or rugby club.

In modern-day sport, sportsmanship is under attack, as winning becomes increasingly important. For example:
+ When a team is winning, they often stretch the rules and waste time to ensure a victory.
+ Some performers have earned a negative reputation for simulation/diving in the penalty area to try to unfairly win a penalty or get an opponent sent off.
+ In addition, violent actions have seemingly replaced the civilised behaviour more evident in the amateur era of many sports.
+ On occasions, performers constantly question the decisions of referees or refuse to adopt sporting etiquette with their opponents (e.g. refusal to shake hands at the end of a match).

Sportsmanship
Conforming to the unwritten rules, spirit and etiquette of a sport.

Simulation Trying to deceive an official by overacting – for example, diving to win a free kick.

> **Now test yourself** TESTED ◯
>
> 1 Define the term 'sportsmanship'.
> 2 Give two examples of how amateurism is still evident in rugby union.
> 3 State who takes the Olympic oath in addition to the athlete representative at the start of each Olympics.
>
> **Answers on p. 272**

> **Exam tip**
>
> For AO1, when defining sportsmanship, students often link it purely to 'playing by the rules' instead of focusing on the key element of playing according to unwritten rules/positive codes of conduct.

While the pressure is on to 'win at all costs', sportsmanship can still be encouraged by the following:
+ Use of NGB campaigns promoting sportsmanship/fair play (e.g. FA Respect).
+ The giving of awards for fair play to encourage it in top-level sport, thereby providing positive role models for youngsters to follow. The UEFA Fair Play

Awards include a place in a European competition awarded on the basis of fair play/sportsmanship.

+ Use of technology to help match officials reach the correct decisions and allow performers to be cited after matches for behaviour that goes against the rules.

+ Introduction of NGB rules promoting fair play (e.g. banning high or late tackles).

+ Punishing foul play and unsporting behaviour on the field of play and within the sporting event (e.g. officials can 'sin bin', book or send a player off).

+ Punishing foul play and unsporting behaviour after the event (e.g. fines or bans imposed by national governing bodies of sport).

+ Use of positive role models to promote sportsmanship and fair play.

+ Use of rigorous drug testing to try to ensure fairness in sporting contests and catch out drugs cheats.

Now test yourself   TESTED ◯

4   Identify different ways in which elite level sports performers fail to adopt the sportsmanship ethic, and suggest ways in which sportsmanship is encouraged and maintained in high-level/elite sport.

Answer on p. 273

Gamesmanship   REVISED ◯

Gamesmanship can be described as the art of winning games by cunning means, but without breaking the rules. However, there is often a fine line between gamesmanship and cheating. Gamesmanship therefore involves stretching the rules to the limit and failing to follow the etiquette of the game or sporting contest. There are many examples of gamesmanship in elite-level, modern-day sport:

+ Delaying play at a restart to get back in defence (e.g. by keeping possession of the ball).

+ Time-wasting when ahead in a game to try to ensure victory.

+ Verbally 'sledging' an opponent to distract or upset them – for example, in cricket, a bowler or fielder might say something to upset the concentration of a batsman in an effort to get them out.

+ Psyching out an opponent at a pre-match press conference.

+ Taking an injury time-out, toilet break or appealing a decision to the umpire even when it is not necessarily needed, to upset the concentration or rhythm of an opponent (e.g. in tennis or cricket).

+ Deliberate deception of an official to try to gain an advantage – for example, over-appealing for a wicket in cricket or a penalty in football, or claiming for a decision that is not necessarily theirs.

+ Over-reacting to a challenge in a bid to put pressure on a referee to book or send off an opponent.

> **Gamesmanship** Bending the rules and stretching them to their absolute limit without getting caught; using whatever dubious methods possible to achieve the desired result.

Exam tip

For an AO1 definition question on gamesmanship you should not refer to breaking the rules, cheating or taking performance-enhancing drugs. Remember, it is about bending the rules to their limit in order to win.

Now test yourself   TESTED ◯

5   Identify the similarities and differences between gamesmanship and negative forms of deviancy in sport.

6   Give two examples of gamesmanship in cricket.

Answers on p. 273

Win ethic   REVISED ◯

The win ethic links to the sporting ethic of 'win at all costs', where coming second is not viewed as an option and the outcome is all that matters.

Check your understanding and progress at **www.hoddereducation.co.uk/myrevisionnotes**

The win ethic has sometimes been called the 'Lombardian ethic' after the Green Bay Packers American football coach, Vince Lombardi. Lombardi claimed that, for him, '…winning was not a sometime thing, it was an all-time thing'.

In modern-day rugby, where the code of amateurism was protected until late in the twentieth century, top-level coaches have even resorted to using fake blood capsules to mimic a blood injury so that a specialist kicker can enter the field at a crucial game stage, when kicking a penalty is required to win.

Performers also try to ensure victory when the stakes are high by cheating in various ways. Diego Maradona was famous for his 'hand of God', which involved illegally punching a ball into the back of the net to help Argentina to victory over England in the 1986 Football World Cup. Seemingly, winning is all that matters when the rewards for winning are high and livelihoods are at stake.

The win ethic is evident in modern-day elite sport via the following examples:
+ No drawn games – for example, there is always a winner in basketball, American football, and League Cup football in England.
+ Managers and coaches are fired if unsuccessful (e.g. Premier League football managers).
+ High amounts of deviance (e.g. violence, over-aggression, doping – see below).
+ Media praise for winners; positive newspaper headlines.
+ Media negativity for losers.

Now test yourself   TESTED ○

7   The Lombardian ethic is a dominant sporting ethic in twenty-first century elite sport. How is such a 'win at all costs' ethic displayed in sporting contests?

Answer on p. 273

Positive and negative deviance   REVISED ○

Positive deviance

Deviance is behaviour that goes against the norms of society and is deemed to be unacceptable.

In terms of sports performers, positive deviance involves over-adherence or over-conformity to the norms and expectations of society. For example, a performer might over-train or try to compete in a sporting event, despite being injured.

Retired marathon runner Paula Radcliffe is one example of an elite performer doing her best to win for her country at the 2004 Athens Olympics, despite carrying an injury that ultimately led to her pulling out of the race part-way through.

Another example of positive deviance is where a performer is striving to win within the rules or etiquette of a sport, who accidentally and without intent injures another player – for example, in November 2019, when Tottenham player Son accidentally broke the leg of Everton midfielder Gomes, which brought Son to tears).

> **Positive deviance**
> Behaviour that is outside the norms of society but with no intent to harm or break the rules. It involves over-adherence to the norms or expectations of society.

Negative deviance

Negative deviance in sports performers involves under-conformity to the norms and expectations of society. The motivation to win at all costs encourages performers who lack moral restraint to act against the norms of society and sport in various ways and cheat. Examples of negative deviance include the following:
+ Taking illegal performance-enhancing drugs.

> **Negative deviance**
> Behaviour that goes against the norms and has a detrimental effect on individuals and society in general.

+ Deliberately fouling or harming an opponent through aggressive or violent actions.
+ Accepting a bribe to lose – match-fixing.
+ Diving to win a penalty or free kick.

Making links

For AO2 you might be required to apply your knowledge and link deviance in sport in a synoptic manner with sport and the law (pp. 225–230).

Exam tips

When defining positive deviance (AO1) you must make reference to the fact that there is no intent to harm or break the rules.

Remember, deviance can be positive or negative. For AO2, make sure that you can provide examples and explanations for both types of deviance, particularly in relation to positive deviance, the more difficult of the two.

Now test yourself   TESTED

8 Using examples, explain the terms 'positive deviance' and 'negative deviance' in relation to the performer.
9 Define the terms (a) gamesmanship and (b) amateurism.

Answers on p. 273

Revision activity

Draw a table with two columns, one identifying the seven key sports ethics terms from the specification, the other stating clear definitions and practical examples of these ethical terms.

Exam practice

1 Which of the following statements best describes the term 'gamesmanship'? [1]
   A Over-adherence to the rules
   B Breaking the rules
   C Stretching the rules to their limit
   D Playing to the rules
2 Using examples, explain the difference between *sportsmanship* and *gamesmanship*. [4]
3 Discuss the suggestion that increased commercialisation of sport has had a negative effect on traditional sports performer values, such as sportsmanship/ fair play and the Olympic oath. [5]
4 Outline strategies sporting authorities such as national governing bodies could use to encourage higher standards of individual performer behaviour. [3]
5 Describe how deviance in sport has increased in the twenty-first century. [5]
6 Define the Olympic oath. [2]
7 Give two examples of positive deviance in sport. [2]

Answers online

Knowledge and skills summary

This topic involves the following knowledge (AO1):
+ Definitions of the following sports ethics terms: amateurism, sportsmanship, the Olympic oath, gamesmanship, win ethic, positive deviance and negative deviance.

AO2 marks will require application of this knowledge – for example, using relevant practical sporting examples linked to these ethical terms.

AO3 marks are for analysis or evaluation in extended questions – for example, an analysis of the continued relevance or existence of the Olympic oath or sportsmanship in modern-day Olympic Games or elite sport.

7.4 Violence in sport

Causes and implications of violence in sport

REVISED

Sporting ethics are introduced and explained on pages 210–214. Of these, the 'win ethic' in particular can help explain why performers become aggressive and ultimately commit violence in sport during sporting contests. On occasions, pre-match media hype and intense build-up to a key contest can 'over-psych' a performer and lead them to become over-aggressive (for example, via a high tackle in rugby).

Frustration with decisions made by match officials might create a sense of injustice and increase frustration for sports performers, which ultimately leads them to become violent on the field of play – for example, performing a late tackle or retaliation against an opponent. Performer violence might also occur as a result of abuse or provocation from opponents and/or the crowd. Some sports are viewed as naturally more violent than others because aggression and high levels of physical contact are viewed as part of the game.

Some of the causes of player violence can be remembered using the mnemonic 'WINNER':

+ **W**in ethic and high rewards for success.
+ **I**mportance/emotional intensity of an event (e.g. local derby/cup final).
+ **N**ature of the sport is aggressive/intense (e.g. rugby union, American football, ice hockey)
+ **N**ational governing bodies are too lenient with their punishments.
+ **E**xcitement/over-arousal
+ **R**efereeing decisions are questionable/poor leading to frustration.

> **Aggression** An emotional response (involving anger) to an individual perceived as an enemy or a frustrating rival; an intent to harm outside the laws of the game.
>
> **Violence in sport**
> Physical acts committed to deliberately harm others, which can occur in sports such as American football, rugby, football and ice hockey.

Now test yourself

TESTED

1 Suggest possible reasons why a performer might become violent during a sporting contest.

2 State three examples of sports that are aggressive or intense, and therefore more likely to lead to player violence than sports that are non-aggressive or less intense.

Answers on p. 273

Making links

You should be aware of the possible synoptic link between the causes of performer violence and sports ethics – in particular, negative deviance and the win ethic.

You should also be aware of the possible synoptic link between the causes of performer violence and theories of aggression as part of sport psychology (pp. 168–170).

Strategies for preventing violence in sport

REVISED

Players can often become aggressive in fast-moving, highly competitive sporting contests. A coach can use a range of strategies to reduce aggressive behaviour in a sports performer, including the following:

+ Remove the performer or player from the pitch or substitute them.
+ Punish aggressive behaviour – for example, by fining them or leaving them out of the team for a certain number of matches.
+ Increase peer pressure (e.g. on the field of play via a teammate/captain) to act less aggressively.
+ Educate the performer; reinforce use of assertive behaviour.
+ Provide positive role model behaviour to aspire to.
+ Highlight their responsibility to the team/negative impact on them if aggression leads to being sent off/banned from future matches.

+ Decrease the emphasis on winning.
+ Use stress management techniques with a sport psychologist (e.g. positive self-talk).
+ Work on improving fitness to decrease the likelihood of fatigue negatively affecting mood/mind-set.

The frustration caused by poor officiating can be decreased by using more officials to help reach decisions as actions occur 'on the field of play'. For example, extra officials have been trialled and adopted in the Europa League, where two additional officials are employed to help with decisions close to goal, and one additional official is situated on each goal line.

'Off the field of play', sporting contests can be stopped and video technology used to help reach the correct decision – for example, via a fourth official. This can help decrease performer frustration with officials and any perceived injustice, because the decision is taken out of the referee's hands and given to an individual in the stands, using technology to help them reach the 'correct' decision. For example, football uses a video assistant referee (VAR), while in rugby league, the television match official (TMO) is an official who reviews plays by looking at video footage when asked to by the on-field referee.

> **Television match official (TMO)** An official, who is a qualified referee, who can review plays by looking at video footage when asked to by the on-field referee.

> **Now test yourself** TESTED ◯
>
> **3** Identify three strategies a rugby coach could use to reduce aggressive behaviour by one of their players.
>
> **Answer on p. 273**

If a lack of punishment or effective deterrents is a cause of violence, then the sporting authorities/NGBs and even the law need to apply tougher sanctions. These sanctions could include longer bans, higher fines on players or the deduction of points from clubs.

In extreme cases, where there are particularly violent actions by performers on the field of play, court action might be taken and a possible prison sentence imposed (as was the case with Rangers player Duncan Ferguson, who received a 3-month prison sentence for his head butt on Raith Rovers player Jock McStay in 1994).

In most sporting situations where particularly aggressive actions have occurred, it is normally the NGB of the sport that is responsible for discouraging performer violence and promoting higher standards of behaviour. Controlling violent behaviour in their sport is therefore an important responsibility of the NGBs, who are keen to present a positive image to fans and future performers, as well as potential sponsors. They can take various actions to try to prevent player violence, including the following:

+ Supporting the decisions of match officials when dealing with violence by performers by using a TMO/video replays to check decisions being made, changing/clarifying rules on violent acts (e.g. high tackles in rugby), and training officials to develop the skills necessary to diffuse or calm down match situations that could potentially develop into aggressive behaviour.
+ Retrospectively punishing violence by performers that was missed by officials, using video evidence. Appropriate action might be taken against the performer and/or the club itself if the latter is deemed not to be in control of its players. Fines and/or point deductions might be imposed on clubs for repeat offences of violence among its players.
+ Use of post-match video evidence, where individuals have been cited by referees as performing violent actions worthy of further investigation. For example, the rugby league 'on-report' system allows a referee who sees what they believe to be an act of foul play to highlight the incident immediately to independent reviewers.

Check your understanding and progress at **www.hoddereducation.co.uk/myrevisionnotes**

- Promoting performers with good disciplinary records as positive role models in their sport.
- Imposing punishments for violent actions on the field of play (e.g. sin bin/ booking/sending off).
- Introducing education campaigns and/or rewards linked to fair play. For example, the FA and its Respect campaign – West Ham qualified for the Europa League after topping the Premier League Fair Play table in 2014–15. From 2016, winning associations of the UEFA Fair Play competition have been awarded prize money to allocate to fair play or respect-themed projects of their choice.

If such strategies do not work, there might be a potential negative impact for a sport as a result of the negative publicity associated with a performers' over-aggressive behaviour. This might take the form of:

- lower attendances/gate receipts at a sporting event
- declining participation numbers in a sport
- negative media reporting/decreased media coverage
- reduced sponsorship/media revenue
- negative role models encouraging an increase in poor behaviour in the sport among the young/amateur performers
- increased pressure on NGBs to introduce strategies to eliminate/decrease negative aggressive behaviour in their sport

Causes and implications of violence in sport in relation to the spectator and the sport

REVISED

Spectator violence has been particularly evident over the years in the sport of football. This section reviews the causes of football hooliganism and considers the negative implications of such violence.

Football hooliganism
Unruly, violent and destructive behaviour by over-zealous supporters of association football clubs.

A variety of factors can be identified as causing football hooliganism:

- Emotional intensity and the ritual importance of the event – for example, a local derby, with team loyalty taken to extremes.
- Too much alcohol and/or the 'highs' caused by drug-taking.
- Pre-match media hype stirring up tensions between rival fans.
- Poor policing, stewarding and crowd control (one of the key reasons identified for the Hillsborough Stadium disaster in 1989).
- Lack of effective deterrents and punishments to discourage individuals from involving themselves in violence at football matches.
- Diminished responsibility by individuals in a large group (i.e. a football crowd); organised violence as part of a gang and peer pressure to get involved in violence.
- Reaction of working class individuals, who perceive the middle class to be taking over 'their game'.
- Poor officiating or frustration with match officials, which heightens tensions between rival fans.

217

+ Violence by players on the pitch being reflected in the crowd.
+ Religious discord – for example, at a Celtic vs Rangers match, where tensions are particularly high between rival fans of the Protestant and Catholic religions.
+ A negative violent reaction occurring as a result of chants and taunts by rival fans; frustration at one's own team losing leading some in the crowd to become violent – for example, when fans of the opposition keep chanting reminders of the score.
+ Violence used by young males as a display of their masculinity, caused by an adrenaline rush when attending a match.

Now test yourself   TESTED

4   Hooliganism is often associated with excessive alcohol consumption. Identify other causes of spectator violence at football matches.

Answer on p. 274

Making links

You should be aware of the possible synoptic link between the implications of performer and spectator violence and sport and the law (e.g. via intent to harm; trespass laws).

Strategies for preventing violence

Strategies being employed to combat crowd violence at football matches include the following:

+ Bans on, or control of, alcohol sales – for example, ban pubs where known trouble makers gather from opening prior to kick-off.
+ Increased use of police intelligence and improved liaison between forces across the country to gather information on known or potential hooligans.
+ Imposing tougher deterrents like bans from matches, higher fines and prosecution/imprisonment for violent offenders; banning individuals from travelling abroad.
+ Using CCTV in and around stadiums to identify and then eject or arrest individuals for crowd disorder.
+ Removal of terraces, building of 'all-seater' stadiums, segregation of fans, and family zones to create a better, 'more civilised' atmosphere at football matches; promoting football as family entertainment.
+ Encouraging responsible media reporting prior to matches; decreasing the hype and potential tensions between rival fans.
+ Playing games at kick-off times imposed by the police – for example, early kick-offs to try to avoid high levels of alcohol consumption.
+ Passing specific laws preventing 'trespass' onto the pitch to try to stop pitch invasions and potential clashes between rival fans in the ground.

Exam tip

If a synoptic question is set linking solutions to hooliganism with sport and the law, you need to make sure the answers you give have a clear link to law enforcement. For example, encouraging responsible media reporting is not a legal solution, but passing a trespass law to discourage pitch encroachment is.

Making links

You should be aware of the possible synoptic link between this topic and sport and the law in relation to strategies being implemented to address (i.e. decrease) performer and spectator violence.

Revision activity

Draw a table to identify the potential causes of spectator violence, alongside possible solutions to such causes.

Now test yourself   TESTED

5   Identify the negative effects of hooliganism for law-abiding football fans.

Answer on p. 274

When football hooliganism was at its height towards the end of the twentieth century (especially in the 1970s and 1980s), there were some **negative consequences** for the sport of football:

Check your understanding and progress at **www.hoddereducation.co.uk/myrevisionnotes**

+ Hooliganism had negative implications for football clubs **as a result of** the ever-increasing costs of security and policing before, during and after matches. This was particularly the case for clubs in the lower leagues, where money was tighter.
+ The negative images of football hooliganism involving English 'fans' at home and abroad were often viewed globally and portrayed England as a nation of violent thugs who were out of control. This then had a negative influence on relations with other countries and on bids to host international sporting events.
+ It also had repercussions for commercial deals and sponsorships of leagues or cup competitions as these came up for renewal.

Now test yourself

TESTED

6 Explain the negative implications of hooliganism for the sport of football.

Answer on p. 274

Exam tips

When you are asked to 'explain' the negatives of spectator violence for a sport (AO2), you should avoid just listing bullet points that lack the detail necessary to score well in exams.

For AO1, you need to develop knowledge of various causes of performer and spectator violence and be able to identify/state a range of possible consequences of this for the performer, spectator and sport. For AO2, you must remember to apply your knowledge of causes and consequences of performer and spectator violence, using appropriate explanation of points being made, backed up by relevant examples where appropriate. For AO3, you need to be able to analyse/evaluate any data given in questions relating to the frequency of performer and spectator violence.

Exam practice

1 Identify the possible solutions to violent behaviour among spectators in high-level sports such as football. [4]

2 Elite sport performers are expected to act as positive role models for others to follow. Outline possible reasons why an elite performer might act in an aggressive way that is deemed unacceptable by society. [4]

3 Explain possible strategies national governing bodies could use to eliminate acts of violence by sports performers. [4]

4 Outline the causes of violent behaviour in high-level sports such as association football. [3]

5 Table 7.9 shows the number of red cards awarded in the English FA Premier League across four seasons. Red cards can be given for aggressive acts.

Table 7.9

Season	Number of red cards
2013/14	73
2014/15	58
2015/16	45
2016/17	41

Instinct theory and the frustration–aggression hypothesis are psychological theories relating to aggression in sport.

Use these theories to analyse why aggressive acts still exist in football and evaluate the effectiveness of strategies used to prevent such violence. [15]

Answers online

This topic involves the following knowledge (AO1):
+ Causes and implications of performer violence in sport.
+ Strategies used to try to combat such aggression among sports performers.
+ Causes and implications of violence in sport in relation to the spectator and sport in general, as well as strategies for preventing hooliganism at football matches.

AO2 marks will ask for application of this knowledge – for example, illustrating your understanding of causes and implications of performer violence in sport, linked to a variety of examples where such violence has occurred.

AO3 marks are for analysis or evaluation. In an AO3 response for this topic make sure that you analyse/evaluate any data given in questions relating to the frequency of performer and spectator violence.

7.5 Drugs in sport

Reasons for using illegal drugs and doping

REVISED

The use of illegal drugs and doping methods to enhance performance at elite level continues to be a major issue in sport in the twenty-first century.

The social reasons for drug taking and using doping methods to enhance performance illegally include the following:
+ A win-at-all-costs attitude, which dominates modern-day elite sport.
+ The fame and fortune attached to success at elite level (i.e. the very high level of extrinsic rewards/money received for sporting success via prize money, sponsorship deals and so on).
+ The high levels of pressure to win from a variety of different sources, including coaches, family and media expectations. (Coaches might persuade athletes to take drugs illegally because the main competitors are doing so, and they will not be able to compete with them on a level playing field if they do not.)
+ The lack of effective deterrents and a firm belief that they will get away with it and not get caught.
+ Poor role models setting a bad example in suggesting that drug taking in certain sports is viewed in some way as being acceptable (e.g. athletics and cycling).

Doping In competitive sports, the use of banned performance-enhancing drugs by athletic competitors.

In addition to the various social reasons, elite performers also use illegal performance-enhancing drugs and doping to aid their **psychological performance** in a variety of different ways:
+ Some might use beta blockers to slow their heartbeat when fine motor control is required (e.g. in archery, pistol shooting and snooker).
+ Others might use anabolic steroids to increase their aggression in high-contact sports (e.g. rugby players).
+ When athletes are suffering from a lack of confidence, stimulants can be used to raise a performer's belief that they can achieve, even when the competition is of the highest standard (e.g. at the Olympic Games).

Stimulants Drugs that induce a temporary improvement in mental and physical function (e.g. increase alertness and awareness).

Now test yourself

TESTED

1 Identify the social and psychological reasons why elite performers continue to take illegal performance-enhancing drugs despite obvious dangers to their health.

Answer on p. 274

Making links

In exam questions, you might be required to make the link between the social and psychological reasons behind elite performers using illegal drugs and doping to aid performance and ethics in sport, the win ethic and negative deviance.

Physiological effects of drugs

REVISED ⬤

All athletes want to improve their performance, and there are both legal and illegal methods, in addition to training, of achieving this. Table 7.10 lists the illegal drugs that some athletes feel the need to use.

Table 7.10 Illegal drugs used by some athletes

Method of enhancement	What are they?	Reasons why this method is used (i.e. physiological benefits)	Which athletes might use them?	Side-effects
Anabolic steroids	Artificially produced hormones, e.g. **tetrahydrogestrinone (THG)**	They aid in the storage of protein and promote muscle growth and development of muscle tissue in the body, leading to increased strength and power; they also lead to less fat in the muscle and a lean body weight They can improve the body's capacity to train for longer at a higher intensity, and decrease fatigue associated with training	They are particularly beneficial to power athletes, such as sprinters	Liver damage, heart and immune system problems Acne and behaviour changes, such as aggression, paranoia and mood swings
Beta blockers	Help to calm an individual down and decrease anxiety by counteracting the adrenaline that interferes with performance, by preventing it from binding to nerve receptors	They can be used to improve accuracy in precision sports through steadying the nerves They reduce anxiety and aid performance by keeping the heart rate low and decreasing tremble in the hands They work by widening the arteries, allowing increased blood flow and reducing involuntary muscle spasms	Particularly relevant in high-precision sports such as archery, snooker and golf	Tiredness due to low blood pressure and slower heart rate, which will affect aerobic capacity
Erythropoietin (EPO)	A natural hormone produced by the kidneys to increase red blood cells Now it can be artificially manufactured to cause an increase in haemoglobin levels	It stimulates red blood cell production, which leads to an increase in the oxygen-carrying capacity of the body; this can result in an increase in the amount of work performed It therefore increases endurance and delays the onset of fatigue; the athlete can keep going for longer and recover more quickly from training	Tends to be used by endurance performers (e.g. long-distance runners and cyclists) who need effective oxygen transport to succeed in their sport	Can result in blood clotting, stroke and, in rare cases, death

Tetrahydrogestrinone (THG) A banned steroid used to increase power, which was tweaked by chemists to make it undetectable by 'normal tests'.

Erythropoietin (EPO) A hormone that is naturally produced by the kidneys, but can also be artificially produced to increase performance in endurance athletes such as long-distance cyclists.

221

Positive and negative implications of drug taking

REVISED ◯

In terms of 'the sport', drug taking/doping has the following implications:

+ It threatens the spirit and integrity of the sport.
+ It is cheating, and damages the reputation of a sport, decreasing interest in it.
+ Certain sports are strongly associated with drugs cheats – for example, Ben Johnson and athletics, Lance Armstrong and cycling.

In terms of 'the performer':

+ Drug taking can *impact positively* on performance, bringing fame and fortune for those who manage to evade detection.

However, there are many negative implications of drug taking for the performer:

+ It provides negative role models, which set a bad example to young people.
+ It can be very damaging to a performer's health (steroids can lead to high blood pressure; EPO can increase the risk of heart disease and strokes; beta blockers can lead to low blood pressure).
+ There are also negative social consequences because athletes involved in doping might lose their good reputation following a positive test.
+ Future career prospects might be negatively impacted, with a loss of income and sponsorship deals resulting from doping infringements being widely reported in the media.
+ In certain cases, it can result in legal action against an individual, who can be fined, banned from competing, stripped of medals and earnings and even end up in jail (e.g. Marion Jones as part of the BALCO scandal).
+ Doping can lead to social isolation from peers, as well as having a negative effect on an individual's emotional and psychological wellbeing.

BALCO The Bay Area Laboratory Cooperative, which was behind one of the biggest scandals in drugs history as the source of THG, with several athletes implicated and subsequently banned from sport, including sprinters Dwain Chambers and Marion Jones.

Strategies for elimination of drugs in sport

UK Anti-Doping (UKAD) is the organisation responsible for protecting UK sport from the threat of drug taking and doping. It administers the testing programmes for over 40 sports and has anti-doping strategies designed to try to eliminate the use of illegal performance enhancers in sport.

Educationally, UKAD works with athletes and their support staff (e.g. coaches) to increase their knowledge and understanding of the dangers of drugs and the moral issues associated with doping. It promotes ethically fair, drug-free sport via its '100% Me' programme. This programme is delivered to athletes at all stages of the performance pathway, and includes rising stars at the School Games as well as elite athletes preparing for the Olympics and Paralympics.

Investment in drug-detection technology, science and medicine are also used by UKAD to try to ensure that it can prevent and detect doping.

It works in a coordinated manner with other organisations involved in drug detection and prevention, such as the World Anti-Doping Agency (WADA) and the national governing bodies of sport. Such a cooperative approach is important when trying to develop and enforce stricter testing procedures to try to catch out the drug takers. These procedures include random testing, out-of-competition testing, and the 'whereabouts system').

Once a drugs cheat has been detected and caught, it is important that organisations punish the athlete as harshly as possible to act as a deterrent to those considering following a similar route. Harsher punishments might include longer or lifetime bans, and the return of career earnings and money gained from sponsorship.

It is important to try to adopt a standardised, consistent approach across different countries and different sports when punishing drugs cheats, so that elite performers who are 'clean' gain confidence from a unified system that deals strongly with convicted drugs cheats.

Where positive role models exist, they should be used to promote ethically fair, drug-free sport – for example, Sir Chris Hoy and the 100% Me campaign, which promotes the fact that winning clean is possible.

In addition, drugs cheats should be 'named and shamed' to try to dissuade others from following their negative example.

You can remember the strategies being used to decrease drug usage as 'DOPING':

+ **D**rug-free culture created via education programmes (e.g. 100% Me).
+ **O**rganisations involved in drug detection/enforcement need to work together.
+ **P**unishments need to be harsher.
+ **I**nvestment is required into new testing programmes/technology.
+ **N**ame and shame negative role models.
+ **G**uilty lose funding/sponsorship deals.

> **WADA (World Anti-Doping Agency)** A foundation created in 1999 through a collective initiative led by the IOC to promote, coordinate and monitor the fight against drugs in sport.
>
> **Whereabouts system** A system designed to support out-of-competition testing, which requires athletes to supply the details of their whereabouts so that they can be located at any time and anywhere for testing, without advance notice.

> **Exam tip**
>
> For AO1, make sure you can identify a number of strategies being used to eliminate performance-enhancing drugs in sport. For AO2, it is important that you can apply your knowledge of these strategies by explaining how they are being implemented. For AO3, make sure that you can evaluate the effectiveness of the strategies in eliminating performance-enhancing drugs in sport.

> **Making links**
>
> Be prepared in exam answers to make the link between the role of technology in sport and its positive and negative impacts (pp. 246–247) and strategies for the elimination of performance-enhancing drugs in sport.

> **Now test yourself**   TESTED
>
> 4 Explain the advantages of all sports in all countries testing for performance-enhancing drugs.
>
> **Answer on p. 274**

Arguments for and against drug taking and testing

Various arguments can be used *for* the legalisation of drugs in sport, allowing them to be just another training aid. These are outlined below:

+ The battle against drugs is expensive and time consuming.
+ Drugs are quite easy to access, and some would argue that they are very difficult to eliminate. The money spent on testing could be better spent on things like participation initiatives and/or investment in elite sport.
+ Detection is not always effective; drug testers are always one step behind because new drugs become available and masking agents are developed.
+ Sometimes it is difficult to define what a 'drug' is, compared with a legal supplement. Other technological aids, such as oxygen tents and nutritional supplements, are not regulated.
+ Drugs are sometimes taken 'accidentally' – for example, stimulants in cold cures, as with skier Alain Baxter).
+ Sacrifices made by a performer are a personal choice.
+ If everyone takes drugs, it levels the playing field and increases performance standards physiologically and psychologically.
+ If drug taking is properly monitored, health risks might be lessened.
+ Athletes do not ask to be role models, and individuals have a right to choose because it is their body.
+ Drugs can be particularly helpful to athletes in allowing them to recover more quickly from gruelling training.

> **Exam tip**
>
> It is too vague to justify legalising drugs by saying that it would make a sport more exciting or that it would lead to money being saved.

Most people, however, would argue *against* the points above, and point out that drugs should continue to be banned in sport for a variety of different reasons. These are outlined below:

+ There can be health risks and dangerous side-effects (addiction/heart disorders).
+ Drug taking creates negative role models, who set a poor example to the young, who might then be tempted to use drugs.
+ Drug use gives a negative image to certain sports (e.g. weight lifting, cycling, athletics).
+ Pressure to take drugs increases from coaches and peers who take drugs.
+ Success in sport should be about hard work and natural talent; drug use is outside this concept.
+ Drugs give an unfair advantage and are immoral, unethical and against the fair-play ethic.
+ Taking drugs is cheating.
+ Only richer countries can afford the drugs.
+ There are several negative consequences if caught doping, such as loss of sponsorship, loss of medals and loss of lottery funding.
+ Drug taking is illegal.

> **Now test yourself**   TESTED ⬤
>
> 5 Identify three sports that have gained a negative reputation resulting from links to elite performers testing positive for illegal performance-enhancing drugs.
>
> **Answer on p. 274**

> **Exam tip**
>
> When discussing the issues surrounding drugs and sport, make sure that you clearly identify (AO1) and outline (AO2) *both* sides of the argument for and against the legalisation of drugs in sport.

Check your understanding and progress at **www.hoddereducation.co.uk/myrevisionnotes**

Exam practice

1 Elite athletes continue to take performance-enhancing drugs despite obvious risks to their health and the negative implications of being caught. Give reasons why drug taking continues at elite sporting events such as the Olympics. [4]

2 Describe the physiological reasons why an elite performer might use anabolic steroids just like any other training aid. [3]

3 Outline the strategies being used by sports organisations to try to decrease the use of drugs by elite performers. [4]

4 Explain the problems faced by drug enforcement agencies in the world of sport (e.g. WADA/UK Anti-Doping) in their fight to eliminate performance-enhancing drugs at the elite performer level. [5]

5 Using the headings coordination and education, outline the strategies being used by sports organisations to decrease the use of illegal performance-enhancing drugs by elite performers. [2]

6 Outline and evaluate the strategies sports organisations use to limit the use of banned performance-enhancing substances by elite sport performers. [8]

Answers online

Knowledge and skills summary

This topic involves the following knowledge (AO1):

+ The different social and psychological reasons why elite performers use illegal performance-enhancing drugs/doping methods to aid performance.
+ The physiological impact on sport performance of drugs such as EPO, beta-blockers and anabolic steroids.
+ The positive and negative implications of drug taking for the sport and the performer.
+ The causes and implications of violence in sport in relation to the spectator and sport in general, as well as strategies for preventing hooliganism at football matches.

+ Identify strategies being used for the elimination of performance-enhancing drugs in sport.
+ Arguments for and against the legalisation of drugs in sport.

AO2 marks will require application of this knowledge – for example, explaining how the strategies being used for the elimination of performance-enhancing drugs in sport are being implemented.

AO3 marks are for analysis or evaluation. For this topic, an AO3 response might involve evaluating the effectiveness of the strategies designed to eliminate performance-enhancing drugs in sport.

7.6 Sport and the law

Uses of sports legislation

Performers

The use of sports law relates to sports performers as outlined below.

+ Protection from violent actions of fellow performers:
    + Injuries sometimes occur to performers while playing sport, and more often than not they are seen as being an expected side-effect of participating in sport.
    + However, they sometimes involve a deliberate act by a participant to injure another. In certain instances, these are illegal. For example, criminal cases have been brought for dangerous tackles and other violent actions, such as punches in football matches, which have resulted in serious career-ending injuries.
    + In such cases, civil claims for damages (e.g. for injuries suffered and/or loss of earnings) can be made against the person who has committed the illegal act. To be successful, claims made by sports performers for injury or loss of earnings (e.g. ex-Reading footballer Chris Casper) need to prove that the act was outside the playing culture of the sport; the incident must be shown to be an unacceptable means of playing the sport.

> **Sports law** The legislation, regulations and judicial decisions that govern sports and athletes who perform in them.
>
> **Damages** Legal redress and compensation sought by individuals for loss of earnings. They must prove that they have, for example, suffered an actual injury as the result of the deliberate harmful, reckless actions of an opponent.

225

+ Rugby union (RFU) and football (FA) have recently faced questions about the protection of their players with regard to head injuries/concussion; this has resulted in changes recommended in training and matches to help protect players far more than in the past.
+ Protection from discrimination (e.g. linked to equality issues in sport):
  + Loss of earnings might also result from a legal 'injustice' or an inequality issue – for example, members of the USA women's soccer team took action against their federation and filed a wage discrimination complaint based on the fact that their male counterparts were paid four times more despite generating less money.
+ Protection in relation to **contractual disputes** with employers:
  + Performers are employees and as such should have the same employment rights as other workers. Rights were greatly improved in 1995 by the Bosman ruling, which gave professional footballers within the EU the right to move freely to another employer (i.e. football club) at the end of their contract, and their existing club could not demand a transfer fee or retain the individual's playing licence. Players within the EU therefore have the right to work anywhere within the EU without restriction.
+ Protection in relation to **contractual disputes** with sponsors/agents:
  + In terms of contracts with sponsors, a rare example of a brand suing an endorser was when Oakley brought an action against golfer Rory McIlroy when he left the sportswear company without allowing it the 'right of first refusal' before he signed a deal with Nike. Eventually the case was resolved amicably without going to court.
  + Wayne Rooney's legal dispute with Proactive Sports Management, however, did go to court. The sports management company claimed it was owed commission by Rooney, but the Court of Appeal ruled that the deal he signed as a 17-year-old was unenforceable and was a 'restraint of trade'.

> **Bosman ruling** A ruling by the European Court of Justice, which gave professional football players the right to a free transfer at the end of their contract.

In addition to performers making loss of earnings claims due to injuries and contractual disputes with employers and sponsors/agents, other possible reasons why the use of sports legislation might be required include:

+ Loss of earnings due to false doping prosecutions via the 'right to appeal' – for example, middle distance athlete Diane Modahl had her drugs ban overturned by the British Athletics Federation in July 1995 following an appeal hearing in London.
+ Protection from injury from spectators/fans, via trespass laws banning movement into the field of play.
+ Equality issues – performers are protected from discrimination (e.g. linked to equality issues in sport) by equality legislation (e.g. the Sex Discrimination Act). Loss of earnings might also result from a legal 'injustice' or an inequality issue – for example, members of the USA women's soccer team took action against their federation and filed a wage discrimination complaint based on the fact that their male counterparts were paid four times more despite generating less money. Online racist abuse against sports performers has also led to legal action being taken to protect players. In September 2021, West Bromwich Albion player Romaine Sawyers welcomed an 8-week prison sentence handed to a fan thought to be the first supporter to be jailed over online racist abuse of a footballer. The Albion supporter was jailed and ordered to pay £500 in compensation over a 'grossly offensive' Facebook post.
+ Protection from negligence of officials/coaches and ensuring they apply their duty of care – for example, legal action that has led to prosecution and imprisonment of football coaches for historical sex abuse cases. British Gymnastics coaches have also faced allegations of abuse in recent years.
+ The Whyte Review into the allegations was published in June 2022. It highlighted a failure to put the welfare of participants at the centre of gymnastics, including inappropriate weight management techniques and verbal harassment, which led to a number of British Gymnastics coaches

> **Restraint of trade** Action that interferes with free competition in a market. In sport, this might involve a clause in a contract that restricts a person's right to carry out their profession.
>
> **Trespass** To enter someone's land without permission (e.g. a football pitch).

Check your understanding and progress at **www.hoddereducation.co.uk/myrevisionnotes**

leaving their posts. UK Sport funding to the sport was tied to the enactment of the Whyte Review recommendations.

+ Protection from media intrusion into private lives, which in some cases might lead to performers taking action for libel if what is printed about them is untrue (e.g. David Beckham and the *News of the World*).

> **Libel** A published false statement that is damaging to a person's reputation.

> **Exam tip**
>
> Make sure you can identify (AO1) reasons why sports performers might need assistance from the law during their sports careers, and can link these to explanations/examples (AO2). For AO3 you would be required to analyse/evaluate the relative success of the use of legislation to protect sports performers.

> **Exam tip**
>
> Use SOCCER MD to help remember the reasons why sports performers might need help from the law:
>
> **S**pectator violence
> **O**pponent violence
> **C**ontracts with employers/commercial deals with sponsors
> **C**oach negligence/failure to ensure duty of care
> **E**quality issues (sex discrimination, race discrimination etc.)
> **R**eferee negligence and failure to ensure the duty of care
> **M**edia intrusion/libel
> **D**oping issues/drugs offences

The law affects sport in twenty-first century Britain in the following ways:

+ Sport is more equal – legislation eliminates discrimination on the basis of gender/race – for example, women/minority groups can no longer be banned from golf club membership.
+ Sport is less violent – the law controls violence among players and spectators – for example, banning orders/passports confiscation for known hooligans when international fixtures occur.
+ Performers are more protected – for example, from on-field violence, which can lead to convictions for assault (e.g. Duncan Ferguson going to jail), and payments are made for loss of earnings. (Note: this goes against the traditions of sport because such incidents would normally have been dealt with by NGBs and not a court of law.) Performers are also protected from contractual disputes (e.g. the Bosman ruling and freedom of contract/wages/transfer rights).
+ Sport is fairer – fair competition is achieved via clarification on issues relating to PEDs/doping (e.g. banning of anabolic steroids), bribery, illegal betting and match-fixing.
+ Sport is safer – this is ensured through legal duty of care for players/fans from organisers and officials/coaches. Prosecutions can result from negligence/failure to ensure duty of care (e.g. rugby referees and collapsing scrums; the Hillsborough disaster).
+ The Court of Arbitration for Sport (CAS) was created in 1981 to deal with disputes in sports law.

> **Making links**
>
> Increased law and order in sport as a reflection of twenty-first-century society can be linked to various topics, including sport and society – solutions to discrimination (pp. 106–111), player and spectator violence solutions (pp. 215–219), and sports ethics (e.g. negative deviance – pp. 213–214).

> **Now test yourself**  TESTED
>
> 1 Identify the reasons why sports performers might need protection from the law during their careers.
> 2 Define the terms libel and restraint of trade.
>
> **Answers on pp. 274–275**

Officials (negligence)

+ Negligence is when someone (e.g. an official) fails to take reasonable care for another person to avoid any dangers that could cause them harm.
+ Officials have a duty of care towards participants to make sure that all dangers around them are eliminated, so they can take part in a contest in a safe environment.
+ When they do not do 'everything possible' to keep participants safe, they might be deemed 'negligent' – for example, allowing a match to be played

> **Negligence** Conduct that falls below a 'reasonable person standard' and leads to a breach of the duty of care, which results in foreseeable harm to another.

> **Duty of care** A legal obligation imposed on someone if they are responsible for a group of people.

227

on a dangerous surface that has not been checked prior to the match starting.

+ To bring a successful personal injury compensation claim in a sporting context, a claimant would have to show: they were owed a duty of care; the defendant (the sporting body, coach, or referee) breached their duty of care; that they suffered damage as a result of the breach.

Negligence cases are being brought against officials at both professional and amateur levels of sport. For example, some court cases have highlighted situations in which a rugby referee can be found liable for injuries sustained by a player during the game.

In the case of *Smoldon v Whitworth and Nolan*, a referee was found liable for serious injuries sustained by the claimant following a scrum collapsing. The court found that the official was at fault because he allowed several scrums to collapse during the course of the fractious match he was refereeing. The referee was found to have failed to follow Rugby Football Board guidelines in relation to collapsed scrums. In this particular matter, it was found that the official had allowed two packs to come into the scrum too hard, leading to a scrum collapse, on more than 20 occasions.

In the case of *Allport v Wilbraham*, a claim against a rugby referee failed. Allport, the claimant, was left paralysed from the neck down following a scrum collapse. He argued that the referee had failed to ensure that the scrum had been adequately controlled. In this case, the court preferred the evidence of the defendant (Wilbraham) and dismissed the claim for compensation.

Such cases show that it is likely that there will continue to be litigation against referees and other officials in rugby, as well as in other sports. They need to do everything in their power to ensure they are not negligent in the performance of their required duties.

> **Now test yourself**   TESTED
>
> 3 Define the term 'negligence' and give an example of how a sporting official might be deemed to be negligent in the execution of their duties.
>
> 4 How would a sports performer make a claim for damages as a result of a referee's failure to ensure a 'duty of care'?
>
> **Answers on p. 275**

Coaches (duty of care)

In terms of sports coaches, the duty of care means that they have a legal obligation to eliminate all potential dangers and risks so that players can participate in a safe environment, to ensure that nobody gets hurt unnecessarily.

Coaches therefore need to be aware of their legal responsibilities, especially with respect to the advice they give sports performers and the way they manage and supervise participation in sport. Coaches have a legal responsibility to their athletes in a variety of different ways:

+ **Health and safety** – coaches are responsible for the health and safety of the performers and athletes in their care. They should have access to first aid facilities and have the means to contact emergency services should this be required. A coach could be deemed to be liable if evidence shows that normal standards and practices were not followed.

+ **Protection from abuse** – coaches have a responsibility to protect children from all forms of abuse, including emotional abuse (threats or taunting) and physical abuse (being hit by someone). All organisations (local sports clubs, local authorities etc.) should have a policy statement and guidelines regarding child abuse, which a coach should adhere to. The issue of sexual abuse rose to prominence at the end of December 2016 in football, with a number of historical cases reported and investigated. Emotional abuse has more recently been investigated in British Gymnastics following claims from several athletes, at grass roots and elite levels, resulting in the highlighting of several inappropriate coaching practices (e.g. weight shaming and continuing with training even when performers were known to be seriously injured, including with broken bones).

+ **Supplements** – coaches have a legal and ethical responsibility to educate their athletes about drug use and abuse, and to provide general and appropriate advice on legal nutrition and supplements that can be used to enhance performance.

+ **Duty of care** – it is widely accepted that, in relation to children and young people, sports organisations and the individuals who work for them have a duty of care. When coaching young children, ensuring the participants' safety and welfare can be due to a *legal* duty of care or a *moral* duty of care.

Legally, liability issues would only arise if an incident occurred and it could be demonstrated that the risk was foreseeable, but no action was taken to remedy it. In the sporting environment, when working with children and young people (e.g. at a sports club), coaches should ensure that they take steps to demonstrate a reasonable standard of care. These include:

+ keeping up-to-date contact details, medical details, registers of attendance
+ maintaining appropriate supervision ratios
+ ensuring that first aid provision is available at the club
+ ensuring that individuals regularly involved in coaching children have a current DBS clearance to assist in making safer recruitment decisions
+ ensuring they have undertaken an appropriate risk assessment for the activities being coached

Morally, coaches have a responsibility for the safety and welfare of those under their control. Where children are involved, those in charge have to act 'in loco parentis', which requires the coach to act as a reasonable parent would.

> **In loco parentis** A Latin phrase that means 'in the place of a parent'. It is the authority parents assign to another responsible adult who will be taking care of their child (e.g. a sports coach at a sports club).

Now test yourself

TESTED ◯

5 Identify the steps a sports coach should follow to demonstrate a reasonable standard in terms of a legal duty of care to children and young people.

6 a Define the term DBS clearance.
  b Give examples of forms of abuse.

Answers on p. 275

> **Exam tip**
>
> Make sure that you can identify (AO1) different ways in which sports coaches can ensure a duty of care for the performers they work with. Explanations and examples of these will be required for questions using the command word 'explain' (AO2).

Spectators (safety, hooliganism)

Spectators at sports events must act within the law. It is now illegal to trespass onto the field of play and chant in a racist manner towards players and opposition fans. Some of these new laws are particularly applicable to the sport of football, where clubs have a responsibility to ensure the health and safety of all spectators.

A range of measures has been introduced to try to ensure safety and overcome hooliganism at sports events, including football matches:

+ Removal of perimeter fences and terraces; all-seater stadia to replace the terraces.
+ Control of alcohol sales on the way to grounds as well as in the grounds.
+ Specified kick-off times imposed by police – for example, in the case of a local derby, an early kick-off time can be imposed to decrease the likelihood of alcohol consumption.
+ Increased security and police presence, intelligence gathering, and improved police liaison between forces across the country and internationally.
+ Tougher deterrents, such as banning orders, fines and imprisonment for offenders.

> **Exam tip**
>
> Make sure that you can be specific when describing **legal measures** taken to control crowd behaviour at football matches. It is not just a case of fining clubs, deducting points, segregating fans or banning alcohol.

229

The various pieces of legislation that have emerged over the years to try to control fan behaviour at sporting events and improve safety can be considered as a 'timeline of crowd safety legislation':

+ **Occupiers' Liability Act (1957)** – considered to be the fundamental law governing spectator safety at sporting events. It states that an 'occupier' of a premises owes a common duty of care to its 'visitors'. An occupier is in charge of the premises, while the visitor is someone who is invited or permitted to be at the premises.
+ **Safety of Sports Grounds Act (1975)** – protects all spectators and covers all grounds in all sports.
+ **Sporting Events (Control of Alcohol etc.) Act (1985)** – introduced to ban possession of alcohol at a football match or on a journey to a match. It also empowers magistrates to impose conditions on licensed premises within sports grounds to ensure that no alcohol can be sold by them during a match.
+ **Fire Safety and Safety of Place of Sport Act (1987)** – a fire security certificate/licence needs to be gained from the local authority for an event to happen. The Act also sets the maximum number of spectators who will be safely allowed into a stand, as well as stating that stands have to be made from fireproof materials.
+ **The Football Spectators Act (1989)** – this allows banning orders to be placed on individuals who have committed offences. The Act prevents them from attending sports events for a certain period of time at home and abroad – for example, at West Ham at the start of the 2016 Premier League season following the move to its new home at the London Stadium, where security issues were experienced.
+ **The Football Offences Act (1991)** – this creats three offences at football grounds to prevent the throwing of missiles, the chanting of racist remarks and trespassing onto the field of play. Supporters face legal consequences for their unacceptable behaviour, such as running onto the pitch (i.e. trespass) and attacking players. In February 2013, Wycombe goalkeeper Jordan Archer was attacked by a fan in the closing stages of his side's 1–0 win at Gillingham. A 17-year-old was arrested and charged with assault. Prior to this, in October 2012, Leeds fan Aaron Cawley was jailed for 16 weeks for attacking Sheffield Wednesday goalkeeper Chris Kirkland.

Now test yourself   TESTED

7 Describe how the use of sports legislation has helped improve spectator safety.

Answer on p. 275

Revision activity

Create a term/definition sheet to ensure that you understand the key sports legislation terms, such as 'sports law', 'contract', 'damages', 'civil claims', 'negligence', 'duty of care' and 'in loco parentis'.

Exam practice

1 Identify the potential benefits of the law becoming more closely linked to the world of sport.   [3]

2 Explain how the law aims to protect spectators from hooliganism at football matches.   [5]

3 Which of the following is *not* a requirement of a coach in relation to their duty of care to participants?   [1]
   A Checking their emergency contact details
   B Checking their medical history
   C Checking their favourite sports
   D Checking their clothing and equipment

4 Describe how law and order has shaped the characteristics of sport in the twenty-first century.   [5]

5 Explain, using examples, the link between the law and deviance in sport.   [4]

Answers online

Check your understanding and progress at **www.hoddereducation.co.uk/myrevisionnotes**

7.7 Impact of commercialisation

Impact of commercialisation, sponsorship and the media

REVISED ⬤

Sport, commercialisation/sponsorship and the media are closely interconnected and form what is known as the 'golden triangle'.

The advantages to elite sport of this golden triangle include the following:
+ Increased income to the sport for allowing events to be televised. This can be spent at all levels of the sport – funding participation initiatives at grassroots level, as well as providing finance to support elite athletes at the top of their profession.
+ Increased promotion of the sport can gain more fans and increase its popularity.
+ Increased sponsorship and income from business sources pays for advertising at grounds and sporting events.
+ Sports are organised and funded, which in turn improves the way they are run (i.e. in a more professional manner).
+ Improved facilities benefit performers and spectators alike.

However, there are also disadvantages to elite sport resulting from its links to the media and sponsorship. These include the following:
+ Sensationalist media reporting might sometimes focus too much on the negative aspects of a sport.
+ The media and sponsors can dictate kick-off times and scheduling of sports events, to the detriment of performers and fans.
+ The media and sponsors can change the nature of a sporting activity – for example, introducing more or longer breaks in play to allow for advertising.
+ The media and sponsors only televise already popular, high-profile sports.
+ Sponsors and the media can be too demanding on elite performers and coaches – for example, in relation to personal appearances and giving interviews.
+ Sponsorship deals can increase the pressure to win to maintain lucrative contracts with companies willing to pay for an association with successful sports and sports performers.

Media Organised means of communication by which large numbers of people can be reached quickly.

Making links

Make sure that you can link the positive and negative impacts of commercialisation, sponsorship and the media with the characteristics and impact of the golden triangle (sport and society, pp. 94–95).

231

The media use sport to gain viewers, or readers, and to increase their income/advertising revenue. For most people, the information and knowledge gained about sport is as a result of what they have seen or heard in the media (including television, newspapers, magazines, radio, the internet and social media). The presence of the media as an influence in modern-day sport has turned it into a highly marketable commodity worth billions of pounds.

Now test yourself   TESTED ◯

1   Discuss the relationship between sport, sponsorship and the media.

Answer on p. 275

The OFCOM Code on Sports and Other Listed and Designated Events provides a series of regulations designed to protect the availability of major listed events in sport. The list of ring-fenced sporting events, however, has declined in recent years as satellite channels have been able to offer financial rewards that the sporting authorities cannot refuse.

Reasons for the continued ring-fencing of certain major sporting events include the following:
+   To access the greatest number and range of viewers.
+   To avoid restricting coverage to subscription channels available only to those who can afford them.
+   To increase access to major sporting events for all viewers, in all parts of the country.
+   To enable viewing of certain events that are seen as part of the UK's sporting heritage and culture.
+   To enable access to sporting events that should be freely available to all to view (e.g. the Olympic Games and the Football World Cup).

> **OFCOM** The communications regulator in the UK – for example, it regulates the television sector.
>
> **Ring-fenced** Relating to the number of sporting events at national and international level that must be available for viewing on terrestrial or free-to-access television rather than on satellite and subscription channels.

Now test yourself   TESTED ◯

2   State the reasons why certain sporting events should continue to be 'ring-fenced'.

Answer on p. 275

Sports that have the following characteristics are particularly attractive to the media:
+   They have high levels of skill for viewers to watch and admire, which comes through a competitive, relatively well-matched competition.
+   They are visually appealing and demonstrate physical challenge, action-packed excitement and aggression (e.g. rugby).
+   They are easily understood, with relatively simple rule structures.
+   The sport or sporting event is easy to televise and has a relatively short timescale that fits into viewers' busy schedules.
+   They are seen as nationally relevant, with easily identifiable personalities and role models. Television companies focus their coverage on sports like these (e.g. association football and golf).

Media coverage presents both advantages and disadvantages for a sport (Table 7.11).

Table 7.11 Advantages and disadvantages of media coverage for a sport

Advantages of media coverage	Disadvantages of media coverage
+ It increases the profile of the sport and individual performers within the sport	+ National governing bodies/sports performers lose control to television/sponsors. The traditional nature of a sport is lost (e.g. rule structures/timings of a sport are adapted to suit the demands of television or sponsors)

Check your understanding and progress at **www.hoddereducation.co.uk/myrevisionnotes**

Table 7.11 continued

Advantages of media coverage	Disadvantages of media coverage
+ Increased participation levels within a sport as a result of television coverage encourage others to take it up (e.g. cycling as a result of the Tour de France or football as a result of World Cup coverage) + More variations of a sport are developed to make it more 'media friendly', leading to more matches/fixtures for fans to watch (e.g. Twenty20 cricket) + It generates higher levels of income and makes a sport more appealing to sponsors; it increases commercial opportunities, which further increases the financial gain for a sport or sports performers (e.g. golf, tennis, football) + Improved standards of performance as well as behaviour result from an increased media focus + Rule changes lead to a speeding up of action, more excitement and entertainment in a sport (e.g. penalty shoot-outs)	+ The media control the location of events, as well as kick-off times and, in some cases, playing seasons (e.g. Super League Rugby switched to being a 'summer' game; there is sometimes too much sport on television, which can lead to boredom among spectators and/or lower attendance at events that are on television + There are inequalities of coverage – more popular sports, such as football, gain at the expense of minority sports, such as squash; certain prestigious events are now available only on satellite television, which requires a subscription payment (e.g. test cricket, golf's Ryder Cup), and means there are fewer viewers for some sports due to the increasing control of Sky and BT Sport + The demands of media and sponsors impact negatively on high-level performers (e.g. demands for interviews, personal appearances) + The media can sometimes over-sensationalise or over-dramatise certain negative events in sport; a win-at-all-costs attitude develops due to high rewards on offer, which leads to negative, deviant acts and players becoming poor role models (e.g. in football – arguing with officials, diving to cheat and trying to win a penalty) + More breaks in play (e.g. for adverts) can disrupt the spectator experience

Now test yourself
TESTED ◯

3 Describe the possible disadvantages of media coverage for a sport.

4 Identify three reasons why Premier League association football coverage is particularly appealing to media companies such as Sky Sports and BT Sport.

Answers on pp. 275–276

Exam tip

Make sure that you can apply your knowledge (AO2) by outlining the advantages and disadvantages of media coverage for a sport, and can analyse/evaluate (AO3) these advantages and disadvantages.

Impact of commercialisation and sponsorship

REVISED ◯

There are several reasons why sport is attractive to businesses. Businesses use television companies to promote and advertise their products.

Businesses give their support to elite teams and performers in a variety of ways, including sponsorship, advertising contracts and product endorsements. Due to the following characteristics, sport becomes very attractive as a commercial enterprise:

+ It has extensive media coverage.
+ It gains large audiences, viewing figures and high levels of ticket sales.
+ It allows media links with professional/high-profile sports.
+ Players are contracted to perform with, or endorse, products.
+ The media offer extensive advertising, merchandising or sponsorship deals to a sport/sports performers.
+ Winning is important because it creates a link with success.
+ The sport is media-friendly/entertaining.

Merchandising The
practice in which the brand or image from one 'product' is used to sell another (e.g. professional sports performers/teams promoting various products, including mobile phones and betting companies).

Revision activity

Using a practical example (e.g. association football), draw a spider diagram to summarise the characteristics of a sport that make it commercially appealing.

Now test yourself
TESTED ◯

5 Identify the characteristics of commercial sport.

Answer on p. 276

The commercialisation of sport has grown alongside the use of sport as part of the entertainment industry. Sports have become increasingly aware of their ability to make money from television via the sale of rights to the highest bidder (e.g. Premier League football to Sky/BT Sport), as well as using this exposure to generate high levels of extra income from business and commerce. Televised sport offers companies an investment opportunity via sponsorship, whereby a company puts money into a sport to better itself financially. This happens through:

+ increased sales and promotion of a product
+ increased brand awareness
+ improved company image linked to the healthy image of sport
+ opportunities to entertain clients through corporate hospitality
+ decreasing the amount of tax a company pays, as sponsorship is tax deductible

There are potential positive and negative effects of sponsorship and commercial deals for elite sports performers and the sports they participate in (Table 7.12).

Sponsorship Provision of funding and/or support for a commercial return.

Table 7.12 Effects of sponsorship and commercial deals for elite sports

Positives	Negatives
+ Increased wages, prize money and extrinsic rewards + Increased availability of professional contracts, with performers able to devote themselves full time to sport, training harder and longer to improve performance + Performers are increasingly in the public eye and well known, so they need to maintain discipline and behave appropriately to protect a positive image (e.g. on-field via fair play and sportsmanship; off-field via community and charitable work) + Increased funding to pay for access to high-quality training support and specialist equipment etc.	+ Increased pressure to win and a win-at-all-costs attitude to maintain high-level prize money, extrinsic rewards, wages, sponsorship deals etc. + An rise in 'deviant' behaviour due to increased pressure to win (e.g. performing when injured or over-training; taking illegal drugs; off-field drinking and gambling) + Performers are treated as commodities, bought and sold for economic reasons; sponsors become too demanding (e.g. requiring personal appearances at sponsorship events when they should be training) + Inequality of funding means performers in 'minority sports' (e.g. badminton, table tennis) miss out on funding and full-time professional opportunities

Now test yourself TESTED

6 Discuss the impact of sponsorship deals on the behaviour of elite sport performers.

Answer on p. 276

Impact of increased media coverage and commercialisation

REVISED

Impact on coaches and managers

Increased media coverage and associated commercialisation of sport not only influences performers, it can also positively and negatively impact on the coaches and managers who are in charge.

Positive effects for coaches and managers include the following:

+ They gain a much higher profile as a result of high levels of media coverage, which increases public awareness of their role.
+ Such coverage has also led to increased salaries being on offer, particularly in high-profile sports such as football.
+ The increased funding received from sponsors and the sale of media rights, which is then invested into the sport, impacts positively on coaches and managers because they are then able to invest some of this money into improving their playing squads, as well as support systems (e.g. training grounds and medical provision).

Check your understanding and progress at **www.hoddereducation.co.uk/myrevisionnotes**

- Media coverage of sport also enables coaches to analyse their opponents more, as well as learn from other high-level coaches.

Negative effects for coaches and managers include the following:
- They are under intense pressure to be successful and win matches. There is a high level of public expectation to produce positive results and, if not, managers can expect the sack relatively quickly.
- When the pressure is on, the expectation to deal with the media (which is often part of media deals, such as that between the Premier League and Sky Sports) and answer their questions can be particularly difficult for managers.
- Inequalities of sponsorship and funding mean that coaches and managers in lower-level clubs and minority sports find it harder to attract the best, high-level performers to their clubs/sports, which means they are financially disadvantaged in relation to their higher-profile colleagues.

> **Now test yourself**   TESTED
>
> **7** Identify three ways in which increased media funding of football has benefited coaches/managers.
>
> **Answer on p. 276**

Impact on officials

Increasing media coverage and the commercialisation of sport have also impacted in both positive and negative ways on the referees and officials who take charge of sporting contests.

The potential *positives* for officials are outlined below:
- Increased profile of officials, which increases public awareness of their important role in ensuring 'fairness' in sport.
- An increase in salary and the possibility of full-time job opportunities as part of an elite group of match officials (e.g. in Premier League football).
- Increased funding to invest in support systems and training to improve standards of officiating; increased ability to learn from other officials.
- Increased funding to invest in technology to aid officials in their decision making.

On the other hand, there are also possible *negative* outcomes of increased media coverage and commercialisation of sport on officials, such as the following:
- Increased pressure on officials to get decisions right (e.g. when television channels including BT Sport have an ex-professional referee such as Peter Walton giving instant reviews of key decisions via replays).
- Increased expectation to respond to media enquiries and give interviews explaining their decisions.
- Risk of possible demotion or loss of job if a 'faulty decision' is highlighted in the media.
- Technology to aid officials in their decision making not always available at lower levels of a sport.
- Officials can become too dependent on media technology when it is made available to them.

> **Exam tip**
>
> The negative impact of increased media coverage and commercialisation of sport for the official can be remembered as 'OFICAL':
>
> **O**ver-use of/over-dependency on technology
> **F**aulty decisions are highlighted
> **I**ncreased pressure to deal with media queries
> **C**onstant **A**nalysis of decisions made
> **L**ack of availability of technology at lower levels of a sport

> **Now test yourself**   TESTED
>
> **8** Identify two possible negative implications of increased media coverage and commercialisation of sport on 'officiating technology'.
>
> **Answer on p. 276**

Impact on spectators/audience

There are many *positive* effects of media coverage and commercialisation of sport for the sporting experience of 'the audience':

235

+ Increased performance standards; players of a higher standard provide a high level of excitement and entertainment.
+ Improved quality of facilities; larger, higher-quality stadia resulting from increased investment.
+ Improved viewing experience via innovations such as changes in ball colour; creation of team merchandise to create team loyalty via the purchase and subsequent wearing of a team's kit.
+ Increased access to watch sport; more opportunities to watch events 'live' as more competitions, more events and more matches are taking place.
+ Development of more variations of a sport format, which provide alternative viewing experiences, extra interest and more excitement for the spectator (e.g. Twenty20 cricket).
+ More funding available to provide entertainment (e.g. cheerleaders/pop stars) at sports events.
+ Increased funding for improved technology at a ground (e.g. video screens) and at home (e.g. interactive technology, HD coverage of sport and referee links).
+ Increased excitement in the audience while awaiting the decisions of off-field officials (e.g. Hawk-Eye in tennis).
+ Increased awareness and knowledge of sport; creation of role models for fans to idolise.
+ A reduction in negative aspects of sport (e.g. hooliganism/player violence).

There are some *negative* effects of media coverage and commercialisation of sport for the sporting experience of 'the audience':
+ Increased costs to watch sport (e.g. on pay-per-view satellite channels).
+ Loss of the traditional nature of the sport (e.g. via the wearing of coloured clothing in cricket).
+ Increased number of breaks in play to accommodate adverts and decisions of officials.
+ Fewer tickets available for the fans; more allocated to sponsors and corporate hospitality.
+ Changes in kick-off times to maximise viewing figures (i.e. scheduled at prime time), which is not always in the best interests of the long-distance travelling fan who wishes to watch an event live.
+ Minority sports might receive less coverage; major sports are likely to dominate the television schedules and become 'over-exposed'.
+ Links to team or player merchandise sometimes viewed negatively due to their high cost and regularity of change.

> **Revision activity**
>
> Draw a table identifying the positives and negatives in relation to the impact of increased commercialisation and media coverage on spectators.

Now test yourself TESTED ◯

9 Explain how the increased level of media coverage of sport and sporting events has positively affected spectators.

Answer on p. 276

Exam practice

1 Discuss the impact of the 'golden triangle' on elite sport. [4]
2 Define the term 'sponsorship' and identify how companies benefit from their involvement in sport. [4]
3 Discuss whether an elite performer should consider the nature of a sponsor before accepting a sponsorship deal. [4]
4 Evaluate the impact of the media and commercialisation of sport on spectators. [5]
5 Discuss the impact of commercialisation on officials. [4]
6 Evaluate the effect of media coverage of sport in the twenty-first century. [6]

Answers online

7.8 Role of technology

High-quality research is vital to understanding all aspects of sport, exercise and health. When undertaking research and collecting information using technology, it is important that you understand some important terms you might come across during your studies, such as sports analytics. Look out for other key terms highlighted below.

> **Research** A systematic process of investigation and study carried out with the aim of advancing knowledge.
>
> **Sports analytics** Studying data from sports performances to try to improve performance.

Now test yourself

TESTED ◯

1 Define what is meant by sports analytics.

Answer on p. 276

Data collection

REVISED ◯

Quantitative and qualitative research

Quantitative research is a formal, objective and systematic process used to gather quantitative data (i.e. factors that can be measured or counted). Most fitness tests used to analyse elite performers use quantitative data – for example, the VO_2 max test on a treadmill.

Qualitative research is generally focused on words as opposed to numbers. It can include factors such as the type of equipment used, or the playing conditions. The qualitative data collected can also be subjective, as they look at feelings, opinions and emotions – for example, a group of coaches expressing an opinion when judging a gymnast performing a competitive routine.

> **Quantitative** Relating to data that can be measured precisely or counted.
>
> **Qualitative** Relating to data that are descriptive, and that can also represent the way people think or feel.

Making links

You should be aware of the possible synoptic link between the use of technology in data collection and an understanding of the key terms relating to laboratory conditions and field tests (preparation and training methods in relation to maintaining physical activity and performance, p. 122).

Examples of areas where *quantitative* data could be gathered to try to prove a hypothesis include the following:

➕ In sport psychology, the potential positive link between motivational self-talk and its relationship to improving self-paced skills (e.g. a golf putt).

➕ In exercise psychology, research of a quantitative nature (e.g. using a numerical scale) to compare the relative effect of different environments on exercisers' moods (e.g. cycle trails in wooded areas versus cycling lanes in urban areas).

Qualitative research data are used to try to gain a better understanding of a participant's experiences.

Objective and subjective

Objective data refer to received information based on facts. They are measurable and observable and therefore highly suitable and meaningful for decision making when feeding back to sports performers – for example, in a performance analysis of a swimmer at the English Institute of Sport (EIS).

Subjective data are based on personal opinions, assumptions, interpretations, emotions and beliefs. With their emphasis on personal opinions, they are seen as less suitable and meaningful when feeding back to performers – for example, a parent talking to their child at half-time during a football match, giving them their opinion on their performance in the first half.

Validity and reliability

Data collection when using technology should be both valid and reliable.

Validity refers to the degree to which the data collected actually measure what they claim to measure. To assess the validity of data collection, an important question to ask is: Do the data collected measure exactly what you set out to measure?

Reliability is when the data collected are consistent, and similar results are achieved when the data collection process is repeated at a later date.

+ In **quantitative** research, reliability can be one researcher conducting the same test (e.g. skinfold measurements) on the same individual on different occasions and getting the same or very similar results. Alternatively, it can be different researchers conducting the same test on the same individual and getting the same or very similar results.
+ In **qualitative** research, reliability relates to the same researcher placing results into the same categories on different occasions, or different researchers placing results into the same or similar categories.

Reliability can be affected by errors occurring when researchers do not know how to use equipment correctly – for example, in the use of skinfold calipers when assessing body composition. Accuracy can also be affected by poorly maintained equipment – for example, weighing devices giving initial incorrect readings that affect calculations such as body mass index (BMI).

Data need to be both reliable and valid in order to be useful. In other words, if data collected are not valid, there is little or no point in discussing reliability because data validity is required before reliability can be considered in any reasonable way.

> **Now test yourself** **TESTED** ⬤
>
> 2 **a** Define the terms 'subjective data' and 'validity'.
>   **b** What term is this description referring to: 'the degree to which data collection is consistent and stable over time'?
>
> **Answer on p. 276**

> **Objective data** Fact-based information that is measurable and usable (e.g. the level achieved on the multi-stage fitness test, which links to a VO_2 max score).
>
> **Subjective data**: Based on personal opinion, which is less measurable and often less usable.

> **Validity** An indication of whether the data collected actually measure what they aim to measure.
>
> **Reliability** The degree to which data collection is consistent and stable over time.

> **Exam tip**
>
> Make sure you can define terms linking technology with data collection (AO1), such as quantitative, qualitative, objective, subjective, validity and reliability.

Video and analysis programs

REVISED ⬤

Coaches and athletes are increasingly using video and other digital technology as a medium to analyse individual technique as well as team performances. At an individual level, video analysis can be used to analyse gait and biomechanical aspects of performance. Any information gained is also potentially helpful in rehabilitation from injury.

Video motion analysis usually involves a high-speed camera and a computer with software that allows frame-by-frame playback of the footage on video.

> **Video motion analysis** A technique used to gather information on moving objects from video footage.

The process of motion analysis has developed into two distinct sport science disciplines:

✦ **Notational match analysis** – used to record aspects of individual/team performance. Notational analysis takes place through the study of movement patterns, strategy and tactics in a variety of different sports. It is used by coaches and sport scientists to gather objective data on the performance of athletes.

✦ **Biomechanics** – used to analyse the sporting impact of body movements. It involves the quantitative study and analysis of sports activities. It is sometimes called **kinematics** – the study of the motion of bodies with respect to time, including displacement, velocity and speed of movement.

The two disciplines use similar methods to collect data and both rely on IT for data analysis. But the main similarity is the use of measured observation (i.e. quantitative analysis) during or after an event to quantify performance in an accurate, reliable and valid way.

Performance analysis (PA) is now acknowledged as an important aid to performance enhancement at all levels. Failure to use it might result in poor immediate decisions being made (e.g. in competition), as well as, in the longer term, choosing the wrong options in relation to an athlete's training programme.

> **Now test yourself**   TESTED ○
>
> 3   Identify the potential problems a sports coach might have if they choose not to use video analysis programs, but instead rely on their own observation and analysis skills.
>
> **Answer on p. 276**

Different PA techniques can be used by coaches and sport scientists to provide them with task, performance and physiological data. Within a training environment, immediate visual feedback software is useful to provide images pre- and post-feedback for the athlete and coach to compare.

In a competitive environment, the coach and performer might look at the statistics of their opponent(s) before discussing the data, alongside any other past experiences against such opposition, to come up with a game-plan to win. In this case, they would look to use particular strategies and tactics to outwit their opponents.

> **Making links**
>
> You should be aware of the possible synoptic link between the use of video and analysis programs and the support services provided by National Institutes of Sport for talent development (development of elite performers in sport, p. 204).

Testing and recording equipment   REVISED ●

A metabolic cart is an electronic medical tool used to measure the body's metabolism through the amount of heat produced when the body is at rest. The metabolic cart uses a process called calorimetry to get this measurement. The result can help tell medics more about a person's overall health condition. The various parts of the device, which include a computer system, monitor and breathing tubes, are typically mounted together on a mobile push-cart, hence the name, so that it can easily be moved from one room to another.

> **Metabolic cart** A device that works by attaching headgear to a subject while the person breathes a specific amount of oxygen over a period of time.
>
> **Calorimetry** The measurement of the heat and energy eliminated or stored in any system.

> **Performance analysis (PA)** The provision of objective feedback to performers in order to achieve a positive change in performance. (Feedback can be gained on a variety of performance indicators, such as the number of passes made, the distance run in km and the number of shots attempted.)

> **Exam tip**
>
> Make sure you can apply your knowledge (AO2) of video and analysis programs to illustrate your understanding of technology for sports analytics.

239

Indirect calorimetry is a technique in which the headgear from the cart is attached to a subject while they breathe for a specific amount of time. The subject's inspired and expired gas flows, volumes and concentrations of oxygen (O_2) and carbon dioxide (CO_2) are all continually measured. These measurements are then translated into a heat equivalent. It is a non-invasive technique and is regarded as being relatively accurate.

Indirect calorimetry
The measurement of the amount of heat and energy generated in an oxidation reaction.

Now test yourself
TESTED ◯

4   Define the terms 'indirect calorimetry' and 'metabolic cart'.

Answer on p. 276

The two figures (concentrations of O_2 and CO_2) provide the result for the metabolic cart, which is generally measured as resting energy expenditure (REE). The REE for a patient can vary quite a bit. The results can change according to a range of conditions. Between individuals, the REE changes with regard to a person's overall weight or height-to-weight ratio. Age and gender can also influence the result of this test. In addition, the chemistry of the body in response to various drugs will change the outcome. Therefore, due to average differences in size, REE is lower in women when compared with men. Smoking and drugs such as amphetamines can both increase someone's REE.

Resting energy expenditure (REE) The amount of energy, usually expressed in kcal, required by the body during rest for a 24-hour period.

Now test yourself
TESTED ◯

5   Identify different reasons for individual variations in resting energy expenditure (REE) over a period of time.

Answer on p. 276

Revision activity

Draw a spider diagram identifying four factors that can cause an individual's REE to vary.

Indirect calorimetry and use of a metabolic cart can help individuals in the following ways:
+ To determine their energy requirements and response to nutrition over time.
+ To calculate energy expenditure, which allows the determination of nutritional requirements/calorific needs.
+ To enable someone to be classified or potentially classified as obese.
+ To calculate their REE, which helps medics determine the amount of food and nutrition needed.

Exam tip

Make sure that you can define terms linking technology with testing and recording equipment (AO1), such as a metabolic cart for indirect calorimetry, as well as apply your knowledge (AO2) of the factors affecting the validity and reliability of using this method.

Possible difficulties or sources of error affecting the validity and reliability of using indirect calorimetry via a metabolic cart include:
+ inaccuracies from air leaks
+ possible inaccuracies from measurement or recording errors
+ difficulty in using on children
+ possible overfeeding or underfeeding, based on results received
+ single snapshots being worse than 'average results/studies' over a longer period
+ the fact that the process measures consumption, not needs

Exam tip

Possible sources of error when using a metabolic cart can be remembered as 'LOSE':

Leakage of air
Overfeeding or underfeeding might occur post-results
Single snapshots are not as good as average results over longer time periods
Errors in taking measurements might occur

Use of GPS and motion-tracking software and hardware

REVISED

GPS software tracking systems are very useful when helping coaches to monitor players during matches, as well as in training. Such systems immediately give coaches a vast amount of computer-based information. For example, they track the speed, distance and direction of the individuals concerned.

GPS can also provide data that help to improve performance by monitoring success rates in technical performance. In high-contact sports (rugby, for example), it can measure the impact in G-forces. It can also help coaches to make objective decisions about possible replacements/substitutions – for example, GPS can help gauge a performer's fatigue level. This can help decrease the risk of injury. If a performer is unfortunate enough to be recovering from injury, GPS can be used to manage workload during their rehabilitation.

In football, GPS tracking of players allows the measurement and monitoring of players' speed and distance covered during a game or a training session. GPS tracking can also be used to measure a player's heart rate, pace, recovery time and the amount of dynamic acceleration. Reasons for using GPS technology for player performance tracking include the following:
+ It makes better use of training time, to ensure training meets game demands.
+ It improves the tactical analysis undertaken at a club.
+ GPS can help a coach compare player performance, and potentially pick the 'best players' for the team.
+ It helps to get injured players successfully through rehab at a faster rate.

GPS (global positioning system) A satellite-based navigation system that provides location and time information.

Hardware The physical components of computers.

Software Any set of machine-readable instructions that direct a computer's processor to perform specific operations.

G-forces Forces acting on the body as a result of acceleration or gravity (e.g. the G-load/force of an American football 'hit' on an opponent).

Exam tip

Make sure that you can define terms linking technology with GPS and motion tracking (AO1), such as software and hardware, as well as apply your knowledge (AO2) of the use of such technology by coaches/sport analysts.

Now test yourself
TESTED

6 Describe the different ways in which GPS technology can help to improve player performance.

Answer on pp. 276–277

Maintaining data integrity
REVISED

The overall intent of data integrity is to ensure that data are entered into the system and recorded exactly as intended; and when they are retrieved later, they should be the same as when they were originally recorded.

Data integrity can be compromised through:
+ human error when data are entered
+ errors occurring when data are transmitted from one computer to another
+ software bugs or viruses
+ hardware malfunctions, such as disk crashes

Data integrity The maintenance of accuracy and consistency of stored data over its entire lifetime.

Ways to minimise threats to data integrity include:
+ regularly backing up data
+ controlling access to data and protecting against malicious intent via security mechanisms
+ designing interfaces that prevent the input of invalid data; taking care when entering data

+ using error detection and correction software when transmitting data
+ not leaving a computer unattended for others to access

The functions of sports analytics

REVISED ⭕

The effective use of sports analytics can help an individual and/or team increase their chances of success, and win more frequently and more consistently. The focus should therefore be more about *how* sports analytics can be used to gather new, meaningful statistical information on player performance and/or game details. Then, it is important to consider how the data can be synthesised and summarised into key points that help improve the efficiency and effectiveness of performance for those involved in sport or physical activity.

Monitoring fitness for performance

Analysing data and assessing fitness levels is common in high-level sport, and is becoming more common in lower levels of performance.

One function of sports analytics is to use it to gain information to help in monitoring fitness for performance, whether this is for individual recreational purposes (e.g. monitoring heart rate or amount of calories being burnt when training for a marathon) or for elite-sport purposes (e.g. elite marathon runners monitoring key aspects of performance, such as distance covered in training, pace of running, sleep statistics, calorie input and output, as well as heart-rate monitoring before, during and post-exercise).

Various smart wearable fitness and sports devices are available to aid such performers in their quest to improve performance based on the key information they provide.

Smart wearable fitness and sports device A device that is worn or attached to a performer's body while in use to provide instant feedback on aspects of performance, such as distance covered and heart rate (e.g. Garmin Vivofit).

Skill and technique development

Sports analytics can be a highly valuable tool in aiding the skill and technique development of elite performers. An analytics program called Dartfish is one example of how technology can be used to capture, create, analyse and share video content on sports performance. The software available via Dartfish combines technical, tactical and statistical information to provide information that can be used to improve skills and techniques on the spot, or to identify areas for improvement in future training sessions. It is particularly useful in sports and activities where visual feedback will be beneficial for the performer and coach.

Injury prevention

Vibration technology can be used for various purposes, including exercise recovery, injury prevention and rehabilitation. Application of vibration therapy can be made both directly (i.e. applied to the affected area) and indirectly (transferred to the whole body or body part affected).

Advocates of vibration therapy claim a variety of possible health benefits that can be gained from both whole-body and localised vibration therapy. These include:

+ increased bone density
+ increased muscle mass/muscle power
+ improved circulation
+ reduced joint pain

Vibration technology Vibration training/therapy, also known as 'whole-body vibration' (WBV). An example of its usage involves the use of vibration plates to induce exercise effects in the body.

- reduced back pain
- alleviated stress
- boosted metabolism
- an overall reduction in pain/delayed onset of muscle soreness (DOMS)
- maintenance of cartilage integrity where weight-bearing activities are difficult to undertake

These benefits help to prevent future injuries.

Now test yourself   TESTED ⭕

8 Identify the possible benefits to health of using vibration technology/therapy.

Answer on p. 277

Revision activity

Draw a spider diagram identifying a range of health benefits of using vibration technology/therapy.

Electrostimulation can aid in the prevention of injuries in the following ways:
- Strengthening and toning the muscles to help prevent injury (e.g. it can strengthen the muscle groups of the legs to give stability and help prevent injury or recurring injuries to the knees and ankles).
- Helping to prevent losses in fitness levels via application to specific muscle groups, which maintains muscle tone during periods of inactivity.
- Assisting in rehabilitation through the gradual strengthening of injured or weakened muscles via small incremental increases in workload on the muscles (i.e. by inducing stronger muscular contractions).
- Helping to get rid of lactic acid after a training session or competition, as well as decreasing muscle tension and potential injury by providing a relaxing effect to muscles.

Electrostimulation The induction of muscular contraction using electrical impulses.

Now test yourself   TESTED ⭕

9 Explain the role of electrostimulation in injury prevention.

Answer on p. 277

Game analysis

Analytics can be used in many different sports (e.g. in team games such as netball and basketball) to gather quantitative data, including player performance metrics that measure the amount of court covered by individual players during matches.

Elite-level sports have embraced the role of technology and sports analytics in providing them with valuable information on player performance. Use has increasingly been made of video and data – captured and displayed on iPads – which are then used to give real-time analysis and feedback to coaches during games. This ultimately aims to give them an edge over the opposition.

On the field or court (e.g. during games of football and netball) sports analytics can also be used to measure the performance of individual performers, which can be used to help further improve player performance and fitness.

Use of small GPS receivers can help measure aspects such as distance covered in games, as well as top speeds and/or acceleration achieved by individual performers during matches. The information received from games can help coaches and physios fine-tune training programmes and optimise rest and recovery times.

The data gained via sports analytics can also assist coaches when looking at tactics, formations and substitutions during games. Access to precise data allows coaches to compare an individual player's performance with their 'normal play', as well as match team tactics to the squad available to them.

243

It is important to appreciate that as the technology available for game analysis develops further, there is more of a need to be selective and choose the most relevant information to capture. Quality of information is more important than quantity of information.

Talent ID/scouting

Sports analytics can be used to provide qualitative data on individual performers in a range of different sports – including written scouting reports commenting on opposition players and/or feedback from players being watched, with a view to recruiting them onto a Talent ID programme.

Technology can be used in 'pathway analytics' as a method of systematically profiling and benchmarking the effectiveness of performance pathways across Olympic and Paralympic sports. Talent ID programmes have developed over the years, forming links between specific technical, physiological and psychological requirements of different sports. For example, Tall and Talented required technically gifted sports performers to be above a certain height for sports such as basketball and rowing. The data on potential recruits need to be systematically gathered and analysed so it can be used effectively to identify the best, most talented athletes who are the 'most likely' to succeed at elite level.

> ### Making links
>
> You should be aware of the possible synoptic link between the use of sports analytics for Talent ID and the support services provided by national institutes of sport for talent ID and development (development of elite performers in sport, p. 204).

> ### Exam tip
>
> It is important for AO1 that you can identify the functions of sports analytics as well as apply your knowledge of sports analytics (AO2) in relation to monitoring fitness, developing skills and techniques, preventing injury, analysing game performance and talent ID/ scouting.

Development of equipment and facilities

REVISED

Adapted equipment for elderly people and people with disabilities

In the twenty-first century, mobility limitations resulting from age or disability no longer need to constitute a barrier to participation in sport and physical activity.

Assistive or adapted technology in sport is an area of technology in which design capability is on the increase. New devices are being created to help elderly and disabled sports enthusiasts to participate at recreational level, and highly advanced equipment is being created for elite Paralympians. Assistive devices can therefore enable training and exercise, as well as providing the opportunity for participation in sport.

+ In athletics, adaptive equipment, such as specially designed wheelchairs, is used on the track; in the field, throwing frames have been designed for use in the shot put and discus.
+ Wheelchairs are an important assistive technology in sport and can be individually designed and adapted to meet the specific requirements of different sports:
  + Sports such as tennis and basketball require lightweight frames to enable fast-paced movements, sharp turns and agility.
  + Contact sports such as rugby require chairs with strong, reinforced frames and impact/foot protection.
+ Prosthetic devices have been designed and developed to meet a number of athletic purposes:
  + Prosthetic leg devices (e.g. the Springlite prosthesis device) have been designed to assist athletes in running via improved gait efficiency.
  + Prosthetic legs have also been designed for use in cycle racing.
  + The introduction of new materials for prosthetic devices, such as carbon flex-fibre, and new developments in wheelchair technology are positively impacting performances in many sports.

Check your understanding and progress at **www.hoddereducation.co.uk/myrevisionnotes**

Technology and facility development – the Olympic legacy

Places People Play is an initiative being delivered by Sport England in partnership with the British Olympic Association. This initiative aims to deliver on the Olympic and Paralympic legacy promise to increase sports participation by providing sports facilities for the local community to access and use.

Iconic Facilities is part of this initiative, designed to transform the places people use to play sport in towns, cities and villages across the country. Iconic Facilities directs funds into a small number of 'best practice' strategic facility projects designed to increase mass participation in sport across England. Best practice is based on high-quality design and long-term sustainability of a facility that delivers multi-sport provision, with a focus on sporting activities that have high participant numbers.

There have been a number of technological developments in surfaces that are suitable for such multi-sport provision, with 4G/5G surfaces increasingly being used. The sand and rubber infill in 3G surfaces gives them playing characteristics similar to those of natural grass. They allow high levels of use in a wide variety of sports and are ideal for sports such as hockey, football and rugby. The benefits of these and the more recent 4G/5G surfaces include the fact that they can be played on more frequently and for longer than natural grass. Synthetic grass also gives consistent conditions, unlike natural grass, which can become very worn and unpredictable.

While there have been benefits associated with artificial surfaces being designed and used in sport, one of the main problems in sports like football is that some do not reflect the true bounce of grass. In addition, they have been criticised for being too rigid, leading to joint or ligament injuries. The more recent 4G/5G surfaces have gone some way to rectifying such problems. Even fully competitive games of rugby are now being played on artificial surfaces – Rugby Super League team Widnes Vikings has re-embraced artificial turf at its home stadium in Halton, as has the rugby union team Saracens at Allianz Park.

4G/5G surface Fourth/fifth-generation artificial synthetic grass covering for pitches etc.

Advances in technology have also led to the development of multi-use games areas (MUGAs). A specific surface for each sport would be ideal, but this is often too expensive and impractical in terms of space for many local authorities, schools and sports clubs. MUGAs, made of artificial grass, are often the best solution to providing multi-sport opportunities, while increasing participation in sport and physical activity helps the Places People Play initiative deliver on its promise.

245

Role of technology in sport and its impact

Sport

Technology can have a *positive* impact on sport in the following ways:

+ Helping to increase participation and make it more inclusive. The development of adapted equipment, such as the carbon-fibre prosthetic blades and lightweight wheelchairs described above, has certainly increased access to sport for people with disabilities.
+ Technology can also benefit sport by improving the quality of surfaces it is played on, as well as providing meaningful data via GPS systems, which can help in the short- and long-term development of players.

There are also possible **negative** implications of using technology for sport, including the following:

+ Pure data can be misleading at times – for example, when a performer has not covered many metres in a game, but the tactics and game context were such that they did not require them to do so.
+ It can be expensive, so inequalities might exist in a sport in terms of access to the latest technology – i.e. only the wealthiest countries and teams are able to succeed. Some might argue that the high costs of technological advancements in sport might be invested better in participation initiatives, as opposed to a few elite performers.
+ It can lead to 'paralysis by analysis'. Players and coaches might become too reliant on data to inform their decision making and unable to react creatively and instantly to onfield problems or issues as they occur.
+ It can have a placebo effect. Are athletes simply gaining increased confidence by using equipment, even though there may be limited scientific evidence to support it?

> **Exam tip**
>
> When 'discussing' the impact of technology on sport, you need to clearly identify and talk about both positive and negative effects (AO2).

The performer

Potential *benefits* of technology for sports performers include:

+ Improved clothing/footwear. This can lead to improved performances – for example, bodysuits used by athletes have helped sprinters increase their speed. Their use in swimming was a little more controversial because it led to some dramatic performance improvements, with several world records being broken in a short space of time following their introduction.
+ Improved sports equipment. This can aid skill/technique development – for example, modern-day footballs have been designed to allow more swing and curve than before. Technological developments in golf have allowed manufacturers to build lighter clubs to increase swing speeds and enable golfers to hit golf balls a lot further and with more control than before. Clubs can now be personalised and designed to meet the individual needs of a golfer. Aerodynamics has improved through driver head designs decreasing wind resistance and increasing club head speed.
+ Improved protective equipment – for example, cricket helmets to withstand increasingly fast-paced deliveries.
+ Improved recovery from training (e.g. via compression clothing); technology can be used to simulate/counter extreme climatic conditions.
+ Improved recovery from injury and better rehabilitation (e.g. oxygen tents).
+ Detailed scientific analysis of performance via GPS data to provide meaningful technical and physiological feedback to performers and coaches.
+ Increased knowledge of diet and sports supplements (e.g. carbo-loading; sports energy drinks).
+ Advancements in drug-testing technology to keep up with performers taking illegal performance-enhancing substances.
+ Improved sleep through monitoring technology and feedback, enabling appropriate rest and recovery from training or competition. Sleep is important for physiological recovery as well as an individual's reaction

> **Compression clothing**
>
> Items such as elasticated leggings, socks or shirts worn to promote recovery by improving circulation. They can decrease the pain suffered from muscle soreness/stiffness and decrease the time for muscle repair.

time. Players at some professional clubs (e.g. in football) who are poor sleepers are given wristbands (e.g. the Fatigue Science ReadiBand), which use movement sensors to assess sleep quality.

> **Making links**
>
> You should be aware of the link between the role of technology in sport and its positive and negative impacts, and the different methods used in injury prevention, rehabilitation and recovery (p. 132), such as compression garments, ice baths and cryotherapy.

Potential *negative* effects of technology for the sports performer include the following:

+ It can lead to injury or over-aggression – for example, from bladed boots or due to the use of protective equipment, which makes some performers feel invincible or less inhibited.
+ It can lead to cheating – for example, effective masking agents or newly developed performance-enhancing substances for which there is no test can allow athletes to take illegal drugs in the belief that they will get away with it.
+ It can be expensive and unaffordable for some, which leads to potential inequalities and unfair advantages if the technology is not available to all.
+ The availability of technological advancements aiding performance might be dependent on an individual or team sponsor, which might positively or negatively impact the chances of success. The use of modern technologies in sport might mean that competition at the very highest level is only affordable to the leading top athletes due to the high costs of specialist sports equipment.

> **Revision activity**
>
> Make a list of the positives and negatives of technology in relation to the sports performer

> **Now test yourself**   TESTED ⬤
>
> 12 Identify the potential negative impacts of technology for performers.
>
> **Answer on p. 277**

Coaches

Coaches can use a variety of different forms of technology – for example, when involved in sports analytics. These include global positioning system (GPS) technology, video analysis programmes and motion tracking software/motion analysis.

Possible benefits for coaches of using technology (e.g. GPS for player performance tracking) include the following:

+ It makes better use of training time, to ensure training meets competition/game demands.
+ It improves decision making with regard to tactics/strategies during competition/matches.
+ It helps a coach compare performances and aids their squad/team selection.
+ It helps a coach make fitness/injury/rehab assessments of performers.
+ It helps with the analysis of the opposition.

However, there are possible negative aspects for sports coaches of using technology:

+ Potentially, a lot of data can be collected, which could lead to an overload of information.
+ Coaches might not be able to understand/interpret the data collected.
+ There might be an over reliance on data/statistics.
+ Faulty equipment/testing procedures might lead to unreliable data.
+ Potential computer hacking might lead to information being accessed by other coaches/teams.

The audience/spectators

Statistics enthusiasts can visit many websites to find out various pieces of information on their favourite teams and players. The data collected in different ways can be organised to make it more easily understandable and digestible to fans and spectators, who can gain improved knowledge about the physical, technical and tactical aspects of performance in a sport.

Advancements in technology have certainly impacted in *positive* ways on the audience. Officials now have microphones (e.g. in rugby) so the audience can hear what is being said on the field of play. This increases involvement and excitement for the audience, and enhances the viewing experience. Increased interest and excitement are also gained as a result of technology being employed to aid officials in their decision making (e.g. Hawk-Eye in tennis).

Other advantages for an audience from the increased use of technology to aid officials in their decision making include the following:
+ It ensures the right decisions are reached, with less frustration at incorrect decisions.
+ It helps officials communicate with one another and the players, which the audience can sometimes hear (e.g. in rugby matches).
+ More accurate data on timing and distances achieved are quickly communicated to the audience (e.g. via big screens in the stadium).
+ There is increased excitement in the audience as they await decisions (e.g. Hawk-Eye at the Wimbledon Tennis Championships).

However, there are also some *disadvantages* of officiating technology as far as the audience is concerned:
+ There might be a loss of respect for the official as the 'final decision maker'.
+ Costs limit the use of technology at events, which can give an inconsistent experience to spectators, as well as performers.
+ Breaks in play can be disruptive for spectators if they take too long or there is an over-reliance on technology, which leads to the official over-using it. For example, in the opening 2015 Rugby World Cup fixture, when England played Fiji, the referee Jaco Peyper was criticised for his over-reliance on the television match official (TMO), which seriously slowed down the action and impacted negatively on the viewing experience. Prior to the 2019 Rugby World Cup, World Rugby highlighted the possible risks of using technology (i.e. the TMO) in reviewing tries scored in relation to a slowing down of the game and limiting the action played out on the pitch.

Exam practice

1 Which of the following is a negative aspect of technology when used to aid officials in their decision making? [1]
   A Increased performer confidence in the correct decisions being made
   B Increased disruption to a sporting event because of a lot of referee referrals
   C Increased excitement in the crowd as decisions are awaited on the big screen
   D Increased accuracy of timings or measurements taken
2 Identify two types of adaptive equipment used in the sport of athletics. [2]
3 State the disadvantages to a sporting event of the increased use of technology to help officials in their decision making. [3]
4 Modern technological products are becoming an increasingly important part of twenty-first-century sport.
   Outline the advantages for performance in sport of using such technology. [4]
5 How have sports spectators benefited from advancements in technology? [3]
6 Discuss the impact of modern technology on participation in sport/physical activity. [6]

7 Using examples, critically evaluate the effect that technology has on the sports spectator. [6]

8 Outline the reasons why some football fans might be against the use of VAR and goal-line technology while others are in favour of its introduction. [4]

Answers online

Knowledge and skills summary

This topic involves the following knowledge (AO1):

+ Definitions of terms linking technology with data collection, such as quantitative, qualitative, objective, subjective, validity and reliability.
+ Examples of the development of equipment and facilities in physical activity and sport.
+ Functions of sports analytics.
+ Identifying how data integrity can be maintained.
+ Definitions of terms linking technology with GPS and motion tracking, such as software and hardware.
+ Definitions of terms linking technology with testing and recording equipment, such as metabolic cart for indirect calorimetry.
+ Positive and negative impacts of technology on sport, performers, coaches and audiences.

AO2 marks will require application of this knowledge – for example, describing the impact of the development of equipment and facilities in physical activity and sport on participation and performance; explaining the use of GPS and motion tracking for coaches/sport analysts; explaining the factors affecting the validity and reliability of using the metabolic cart for indirect calorimetry; linking the positive and negative impacts of technology on sport, performers, coaches and audiences.

AO3 marks are for analysis or evaluation. For this topic, an AO3 response might involve an analysis of the role of sports analytics and video analysis programs in sport; or evaluating the possible impact of technology on sport, performers, coaches and audiences.

Glossary

Term	Definition	Page
1 rep max (1RM)	The maximum amount a performer can lift in one repetition.	127
4G/5G surface	Fourth/fifth-generation artificial synthetic grass covering for pitches etc.	245
Abduction	Movement away from the midline of the body.	30
Acceleration	Rate of change of velocity.	134
Acute injury	Sudden injury caused by a specific impact or traumatic event, where a sharp pain is felt immediately.	129
Adduction	Movement towards the midline of the body.	30
Adenosine triphosphate (ATP)	The only usable form of energy in the body.	35
Adrenaline	A stress hormone released by the nervous system to increase heart rate.	13
Aerobic	A reaction that occurs in the presence of oxygen.	9
Aggression	An emotional response (involving anger) to an individual perceived as an enemy or a frustrating rival; an intent to harm outside the laws of the game.	168, 215
All or none law	Where a sequence of impulses has to be of sufficient intensity to stimulate all of the muscle fibres in a motor unit in order for them to contract. If not, *none* of them contracts.	27
Amateur	A person who plays sport for the love of it and receives no financial gain.	83
Amateurism	Participation in sport for the love of it, receiving no financial gain; it is based on the concept of athleticism (i.e. physical endeavour with moral integrity).	210
Anaerobic	Involving a reaction that can occur without the presence of oxygen.	36
Angle of attack	The tilt of a projectile relative to the air flow.	155
Angular motion	The motion of a body about a fixed point or axis.	147
Approach behaviour	Having the competitive drive to persist and achieve success.	172
Arteriovenous difference (A-VO$_2$ diff)	The difference between the oxygen content of the arterial blood arriving at the muscles and that of the venous blood leaving the muscles.	18
Articulating bones	Bones that meet and move at a joint.	30
Assertion	Hard but fair play. More effort than normal may be exerted, but there is no intention to harm.	168
Atherosclerosis	When arteries harden and narrow, and become blocked with fatty deposits.	9, 116
Athleticism	A fanatical devotion to sport involving high levels of physical endeavour and moral integrity.	77
Autogenic inhibition	Where there is a sudden relaxation of the muscle in response to high tension. The receptors involved in this process are Golgi tendon organs.	29
Avoidance behaviour	Steering clear of situations where evaluation might take place, i.e. competitive situations.	172
BALCO	The Bay Area Laboratory Cooperative, which was behind one of the biggest scandals in drugs history as the source of THG, with several athletes implicated and subsequently banned from sport, including sprinters Dwain Chambers and Marion Jones.	222
Ballistic stretching	Performing a stretch with swinging or bouncing movements, to push a body part even further.	123
Baroreceptors	Receptors that detect changes in blood pressure.	24
Bernoulli principle	Where air molecules exert less pressure the faster they travel, and more pressure when they travel slower.	155

Check your understanding and progress at **www.hoddereducation.co.uk/myrevisionnotes**

Beta oxidation	A process in which fatty acids are broken down to generate acetyl-CoA, which enters the Krebs cycle.	36
Bohr shift	When an increase in blood carbon dioxide and a decrease in pH results in a reduction of the affinity of haemoglobin for oxygen.	16
Bosman ruling	A ruling by the European Court of Justice, which gave professional football players the right to a free transfer at the end of their contract.	89, 226
Bradycardia	When there is a decrease in resting heart rate to below 60 beats per minute.	11
British Empire	A worldwide system of dependencies that, over a timespan of some three centuries, were brought under the rule and administration of Great Britain.	80
Broken-time payments	Financial payments made to factory workers/amateurs to compensate them for the time they had to take off work to compete.	77
Buffering	A process that aids the removal of lactate and maintains acidity levels in the blood and muscle.	40, 120
Calorimetry	The measurement of the heat and energy eliminated or stored in any system.	239
Cardiac hypertrophy	When the heart becomes bigger and stronger due to a thickening of the muscular wall.	11
Catharsis	The release of emotions, including aggression.	168
Centre of mass	The point from which the whole mass appears to act, or the point in the body at which the force of gravity can be thought to act.	136
Channelling	When people from minority ethnic groups might be pushed into certain sports, and even certain positions within a team, based on stereotypical assumptions about them.	109
Characteristics	Key features used to identify a particular concept (e.g. fun/enjoyment in physical recreation or a serious attitude in sport).	193
Chemoreceptors	Receptors that detect changes in blood acidity.	24
Chronic injury	A slowly developing injury that can last a long time. Often referred to as an overuse injury.	129
Chunking	Grouping information together to expand the capacity of the short-term memory.	67
Codification	The gradual organisation and defining of the rules – for the actual playing of a sport, as well as the conduct and behaviour of participants.	73
Cognitive	Relating to the mind.	162
Commercialisation	Treating sport as a commodity, involving the buying and selling of assets, with the market as the driving force behind sport.	95
Compression clothing	Items such as elasticated leggings, socks or shirts worn to promote recovery by improving circulation. They can decrease the pain suffered from muscle soreness/stiffness and decrease the time for muscle repair.	246
Concentration/diffusion gradient	This explains how gases flow from an area of high concentration to an area of low concentration.	22
Cori cycle	The process in which lactic acid is transported in the blood to the liver, where it is converted to blood glucose and glycogen.	41
County Sport Partnerships (CSPs)	Now known as Active Partnerships, these comprise 43 national networks of local agencies spread across England, which are working together to increase numbers participating in sport and physical activity.	113
CRAC	Contract–relax–antagonist–contract	28
Cryotherapy	The use of cold temperatures to treat an injury.	131
Cycle ergometer	A stationary bike that measures how much work is being performed.	44
Damages	Legal redress and compensation sought by individuals for loss of earnings. They must prove that they have, for example, suffered an actual injury as the result of the deliberate harmful, reckless actions of an opponent.	225

Data integrity	The maintenance of accuracy and consistency of stored data over its entire lifetime.	241
Dehydration	A condition that occurs when the body is losing more fluid than it is taking in.	119
Diastolic	The ventricles are relaxing.	17
Diffusion	The movement of gas molecules from an area of high concentration or partial pressure to an area of low concentration or partial pressure.	21
Digital Terrestrial Television (DTT)	The most common type of television service across the world. In the UK it is known as Freeview, and replaced the old analogue television service, which consisted of five channels. With Freeview you can get up to 70 free-to-air standard channels, 15 HD channels and around 30 radio services.	89
Direct gas analysis	A laboratory technique that measures the concentration of oxygen that is inspired and the concentration of carbon dioxide that is expired.	44
Discrimination	The unfair treatment of a person or minority group; distinguishing and acting on prejudice (e.g. reduced access to clubs or coaches).	106
Distress	A negative response to a stressful situation.	190
Dominant response	A well-learned skill that the performer will use under competitive pressure.	162
Doping	In competitive sports, the use of banned performance-enhancing drugs by athletic competitors.	220
Drag force	A force that acts in opposition to motion.	153
Duty of care	A legal obligation imposed on someone if they are responsible for a group of people.	227
Ejection fraction	The percentage of blood pumped out by the left ventricle per beat.	18
Electron transport chain	A series of chemical reactions in the cristae of the mitochondria in which hydrogen is oxidised to water and 34 ATP are produced.	35
Electrostimulation	The induction of muscular contraction using electrical impulses.	243
Elite	The best, highest level sports performers at 'excellence' level.	201
Emergent leader	Chosen from within the group.	187
Energy continuum	A term that describes which type of energy system is used for different types of physical activity and sport. The contribution of each system depends on the intensity and duration of exercise.	37
EPOC	The amount of oxygen consumed during recovery above that which would have been consumed at rest during the same time.	41
Equal opportunities	Treating people fairly; giving people the same chance (e.g. in relation to gender).	106
Erythropoietin (EPO)	A hormone that is naturally produced by the kidneys, but can also be artificially produced to increase performance in endurance athletes such as long-distance cyclists.	221
Ethnic groups	People who have racial, religious or linguistic traits in common.	108
Eustress	A positive response to a stressful situation.	190
Expiratory reserve volume (ERV)	The volume of air that can be forcibly expired after a normal breath.	20
Extrovert	A performer who is outgoing and likes social situations.	163
Fascia	A layer of fibrous connective tissue that surrounds the muscle or group of muscles.	132
Fast replenishment stage	The restoration of ATP and phosphocreatine stores, and the resaturation of myoglobin with oxygen.	41
Feudal system	Broadly defined, this was a way of structuring society around a relationship derived from the holding of land in exchange for service or labour.	73
Football hooliganism	Unruly, violent and destructive behaviour by over-zealous supporters of association football clubs.	217

Check your understanding and progress at **www.hoddereducation.co.uk/myrevisionnotes**

Form drag	The resistance caused by an object's shape as it moves through a fluid.	153
Gamesmanship	Bending the rules and stretching them to their absolute limit without getting caught; using whatever dubious methods possible to achieve the desired result.	212
Gaseous exchange	Movement of oxygen from the air into the blood, and of carbon dioxide from the blood into the air.	21
G-forces	Forces acting on the body as a result of acceleration or gravity (e.g. the G-load/force of an American football 'hit' on an opponent).	241
Globalisation	The process whereby nations are increasingly being linked together and people are becoming more interdependent via improvements in communication and travel.	96
Glycolysis	The breakdown of glucose into pyruvic acid.	35
Golgi tendon organs	Structures that detect levels of tension in a muscle.	29
GPS (global positioning system)	A satellite-based navigation system that provides location and time information.	241
Grooved	Overlearned or practised to perfection.	51
Hardware	The physical components of computers.	241
HDL (high-density lipoprotein)	Transports excess cholesterol in the blood back to the liver, where it is broken down. It is classed as 'good' cholesterol because it lowers the risk of developing heart disease.	116
Horizontal component	The horizontal motion of an object.	151
Horizontal displacement	The shortest distance from the starting point to the finishing point in a line parallel to the ground.	150
Hydrogen ions	Responsible for the acidity of the blood.	120
Hydrotherapy	The use of water to treat injuries.	131
Impulse	The time it takes a force to be applied to an object or body, given by force × time.	145
Indirect calorimetry	The measurement of the amount of heat and energy generated in an oxidation reaction.	240
Industrial patronage	The setting up of factory teams by factory owners as a way of decreasing absenteeism and encouraging loyalty in the workforce.	77
Industrial Revolution	A period deemed to have occurred from the mid-eighteenth to the mid-nineteenth century that marked a change in Britain from a feudal, rural society into an industrialised, machine-based, capitalist society, controlled by a powerful urban middle class.	74
Inequality	The unfair situation in which resources or opportunities are distributed unevenly within a society.	101
In loco parentis	A Latin phrase that means 'in the place of a parent'. It is the authority parents assign to another responsible adult who will be taking care of their child (e.g. a sports coach at a sports club).	229
Inspiratory reserve volume (IRV)	The volume of air that can be forcibly inspired after a normal breath.	20
Institution	An established organisation founded for a religious, educational, professional or social purpose.	100
Internalisation	The learning of values or attitudes that are incorporated within yourself.	99
Introvert	A performer who is reserved and avoids social situations.	163
Krebs cycle	A series of cyclical chemical reactions that take place using oxygen in the matrix of the mitochondria.	35
Lactate threshold	The point at which lactic acid accumulates rapidly in the blood.	39
Lactic acid	A by-product of anaerobic respiration. As it accumulates, it causes fatigue.	120
Lawn tennis	Originally called 'sphairistike' and played on an hourglass-shaped court, before its name and court shape were quickly replaced.	84

LDL (low-density lipoprotein)	Transports cholesterol in the blood to the tissues, and is classed as 'bad' cholesterol, because it is linked to an increased risk of heart disease.	116
Learned helplessness	A performer's belief that failure is inevitable.	184
Libel	A published false statement that is damaging to a person's reputation.	226
Lift force	The force that causes a body to move perpendicular to the direction of travel.	155
Linear motion	Motion in a straight or curved line, with all body parts moving at the same speed in the same direction.	134
Locus of causality	Where the performer places the reason for winning or losing. Can be internal or external.	183
Long-term memory	Where unlimited amounts of information (e.g. motor programmes) are stored and recalled.	66
Macro cycle	A long-term planning form of periodisation.	125
Mass	The quantity of matter a body has.	136
Maximal oxygen deficit	The difference between the estimated oxygen cost of exercise and the accumulated oxygen uptake.	41
Mechanical advantage	Where the effort arm is longer than the resistance arm.	139
Mechanical disadvantage	Where the resistance arm is longer than the effort arm.	139
Media	Organised means of communication by which large numbers of people can be reached quickly.	95, 231
Medulla oblongata	The most important part of the brain, because it regulates the processes that keep us alive.	13
Merchandising	The practice in which the brand or image from one 'product' is used to sell another (e.g. professional sports performers/teams promoting various products, including mobile phones and betting companies).	233
Meso cycle	Usually a 4–12 week period of training, with a particular focus, such as power.	125
Metabolic cart	A device that works by attaching headgear to a subject while the person breathes a specific amount of oxygen over a period of time.	239
Micro cycle	Planning for a week, a few days or an individual training session.	126
Minute ventilation	The volume of air inhaled or exhaled per minute.	20
Mitochondria	Components of cells that are often referred to as the 'powerhouses' of the cells because respiration and energy production occur there.	15
Moment of inertia	The resistance of a body to having its speed of rotation about an axis altered by the application of a turning force.	148
Motivation	The drive/desire/need to achieve a goal.	171
Motor neurone	A nerve cell that sends impulses from the brain and spinal cord to the muscles.	27
Motor unit	A motor neurone and muscle fibres.	27
Muscle spindles	Proprioceptors that detect how far and how fast a muscle is being stretched, and produce the stretch reflex.	29
Myoglobin	Myoglobin A protein found in muscle cells which stores and provides oxygen.	15
National governing body (NGB)	An organisation that has responsibility for managing its own particular sport (e.g. British Cycling).	205
National identity	A person's sense of belonging to one state or to one nation. It is the sense of a nation as a cohesive whole, as represented by distinctive traditions, culture, language and politics.	98
National pride	A feeling of attachment to one's homeland, and alliance with other citizens who share the same (i.e. patriotism).	98
Negative deviance	Behaviour that goes against the norms and has a detrimental effect on individuals and society in general.	213

Check your understanding and progress at **www.hoddereducation.co.uk/myrevisionnotes**

Negligence	Conduct that falls below a 'reasonable person standard' and leads to a breach of the duty of care, which results in foreseeable harm to another.	227
Newton's first law	A force is required to change the state of motion.	134
Newton's second law	The magnitude (size) and direction of the force determines the magnitude and direction of the acceleration when the mass remains constant.	134
Newton's third law	For every action force there is an equal and opposite reaction force.	134
Non-REM sleep (NREM)	Sleep with no rapid eye movement. It consists of three stages of sleep, which get progressively deeper.	133
Objective data	Fact-based information that is measurable and usable (e.g. the level achieved on the multi-stage fitness test, which links to a VO_2 max score).	122, 238
OBLA	The point at which lactate levels go above 4 millimoles/litre.	39
OFCOM	The communications regulator in the UK – for example, it regulates the television sector.	232
Open era	When professional tennis players were allowed to compete alongside amateurs and earn money.	92
Outdoor education	Activities that take place in the natural environment and utilise nature/geographical resources, such as mountains, rivers, and lakes.	197
Oxidation	The gain of oxygen by a substance.	41
Oxygen consumption	The amount of oxygen we use to produce ATP.	40
Partial pressure	The pressure exerted by an individual gas when it exists within a mixture of gases.	21
Participation level	An emphasis on taking part recreationally, with enjoyment as a key motivator to participate.	193
Peaking	Planning and organising training so that the performer is at their peak, both physically and mentally, for a major competition.	126
Perceived risk	A sense of danger and adventure stimulated by challenge facing beginners or inexperienced performers in a safe environment, with danger minimised via stringent safety measures (e.g. wearing a harness when climbing).	198
Perception	How environmental information is judged, understood and interpreted by the performer.	166
Performance analysis (PA)	The provision of objective feedback to performers in order to achieve a positive change in performance. (Feedback can be gained on a variety of performance indicators, such as the number of passes made, the distance run in km and the number of shots attempted.)	239
Performance Pathway Team	A combination of EIS and UK Sport expertise used to identify and develop world-class talent.	206
Periodisation	Dividing the training year into specific sections for a specific purpose.	125
Personal qualities	The attributes and personality characteristics of an individual person.	201
Personality	The unique, psychological, temperamental features of an individual.	157
Philanthropists	Kind, generous, middle-class individuals who had a social conscience and were keen to try to provide for a better life among the working class.	80
Phosphocreatine (PC)	An energy-rich phosphate compound found in the sarcoplasm of the muscles.	36
Plyometrics	Repeated, rapid stretching and contracting of muscles to increase muscle power.	45
Popular recreation	Sports and pastimes associated with the lower-class society in pre-industrial Britain.	73
Positive deviance	Behaviour that is outside the norms of society but with no intent to harm or break the rules. It involves over-adherence to the norms or expectations of society.	213

Prejudice	An unfavourable opinion of an individual, often based on inadequate facts (e.g. lack of tolerance, dislike of people of a specific ethnicity, religion or culture), which can negatively affect the treatment of a performer from a minority ethnic group by a coach, for example.	106
Prescribed leader	Chosen from outside the group.	187
Professional	A person who plays sport for financial gain.	83
Progression	The process of gradually developing towards a more advanced state.	104
Proprioceptors	Receptors that detect changes in muscle movement.	24
Public provision	Local council provision of facilities (e.g. sport/recreational) to allow the masses to participate.	81
Public school	A private, fee-paying secondary school, especially one for boarders.	80
Pulmonary ventilation	The process of breathing.	23
Qualitative data	Descriptive information, perhaps relating to the way people think or feel.	122, 237
Quantitative data	Data that can be measured (e.g. height) or counted (e.g. number of people).	122, 237
Race	A categorisation of humans based on shared physical or social qualities into groups generally viewed as distinct within a given society.	109
Racism	A set of beliefs or ideas based on the assumption that races have distinct hereditary characteristics that give some an intrinsic superiority over others; it might lead to physical or verbal abuse.	108
Reliability	The degree to which data collection is consistent and stable over time.	122, 238
Repetitions	The number of times you do an exercise (often referred to as reps).	127
RER	The ratio of carbon dioxide produced to oxygen consumed.	44
Research	A systematic process of investigation and study carried out with the aim of advancing knowledge.	237
Residual volume	The amount of air that remains in the lungs after maximal expiration.	20
Resting energy expenditure (REE)	The amount of energy, usually expressed in kcal, required by the body during rest for a 24-hour period.	240
Restraint of trade	Action that interferes with free competition in a market. In sport, this might involve a clause in a contract that restricts a person's right to carry out their profession.	226
RICE	Rest, ice, compression, elevation.	131
Ring-fenced	Relating to the number of sporting events at national and international level that must be available for viewing on terrestrial or free-to-access television rather than on satellite and subscription channels.	232
SAN	A small mass of cardiac muscle (sinoatrial node or SAN) found in the wall of the right atrium that generates the heartbeat. It is more commonly called the pacemaker.	12
Sarcoplasm	The fluid that surrounds the nucleus of a muscle fibre – the site where anaerobic respiration takes place.	35
Scalar quantity	A quantity that has size only.	135
School Games	An initiative to increase participation in school sport from intra-/interschool level through to county and national levels.	198
School Sport Partnerships	The creation of increased opportunities for school sport via junior/primary schools working together with secondary schools and further education providers.	198
Selective attention	Focusing on the relevant information/cues in the sporting environment and disregarding the irrelevant.	63
Self-efficacy	Describes the amount of confidence you have in a particular sporting situation.	185
Self-serving bias	Attributing the reason for winning internally and for failure externally.	184
Sets	The number of cycles of repetitions (reps).	127
Short-term memory	The working memory where the motor programme is initiated.	65

Check your understanding and progress at **www.hoddereducation.co.uk/myrevisionnotes**

Significant other	A person who is held in high esteem, such as a family member, friend, role model in the media or a coach/teacher.	59, 157
Simulation	Trying to deceive an official by overacting – for example, diving to win a free kick.	211
Smart wearable fitness and sports device	A device that is worn or attached to a performer's body while in use to provide instant feedback on aspects of performance, such as distance covered and heart rate (e.g. Garmin Vivofit).	242
Social action theory	A way of viewing socialisation that emphasises the proactive role of people in shaping social life (i.e. social action).	104
Social change	An alteration in the social order of a society, i.e. significant changes in social behaviours and/or cultural values over time, leading to long-term effects.	101
Social class	A term used to reflect social inequalities, i.e. where certain groups have more access to wealth, income and power than others. Factors that contribute to social class include a person's job, family background, education and income.	80
Social control	A concept that refers to the way in which people's thoughts, feelings, appearance and behaviour are regulated in social systems.	100
Social facilitation	The positive effects experienced by a performer while in the presence of an audience.	174
Social inhibition	The negative effects experienced by a performer while in the presence of an audience.	174
Social issues	Problems or conflicts that influence or affect a considerable number of people in society – for example, discrimination based on gender, disability or ethnic group, drug abuse and low activity patterns linked to obesity and health problems.	101
Social processes	Forms of social interaction between individuals and groups that occur again and again.	100
Social stratification	A type of social inequality in which society is divided into different levels based on a social characteristic, such as wealth, social status or derived power.	102
Socialisation	A lifelong process whereby members of a society learn its norms, values, ideas, practices and roles in order to take their place in that society.	98, 157
Society	An organised group of people associated for some specific purpose or with a shared common interest.	98
Socioeconomic status	An individual's position in the social structure, which depends on their job, level of income and area they live in.	202
Soft tissue	Includes tendons, ligaments, muscles, nerves and blood vessels.	132
Software	Any set of machine-readable instructions that direct a computer's processor to perform specific operations.	241
Somatic	Relating to the body.	162
Spatial summation	When the strength of a contraction changes by altering the number and size of the muscle's motor units.	28
Sponsorship	When a company pays for its products to be publicly displayed or advertised, usually in an attempt to increase the sales of their goods.	95, 234
Sporting development continuum	Participation in various forms of physical activity at various stages of development. For example, the grass-roots 'foundation stage' in primary school PE or 'participation stage' involvement as an adult in physical recreation.	193
Sports analytics	Studying data from sports performances to try to improve performance.	237
Sports law	The legislation, regulations and judicial decisions that govern sports and athletes who perform in them.	225
Sportsmanship	Conforming to the unwritten rules, spirit and etiquette of a sport.	211

Stability dimension	How fixed the attributions are. Stable attributions are relatively permanent, whereas unstable attributions are highly changeable.	183
Stacking	The disproportionate concentration of people from minority ethnic groups in certain positions in a sports team, which tends to be based on the stereotype that they are more valuable for their physicality than for their decision-making and communication qualities.	109
Static stretching	When the muscle is held in a stationary position for 30 seconds or more.	123
Stereotyping	A standardised image/belief shared by society; making simple generalisations about all members of a group, which allows others to categorise and treat them accordingly (e.g. negative stereotypes about women that negatively impact on their participation in sport in general and/or allow certain sports to be deemed 'inappropriate').	106
Stimulants	Drugs that induce a temporary improvement in mental and physical function (e.g. increase alertness and awareness).	220
Streamlining	Shaping a body so it can move effectively and quickly through a fluid.	153
Stress	An individual's physical response that prepares the body for action when a threat is perceived.	190
Stressor	The *cause* of the stress response – for example, playing in an important competitive situation (final or semi-final), sustaining an injury, being fouled/injured, the perception that you are playing badly/feel that you are letting the team down, fatigue or the weather/conditions.	190
Subjective data	Data based on opinions, which is less measurable and often less usable than objective data.	122, 138
Submaximal oxygen deficit	When there is not enough oxygen available at the start of exercise to provide all the energy (ATP) aerobically.	41
Surface drag	The resistance that occurs from friction between the surface of a body and the fluid through which it is moving.	153
Systolic	The ventricles are contracting.	17
Talent identification	The multidisciplinary screening of athletes to identify those with the potential for world-class success.	202
Tapering	Reducing the volume and/or intensity of training prior to competition.	126
Television match official (TMO)	An official, who is a qualified referee, who can review plays by looking at video footage when asked to by the on-field referee.	216
Tetanic contraction	A sustained, powerful muscle contraction caused by a series of fast repeating stimuli.	28
Tetrahydrogestrinone (THG)	A banned steroid used to increase power, which was tweaked by chemists to make it undetectable by 'normal tests'.	221
Tidal volume	The volume of air breathed in or out per breath.	20
Torque	A rotational force.	147
Transfer	The effect that one skill has when learning and performing another skill.	49
Trespass	To enter someone's land without permission (e.g. a football pitch).	226
Urbanisation	Large numbers of people migrating from rural areas into towns and cities, seeking regular work in the factories.	77
Validity	An indication of whether the data collected actually measure what they aim to measure.	122, 138
Vascular shunting	The redistribution of cardiac output to where oxygen is needed most.	14
Vasoconstriction	The narrowing of the blood vessels to reduce blood flow into the capillaries.	15
Vasodilation	The widening of the blood vessels to increase the flow of blood into the capillaries.	15
Vector quantity	A measurement described in terms of both size and direction.	143
Venous return	The return of blood to the right side of the heart via the vena cava.	17
Vertical component	The upward motion of an object.	151

Check your understanding and progress at **www.hoddereducation.co.uk/myrevisionnotes**

Vibration technology	Vibration training/therapy, also known as 'whole-body vibration' (WBV). An example of its usage involves the use of vibration plates to induce exercise effects in the body.	242
Video motion analysis	A technique used to gather information on moving objects from video footage.	238
Violence in sport	Physical acts committed to deliberately harm others, which can occur in sports such as American football, rugby, football and ice hockey.	215
VO$_2$ max	The maximum amount of oxygen that can be utilised by the muscles per minute.	39
WADA (World Anti-Doping Agency)	A foundation created in 1999 through a collective initiative led by the IOC to promote, coordinate and monitor the fight against drugs in sport.	223
Wave summation	Where there is a repeated nerve impulse with no time to relax, so a smooth, sustained contraction occurs rather than twitches.	27
Whereabouts system	A system designed to support out of competition testing, which requires athletes to supply the details of their whereabouts so that they can be located at any time and anywhere for testing, without advance notice.	223

Now test yourself answers

1.2 Cardiovascular system

1 + Lowers blood pressure
  + Lowers LDL cholesterol levels and increases HDL cholesterol levels.
2 + Cardiac output is the amount of blood pumped out of the ventricles per minute.
  + Stroke volume is the amount of blood pumped out of the ventricles per beat.
  + Relationship: cardiac output = stroke volume × heart rate
3 Elite football player:
  + has a lower resting heart rate of below 60 bpm/bradycardia
  + has a higher resting stroke volume
  + will train regularly, which leads to cardiac hypertrophy
  + will therefore have stronger heart/more forceful contraction
4 Trained performer's maximal cardiac output would be higher because of:
  + a greater maximum stroke volume
  + cardiac hypertrophy
5 SAN → atrial systole (contract) → AVN → bundle of His → bundle branches → Purkinje fibres → ventricular systole (contract)
6 + Chemoreceptors – an increase in blood carbon dioxide results in impulses sent to the cardiac control centre in the medulla oblongata. This then sends impulses through the sympathetic system to the SAN to increase heart rate.
  + Proprioceptors – an increase in muscle movement results in impulses sent to the cardiac control centre in the medulla oblongata. This then sends impulses through the sympathetic system to the SAN to increase heart rate.
7 + Blood flow to the skin increases so that heat can be released.
  + Blood flow to the heart increases because the heart needs more oxygen for energy to beat faster and with more force.
8 + Muscles need oxygen for energy.
  + An increase in CO_2 is detected by chemoreceptors.
  + An increase in movement is detected by proprioceptors.
  + They send impulses to the vasomotor centre in the medulla oblongata of the brain.
  + Through the sympathetic nervous system the brain sends impulses causing:
    + vasodilation to areas needing blood, such as the muscles
    + vasoconstriction to areas not needing as much blood, such as the kidneys/liver/gut

+ Precapillary sphincters relax, so blood flow is increased.
9 + They are closest to the pumping action of the heart.
  + They have more of an elastic outer layer to cope with fluctuations in pressure.
  + They have strong, muscular walls.
10 + One cell thick – means a short diffusion pathway.
  + Tiny lumen slows blood flow down for diffusion to occur.
11 + Haemoglobin transports oxygen in the blood.
  + Myoglobin stores oxygen in the muscles.
12 + The Bohr shift is when an oxyhaemoglobin disassociation curve moves to the right.
  + Haemoglobin has a lower affinity for oxygen at working muscles/gives up oxygen more easily/at higher partial pressures.
13 Occurs as a result of increased CO_2 in the blood/increased blood acidity/decreased blood pH/increased temperature.
14 + Systolic: the ventricles are contracting.
  + Diastolic: the ventricles are relaxing.
15 + Arteriovenous difference is the difference between the oxygen content of the arterial blood arriving at the muscles and the venous blood leaving the muscles.
  + It increases during exercise.

1.3 Respiratory system

1 Residual volume will stay the same during exercise, so the graphical representation will remain the same.
2 + One cell thick, which means there is a short diffusion pathway.
  + Extensive capillary network surrounds the alveoli, so they have an excellent blood supply, which means greater diffusion can take place.
  + Large surface area, which allows for a greater uptake of oxygen.
3 Through diffusion, where O_2 and CO_2 move from an area of high concentration/partial pressure to a low concentration/partial pressure, down a concentration/diffusion gradient:
  + There is a high pO_2 in the blood and a lower pO_2 in the muscles, so oxygen moves from the blood into the muscles.
  + There is a high pCO_2 in the muscles and a lower pCO_2 in the blood, so carbon dioxide moves from the muscles into the blood.
4 + Proprioceptors detect an increase in muscle movement and send impulses to the respiratory centre in the medulla oblongata to increase breathing during exercise.

- When baroreceptors detect a decrease in blood pressure, they send impulses to the respiratory centre in the medulla oblongata, which results in an increase in breathing rate.

5 Answers can include:
- Carbon monoxide combines with haemoglobin in lungs rather than oxygen
- Bronchioles constrict
- Damage to cilia
- Number of alveoli reduces

1.4 Neuromuscular system

1 Any sporting examples that are long duration and low to medium intensity, e.g. triathlon, marathon, long-distance cycling/swimming.

2 Type IIx

3 Characteristics:
- Large motor neurone size
- High PC stores
- High glycogen stores
- Low mitochondrial density
- Low myoglobin content
- Low capillary density
- High myosin ATPase/glycolytic enzyme activity
- High fatigability/low aerobic capacity/high anaerobic capacity
- High force production/speed of contraction

4 A motor unit comprises a motor neurone and muscle fibres. It contains either all fast-twitch or slow-twitch fibres.
   Spatial summation causes an increase in strength of contraction/more force in muscles:
   - uses bigger/larger motor units
   - uses more motor units
   - fast-twitch units produce more force than slow-twitch units

5 Proprioceptors are sensory organs in the muscles, tendons and joints that inform the body of the extent of movement that has taken place.

1.5 Musculoskeletal system and analysis of movement

1 Shoulder = abduction, hip = abduction

2

Joint	Joint action	Plane and axis	Agonist	Type of contraction
Hip	Extension	Sagittal plane/transverse axis	Gluteals	Concentric
Knee	Extension	Sagittal plane/transverse axis	Quad-riceps	Concentric
Ankle	Plantar flexion	Sagittal plane/transverse axis	Gastro-cnemius	Concentric

1.6 Energy systems

1
- Pyruvic acid combines with acetyl CoA/acetyl coenzyme A.
- Fatty acids are broken down to form acetyl CoA/beta oxidation.
- Oxaloacetic acid combines with coenzyme A and forms citric acid.
- Hydrogen is removed from citric acid.
- Carbon dioxide is produced.
- Hydrogen is passed onto the electron transport chain/electron transfer chain.
- The process forms two ATP molecules.

2
- An anaerobic process
- Controlling enzyme is creatine kinase
- Breaks down phosphocreatine in muscles to phosphate and creatine
- Releases energy to make one ATP molecule

3 a Short 10-metre sprint into space to receive the ball = ATP/PC system
   b Making a quick break in attack over the length of the pitch = anaerobic glycolytic system
   c Jogging to keep in position = aerobic system

4 Factors that affect lactate accumulation:
- Intensity of exercise – the higher the intensity the faster lactate accumulation occurs.
- Fitness of the performer – physiological adaptive responses due to training, for example having more mitochondria, greater capillary density, improved gaseous exchange.
- VO_2 max of a performer – the higher the level, the more lactate accumulation is delayed.
- Respiratory exchange ratio/RER – the closer the value is to 1.00, the quicker lactate accumulation occurs.
- Muscle fibre type used – if slow-twitch fibres used, lactate accumulation is delayed.

5 Any two from:
- Oxidation into carbon dioxide and water in inactive muscles and organs, and used by muscles as an energy source
- Converted to blood glucose and glycogen (Cori cycle)
- Converted into protein
- Removed in sweat and urine

6
- VO_2 max – the maximum volume of oxygen utilised per minute.
- Lactate threshold – the point at which lactic acid rapidly starts to accumulate in the blood/OBLA.
- Lactate threshold is a percentage of VO_2 max.
- The higher the VO_2 max, the more the delay in lactic acid build-up/as VO_2 max increases, so does the lactate threshold.
- Trained athletes can exercise for longer periods at the same/higher intensity compared with untrained athletes.

7 Improves speed and agility; with a relevant example, such as quicker to change direction to get free or dribble more effectively to beat a player.

2.1 Skill, skills continuums and transfer of skills

1 + Aesthetically pleasing means the skill is good to watch.
  + Goal directed means the performer has a clear aim in mind.

2 + Fluency – the skill is performed smoothly, without stopping and starting. For example, when performing a triple jump, the athlete transitions from one phase of the jump to the next without it being jerky/uncoordinated.
  + Efficiency – the skill is produced with the least amount of energy and in the quickest time. For example, a trampolinist swiftly completes a ten-bounce routine, and their energy levels are maintained throughout.

3

Classification	Definition
Open	The sporting environment changes while the skill is being performed. Performers must adapt and a high amount of decision making is involved.
Closed	The sporting environment/playing conditions are stable, enabling the performer to repeat the same movement pattern. There are few decisions to make.
Gross	Large muscle groups are used to perform the skill.
Fine	Small muscles are used to perform skills that require precision.
Self-paced	The performer is in control of the speed and timing of the skill.
Externally paced	The performer must adapt because they have no control over the speed and timing of the skill. It is in the control of the sporting environment.
Highly organised	The skill is difficult to break down into subroutines/parts due to the speed at which it is performed. Whole practice is recommended for these skills.
Low organisation	The skill can easily be broken down into subroutines/parts. Subroutines can be practised in isolation.
Simple	Limited decision making is required.
Complex	Several decisions must be made.
Discrete	The skill has a clear beginning and ending and is one distinct action.
Serial	A number of discrete skills are performed together sequentially, creating another skill.
Complex	The skill has no clear beginning or ending. The end subroutine of one skill becomes the beginning subroutine of the next. The movement is cyclical.

4 Positive transfer – learning a skill facilitates the learning of an additional skill.
Negative transfer – learning a skill inhibits the learning of an additional skill.
Zero transfer – there are no similarities between the tasks; therefore, there is no effect on either skill.
Bilateral transfer – the learning and performing of a skill on one side of the body is then transferred to the opposite side.

2.2 Impact of classification on practice

1 Advantages:
  + Kinaesthesis is developed
  + Fluency between subroutines is maintained
  + Not time-consuming
  + Creates a clear mental image
  + Easily transferred into full game
  + Aids understanding
  Disadvantages:
  + Not ideal for cognitive performers
  + Can cause information overload
  + Can cause fatigue
  + Must be physically capable of producing the full skill

2 + The first subroutine is taught and then grooved – for example, in swimming front crawl, the arm action is taught and grooved
  + The second subroutine is taught and then grooved – for example, the leg kick is taught and grooved.
  + The two subroutines are linked and practised together until grooved – for example, the arm and leg actions are grooved together.
  + Each additional subroutine is grooved on its own and added on sequentially.

3 Variable practice involves practising skills and drills in a constantly changing environment.
  Advantages:
  + Develops schema
  + Increases motivation
  + Performer gains experience in a range of situations
  + Positive transfer from training to game
  Disadvantages:
  + Time-consuming
  + Can cause fatigue
  + Possibility of information overload

2.3 Principles and theories of learning and performance

1 Any two from each:
  Autonomous:
  + Fluent
  + Efficient
  + Automatic movements
  + Motor programmes formed and stored in the LTM

Check your understanding and progress at **www.hoddereducation.co.uk/myrevisionnotes**

- Focus can be shifted on to fine details
- Intrinsic feedback can be utilised

Associative:
- Practice essential to maintain standard
- Fewer mistakes made
- Some performers do not leave this stage
- Focus can begin to be shifted on to fine details
- Smoother movements/more coordinated
- Feedback important/kinaesthesis begins to develop

Cognitive:
- Mental images created
- Accurate demonstrations required
- Practice/mental rehearsal necessary
- Several mistakes made
- Trial-and-error learning used
- Jerky/uncoordinated movements
- No motor programmes
- Reliant on extrinsic feedback

2 Cognitive stage:
- Performer reliant on extrinsic feedback
- Feedback is positive
- Some knowledge of results is used

Associative stage:
- Performer begins to develop kinaesthesis and uses intrinsic feedback to correct movement
- Extrinsic feedback used less frequently – to refine actions
- Begin to use knowledge of performance

3

Causes	Solutions
Loss of motivation/boredom	+ Set new tasks/challenges + Use variable practice + Offer tangible rewards
Mental/physical fatigue	+ Allow the performer to rest + Use distributed practice
Limit of ability reached	Allow the performer to compete against others of similar ability
Poor coaching	+ Try a variety of coaching methods + Try an alternative coach
Incorrect goals set	Set goals using the SMARTER principle

4 Gestaltists believe that part learning is not effective and that by learning the skill as a whole, kinaesthesis and the flow of the skill are maintained, and the performer gains a greater understanding of the task they are facing.

5 + Positive reinforcement is endorsing a performer's action when it is correct.
+ Negative reinforcement is saying nothing when a correct action is shown, after a period of criticism about a performance.
+ Punishment is a method of reducing or eliminating undesirable actions.

6 Attention:
- The performer has to concentrate on the model.
- The coach highlights key cues in the demonstration.

- The model should be attractive (e.g. use a role model).
- The model should be accurate.

Motor (re)production:
- The performer must be physically and mentally able to copy the model demonstration.

7 A more knowledgeable other (MKO) is a person – normally a coach or teacher – who has a greater understanding of the task than you do. They are important because they give you technical advice and feedback on how to produce the skill.

2.4 Use of guidance and feedback

1 Negative feedback is information about incorrect actions, so that they are not repeated and errors are corrected. For example, a coach tells you that you do not have enough height on the three-point shot in basketball, so you adjust this next time.

Knowledge of results (KR) is information about whether or not the skill/action was successful (if so, repeat) or unsuccessful (if so, adjust next time). For example, the three-point shot missed the basket.

2 Advantages:
- It can be given immediately during performance.
- It is useful for open skills in which performer needs to make decisions and adapt quickly.
- It is used effectively in conjunction with visual guidance.

Disadvantages:
- There may be a chance of information overload if too many instructions are given together.
- Lengthy explanations may cause the performer to lose concentration.
- Cognitive performers may not understand specific technical instructions.

2.5 Memory models

1 Perceptual mechanisms:
- A judgement is made regarding the incoming information received by the sense organs.
- Includes the DCR process (detection – receive cues; comparison – cues compared with those already stored in the memory system; recognition – understand what response is required based on the stored memories).
- Selective attention occurs. Only the relevant information is acted upon, while the irrelevant information is disregarded.

Effector mechanisms:
- Decision is put into action by sending impulses to the relevant working muscles in order to carry out the movement.

2 Central executive:
- Maintains overall control
- Links with the long-term memory
- Focuses and switches attention
- Identifies which information goes to which subsystem

Episodic buffer:

+ Stores three/four chunks or 'episodes'
+ Allows different parts of working memory system to talk to each other
+ Produces sequences of information to send to the LTM
+ Gathers perceptual information

3 + Receives the relevant information that has been filtered away from the irrelevant by selective attention.
+ Limited capacity – stores 7 ± 2 items
+ Limited duration – up to approximately 30 seconds
+ Practice/rehearsal required to transfer to and store information in the LTM
+ Produces a memory trace
+ Compares information with that stored in the LTM
+ Initiates the motor programme

4 Reaction time – time from the onset of the stimulus to the onset of the response.

Movement time – time from the onset of the movement to the completion of the task.

Response time is reaction time plus movement time – time from the onset of the stimulus to the completion of the task.

5 Anticipation – predicting that a movement will happen before it occurs.

Temporal – predicting when the action will be performed.

Spatial – predicting what action is going to be performed, and where.

6 Recall schema:
+ Stores information about the movement
+ Initiates the movement
+ Includes:
  + initial conditions
  + response specifications

Recognition schema:
+ Controls the movement
+ Evaluates the movement
+ Includes:
  + sensory consequences
  + response outcome

3.1 Emergence of globalisation of sport in the twenty-first century

1 + Played occasionally – because of limited free time; linked to seasons/religious festivals.
+ Local – because of limited transport/communications.
+ Limited organisation/few rules – because the lower class in society were illiterate.
+ Violent – because society was harsh/violent in nature.
+ Lower-class participation – mob games were viewed as suitable activities for the lower classes.

+ Rural – society was agrarian in nature with the population spread out in the countryside.
+ Natural/simple – because people used what was readily available to them (e.g. open fields).

2 + Limited communications/transport
+ Widespread illiteracy
+ Cruel/violent
+ Limited free time
+ Rural

3 + Violent/unruly nature of the activity
+ Injuries it caused
+ Damage to property it caused

4 + It was courtly/exclusive/played by the upper class.
+ It had complex written rules.
+ It was non-violent; had etiquette; respect for opponents.
+ It was played regularly.
+ It was played in purpose-built facilities; it used specialist equipment.
+ It was non-local; the upper class could travel to play.
+ It required the use of complex skills (and not violence).

5 The lower class worked very long hours and so had very little free time to participate (i.e. occasional – participation in mob football on an annual basis).

The upper class had lots of free time to participate (e.g. regular participation in real tennis).

6 + Improved health and fitness, leading to more energy/improved general wellbeing.
+ Increased income/more time to play sport due to increased wages and decreased working hours.
+ Positive influence of the new middle class, leading to more provision/increased acceptability of working-class participation.
+ Employer provision/industrial patronage, leading to factory teams being formed/broken-time payments being made.
+ Improved transport/communications, leading to increased travel distances/regular nationwide fixtures.
+ Improved public provision (e.g. public parks).

7 + Factory teams were set up.
+ Sports facilities were provided.
+ Excursions were organised to the seaside for fresh air/exercise.

8 + Lack of space and the development of purpose-built facilities.
+ The large numbers of working-class people in towns and cities needed entertaining.

9 + Development of the railways allowed transport of teams and spectators; spectator sport developed.
+ Third-class travel was relatively cheap/affordable for the working classes.
+ Fixtures could be played more regularly.
+ Competitions developed nationally (e.g. FA Cup; Football League).
+ Professional sport developed.

Check your understanding and progress at **www.hoddereducation.co.uk/myrevisionnotes**

- Improved access to the countryside was possible (e.g. for rambling/climbing); escape from urban pollution.
- Road improvements led to the development of cycling clubs.

10
- It meant the working class could read newspapers.
- These contained lots of information, improving interest in/access to sport – for example, upcoming fixtures, results of matches, league tables, and names of players.

11
- By giving its 'approval'.
- By providing facilities – a place to play (e.g. on church land or in church halls).
- By establishing it as a social activity to increase the opportunity to play the game (e.g. in Sunday school teams).
- By establishing clubs/youth sections in the Church, which encouraged football (e.g. the Boys Brigade).

12
- The middle class acted as agents for working-class players.
- The middle class promoted events (e.g. athletics meetings).
- Middle-class factory owners set up factory teams and paid broken-time payments for workers to play in matches organised when they should have been at work.

13
- To increase the health and fitness/personal hygiene of the working class.
- Via civic responsibility, in times of social responsibility/social justice/philanthropy.
- To gain prestige for the local area.
- To increase social control/civilise society; the temperance movement wanted to keep the working class out of the pubs and away from alcohol; to encourage middle-class values.
- To improve the productivity of the workforce/raise morale of the community.

14
- Boarding/non-local/rural/residential
- Single sex – boys only
- Fee paying – for the elite of society (upper class; then spread to middle class)
- Set in large grounds – provided facilities for sport (e.g. rugby pitches)
- Had strict systems of discipline (e.g. 'fagging' – younger boys fetched and carried for the older sixth-form boys).

15
- Women could play in seclusion/the privacy of their own garden, away from view.
- Tennis became a social game, which could be played as a mixed-sex activity.
- It was an opportunity to be athletic/energetic, but it did not need to be vigorous – women could retain their decorum and stay 'ladylike'.
- No special kit was initially required; women could dress modestly to play tennis.
- The acceptance of exercise in fresh air as therapeutic.
- There were positive female role models (e.g. Lottie Dod as an early Wimbledon champion).
- The middle classes set up tennis clubs to join.

16
- Promote moral development
- Promote physical improvement
- Promote intellectual improvement

17
- Large numbers in a small space provided a mass audience for football.
- Lack of space led to purpose-built facilities for playing and watching football.

18
- It means freedom of movement (to another club) within the EU.
- Able to move clubs with no transfer fee being paid at the end of a contract.
- Players have a lot of 'bargaining power', particularly towards the end of their contracts.
- Many benefit from big wage increases/huge salaries.

19 In relation to both coaching and refereeing, there are:
- Far fewer women in these roles than men
- Far fewer people from a BAME background in these roles than from the indigenous population

20
- Increased sponsorship
- Increased revenue to be invested via WSL/Championship clubs
- Higher profile for the game, generating more interest and role models to relate to/aspire to
- More people inspired to participate

21
- Stereotypes/sexism/hostile attitudes from male players; lack of adherence to FA Respect protocols
- Lack of role models
- Lack of full-time opportunities/lack of sponsorship
- Too many demands on time; lack of leisure time
- Fewer opportunities/competitions to potentially officiate

22
- She founded the organisation specifically designed to develop women's tennis at elite level (WTA).
- She established a year-round global circuit for female players.
- It was good for income generation (e.g. from media/sponsors).
- It provided full-time tennis occupational opportunities for a large number of elite female players.
- Initial interest quickly grew from corporate sponsors, with growth in sponsorship and extreme wealth in top players (e.g. Navratilova was the first female player to earn over $1 million in a calendar year, with Serena Williams now far exceeding this).
- The WTA fought for equality in prize money between men and women at all four Grand Slams, which has now been achieved.
- It provided positive role models to aspire to via highly visible/high-profile tennis competitions at elite level.

23
- False scientific/physiological claims about women – for example, the belief that long-distance running was harmful to women and would damage their fertility.

+ Beliefs on 'masculinity/femininity' led to women being excluded from power events in athletics (e.g. the shot put and hammer throwing).

24 + National relevance/traditional part of culture/large audiences
+ High levels of skill in evidence/professional sport/high profile/competitive
+ Competitive/opponents potentially well matched
+ Demonstrate aggression/physical challenge/entertainment
+ Understandable rules/scoring systems
+ Relatively short timescale
+ Well-known performers/role models
+ Linkage to sponsorship/business; players are contracted

25 The process whereby nations are increasingly linked and people are becoming more interdependent via improvements in communication and travel, which enables sport to become truly worldwide (e.g. football).

26 + National Football League
+ Major League Baseball
+ National Basketball Association
+ National Hockey League

3.2 The impact of sport on society and of society on sport

1 + Socialisation – a lifelong process where members of society learn its norms, values and beliefs.
+ Primary socialisation – socialisation during the early years of childhood.
+ Secondary socialisation – socialisation that occurs during the 'later years', i.e. as teenagers/adults.

2 Primary: mother, brother, father, sister
Secondary: friends, newspapers, peer groups, social media, secondary school teachers, television

3 Verbal communication, non-verbal communication, social media communication, gestures, criticism, smiles, greetings, humour

4 + Significant changes in social behaviours and/or cultural values.
+ Over time these lead to long-term effects.

5 + Lack of money/cost of participating
+ Lack of confidence/self-esteem
+ Lack of role models to aspire to as participants/coaches/leaders of sports organisations in positions of responsibility.
+ Myths or stereotypes in some sections of society about the capabilities of women, people in minority ethnic groups and people with disability.

6 Participation can be increased by:
+ increased publicity/advertisement of opportunities available
+ making sure they are affordable/decreasing costs/subsidising
+ providing taster sessions
+ providing appealing activities
+ investing in areas of social deprivation

7 Traditional social action: actions are controlled by traditions/engrained social habits; long-standing

beliefs – people engage in this type of action often unthinkingly – 'the way it has always been done' (e.g. take up cycling as this is what the family has always done, or go to university because this is what the family has always done).

Affective action: your actions are controlled by your emotional state; it results from the affections/feelings/emotional state of mind of 'the actor'/person; if you enjoy doing something, you are more likely to continue with that action (e.g. you regularly go long-distance running because it makes you feel good/you like doing it.

Value rational action: individuals take actions for self-gain that are determined by a conscious belief in the inherent value of a type of behaviour (e.g. regular exercise/healthy diet to ensure positive health and wellbeing; going to church/mosque to ensure spiritual wellbeing).

Instrumentally rational action: individuals consider the best action/most appropriate steps to take that will lead most effectively to achieving the set goal/desired result (e.g. volunteering as a sports coach to help get a job).

8 + Treating people fairly/giving people the same chance
+ In relation to disability/gender/race etc.
+ Based on inclusiveness/legal acts (e.g. Sex Discrimination Act)

9 Discrimination is:
+ treating people differently
+ acting on a prejudice/excluding from participation
+ based on stereotyping on the basis of race/ethnicity

10 Overt – unfair treatment that is highly visible
Covert – unfair treatment that is harder to uncover

11 Barriers to participation for minority ethnic groups:
+ Racism/discrimination still exists
+ Actively discouraged by parents/peers
+ Low status given to sport/preference for academic work
+ Conflict with religious observances/dress codes
+ Fewer minority ethnic role models/less media coverage
+ Stereotyping/channelling still exists
+ Fear of rejection/lower self-esteem

12 + Aerobic activity leads to a decreased risk of developing heart disease/suffering a stroke.
+ Avoidance of high/low blood pressure.
+ Decreased risk of type 2 diabetes.
+ Maintaining a healthy weight/decreased risk of obesity.
+ Weight-bearing exercise leads to a strengthening of bones and decreased risk of osteoporosis.
+ Improved psychological/mental health and stress management; decreased risk of conditions such as anxiety/depression/emotional disturbance.
+ Decreased risk of some cancers (e.g. colon cancer and breast cancer).

4.1 Diet and nutrition and their effects

1 + Both are important energy sources.
  + Fats are important to last the match/used for long-duration, low-intensity work.
  + Fats are a good source of vitamins A, D, E and K.
  + Carbohydrates are the main energy provider.
  + Carbohydrates are the only food source that can be broken down anaerobically, which will be needed for high-intensity activity during a game, for example sprinting.
2 + Helps form haemoglobin, thus increasing the oxygen-carrying capacity of the blood.
  + Helps the body to use and store energy from protein and carbohydrate in food.
3 + Needed for strong bones
  + Needed for muscle contraction/nerve transmission (important during exercise)
4 1500 m runner

4.2 Preparation and training methods

1 Subjective data:
  + Data that involve opinions/assumptions/ interpretations/beliefs/feelings/emotions
  + Self-analysis/questionnaire/surveys/ observation/interviews
  Objective data:
  + Data based on facts, and which are measurable
  + Wingate test, multi-stage fitness test
2 + Static stretching is when the muscle is held in a stationary position for 30 seconds or more.
  + Ballistic stretching involves performing a stretch with swinging or bouncing movements to push a body part even further.
  Whatever the stretch, it should:
  + start slowly
  + be sport-specific
  + be stopped if painful
  + be balanced between agonists and antagonists
  + be held for approximately 30 seconds if static
  + only be done by performers who are very flexible (e.g. gymnasts) if ballistic
3 The football player will:
  + use specificity to ensure the strength training programme is relevant/best suited to football
  + specifically target muscle groups/energy systems/movements/muscle fibre types
4 Time:
  + Increase the time in which you work, or equivalent example
  + Decrease the time of rest periods
  Type:
  + Method relevant/specific to the area of fitness/ sport
  + Example: continuous training for a marathon runner
5 + Macrocycle – long-term planning
  + Mesocycle – usually a 4–12-week period of training with a particular focus such as power
  + Microcycle – planning for a week, a few days or an individual training session
6 a circuits
  b interval

4.3 Injury prevention and rehabilitation

1 + Screening identifies those at risk of complications from exercise/detects a problem early before any symptoms occur/reduces risk of injury/saves lives.
  + It prepares performers for their sport/enhances performance.
  + The musculoskeletal condition of an athlete can be assessed by screening to highlight any past or current injuries.
  + This will enable the performer to select a relevant conditioning training programme that will prevent further injury.
  + However, some screening tests are not 100 per cent accurate and may miss a problem (false negative) or identify a problem that does not exist (false positive).
  + It can increase anxiety when an athlete finds out they have a health problem or are more susceptible to injury.
2 + Active stretching – holding a stretched position by contraction of your own agonistic muscles.
  + Passive stretching – stretch position being held by something other than the agonistic muscles.
  + Static stretching – holding the muscle in a stationary position for 30 seconds or more.
  + Ballistic stretching – using movement to 'bounce' in and out of a stretch position.
3 + Improves blood circulation, relieves pain and relaxes muscles.
  + The buoyancy of the water helps to support body weight, reducing the load on joints.
  + Allows for more exercise than is permitted on land.
  + Exercise is done against the resistance of the water to strengthen the injured area.
4 + Involves sitting in ice cold water for between 5 and 10 minutes.
  + Causes blood vessels to tighten/vasoconstrict, restricting blood flow to the area.
  + Reduces swelling/tissue breakdown and aids muscle repair.
  + After leaving the ice bath, the area is flooded with new blood/vasodilation.
  + It removes lactic acid.
5 + More sleep is needed following a heavy exercise programme.
  + A deep sleep rebuilds the damage done to muscle cells.
  + Blood is directed towards the muscles to restore energy.
  + 8+ hours is a guide for an elite athlete.

5.1 Biomechanical principles

1 Newton's first law of motion/law of inertia:
    + Performer will remain on the blocks unless a force is applied.
    + Force is applied by the muscles.
    Newton's second law of motion/law of acceleration:
    + The mass of the swimmer is constant.
    + The greater the force exerted on the blocks, the greater the acceleration/momentum.
    + Force governs direction.
2 Answer needs to be given in hours: 40 minutes = 0.66 hours
    + speed = distance/time
    + $8/0.66 = 13.3 \, \text{km h}^{-1}$
3 + Lower the centre of mass.
    + Keep the line of gravity central over the base of support.
    + The more contact points, the larger the base of support becomes (e.g. keep two feet on the ground wherever possible).

5.2 Levers

1 First-class lever

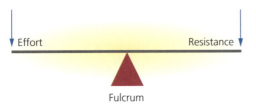

Effort   Resistance

Fulcrum

5.3 Linear motion

1 + Weight/gravity
    + This will be pulling the jumper downwards towards the sand pit.
2 momentum = mass × velocity
    $110 \times 10 = 1100 \, \text{kg m s}^{-1}$
3 Graph (a)
4 impulse = force × time; units are newton seconds, Ns

5.4 Angular motion

1 + Newton's second law: the rate of change of angular momentum of a body is proportional to the force (torque) causing it and the change that takes place in the direction in which the force (torque) acts.
    + The greater the force, the faster the spin.
2 Angular displacement (rad) divided by time taken (s)

5.5 Projectile motion

1 + Angle of release
    + Speed of release
    + Height of release
2 This arrow represents the horizontal component:

→

This arrow represents the vertical component:

5.6 Fluid mechanics

1 + Surface drag is the friction that exists between the surface of an object and the fluid environment. Swimmers wear specialised/smooth clothing to try to overcome this.
    + Form drag relates to the forces that act on a moving body. Streamlining in cycling helps to overcome this, as the cyclist uses another rider's slipstream.
2 + Cyclist leans forward over the handlebars.
    + This reduces air resistance by reducing their frontal cross-sectional area.
    + Cyclist wears tight-fitting body suit and uses specially designed/shaped helmet, shoes and bike.
    + These reduce air resistance by being more streamlined.
3 Discus – upward lift force
    Racing car – downward lift force
    Cycling – downward lift force
    Speed skier – downward lift force

6.1 Psychological factors that can influence an individual in physical activities

1 Trait learning approach:
    + Born with personality/genetically determined
    + Shown in all situations, so personality and behaviour can be predicted
    + Personality is stable and enduring
    Social learning approach:
    + Personality learned from experiences
    + Personality changes according to the situation
    + Personality and behaviour cannot be predicted
    + Observe and copy the behaviour and personalities of significant others
    + More likely to imitate:
        + successful behaviour/personality
        + behaviour/personality that is praised
        + those who share similar characteristics, such as gender, age and ability level
2 If the model:
    + is a significant other
    + shares characteristics with the performer, such as gender/ability level
    + has had their actions reinforced
    + is successful
3 B = f(P × E)
4 + The core/the real you
    + Typical responses/how you usually respond
    + Role-related behaviour/how you respond in a specific environment
5 + Cognitive – beliefs/thoughts (e.g. I believe/think that pre-season training is an essential part of my preparation).

Check your understanding and progress at **www.hoddereducation.co.uk/myrevisionnotes**

+ Affective – emotions/feelings (e.g. I enjoy pre season training).
+ Behavioural – actions/responses (e.g. I attend all pre-season training sessions).

6 Cognitive, affective, behavioural
7 Low arousal
8 Low arousal
9 High arousal
10 Cause – high cognitive anxiety combined with high somatic anxiety
   Result – a dramatic decrease in performance
11 Any three from:
   + Performing at optimum arousal levels
   + Feeling completely calm
   + Complete attentional control – fully concentrated on the task
   + Performing on 'autopilot' – some performers have no memory of it
   + Feeling completely confident that success is inevitable
   + Performing smoothly, efficiently and effortlessly
12 + Fully concentrated on the task.
   + Absolute control over their actions.
   + The performance feels effortless.
   + They feel something like an 'out-of-body' experience that they have difficulty remembering.
13 Competitive trait anxiety – performer has a natural tendency to become anxious in all sporting situations; a genetic predisposition.
   Competitive state anxiety – performer is only anxious in specific sporting situations; often seen in high-pressure moments; can be caused by negative past experiences.
14 Must relate to team sports, not to individual:
   + Task importance (e.g. playing in a final)
   + Losing/fear of failing
   + Perceived inaccuracy of official's decisions
   + Being fouled
   + Injury/fear of being injured
   + Lack of self-confidence/efficacy
   + Audience effects (e.g. an abusive crowd)
   + Evaluation apprehension
15 Advantages:
   + Real-life method
   + Cheap and quick
   + Can gain a vast amount of information in competitive situations
   Disadvantages:
   + Subjective
   + Time consuming
   + Need to be aware of the performer's 'normal' anxiety levels
   + Performer will change their behaviour as soon as they realise they are being observed
16 Releasing and feeling relief from aggression
17 + When a performer has their goal blocked.
   + If learned cues or triggers are present.
18 Cognitive:
   + Mental rehearsal
   + Imagery

+ Visualisation
+ Selective attention
+ Negative thought-stopping
+ Positive self-talk
Somatic:
+ Relaxation techniques
+ Deep breathing
+ Biofeedback

19 Extrinsic motivation:
   + Received from an outside source
   + Can be tangible or intangible
   Intrinsic motivation:
   + Comes from the performer
   + For the 'love' of the sport, self-satisfaction or pride of achieving own goals
20 + Extrinsic – money, medals, trophies, T-shirts, certificates, badges (or equivalent)
   + Intrinsic – the pride of achieving a new personal best time; the drive to land a back somersault; the desire to throw the javelin further than last season
21 Situations with:
   + a low probability of success
   + a high incentive value
22 + Exhibits avoidance behaviour
   + Has low self-efficacy/confidence
   + Dislikes competition and challenge
   + Will take the easy option
   + Gives in easily, especially if failing
   + Does not welcome feedback
   + May experience learned helplessness
   + Attributes failure internally
   + Dislikes performing in front of an audience
   + Is not competitive – likes tasks with:
      + a high probability of success, i.e. an easy task
      + a low incentive, i.e. little satisfaction in achieving their goal
23 + Audience
   + Co-actors
   + Competitive co-actors
   + Social reinforcers
24 Performance will be inhibited. The performer cannot cope with the extra arousal, which means their performance will deteriorate.
25 Cognitive (any two):
   + Psychological skills training
   + Mental rehearsal
   + Visualisation
   + Imagery
   + Positive self-talk
   + Negative thought-stopping
   + Attentional control and cue utilisation
   Somatic (any two)
   + Biofeedback
   + Progressive muscular relaxation
   + Breathing control
   + Centring
   + Warm-up
26 1 Forming, 2 Storming, 3 Norming, 4 Performing
27 Two or more people who:
   + interact with each other
   + share a common goal

+ have mutual awareness
+ have a collective identity

28 Task cohesion – group members work in unity to meet a common aim.

Social cohesion – group members get along and feel attached to others.

29 + Personal
+ Environmental
+ Leadership
+ Team

30 actual productivity = potential productivity – losses due to faulty processes

31 + The things that go wrong in a team
+ Coordination and motivation problems faced by the team
+ Reduces the level of cohesion
+ Lowers the actual productivity

32 Process goals – short-term goals set to improve technique.

Performance goals – goals set against yourself to improve performance from last time.

Outcome (product) goals – long-term goals set against others and based on the outcome – to win.

33 Locus of causality:
+ Describes where the performer places the reason for the win/loss
+ Can be internal or external

Stability dimension:
+ Describes how fixed the attributions are
+ Can be stable or unstable

34 + Performers attribute failure internally to stable reasons
+ Performers have low self-confidence
+ Unrealistic goals set by the coach

35 Trait sports confidence (SC–trait) – natural, innate confidence levels.

State sports confidence (SC–state) – a performer's level of confidence in a particular situation

Competiveness orientation – how driven the performer is and the types of goals they may have set.

36 + Performance accomplishments
+ Vicarious experiences
+ Verbal persuasion
+ Emotional arousal

37 + Ambitious
+ Has clear vision or goal
+ Ability to motivate/motivated
+ An effective communicator
+ Charismatic
+ Knowledgeable about the sport/skilful
+ Empathetic
+ Confident
+ Flexible

38 Prescribed leaders are chosen from outside the group, whereas emergent leaders are selected from within the existing group, often because they are nominated by the other group members.

39 Autocratic

40 Situation:
+ Strength of opponents
+ Level of danger involved
+ Time available

Group:
+ Ability levels
+ Relationships with each other
+ Relationships with the leader
+ Size of group
+ Group traditions

Leader:
+ Ability
+ Personality
+ Preferred leadership style

41 Eustress – positive responses to stressful situations. The performer rises to the challenge they are facing.

Distress – negative responses to stressful situations. The performer finds the stressor threatening.

42 Broad–narrow:
+ How many cues are being focused on.
+ Broad is many cues, while narrow is one or two.

Internal–external:
+ Where the focus is being placed.
+ Internal is the thoughts and feelings of the performer.
+ External is a focus on the environmental cues.

7.1 Concepts of physical activity and sport

1 + It is fun, enjoyable, non-serious and informal in nature, so winning is not important.
+ It is physically energetic, i.e. it involves effort being applied to physical activity.
+ Participating is a matter of choice; it is voluntary and up to you whether you take part or not in the free time you have available.
+ It tends to involve adults at the 'participation level' of the sporting development continuum.
+ It is flexible in nature, so how long you take part for and the rules being followed can be adjusted by participants as they wish.
+ It is self-officiated/self-regulated (i.e. any decisions during activities are made by the participants).

2 Sports development continuum – participation in various forms of physical activity at various stages of development.

3

Stage/level of sports development continuum	Definition	Example (i.e. link to concept)
Foundation level	First introduction to physical activity	Primary school PE
Participation level	Relaxed, fun participation in physical activity	Physical recreation
Performance level	More serious; emphasis on winning; commitment to regular involvement	Sport

Check your understanding and progress at **www.hoddereducation.co.uk/myrevisionnotes**

4 + Increased health and fitness decreases strain on the NHS, and lowers obesity rates.
   + Increased social integration occurs as individuals from different social communities join clubs and interact socially.
   + Increased employment/economic benefits result from more people using facilities and buying equipment to participate.
   + A more positive use of free time increases social control and decreases crime statistics in a more socially inclusive society.
   + Increased skill levels at the 'participation' stage lead to more individuals potentially progressing to 'elite level'.
5 + It has set/strict rules (e.g. set time limits; set boundaries).
   + It involves use of specialist equipment/set kit.
   + Officials appointed by national governing bodies are present to enforce the rules.
   + Strategies and tactics are involved to try to outwit opponents.
   + High skill levels/high prowess are visible in the sporting performance.
   + High levels of commitment/strict training are involved.
6 Three from:
   + Praise from coach/family etc.
   + Trophy
   + Medal
   + Certificate
7 For individuals, sport:
   + increases their self-confidence as a result of skill improvement and success
   + provides more opportunities to communicate/socialise/work as part of a team/make friends at sports clubs
   + develops positive sporting attitudes (e.g. fair play/sportsmanship)
8 Two from: fair play, sportsmanship, morality, respect for opponents/officials
9 + Learning to appreciate and engage with the natural environment
   + Learning to develop new physical skills/survival skills (e.g. abseiling, climbing)
   + Increased self-esteem
   + Increased health and fitness
   + Increased cooperation; improvement in social skills
   + Increased cognitive skills; decision making; leadership skills
   + Increased awareness of conservation skills
   + Increased commitment to active leisure
   + Opportunity to experience challenge/excitement/adrenaline rush/perceived risk
10 Two from: mountain hiking, caving, climbing, abseiling
11 Two from: extracurricular time, competitive, use of teachers/sports coaches
12 Similarities:
   + Both develop physical skills.
   + Both develop health and fitness.

   + Both help individuals achieve intrinsic benefits/have fun.
   Differences:

Physical recreation	Physical education
Voluntary/choice	Compulsory
In a person's free time	In school time
Informal/relaxed	Formal teaching and learning
Participants control activity; self-regulated	Teacher in charge
Participation level	Foundation level
Simple/limited organisational structure	Highly structured

13

National Curriculum PE	School sport
In lesson time; curriculum time	In free time; extracurricular
Compulsory	Element of choice; voluntary involvement
For all	For the chosen few; elitist
Emphasis on taking part	Emphasis on winning; competitive
Teacher-led	Coaches involved
Wide variety of activities experienced	Specialisms developed

14 + If optional as an extracurricular activity, it does not necessarily reach the maximum number, and some talented individuals might miss out; it might be viewed as 'elitist' if only a 'minority' of pupils stay behind at school/compete for the school at weekends.
   + It relies heavily on teacher goodwill; teachers may sometimes opt out due to other pressures on their time (e.g. attendance at staff meetings).
   + School sporting facilities may not be used to their full capacity.

7.2 Development of elite performers in sport

1 + Clear focus/goals to achieve/goal-orientated
   + Patient
   + Dedicated/committed/self-disciplined
   + Determined to succeed
   + High levels of self-motivation
   + High levels of confidence/self-efficacy
   + Highly resilient
   + Ability to control arousal
   + Ability to accept feedback
   + Mentally tough/high pain tolerance
2 + Level of media coverage/status of sport/role models to aspire to
   + Equal opportunities policies/antidiscriminatory practice/sports equity

+ A positive educational experience (e.g. at school/FE college/university)
+ Access to specialist clubs to develop sporting talents (e.g. via high-quality facilities; top-level coaching)
+ Support from family/friends/peers
+ Social class/socioeconomic status

3 + Works on an overall strategy to increase sporting excellence in the UK (e.g. funding/financial decisions – invests National Lottery money into elite performer development in Olympic and Paralympic sports).
+ Responsible for the development of the World Class Coaches strategy/elite-level coaches.
+ Lead agency overseeing the running of Talent ID (e.g. Talent Search–Talent Confirmation).
+ Lead agency in providing performance lifestyle advice/support (providing mentor advice on time management etc.).
+ Development and management of the UK's international sporting relationships (via International Voice programme); it also works to attract major international events to the UK (e.g. via the Gold Events Series).
+ Cooperative/coordinated approach working with other organisations involved in elite performer development (e.g. the EIS); promoting ethical behaviour at the highest level (e.g. 'Win Clean').
+ Responsibility for performance innovation (e.g. British Aerospace and British Cycling technology partnership).

4 Athlete Performance Award

5 + Offer a range of sport support services to NGBs to develop elite performers, including: sports science, physiotherapy, diet and nutrition, biomechanics, performance analysis, psychology and technology.
+ Provide performance lifestyle advice and personalised support to athletes on the World Class Programme, including mentor support and help with time management (e.g. the demands of elite sport and education).
+ Provide top-quality/world-class facilities and the best coaches to develop elite performers to their full potential.
+ Provide host venues for Talent ID assessments and Talent Confirmation; home to the UK Talent Team.
+ Performance innovation, research and innovation, such as research into how technology and engineering can be used to develop kit/equipment to give athletes an edge (e.g. marginal gains in cycling).

6 + Mentor support
+ Time management (e.g. demands of education and elite performance)
+ Media training
+ Balancing family/friends
+ Budgeting/financial advice

7 + Development of effective Talent ID schemes to maintain the talent factory in its sport (e.g.

use of regional scouts/schemes specific to the demands of its sport).
+ Decisions on allocation of UK Sport lottery funding to athletes in its sport (e.g. via World Class Programme funding/Athlete Performance Awards).
+ Development of top-level coaches in its sport. Providing a developmental coaching structure through to a very high level in the sport it is responsible for.
+ Provides developmental training squads. Different levels are provided with progressive levels of competition to work through.
+ Provides support services to elite performers – for example, via links with EIS centres/payment to the EIS for various support services (e.g. performance lifestyle advice, performance innovation, sport science support).
+ By developing and applying equal opportunities policies to ensure all individuals with the necessary talent have the chance to progress to their fullest potential.

8 + It means all potential performers can be screened.
+ Performers can be directed to the sports most suited to their talents.
+ The development process can be accelerated as a result of the information gained.
+ Efficient use can be made of available funding for Talent ID schemes.
+ The chances of producing medallists are improved.
+ It provides a coordinated approach between organisations such as NGBs, the EIS and UK Sport.

9 + Supporting high-performance success.
+ Creating high-profile opportunities for people to engage in sport.
+ Using and demonstrating the legacy of London 2012 and Glasgow 2014.
+ Driving positive economic and social impacts for the UK.

10 Pathway Analytics enables sports to measure and benchmark the effectiveness of their performance pathways, using a Talent Health Check, which is delivered every 4 years by the Performance Pathway team.
It discusses topics such as junior to senior transition, as well as retention and attrition rates of athletes on the pathway.

7.3 Ethics in sport

1 Sportsmanship is conforming to/playing by the unwritten rules of sport/etiquette/fair play.

2 + Shaking hands at end of the game
+ Applauding each other off the field of play
+ Immediate acceptance of refereeing decisions
+ Players calling a referee 'Sir'

3 One judge/official; one coach

4 Sports performers fail to adopt the sportsmanship ethic by:
  + time-wasting
  + cheating/playing unfairly (e.g. diving to win a free kick/penalty in football)
  + deliberately trying to injure an opponent through over-aggressive/violent actions
  + refusing to shake hands with an opponent before/after a sporting contest
  + arguing with officials

  Ways to encourage sportsmanship:
  + Use of national governing body campaigns promoting sportsmanship/fair play (e.g. the FA's Respect campaign).
  + Giving awards for fair play, to encourage it in top-level sport, thereby providing positive role models for youngsters to follow (e.g. the UEFA Fair Play Awards, which include a place in Europe awarded on the basis of fair play/ sportsmanship).
  + Use of technology to help match officials reach the correct decisions and allow performers to be cited after matches for behaviour that goes against the rules (e.g. a dangerous tackle missed by the referee in rugby).
  + Introduction of NGB rules promoting fair play (e.g. banning high tackles/late tackles).
  + Punishing foul play/unsporting behaviour within the sporting event (e.g. officials can sin bin, book or send a player off).
  + Punishing foul play/unsporting behaviour after the event (e.g. fines/bans imposed by NGBs)
  + Use of positive role models to promote sportsmanship/fair play.
  + Use of rigorous drug testing to try to ensure fairness in sporting contests and catch out drugs cheats.

5 Similarities:
  + Both are more evident in professional sport, where a win-at-all-costs ethic dominates.
  + Both conflict with amateur ethics/ sportsmanship.
  + Both lower the status of sport/give sport a bad name/create negative role models.

  Differences:
  + Gamesmanship is pushing the rules to the absolute limit (e.g. sledging an opponent/time-wasting). Deviance is cheating (e.g. taking illegal performance-enhancing drugs/match fixing).
  + Gamesmanship is increasingly coached, whereas deviance is usually not.

6 + Verbal sledging of opponent(s)
  + Taking an injury/toilet break when not necessarily needed
  + Appealing a decision that is highly unlikely to be out
  + Over-appealing for a wicket to pressurise the umpire

7 + No drawn games (e.g. there is always a winner in basketball, American football and League Cup football in England.
  + Managers/coaches are fired if unsuccessful

  + Via high amounts of deviance (e.g. violence/over-aggression/doping)
  + Via media praise for winners/positive newspaper headlines
  + Via media negativity for losers

8 Positive deviance involves behaviour that is outside the norms of society, but with no intent to harm or break the rules. It involves over-adherence to the norms/expectations of society. For example:
  + competing when injured
  + training when injured
  + unintentionally injuring an opponent when striving to win (within the rules/etiquette of a sport)

  Negative deviance involves behaviour that goes against the norms and has a detrimental effect on individuals and society in general. For example:
  + taking drugs
  + violent/over-aggressive actions deliberately harming an opponent
  + match-fixing
  + diving to win a free kick/penalty

9 Gamesmanship is bending the rules and stretching them to their absolute limit without getting caught.

  Amateurism is a nineteenth-century code of sporting ideals, which involved participation in sport for the love of it, while receiving no financial gain.

7.4 Violence in sport

1 + Win-at-all-costs ethic/pressure to win/high financial rewards at stake/job at stake
  + Retaliation against an opponent/crowd
  + Frustration with officiating
  + Importance of event (e.g. local derby/local rivalry/pre-match hype/over-psyched)
  + Nature of game – violence is part of it (e.g. ice hockey)
  + Lack of effective deterrents (e.g. NGB punishments/sanctions)

2 Any relevant examples, such as American football, rugby league, rugby union, ice hockey

3 + Remove the performer/player from the pitch/ substitute them.
  + Punish aggressive behaviour (e.g. by fining them/leaving them out of the team for a certain number of matches).
  + Increase peer pressure (e.g. on the field of play via a teammate/captain) to act less aggressively.
  + Educate the performer/reinforce the use of assertive behaviour.
  + Provide a positive role model behaviour to aspire to.
  + Highlight their responsibility to the team/ negative impact on them if aggression leads to being sent off/banned from future matches.
  + Decrease the emphasis on winning.
  + Use stress management techniques with a sport psychologist (e.g. positive self-talk).
  + Work on improving fitness to decrease the likelihood of fatigue negatively affecting mood/ mind-set.

4   + Emotional intensity/ritual importance of the event (e.g. a local derby; team loyalty taken to extremes).
    + Pre-match media hype stirring up tensions between rival fans.
    + Poor policing/stewarding/crowd control (e.g. this was one of the key reasons identified for the Hillsborough Stadium disaster in 1989).
    + Lack of effective deterrents/punishments to discourage individuals from involving themselves in violence at football matches.
    + Diminished responsibility by individuals in a large group (i.e. a football crowd); organised violence as part of a gang/peer pressure to get involved in violence.
    + Reaction of working-class fans to the middle class taking over 'their' game.
    + Poor officiating or frustration with match officials, which can heighten tensions between rival fans.
    + Violence by players on the pitch being reflected in the crowd.
    + Religious discord (e.g. at a Celtic versus Rangers match, where tensions are particularly high between rival fans).
    + A negative violent reaction occurring as a result of taunts by rival fans.
    + Frustration at one's own team losing, which can lead some in the crowd to become violent.

5   + Fan violence can lead to poor treatment of legitimate fans/supporters.
    + Fans are 'herded' through the streets to reach the stadium and, after the game, to take transport home.
    + All fans following a particular team are treated with suspicion and distrust.
    + All fans of a particular team are banned from certain matches/for a certain time period as a result of the violent/negative actions of individuals following their club.

6   + A negative image of the sport causes a decline in participation rate/smaller foundation base in football.
    + A negative image of football leads to a decrease in live spectator attendances.
    + Supporters are banned from attending matches, or matches are played behind closed doors.
    + All supporters at football matches are treated as hooligans as a result of police suspicions and frequent violence.
    + Teams are banned from competing, or they may lose points or be fined, which punishes the football clubs for the acts of their 'fans'.
    + Sponsors/commercial deals are withdrawn from clubs/players/NGBs due to the negative publicity/poor image of the game.
    + Additional costs to police events/provide more stewards can place financial pressures on clubs, particularly at lower levels of the game.
    + The relationship with other countries declines/negative impact for hosting future major football competitions as a result of the negative reputation of a country's sporting followers.

7.5 Drugs in sport

1   Social reasons:
    + A win-at-all-costs attitude, which dominates modern-day elite sport.
    + The fame and fortune attached to success at elite level (i.e. the very high level of extrinsic rewards/money received for sporting success via prize money, sponsorship deals and so on).
    + The high levels of pressure to win from a variety of different sources, such as coaches, family and the media (e.g. coaches might persuade athletes to take drugs illegally because their main competitors already do so, and they will not be able to compete with them on a level playing field if they do not).
    + The lack of effective deterrents, and a firm belief that a performer will get away with it and not get caught.
    + Poor role models setting a bad example that drug taking in sport or certain sports is viewed in some way as being acceptable (e.g. athletics, cycling).
    Psychological reasons:
    + To steady nerves/decrease anxiety.
    + To increase aggression.
    + To increase confidence/self-belief.

2 a Reasons for using a beta blocker:
    + Counteracts adrenaline, which interferes with performance by binding to nerve receptors
    + Keeps heart rate low
    + Decreases trembling in the hands
    + Increases blood flow through the arteries
    + Decreases muscle spasms
  b Reasons for using EPO:
    + Stimulates red blood cell production
    + Increases endurance; performer can keep going for longer
    + Delays onset of fatigue
    + Aids recovery from training

3   Anabolic steroids: high blood pressure; liver problems/heart problems; behavioural changes
    EPO: increased risk of heart disease, strokes, blood clotting
    Beta blockers: low blood pressure

4   + Upholds the traditions of sport/sporting ethics/all competitors are equal
    + Standard list of banned substances/same testing procedures/similar punishments
    + Random tests more effective
    + Shared costs between all sports
    + Performers not able to 'pick and choose' sports based on drug-testing procedures

5   Cycling, athletics, weight lifting

7.6 Sport and the law

1   + Protection against foul play/violent acts of opponents (leading to compensation claims)
    + Protection from fans/violent spectators during a game

Check your understanding and progress at **www.hoddereducation.co.uk/myrevisionnotes**

- Protection from contractual issues with employers
- Protection from contractual issues with sponsors/commercial deals
- Protection from issues linked to equality of opportunity (e.g. racism from fans/opponents)
- Appeals against NGB decisions/disciplinary issues
- Protection against negligence of poor referees

2 Libel – a published false statement that is damaging to a person's reputation.
Restraint of trade – action that interferes with free competition in a market.

3 Negligence is a failure in the duty of care to a player (e.g. not enforcing rules properly).
Examples of negligence linked to rugby officials:
- Repeatedly allowing dangerous incidents to occur (e.g. scrum collapses).
- Failure to follow NGB rules/guidelines in relation to safe procedures/practice.
- Failure in duty of care to a player (e.g. not enforcing rules properly).

4 In order to bring a successful personal injury compensation claim in a sporting context, a claimant would have to show: they were owed a duty of care; the defendant (the referee) breached their duty of care; that they suffered damage as a result of the breach.

5
- Keeping up-to-date contact details/medical details/registers of attendance.
- Maintaining appropriate supervision ratios.
- Ensuring that first aid provision is available.
- Ensuring that individuals regularly involved in coaching children have current DBS clearance.
- Ensuring that an appropriate risk assessment has been undertaken for the activities being coached.

6 a A check implemented by the Disclosure and Barring Service, which is the body in England and Wales that looks after providing criminal record checks for employers and employees.
   b Physical, emotional and social

7
- Placed a legal responsibility on clubs for a duty of care to provide a safe spectator environment to 'visitors' (e.g. prevention of overcrowding by setting maximum numbers allowed into a stand/setting fire safety standards to adhere to in order to obtain a fire certificate necessary to stage a match).
- Controlled who can attend matches by placing banning orders on certain known trouble makers; tougher deterrents; increased police presence/police liaison/intelligence gathering on known/potential trouble makers.
- Controlled rival fans chanting racist remarks at each other/players.
- Controlled alcohol sales/alcohol consumption prior to and at football matches.
- Removal of perimeter fencing/creation of all-seater stadia to replace terraces.

- An Act controlling missile throwing/trespassing onto the field of play (and potentially attacking rival fans).

7.7 Impact of commercialisation

1
- The media use sport to gain viewers/readers.
- The media are used by businesses/sponsors for advertising purposes, promoting the company name and the products it sells.
- Businesses/sponsors pay the media for advertising time and space on television, online, on the radio and in the newspapers.
- They also pay large amounts to sports/sports performers to act for them as an advertising medium to sell more of their goods.
- Sports are aware that they need to appear in the media to attract sponsorship, increase their profile and appeal to a wide audience.
- Sports need to be more professionally managed as a result of the increasingly commercialised nature of sport.

2
- To access the largest number/widest range of potential viewers.
- To avoid restricting coverage to subscription channels available only to those who can afford them.
- To increase geographical access for all viewers in all parts of the country to major sporting events.
- To enable viewing of certain events that are seen as part of the UK's sporting heritage/sporting culture.
- To enable access to sporting events that should be freely available to all to view (e.g. the Olympic Games and Football World Cup).

3
- National governing bodies/sports performers lose control to television/sponsors; the traditional nature of a sport is lost – for example, rule structures/timings of a sport are adapted to suit the demands of television/sponsors.
- The media control the location of events, as well as kick-off times and, in some cases, playing seasons (e.g. Super League Rugby switched to being a summer game). There is sometimes too much sport on television, which can lead to boredom among spectators and/or lower attendance at events that are being televised.
- There are inequalities of coverage – more popular sports (e.g. football) gain at the expense of minority sports (e.g. squash). Certain prestigious events are now available only on satellite television, which requires a subscription payment (e.g. test cricket and Ryder Cup golf). This means that there are fewer viewers for some sports due to the increasing control of Sky/BT Sport.
- Demands of media/sponsors impact negatively on high-level performers (e.g. demands for interviews/personal appearances).

- The media can sometimes over-sensationalise or over-dramatise certain negative events in sport. A win-at-all-costs attitude develops due to high rewards on offer, which leads to negative, deviant acts and players becoming negative role models (e.g. in football, arguing with officials or diving to win a penalty).
- More breaks in play (e.g. for adverts) can disrupt the spectator experience.

4
- Increased revenue/income via selling more subscriptions
- High skill levels on show
- Competitive/well-matched opponents
- Visually appealing/action-packed excitement
- Easy to televise/relatively short timescale
- Role models/easily identifiable personalities

5
- It has extensive media coverage.
- It gains large audiences/viewing figures/high levels of ticket sales.
- It links to professional sport.
- Players are contracted to perform/endorse products.
- Extensive advertising/merchandising/sponsorship deals are evident.
- Winning is important, because it creates a link with success.
- Sport is media friendly/entertaining.

6 Positive impacts:
- Train harder to produce higher-quality performances.
- Increased need to maintain discipline to protect the positive image that sponsors require.
- Increased need to display sportsmanship/fair play on the field of play.
- Increased need to develop good image off the field of play (e.g. community/charity work).

Negative impacts:
- Increased pressure to win/win-at-all-costs attitude.
- Increased deviancy/temptation to cheat (e.g. drugs/increased use of gamesmanship/over-aggression).
- Negative off-field behaviour (e.g. drinking/gambling).
- Increased pressure to compete when injured/overtraining.
- Increased control of sponsors, which impacts negatively on performance.

7
- Increased wages
- Increased investment in best players from across the world.
- Increased investment in training facilities/sport science/medical provision.
- Increased investment in analytics/technology (e.g. to assess opposition strengths and weaknesses).

8
- Not always available (e.g. in certain competitions; at lower league levels).
- Possibility of too much reliance on officiating technology.
- Decisions not always right/are controversial (e.g. VAR); take too long.

9
- Increased performance standards; players are of a higher standard and provide a high level of excitement and entertainment.
- Improved quality of facilities; bigger, higher-quality stadiums result from increased investment.
- Improved viewing experience via innovations such as changes in ball colour; creation of team merchandise to create team loyalty.
- Increased access to watch sport; more opportunities to watch events live via more competitions/events/matches taking place.
- More variations of a sport format develop, which provide alternative viewing experiences.
- More funding available to provide entertainment (e.g. cheerleaders/pop stars) at sports events.
- Rule changes provide extra interest and excitement for the spectator (e.g. Twenty20 cricket).
- Increased funding for improved technology at grounds (e.g. video screens) and at home (e.g. interactive technology/HD coverage of sport/referee link).
- Increased excitement in the audience while awaiting the decisions of off-field officials (e.g. Hawk-Eye in tennis).
- Increased awareness/knowledge of sport; creation of role models for fans to idolise.
- Increased elimination of negative aspects of sport (e.g. hooliganism).

7.8 Role of technology

1 Studying data from sports performances to try to improve performance.

2 a Subjective data – based on personal opinion, which is less measurable and often less usable.
Validity – an indication of whether the data collected actually measure what they claim to measure.

b Reliability

3
- Issues with memory retention of the performance observed.
- May lead to incorrect decisions during matches/competitions (e.g. when making substitutions).
- May lead to incorrect training programmes being implemented.

4 Indirect calorimetry – the measurement of heat and energy generated in an oxidation reaction.
Metabolic cart – a device that works by attaching headgear to a subject while they breathe a specific amount of oxygen over a period of time.

5
- Overall weight/obesity
- Height; height/weight ratio
- Chemistry of body in response to drugs
- Illnesses

6
- It helps to monitor player performance overall (e.g. is it 'as expected'?).
- It can measure impact (e.g. G-forces).
- It can help make objective decisions about substitutions.

+ It can decrease injury risk by gauging levels of fatigue.
+ It can help manage workload during rehabilitation, and ultimately get the player through it at a faster rate.
+ It can help make better use of training time and ensure that training meets game demands.
+ It improves tactical analysis.
+ It enables player comparisons.

7 + Regularly backing up data.
+ Controlling access to data and protecting against malicious intent via security mechanisms.
+ Designing interfaces that prevent the input of invalid data; taking care when entering data.
+ Using error detection and correction software when transmitting data.
+ Not leaving a computer unattended for unauthorised individuals to access.

8 + Improving bone density
+ Increasing muscle mass/power
+ Improving circulation
+ Reducing joint pain
+ Reducing back pain
+ Alleviating stress
+ Boosting metabolism
+ An overall reduction in pain/in delayed onset of muscle soreness (DOMS)
+ Maintenance of cartilage integrity where weight-bearing activities are difficult to undertake

9 + Strengthening and toning the muscles (e.g. it can strengthen the muscle groups of the legs to give stability and help prevent injury or recurring injuries to the knees and ankles).
+ Helping to prevent losses in fitness levels via application to specific muscle groups, which maintains muscle tone during periods of inactivity.

+ Assisting in rehabilitation through the gradual strengthening of injured or weakened muscles via small incremental increases in workload on the muscles (i.e. by inducing stronger muscular contractions).
+ Helping to get rid of lactic acid after a training session or competition, as well as decreasing muscle tension and avoiding potential injury by providing a relaxing effect on muscles.

10 a Rugby
   b Rugby
   c Tennis
   d Basketball

11 + They can be played on more frequently (e.g. matches/training).
+ They give consistent conditions.
+ They enable fixtures to be played without disruption.
+ They have had a very positive impact on certain sports (e.g. hockey).

12 + It can lead to injury or over-aggression (e.g. from bladed boots or due to the use of protective equipment, which makes some performers feel 'invincible'/less inhibited).
+ It can lead to cheating (e.g. effective masking agents or newly developed performance-enhancing substances for which there is no test can allow athletes to take illegal drugs in the belief that they will get away with it).
+ It can be expensive and unaffordable to some, which leads to potential inequalities and unfair advantages if the technology is not available to all.
+ The availability of technological advances aiding performance might be dependent on an individual/team sponsor, which might positively/negatively impact on the chances of success.

277